Your guide to Wyoming's campgrounds:

on the way,
by the way
and
out-of-the-way

156   RV Parks (54 horse friendly)

154   Forest Service Camps

32   BLM Camps

11   State Parks

34   City or County Camps

47   Game and Fish Access Areas

1000's of free campsites at 135

Free Camping Areas

PLUS

A Guide to Cities and Towns
- Points of interest
- Museums
- Rec centers
- Swimming pools
- Local events

AND

87 Hand-Drawn Maps

Camping

Wyoming

Michael McClure

WigRaf Publishing, Inc.
Atlantic City, WY 82520
(PO 258 • Lander WY 82520)

Camping Wyoming

Published by:

WigRaf Publishing, Inc.
Atlantic City, WY 82520
(PO 258 • Lander WY 82520)   1st edition—May 1999

Library of Congress Catalog Card Number: 99-93832

ISBN 1-928786-00-6 (paper back)

Text — Michael McClure
Design and photography —
    McClure Photography and Media Works • Lander, Wyoming
Map renditions, illustrations and cover art —
    Miss Emily Designs • Jackson, Wyoming
Editorial assistants —
    Geoffrey O'Gara - Plurabelle Productions • Lander, Wyoming
    Lynn Dickey - The Book Shop • Sheridan, WY

Printed at — Publishers Press
              1900 West 2300 South
              Salt Lake City, Utah 84119

Revisions and Updates

The subject matter of this book
is in constant flux.

As new information becomes available
revisions will be posted on the internet at
http://www.campwyo.com.

The author and publisher would
appreciate all comments, corrections,
updates, additions,
amendments and critiques.

Please send to:

WigRaf Publishing, Inc.
PO 258
Lander WY 82520

Contents — General

Introduction

— About the book —

This book is your complete source for locating the right camp for you in Wyoming. Whether you are camping in a luxury motor home or in canvas tent, this book gives you detailed directions— including 87 hand-drawn maps— and information to choose the most convenient camp along your route, or an off-route camp in a more natural setting, or a decidedly remote camp with serenity and solitude at a premium.

It is not a how-to book on camping nor is it a recommendation for any camp or style of camping. I see campers as being a little like snowflakes: they may resemble one another and be searching for similar experiences and rewards, but each is a little different. They differ in their needs, style and approach to the perfect camp; each has a little different interpretation of the freedom, mobility and independence offered by camping, and to no small degree, that's what it's all about.

Wyoming is known as the 'Cowboy State' and the cowboy personifies freedom, mobility and independence. Like the pioneers on their way to a new life on the frontier of the Great American West, people come to Wyoming expecting the freedom to shape their life-styles.

The sense of space in Wyoming attracts us to its rugged landscapes and drives the engine of the experience; it is space that gives man a better sense of scale in the environment; it is space that forces the issue of self-reliance; and it is space that allows for the personal freedom, the mobility and the independence embodied in the life-style of the cowboy, as well as the modern camper.

Campers will find Wyoming has unparalleled quantities of available space to explore in the quest for freedom, mobility and independence. This book will provide the information and direction you need for a memorable camping experience and a unique partnership with the Wyoming landscape.

Enjoy,   Michael McClure

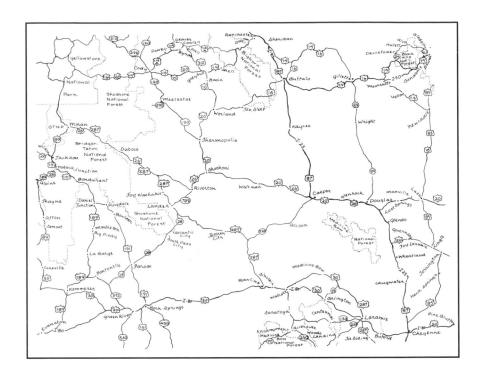

—About Wyoming—

There are less than five people per square mile in Wyoming. It has often been said that the state is just a small town with a really long main street.

But on the way 'crosstown' there are five national forests, over 18 million acres of public BLM lands, 15 wilderness areas, a national monument, two national recreational areas, two national parks, nine mountain ranges, the Great Divide Basin with 55 miles of sand dunes, an Indian reservation, seven scenic highways and three BLM back country scenic byways, 23 state parks and historic sites, 35 state wildlife habitat management areas and 74 public access areas, as well as lakes, streams, creeks and other bodies of water beyond tallying during a normal life-span.

The landscape varies from high desert and rolling sagebrush grasslands to mountain ranges topped by snow-capped granite monoliths. The Continental Divide transects Wyoming, with mountain runoff contributing to the flow of three major American river systems: the Columbia, the Colorado and the Missouri. Within the state, rivers have carved compelling canyons into the landscape and deposited rich soils in long fertile valleys.

Wyoming enjoys an unusually diverse and large wildlife population. This is partly due to its 10,000 foot variation in altitude, and partly due to sparse and late-arriving human settlement.

Elevations vary from the lowest point at 3, 125', in the northeast corner of the state near South Dakota, to 13,804' atop Gannett Peak in the Wind River Range. Weather can vary dramatically and snow storms, although usually brief, have been known to occur during the summer months. Normally, you can expect cool nights during the summer with daytime temperatures rarely over 90° Fahrenheit.

The geology of Wyoming has been referred to as an 'open book.' With miles of unaltered landscapes there is no shortage of opportunities to explore the state in the context of geologic time. The geological landscape played a significant role in early settlement, especially on South Pass, which served in the 1840's, as the natural and least formidable westward passage through the Rocky Mountains. The history of the emerging west is etched in the trail ruts crossing these high plains.

Wyoming was a thoroughfare to a better life elsewhere. Wyoming, viewed by the pioneers as a great barren desert with nothing but high mountains, big rocks and sagebrush, was a far cry from the earthly paradise promised further to the west. The pot of gold at the end of the rainbow was in Oregon or California. Most immigrants elected to stay on the trail to the end of the road, with settling in Wyoming of questionable fulfillment.

Only Indians and a few mountain men and trappers showed an interest in settling in Wyoming up until about 1860. A few hundred white traders, blacksmiths and the like found a niche serving the needs of those on the westward passage and made Wyoming their home. A few settlers followed mountain men and trappers, a few dropped off the wagon trains, and a few, like the wildlife, found the other lands increasingly crowded and returned to Wyoming.

The railroad reached Cheyenne in 1867, and Wyoming, although still known as a high, dry and empty land, was noticed to a greater degree. In 1868, tracks were put down all across southern Wyoming to the Utah line. Communities, founded along the tracks, overflowed and emptied as the transient construction crews moved westward with the new rails: The boom and bust cycles indigenous to the Wyoming economy were born.

With the railroad came a new interest in Wyoming. Construction and completion helped bring people of ethnic diversity who would start businesses, raise livestock and discover the vast energy wealth underlying the state. As emigration and exploration increased mineral discoveries were made: In the South Pass Mining District about $3,000,000 in gold was mined between 1869 and 1871, adding another chapter to the boom and bust history of the state. Oil, gas, coal, trona and uranium have added unfinished chapters to this economic legacy. For years, Wyoming has been dependent on a mixture of agriculture and extractive industries. State coffers have been tied to the price of beef or oil and gas.

As the state searched for economic diversity in the late 20th century an awareness of its potential for a tourist economy grew along with an appreciation for protection and preservation of the natural beauty of the land.

Wyoming has unparalleled recreational opportunities in unique rugged landscapes in the heart of frontier America. If you know where to go, the camping in Wyoming is the pot of gold at the end of the rainbow.

—Using the book—

In a few cases there are many camps listed in or near one particular city. In an effort to present information in a logical and easy-to-use fashion, the camps are ordered as follows:

(1) Urban, privately-owned RV camps with hookups are listed first and in alphabetical order;

(2) Should any town have primitive camps, such as a free camping park, such options are listed following the private listings;

(3) All other camps near that particular city are listed by compass point and in order of their proximity to that city or town, regardless of whether they are privately-owned camps with hookups, or primitive camps.

Simply put, if you want to stay in a particular city or town and enjoy hookups, check the alphabetical listings starting at the top of the heading. If it is your desire to enjoy the countryside, search lower in the listings.

— About the camps —

This book lists every type of camping option available in Wyoming: Privately-owned, Forest Service, BLM, National Recreation Areas, State Parks, county, city and town parks, and Game and Fish habitat and access areas. While easily accessible in your vehicle, many of these areas offer the option of solitude and a near-wilderness experience.

Many of the private camps cater to the needs of the RV user, but most have some tent sites available and the comfort of indoor plumbing and hot showers. Many of these camps have cable TV hookups and some have swimming pools, miniature golf and recreation areas. In general they are more costly than primitive camps, and often they are located in or near urban areas along primary travel routes.

The remainder of the camps listed are primitive camps. While some have conveniences like vault toilets, potable water, tables, fire rings with grates and/or grills, others have absolutely nothing but space.

Generally, Forest Service, BLM, Wyoming State Parks, county and city parks have many of the conveniences. Generally, the Wyoming Game and Fish Wildlife Habitat Management and Access Areas have limited, if any, of the niceties.

The trade-off when you opt for the Game and Fish camping options and others with few conveniences is that they are free. Camping fees are generally lower in direct proportion to the remoteness of the camp and lack of conveniences such as water, garbage collection and vault toilets.

The logic of reduced fees or free camping is that a share of the maintenance responsibility is transferred to the individual camper. In all cases we should take care of our campsites but, when rates are reduced or free we should expect to practice low impact camping (see 'Leave No Trace' page 10).

—Other pertinent information—

In addition to the camps listed under the heading for a particular city or town, other information that should be helpful is included. That information generally includes:

(1) Public swimming pools, open for a shower and relaxing dip, and recreation centers where one can exercise as well as shower. Most of the recreation centers have aerobics equipment, free weights and racquet courts, while many also have pools, spas, saunas, and steam rooms. For a quicker cleanup, try the private camps that rent showers. Under the amenities the (Showers only: $---) informs you that this camp will rent showers and the cost;

(2) The availability of groceries in the city or town which may be limited to snacks and ice or nonexistent. 'Groceries' indicates a major super market, while 'basic groceries' translates to a small market, which generally has some fresh meats and produce; 'limited groceries' signals bread, milk, eggs, some canned goods and condiments and maybe some frozen meats;

(3) Hardware and sporting goods supplies available in the area. Most of the smaller towns in Wyoming have some form of hardware outlet, but generally speaking, if you need such things as a particular brand of fishing line, lantern mantles or a cooler the selection and availability will be best in the larger communities;

(4) A few businesses which might be of special interest to campers, such as makers of custom-designed tents, packs and soft luggage;

(5) Some of the historical sites and small town museums which are favorites of the author and generally free: ($) indicates admission is charged, and

(6) A few major summer events in that area so the traveler can either make plans to attend or avoid, assuming the camps and the town will be fully booked during these celebrations. From year to year, dates for these annual events will change. Current information is available from area Chambers of Commerce. See page 350.

—How to get more information—

This book is focused on camping options and how to get to them, and provides only a brief introduction to the history and attractions of the towns. Should you want to learn more about a particular area, information is available from a variety of sources (addresses, phone numbers and web sites are listed in the back of the book). If you're planning a Wyoming vacation and like many enjoy pondering the possibilities well in advance, brochures, maps and information are easily available by phone and mail. Getting information in advance will also avoid any problems on the road when the offices distributing information may be closed.

For general information about the state, the Wyoming Business Council Division of Tourism may be your best source. They can answer phone questions and provide packets of information, including a highway map for the

State of Wyoming, which they will gladly mail upon request. For more detailed information about a certain area, most cities and towns have Chambers of Commerce that will answer questions and mail information pertinent to their region.

If you're planning a trip to one of Wyoming's national forests, advance information is available by mail, telephone or at one of the ranger district offices along the way. (All of Wyoming's national forests also have web sites, which are listed in the back of the book.) The Bureau of Land Management has offices throughout the state where information is available, but for information prior to your arrival; call or write the Cheyenne office.

This book covers most of the Wyoming Game and Fish Department areas which permit camping, but if you're visiting to fish, you may want information about all of the wildlife habitat management areas and public access areas. The Game and Fish Department's *Access to Wyoming's Wildlife* is a 164 page book available from the Cheyenne office at a cost of $7 with $4 postage and handling.

—Camping on Game and Fish areas—

The Wyoming Game and Fish department is progressive in its attitude toward the beneficial uses of lands under its control and has opened up many of its wildlife habitat management and public access areas to camping and recreational pursuits other than hunting and fishing.

One plaque at an area near Torrington states, "Experiences such as photography, nature study and observation, bird watching, wildlife education, and refuge from an increasingly 'unnatural world' are beginning to take their place alongside the more conventional outdoor pursuits of hunting and fishing." Camping at these areas is primitive. Many public access areas have vault toilets and stone fire rings constructed by earlier visitors, but there is no potable water and rarely are there tables. In most cases, access to these areas has been achieved only through negotiated leases with private land owners. The recreationist and sportsman are responsible for determining land boundaries, and are expected to practice low impact camping.

Wildlife habitat management areas are larger than access areas and offer more varied options for camping. Some offer vehicular access, and all offer parking areas. You can frequently enjoy the serenity and solitude of a near-wilderness camping experience within an easy walk of your vehicle.

The Wyoming Game and Fish Department has gone to considerable effort and expense to provide recreational access areas, but if they are abused, they will be stricken from the list of camping options. At these sites be certain to practice 'Leave No Trace' camping ethics: pack it in, pack it out and keep it clean. If all campers exercise caring stewardship at these sites, the future will be bright. Game and Fish managers and landowners will come to the table with a positive attitude about renewing existing leases and providing more public access areas around the state.

Camping limits are 5 or 14 days depending on the area. Campfires are permitted, but at many of the Game and Fish areas there is no source of wood, and gathering wood from the adjoining private property is not allowed. Bring your own firewood for many of these areas.

—Dispersed camping on public lands—

In Wyoming there are five national forests, a national grassland and the Bureau of Land Management manages 17.8 million acres of public land, which is concentrated largely in the western part of the state. The varied landscapes include deserts and dunes, badlands and grasslands, rolling foothills and lakes and streams, as well as deep gorges and canyons.

This vast amount of public land is available for multiple use, including hiking, photography, wildlife viewing and, of course, camping.

While some few areas of these public lands are closed to overnight camping much of the land is yours to camp where you please. Areas that you might expect to be closed are those within sight of scenic highways or byways and any areas where logging or oil production activities are in progress.

There are, of course, some limits and guidelines. Dispersed camping is generally limited to 14 days at the same location in any 28 day period by the BLM and 16 days in most of the forests. The exception here is the Medicine Bow National Forest where dispersed camping at the same location is limited to 21 days.

Regulations for dispersed camping are similar to wilderness regulations. Campfires, other than a self contained stove, are not allowed within 300 feet of lakes, streams or trails. Camping is not permitted within 100 feet of any lake or stream. Camping at sites posted as closed is not permitted. Camping structures such as hitching racks, tent frames, pegs, and fire rings must be dismantled after use.

With the exception of periods of extreme fire danger, campfires are allowed while enjoying remote undeveloped camping on public lands. You are encouraged to use existing stone fire rings or fire pans and you are permitted to gather 'dead and down' firewood for use at your campsite. You are expected to practice low impact camping and pack it in, pack it out (see "Leave No Trace" page 10.)

You also have the responsibility to ensure that you are on public lands and not on private lands or Wyoming State Trust lands, where campfires and overnight camping are not allowed. If dispersed camping is your preference, visit the nearest BLM office and acquire land status maps for the area you intend to visit.

—Sources for maps—

Using the phone, mail or internet, most maps can be obtained well in advance of your trip to your Wyoming campsite. A Wyoming highway map will be provided in your information packet from the Wyoming Division of tourism and is a likely enclosure with materials from area Chambers of Commerce. Forest Service maps, for any particular forest are available from Ranger District Offices or through the Grand Teton Natural History Association in Jackson (WY). The association is the best source for a variety of maps of that region and markets some maps for all of Wyoming's national forest (the mail order number is (307) 739-3403, with information and orders also possible on the web (http://www.fs.fed.us/btnf/gtnha.htm or http://www.grandteton.com/gtnha). All regional BLM offices have a supply of maps for the whole state, but they can be acquired in advance of your trip through the Cheyenne office. Map information is available on the web at: http://www.wy.blm.gov/Information/fai/wynf.0014(98).pdf. Orders must be placed by phone or mail with the Cheyenne office (see page 353). Maps for the national forests in Wyoming are available by calling the appropriate ranger district office with your request and following up with the correct amount money, including postage, by mail. At this time, they do not accept credit cards. Forest Service maps also include an informative panel which breaks out, by area and name, the more detailed United States Geological Survey (USGS) maps covering that forest. Should you need USGS maps for any part of Wyoming, they are available by contacting: Map Distribution, USGS Map Sales, Box 25286, Federal Center, Bldg. 810, Denver, CO 80225.

—Bear Rules—

Due to the proximity to Yellowstone National Park and high isolated mountain country, bear rules apply in many campgrounds. These rules are generally concerned with food odors and storage to minimize the likelihood of any interest bears might have in joining your group in camp. A few camps, where bear sightings are most likely, are restricted to hard-sided camper units. In these and some of the other camps, steel boxes are provided for the storage of food and other odoriferous items that might attract a bear. These 'Bear Boxes', usually mounted chest high on a steel pole, are steel food storage boxes about 4' long and 1.5' high and deep. They will hold a cooler and other items with food odors that might attract a bear. The neat thing about them is that the lid opens outward and downward, suspended on a chain, so it serves as a nice meal staging area or buffet area for campers. Then, when the lid is closed any odors from the cooking or spilling of food are closeted away with the cooler and other groceries. You may want to get some of the available information on preferred strategies should you meet a bear in the forests. Basically experts say to avoid eye contact and never run, but back away slowly. If hiking in bear country, experts suggest making noise to let the bears know you are nearby, as they will be more likely to clear the area than want to join your group.

—Passports—

The Golden Age Passport is available after reaching the age of 62 with a onetime $10 fee. The Golden Access Passport is free. Both provide lifetime entrance to National Parks, Monuments, and Recreation Areas which charge entrance fees and are Federally managed. They also provide a 50% discount on federal use fees, such as fee campgrounds. Both passports may be issued to citizens or permanent residents of the U. S. who meet the application criteria.

The Golden Eagle Passport is used at all Parks and Monuments which charge entrance fees. This passport costs $50 and is good for one year.

—Long Term Rates—

Many of the privately-owned RV camps have weekly and monthly rates. Inquire if you are planning to be in an area for several days or longer

—Opening and closing dates of camps—

Weather is always a question mark. All dates with regard to opening and closing are "weather permitting,"and many of the RV parks that operate year around will have limited services in the winter months.

—Maps and key—

The maps in this book are artist's drawings and, while basic, used in conjunction with the detailed directions provided you will find any of these camps with ease. Mileages are provided to the one-tenth mile and all mileages were determined using the trip meter in the same vehicle. Your trip meter may not give exactly the same distances but, if your readings are a little long or a little short, you should be able to count on consistency. Traditional symbols for interstates, state highways, BLM roads, Forest Service roads and county Roads were used and are at right.

Roadways

U.S.

State

County

BLM

—I·25— Interstate

Worth mentioning - If the places you want to go entail traveling on some of Wyoming's dirt roads, be advised these roads are usually good and well maintained but wet weather can turn many good roads into disaster areas. Wyoming is not known for its rainfall, but should it rain and you're heading into the backcountry check with locals on road conditions.

— Leave No Trace —

The lore of the West embraces and even glorifies a lawlessness exemplified by the likes of Butch Cassidy and the Sundance Kid. These hombres were likely reckless with few concerns about leaving bean cans or glowing embers for the posse's review. Modern camping, however, has lots of folks using the same campsites over and over during the few fair-weather months of spring, summer and fall.

The "Leave No Trace" program is an educational effort seeking to minimize impacts on public lands as more people use them for recreational purposes. Increasing outdoor recreation threatens both the vitality of the natural resources and the quality of recreational experiences.

Seven basic principles of the "Leave No Trace" program address low impact land use for everything from car camping to wilderness use:

(1) Plan ahead and Prepare — Expectations and equipment will vary with the type of area you intend to visit. Plan your trip accordingly, get necessary permits and follow all agency guidelines.

(2) Travel and Camp on Durable Surfaces — Many popular areas already have man-made features such as stone fire rings. Use these features when they are present, minimize changes to area and confine your activities to preserve the natural surroundings of the area. Stay on existing paths and camp at least 200 feet from lakes and streams.

(3) Dispose of waste properly — Remove litter and leave a clean campsite. Properly dispose of human waste if vault toilets are not provided (bury in "catholes" 6-8 inches deep and at least 200 feet from water). Sites in popular car camping areas are frequently plagued with unsightly gum wrappers, cigarette butts and bottle tops. Much can be done to improve your camping experience as well as those who follow. Remember the popular phrase, "Pack it in, pack it out."

(4) Leave What You Find — This does not mean leaving litter as you found it. It addresses disturbance to natural features, including rocks, plants and archaeological artifacts. As the popular saying goes, "Take nothing but pictures; leave nothing but footprints."

(5) Minimize Campfire Impacts — Campfires are one of the great joys of camping, but impacts should be minimized. Use fire pans or established fire rings while keeping fires small by burning dead and down wood no larger than your wrist. Consider using portable camp stoves.

(6) Respect Wildlife — Avoid impacts to wildlife such as habitat alteration, disturbance and harassment by humans or pets. You should enjoy wildlife from a distance, never feed wild animals, store your food securely, minimize noise and avoid sensitive wildlife habitat.

(7) Be Considerate of Other Visitors — To reduce the likelihood of conflicts with other visitors, crowding, and noise, one should make every effort to respect the privacy of other visitors, keep a quiet camp, manage your pets and let nature's sounds prevail.

The program is managed by LNT Inc., a nonprofit organization located in Boulder, Colorado. LNT Inc. oversees memberships, marketing, fund-raising and program development efforts. The National Outdoor Leadership School (NOLS) maintains the educational component of Leave No Trace by offering LNT educational courses, developing educational materials and supporting the efforts of course graduates who teach LNT to the public. This program was developed, in cooperation with Leave No Trace, Inc., a nonprofit educational corporation authorized by the National Park Service, U.S. Fish and Wildlife Service, U.S. Forest Service, Bureau of Land Management, and U.S. Fish and Wildlife Service, to promote the Leave No Trace educational message.

Fifteen 16- to 24-page pamphlets are available from LNT, Inc., including:

Alaskan Tundra	Rocky Mountains
Backcountry Horse Use	Sierra Nevada
Caving	Southeastern States
Desert and Canyon Country	Temperate Coastal Zones
North American Edition	Tropical Rainforests
Northeastern Mountains	Tropical Rainforests, Spanish Edition
Pacific Northwest	Western River Corridors
Rock Climbing	

For additional information

 LNT Inc.
(800) 332-4100
www.lnt.org

 NOLS Outreach
(307) 332-1292
outreach@nols.edu

—Wyoming State Parks—

The rates for individual state parks published in this guide reflect the action taken by the State Legislature, which raised camping and day use and camping fees for state parks effective January of 2000. For the remainder of 1999 camping at Wyoming's State Parks will be a bargain. Nonresidents will pay an entrance fee of $3 and a camping fee of $4. Annual permits for entrance to the state parks are available for residents ($25) and nonresidents ($30). An annual camping permit is available for residents only ($25).

Contents — Southeast

Southeast

Once bison cloaked the rolling grasslands of southeast Wyoming in the ermine robes of gigantic herds; then it was cattle, raised by England-born "barons" who for awhile made Cheyenne the "richest per capita" city in the world. Empires come and go, but the wealth of the tall grass and peaceful valleys on this vast prairie is undiminished.

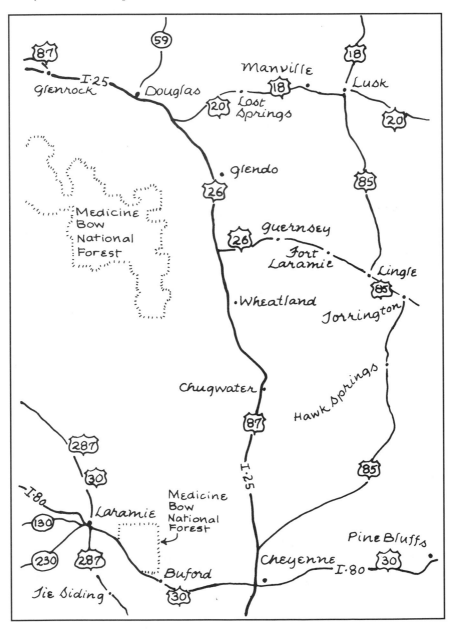

The area is surprisingly good for water sports, with four state parks and 9 of the 14 Game and Fish areas located on reservoirs; remnants of the historic pioneers who passed along the Oregon Trail can be found here; wildlife and birdwatching are excellent. Rock climbing is popular among the unique and sometimes spooky geological formations at Vedauwoo.

This section features 67 camping options, with 36 listings for privately-owned camps with hookups. Remaining options include 13 free Wyoming Game and Fish Areas, 4 Wyoming State Parks, 7 Forest Service camps, 1 free county camp and 6 free town parks. The camps are listed under headings for 16 cities and towns including Cheyenne, Chugwater, Douglas, Fort Laramie, Glendo, Glenrock, Guernsey, Hawk Springs, LaGrange, Laramie, Lusk, Manville, Pine Bluffs, Torrington and Wheatland.

Cheyenne

Cheyenne began life as a railroad camp and shares in the history of the 'Hell on Wheels' era of railroad construction in Wyoming. With the railroad and the discovery of gold in the Black Hills, Cheyenne in the 19th century became a freighting center carrying goods to the miners and gold from the smelters. Soon the vast lands, passed by thousands of emigrants, became the cattle empires of southeast Wyoming. Today, Cheyenne is Wyoming's capital city and a major commercial area.

Free tours are available at the **Wyoming State Capitol** patterned after the capitol in Washington D.C., with an impressive interior and a 146-feet-tall gilded dome; at the **Historic Governor's Mansion**, at 300 E. 21st St., and at the newly renovated **Wyoming State Museum**, in the Barrett Building at 24th and Central Ave. The **Cheyenne Frontier Days Old West Museum** in Frontier Park is one of the best in the state, at 4501 Carey Ave., open all year, seven days a week, Ph: (307) 778-7290 ($). The **Cheyenne Botanic Gardens**, at 710 S. Lions Park Dr., Ph: (307) 637-6458, has outdoor flower gardens to enjoy with a stroll on the pathways or more exotic flora for examination in the greenhouse (free). Cheyenne pulls out all the stops and the city is fully booked during the last full week in July, when they celebrate **Cheyenne Frontier Days**, the world's oldest and largest outdoor rodeo, known as the 'Daddy of 'em All.'

The **Wyoming Game and Fish Department**, at 5400 Bishop Blvd., has a short interpretive nature trail and is a good source for free publications on the state's flora and fauna as well as *Access to Wyoming's Wildlife*, the complete guide to Game and Fish Wildlife Habitat Management Areas and Access Areas ($7). The **US Bureau of Land Management**, at 5353 Yellowstone,

is another good source of information and maps: BLM maps as well as maps of the Medicine Bow National Forest. Other information is available at the **Wyoming Visitors Center** located at I-25 and College Drive (exit 7) in southeast Cheyenne (www.wyomingtourism.org).

There are nine privately-owned RV campgrounds in or near the city with all but one offering some tenting. The sole source of 'country' camping in the area is Curt Gowdy State Park west of the city, which you find in the Laramie listings. Workouts and a swim are available at the **Cheyenne YMCA** at 1426 E. Lincolnway (Day pass: $5). Ph: (307) 634-9622 and at the **Millennium Fitness Spa** at 1700 W. Lincolnway in the basement of the Hitching Post Inn, with your first visit free and $3 day pass thereafter, Ph: (307) 638-9278. Groceries, hardware, sporting goods, bicycle sales and service and RV sales and service are available in Cheyenne. The best single source in Wyoming for outerwear, tents, boots and sleeping bags is the **Sierra Trading Post** at 5025 Campstoll Road, Ph: (307) 775-8050.

AB Camping

(Private, Open March 1 to Oct. 31)
1503 West College Drive, Cheyenne, WY 82007 Ph/Fax: (307) 634-7035
E-mail: abcamping@juno.com

About the camp – Three sides of this camp south of downtown Cheyenne are bordered with trees creating a surprisingly secluded feeling for an urban campground. The camp has 150 RV sites — some shaded, and some with tables and grills — with a mix of gravel, gravel with grass 'yards' and native grass. 92 sites are pull-thrus (up to 23x65) with 58 back-ins (up to 17x40). 89 sites are full hookups (20/30/50 amp on city water). There are 40 tent sites on grass with some tables.

Amenities – Rest rooms and showers at two locations with one handicapped accessible (showers only: $4), two laundry rooms; playground, free videos with deposit; pop and ice, gifts, limited RV parts, dump station, modem jack in office and pay phone. This location is on a city bus route to Frontier Days and/or downtown.

Rates – Full hookups for 2 persons: $19.50. Electric only for 2 persons: $17.50. Tent sites for 2 persons: $12.50. Additional persons: $2. Discounts for Goodsam, AAA and FMCA. V MC D Personal checks okay. Reservations: Phone, E-mail, fax or mail.

Getting there – Westbound on I-80 use exit 364 and go to the stop sign on College Drive; then left 4.1 miles to the camp on the left.

Eastbound on I-80 use exit 359A to I-25 south; then south .5 miles on I-25 to exit 7; then left 1.5 miles on College Drive to the camp on the right.

North or southbound on I-25 use exit 7; then east 1.5 miles to the camp on the right. *See map page 18.*

Cheyenne KOA

(Private, Open April 1 to Oct. 31)
8800 Archer Frontage Rd., Cheyenne, WY 82007 Ph: (307) 638-8840 or 1-800-KOA-1507 Fax: (307) 432-9746
E-mail:manager@cheyennekoa.com

About the camp – This camp, new in 1997, is near the interstate and only 3 miles east of Cheyenne. The camp has 42 gravel pull-thrus (30x60) and grass 'yards' with some tables and grills. 12 sites are full hookups (20/30/50 amp) and 30 water and electric only. There are 10 designated tent sites on sand, with tables and grills and 5 kamper kabins. *Horses okay: free with camping and own feed.*

Amenities – Handicapped-accessible rest rooms and showers (showers only: $5), laundry; game room, playground and heated outdoor pool; limited groceries and RV parts, gift shop, modem jack in office, dump station, propane, and pay phone.

Rates – Full hookups for 2 persons: $26.95. Water and electric for 2 persons: $24.95. Tent sites for 2 persons: $19.95. Kamper Kabins for 2 persons: $34.95. Additional persons age 4 and over: $3. All major cards. Personal checks okay. Reservations: Phone, E-mail, fax or mail.

Getting there – From I-80 use exit 367; then north to the frontage road; then east .5 miles to the camp on the left. *See map page 18.*

Greenway Trailer Park

(Private, Open all year)
3829 Greenway St., Cheyenne, WY 82001 Ph: (307) 634-6696

About the camp – This camp has 32 gravel RV sites: All pull-thrus (15x50) and all full hookups (20/30/50 amp).

Amenities – Rest rooms and showers (showers only: $3), laundry; chain grocery store across street, ice, pop and pay phone.

Rates – Full hookups per site: $14. No credit cards. No personal checks. Reservations: phone or mail.

Getting there – From I-80 use exit 364 (*College Drive*); then north on College Drive 1.4 miles to E. Lincolnway; then straight across the intersection to the camp on the left. *See map page 18.*

Hide-Away

(Private, Open all year)
214 South Greeley Hwy, Cheyenne, WY 82007 Ph: (307) 637-7114

About the camp – This camp is located in south Cheyenne close to groceries, gas, restaurants and other city services. There are 25 gravel and grass RV sites with some tables and grills: one pull-thru and 24 back-ins (all up to 12x40). 9 sites are full hookups (30/50 amp). 5 tent sites are available on grass with tables and grills.

18

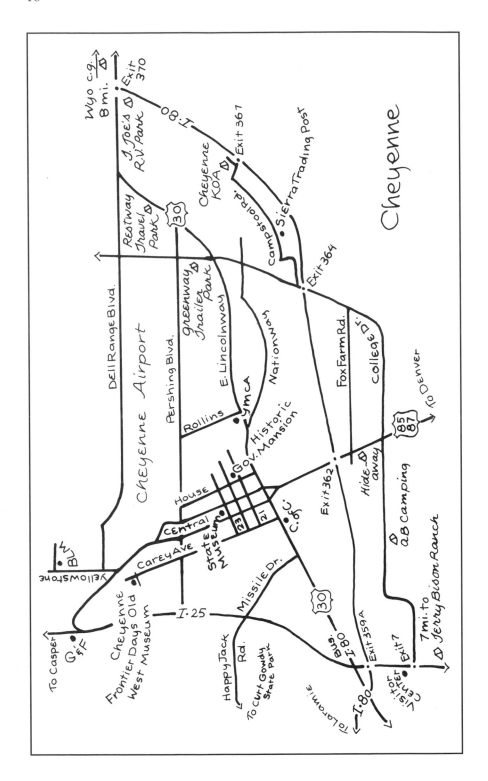

Amenities – Rest rooms and showers (showers only: $5), laundry; pay phone and close proximity to a variety of city services .

Rates – Any RV site for 2 persons: $14. Tent site for 2 persons: $14. Additional persons: $2. No credit cards. Personal checks okay. Reservations: Phone or mail.

Getting there – From I-80 use exit 362; then south on S. Greeley Hwy to the traffic light at Fox Farm Road; then straight ahead .1 miles on S. Greeley Hwy to the camp on the right. *See map facing page.*

Restway Travel Park

(Private, Open all year)
4212 Whitney Road, Cheyenne, WY 82001 Ph: (307)634-3811 or (800) 443-2751 Fax: (307) 635-6744

About the camp – This camp has 112 RV sites: 76 pull-thrus (up to 22x50) and 36 back-ins (up to 30x35). 57 sites are full hookups (30/50 amp) with 65 water and electric only. Sites are gravel with grass 'yards' and most have tables with some grills. 13 tent sites are designated with grills and tables.

Amenities – Rest rooms and showers (showers only. $5), laundry; cable available at full hookups ($2), heated outdoor pool, game room, playground, free miniature golf, badminton, group campfire on demand and weather permitting; limited groceries and RV parts, dump station and pay phone.

Rates – Full hookups for 4 persons: $15.50. Water and electric for 4 persons: $14.50. Tent sites for 4 persons: $12.50-13.50. Additional persons: $2. Discounts on all current camping cards. No credit cards. No personal checks. Reservations: Phone, fax or mail.

Getting there – From I-80 use exit 364; then north .5 miles to E. Lincolnway; then east .5 miles on E. Lincolnway to Whitney St.; then north .1 miles to the camp on the left. *See map facing page.*

Terry Bison Ranch

(Private, Open all year)
51 I-25 Service Road East, Cheyenne, WY 82007 Ph: (307) 634-4171 Fax: (307) 634-9746

About the camp – Terry Bison Ranch is about 7 miles south of Cheyenne on 27,500 acres with lots of western flavor. The camp has 93 RV sites: all are pull-thrus (24x70) with full hookups (20/30/50 amp) on gravel with grass 'yards' and tables. Tent sites or 'dry' sites are available as well as 3 full-service cabins which sleep 4 and 17 bunk house rooms which sleep 2 and share a bath. *Horse boarding available.*

Amenities – Handicapped-accessible rest rooms and showers, laundry; playground; limited groceries and RV supplies, gift shop, full-service restaurant, saloon, Wyoming's only winery and pay phones. The ranch offers activities such as trail rides, pony rides, horse-drawn wagon rides, private (no license required) fishing pond with own tackle, paddle boat and canoe rentals, bus tours to the buffalo herd, chuckwagon dinners (summer only) and Tuesday and Saturday night rodeos (summer except during Frontier Days).

Rates – Full hookups per site: $16.50-19.50. Tent sites or no hookups: $12.50-$14.50. Discounts for Goodsam, FMCA, AAA and AARP. V MC D Personal checks okay. Reservations: phone.

Getting there – From I-25 use exit 2 about 7 miles south of Cheyenne; then east to the service road; then south 2.5 miles to the camp on the left. *See map page 18.*

T-Joe's RV Park

(Private, Open all year)
PO Box 2267 (12700 East I-80 Service Road), Cheyenne, WY 82003 Ph: (307) 635-8750

About the camp – This open 3-acre camp is located near I-80 and just east of Cheyenne proper. The camp has 38 gravel pull-thru sites (up to 26x52) with some tables. 20 sites are full hookups (30/50 amp) with 18 water and electric only. 10 grass tents sites with tables and grills are available. *Horses okay.*

Amenities – Rest rooms and showers (showers only: $3), laundry; adjacent to steak house and saloon with game room, limited gifts, dump station and pay phone. Reservations: Phone or mail.

Rates – Full hookups for 2 persons: $18-20. Water and electric for 2 persons: $14-16. Tents for 2 persons: $13. Additional persons: $2.

Getting there – From I-80 use exit 370; then north to the service road; then left to the camp on the right. *See map page 18.*

WYO Campground

(Private, Open May 1 to Oct. 31)
PO Box 5201, Cheyenne, WY 82003 Ph: (307) 547-2244

About the camp – This camp ground is spacious, level, near I-80 and only about 15 miles east of Cheyenne. The camp has 70 sites: 50 pull-thrus and 20 back-ins (all up to 24x60). 50 sites are full hookups (20/30/50 amp) and 20 electric only. The sites have gravel spurs with native grass 'yards' and some tables. 50 tent sites are available. *Horses okay: with own feed $4.*

Amenities – Rest rooms and showers (showers only: $5), laundry; game room, heated outdoor pool, large common covered patio with grills and tables at pool-side; pop and ice, dump station and pay phone.

Rates – Full hookups for 2 persons: $14.50-22.50. Electric only for 2 persons: $13.50-20.50. Tent sites for 2 persons: $12.50-18.50. Additional persons: $2. Discount: $1 on all current camper cards. V MC Personal checks okay. Reservations: Phone or mail.

Getting there – From I-80 use exit 377; then north to the stop sign on the frontage road; then east .3 miles to the camp on the left. *See map page 18.*

Chugwater

In mid-May, Chugwater hosts the **Chugwater Chili Cookoff**, the largest single-day event in the state. Chugwater is also the headquarters for **Chugwater Chili®**, a gourmet spice mix for chili and dips sold nationally. The **Chugwater Soda Fountain**, on Main St., is the place for a nostalgic ice cream treat, with sundaes, sodas and 30 flavors of malts and shakes. There is a small museum across the street from the soda fountain open summers, Sat. and Sun. from 1-5 p.m. In Chugwater there is one small privately-owned camp for RVs only and to the west a resort ranch with camping for RVs or tents as well as a variety of recreational pursuits. Limited groceries are available at the C-store near exit 54 on I-25 and at the soda fountain.

Diamond Guest Ranch

(Private, Open all summer)
PO Box 236, Chugwater, WY 82210 Ph: (307) 422-3564 or (800) 932-4222

About the camp – This resort ranch camp is located about 12 miles west of Chugwater at the headquarters of the 75,000-acre Diamond Ranch. There are 106 grass RV sites with tables and some grills: 10 pull-thrus and 96 pull-ins (all up to 18x45). 27 sites are full hookups (20/30 amp) and 79 are water and electric only. 25 tent sites with tables are also available. This camp has 25 lodging options in cabins, stalls and ranch rooms.

Amenities – Rest rooms and showers (showers only: $2), laundry; heated pool, game room, playground, volleyball, basketball, horseshoes, mountain biking, trail rides, pony rides, hayrides, fishing and hunting; restaurant, lounge, limited groceries and RV parts, gift shop, dump stations, and pay phone.

Rates – Any RV site for 2 persons: $18. Tent site for 2 persons: $14. Additional persons: $2. Cabins, stalls and rooms: $20 to $70 per night. Discounts: GoodSam and FMCA. MC V Personal checks okay. Reservations: phone.

Getting there – From I-25 use exit 54; then go west .1 miles to Diamond Road; then right 12.5 miles to the camp on the left (*Diamond Road is paved for the first 7 miles*).

Pitzer RV Park

(Private, Open all year)
PO Box 56, Chugwater, WY 82210 Ph: (307) 422-3421

About the camp – This open, level camp is located in a residential area 2 blocks from Business I-25 through Chugwater. There are 8 full hookup (20/50 amp on city water) back-in RV sites with gravel spurs and grass 'yards'. No showers or rest rooms. No water hookups from Nov. to April 15.

Amenities – Cable TV at all sites ($1).

Rates – Full hookups per site: $10. No credit cards. Personal checks accepted. Reservations: phone or mail.

Getting there – Southbound on I-25 use exit 57 and follow Business I-25 into Chugwater 2.8 miles to Clay St.; then right 2 blocks to camp on left.

Northbound on I-25 use exit 54 and follow Business I-25 into Chugwater .6 miles to Clay St.; then left two blocks to camp on left.

Douglas

Douglas is the self-proclaimed lair of Wyoming's mythical **Jackalope**, a hybrid of the jack rabbit and the pronghorn antelope that breeds in taxidermy salons across the state. Surely you've noticed these creatures, on post cards (the only verified sightings of the beast). Douglas hosts the annual **Jackalope Days** in June and the **Wyoming State Fair** with three-days of professional rodeo in August (expect camps to be full). On the fairgrounds you find the excellent and free **Pioneer Memorial Museum**, Ph: (307) 358-9288, open M-Sat, during the summer. About 11 miles north of town is **Fort Fetterman**, open daily from Memorial Day to Labor Day; to the west off of I-25 are **Ayres Park and Natural Bridge**, and to the south the northern part of the **Medicine Bow National Forest**.

In Douglas, there are two privately-owned camps, a free city park and caravan camping at the state fair grounds. Outside of town, there are six camps: a free county-owned camp, four Forest Service camps and a small camp at Esterbrook Lodge. *Horse stalls are also available at the fair grounds: $5 per horse with own feed.* Groceries, hardware and sporting goods are available. There is a free (all you need is a any kind of photo ID) rec center with pool and sauna, at 1701 Hamilton, Ph: (307) 358-4231 and in summer an outdoor pool with modest fees in Washington Park, at 701 E. Center St.

Douglas Jackalope KOA Kampground

(Private, Open April 1 to Nov. 1)
PO Box 1190, Douglas WY 82633 Ph: (307) 358-2164

About the camp – This camp, located just west of Douglas, is nicely landscaped on a grassy slope with trees and flowers. The camp has 60 gravel RV sites: 30 pull-thrus and 30 back-ins (all 30x50). 57 sites are full hookups (20/30/50 amp) and 3 are water and electric only. Tent sites are grass with grills and tables.

Amenities – Rest rooms and showers, laundry; cable TV at 41 sites ($2), heated swimming pool, video games in office/store area and miniature golf ($3); limited groceries and RV parts, gift shop with curios, jewelry, caps and T-shirts.

Rates – Full hookups for 2 persons: $21. Water and electric for 2 persons: $19. Tent sites for 2 persons: $16. Kamper kabins for 2 persons: $27. Additional persons: $2. Discounts: KOA and Goodsam. V MC D Reservations: phone or mail.

Getting there – Northbound on I-25 use exit 140; then follow Business I-25 to the 4-way stop; then right .3 miles to the junction of Hwys 91 and 94; then right .2 miles, going under I-25; then right 1.8 miles on Hwy 91 to the camp on the left.

Southbound on I-25 use exit 146; then west to the frontage road; then left 4.4 miles to the camp on the right. *See map page 24.*

Lone Tree Village RV Park

(Private, Open April to Nov.)
401 S. Russell, Douglas, WY 82633 Ph: (307)358-6669

About the camp – This camp is open and convenient to I-25. The camp has 26 full hookup (30/50 amp), gravel and native grass RV sites: 18 pull-thrus (20x75) and 8 back-ins (20x60). Grass tent sites, with some tables, are available throughout the camp.

Amenities – Rest rooms and showers, laundry; cable included in full hookups and pay phone.

Rates – Full hookups per site: $10.70. Electric only per site: $7.50. Tent sites: $5. No credit cards. Personal checks okay.

Getting there – From I-25 use exit 140; then follow Business I-25 to the 4-way stop; then right for .5 miles to the camp on the left. *See map page 24.*

Riverside Park

(City of Douglas, Open all year)

About the camp – This pleasant city park is located in the northeast part of Douglas along the North Platte River. The park is level and trees are abundant. There is plenty of gravel parking for RV's, a dump station, dumpsters and large grass areas with tables and grills. Tenting is allowed on the grass, but take care as there are buried lines for a sprinkler system and watering starts automatically at 8 a.m. Clean, spacious rest rooms have hot showers, automatic hand blow dryers, electric outlets at the mirrored sinks and feature a western decor with local brands on the woodwork and horseshoes for towel and clothes racks. From this park, you access a two-mile long paved walking or bicycling path along the west bank of the North Platte River. All in all, it's a five-pine-cone rating in the world of free camping, as well as a prime example of western hospitality.

Rates – Free, but the stay is limited to 48 hours, starting at 8 a.m. on your first day.

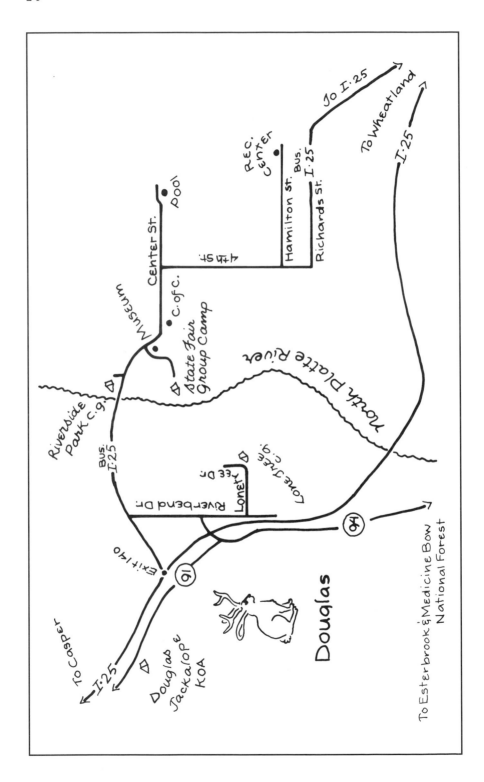

Getting there – From I-25 use exit 140; then follow Business I-25 to the 4-way stop; then straight .7 miles to the camp on the left (*just across the bridge over the North Platte River*). *See map facing page.*

State Fair Group Camper Park
(State Fair Grounds, Open all year)

About the camp – This camp is only for groups with a minimum of 10 campers, RVs or trailers. There are approximately 600 sites: 334 full hookups, 217 water and electric and the remainder no hookups. Most sites are on native grass. The camp has rest rooms, shower, potable water and a dump station. *Horse stalls are also available at the fair grounds: $5 per horse with own feed.*

Rates – Camping per night, per camper unit: $5 (with minimum of 10 camper units).

Getting there – From I-25 use exit 140; then follow Business I-25 to the 4-way stop; then straight .8 miles to the fair grounds on the right. *See map facing page.*

Ayres Natural Bridge
(County owned, Open April to Oct. - 8 a.m. to 8 p.m.)
Rt. 1- 208 Natural Bridge Road, Douglas, WY 82633 Ph: (307) 358-3532

About the camp – This camp is tucked into a little green basin with lots of grass and trees, and a stream running under the natural bridge for which the area is named. The camp has 9 RV sites with combo grills/ fire rings and tables, and 5 tent sites with fire rings, grills and tables.

No hookups, no wood, no showers, no dump, no potable water and no pets. There are 5 vault toilets throughout the park: one is handicapped accessible. Late arrivals and early risers take note: The gate at this park is locked nightly (8 p.m. to 8 a.m.). Stay limited to three continuous nights with permission of the on-site caretaker.

Amenities – Fishing, swimming and tubing in the river which flows under the natural bridge, hiking on adjacent state land, and volleyball and horseshoes with deposit. In the picnic areas there are five large covered group shelters, which can be reserved, and a playground. Ayres Natural Bridge is a local favorite and the frequent setting for family reunions and weddings.

Rates – Overnight camping is free, but donations to help defray the cost of operating the park are welcome and greatly appreciated.

Getting there – From I-25 use exit 151; then south five miles on CR 13 to the camp. *See map page 27.*

Campbell Creek Campground
(Medicine Bow National Forest, Open June 10 to Oct. 31)

About the camp – This camp is in a conifer forest mix with 9 sites on a short loop road. The camp has a vault toilet and potable water. Sites have tables and fire rings with grates. Stay limited to 14 days.

Rates – Campsite per night: $5. Rates half with Golden Age or Access Passports.

Getting there – From I-25 use exit 146 (*about 6 miles north of Douglas*); then west to the frontage road; then south 3 miles to Hwy 91; then right 20.5 miles where Hwy 91 becomes CR 24; then 2 miles on CR 24 to a fork in the road; then right 11.3 miles on CR 24 (*Cold Springs Road*) to the camp on the left. *See map facing page.*

Curtis Gulch Campground
(Medicine Bow National Forest, Open May 1 to Oct. 31)

About the camp – This camp is in light forest along LaBonte Creek in LaBonte Canyon. The camp has 6 sites on a short loop road. The camp has a vault toilet and potable water. Sites have tables and fire rings with grates. Stay limited to 14 days.

Rates – Campsite per night: $5. Rates half with Golden Age or Access Passports.

Getting there – From I-25 use exit 146 (*about 6 miles north of Douglas*); then west to the frontage road; then south 3 miles to Hwy 91; then right 20.5 miles where Hwy 91 becomes CR 24; then 2 miles on CR 24 to a fork in the road; then left 13.0 miles on CR 16 (*Ft. Fetterman Road) to FSR 658 (*Labonte Road*); then left 4.5 miles on 658 to the camp. *See map facing page.*

Worth mentioning – When you first turn off on FSR 658 (*LaBonte Road*) you see private property signs. There is, however, an access to the forest boundary .8 miles in on this road. Should you prefer a more isolated camp, about 1 mile in on LaBonte Road, and for the next 2 miles, note the various dispersed camping options available along the creek to the left of the road.

Esterbrook Campground
(Medicine Bow National Forest, Open June 1 to Oct. 31)

About the camp – This camp, in forest of primarily lodgepole pine, has 12 roomy sites with good tenting options. The camp has vault toilets and potable water. Site 1 is a group site (15 people and 4 vehicles maximum). Sites 3-5 are shady walk-in sites. Sites have tables, fire rings with grates and grills. Stay limited to 14 days.

Rates – Campsite per night: $5. Group site per night: $8. Rates half with Golden Age or Access Passports.

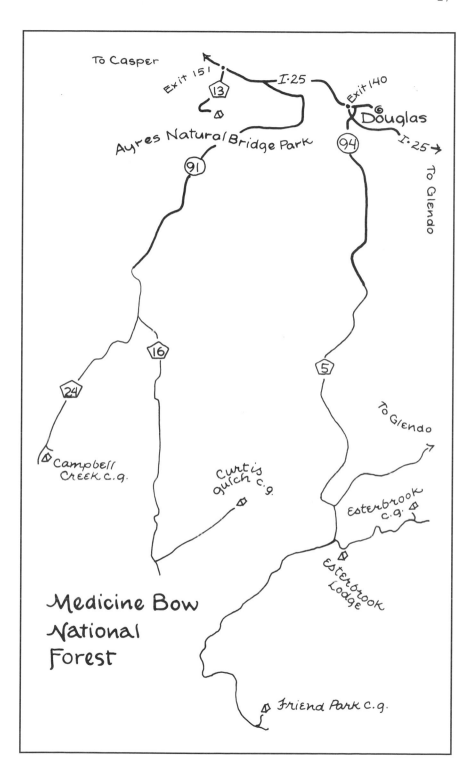

To Casper

Exit 151

I-25

Exit 140

13

94

Douglas

I-25 →

To Glendo

Ayres Natural Bridge Park

91

16

5

24

To Glendo

Campbell Creek c.g.

Curtis Gulch c.g.

Esterbrook c.g.

Esterbrook Lodge

Medicine Bow National Forest

Friend Park c.g.

Getting there – Use I-25 exit 140 and follow Business I-25 to the 4-way stop: then right .3 miles to the junction of Hwys 91 and 94; then right 16.5 miles on Hwy 94 (where the pavement ends) to the fork of CR 5 (Esterbrook Road) and CR 7 (Braae Road); then left about 10 miles on CR 5 to the junction of FSR 633; then straight .3 miles on 633; then left 3.2 miles on 633 to the camp on the left. *See map page 27.*

Esterbrook Lodge

(Private, Open all year)
32 Pine-Esterbrook, Douglas, WY 82633 Ph: (307) 358-6103

About the camp – This small camp is grassy in an open forest of lodge-pole pine behind Esterbrook Lodge. The camp has 4 RV sites: all pull-thrus (up to 18x45) and all with water and electric (20/30 amp) only. Sites are gravel with grass 'yards' and have tables and some grills. Grass tent sites are available with some tables and grills. The lodge also has two cabins sleeping 2 each and one cabin sleeping up to 6. *Horses okay in free corrals.*

Amenities – Rest rooms and showers (showers only: $3); play area and horseshoes; restaurant, lounge, banquet facility and catering and propane.

Rates – Water and electric per site: $15. Tent sites: $5. No credit cards. Personal checks okay. Reservations: Phone or mail

Getting there – Use I-25 exit 140 and follow Business I-25 to the 4-way stop: then right .3 miles to the junction of Hwys 91 and 94; then right 16.5 miles on Hwy 94 (where the pavement ends) to the fork of CR 5 (Esterbrook Road) and CR 7 (Braae Road); then left about 10 miles on CR 5 to the junction of FSR 633; then straight .5 miles on 633 to the lodge. *See map page 27.*

Friend Park Campground

(Medicine Bow National Forest, Open June 1 to Oct. 31)

About the camp – This camp in light lodgepole pine forest at the Laramie Peak Trailhead has 11 roomy sites with good tenting options, vault toilets and potable water. Sites 4-6 are walk-in sites and sites 7-9 have decent tenting options, but they are a little cozy. Sites have tables, fire rings with grates and grills. Stay limited to 14 days.

Rates – Campsite per night: $5. Rates half with Golden Age or Access Passports.

Getting there – Use I-25 exit 140 and follow Business I-25 to the 4-way stop; then right .3 miles to the junction of Hwys 91 and 94; then right 16.5 miles on Hwy 94 (where the pavement ends) to the fork of CR 5 (Esterbrook Road) and CR 7 (Braae Road); then left about 10 miles on CR 5 to the junction of FSR 633; then right on CR 5 about 16 miles (*CR 5 will change to CR 710 at the county line*) to the junction of FSR 671; then left 2.6 miles to FSR 661; then left 1.1 miles to the camp. *See map page 27.*

Fort Laramie

The small town of Fort Laramie—not to be confused with Laramie the university town— is of the same name as the **Fort Laramie National Historic Site** three miles south of town. Historically, Fort Laramie served as an Indian Trading Post, an emigrant way station along the Oregon Trail and a military outpost. The site is well preserved and a visit is a quality trip through time, led by staff donning period attire of outpost life on the frontier. Visitors Center Ph: (307) 837-2221. The town of Fort Laramie hosts the **One Summer Day Rendezvous** on the third weekend in July.

There are two privately-owned camps in town, and two others rural; one just to the south of the historic site and another five miles southwest along Hwy 26. Another option is free camping in town at Fort Laramie South Town Park. Limited groceries, snacks and ice are available.

Bennett Court and Campground

(Private, Open all year)
PO Box 54, Fort Laramie, WY 82212 Ph: (307)837-2270

About the camp – This small grassy camp in residential Fort Laramie is just off US 26. The camp has 6 grassy, full hookup (30 amp) sites. Three sites are pull-thrus (17 x 55) and 3 are back-ins (25 x 35). There are 2 grass tent sites.

Rates – Full hookups per site: $12 incl. tax. Tent sites: $9 incl. tax. No credit cards.

Amenities – Rest rooms and showers (showers only: $1.) and laundry. Reservations: Phone or mail.

Getting there – From US 26 in downtown Fort Laramie, turn north on N. Laramie Ave.; then 3 blocks to the camp on the right. *See map page 30.*

Carnahan Ranch

(Private Open May 1 to Oct. 1)
HC 72 Box 440, Fort Laramie, WY 82212 Ph/Fax: (307) 837-2917 or (800) 837-6730

About the camp – This native grass camp, located on 10 acres, near the headquarters of this 2400 acre ranch, is a little over 3 miles from the town of Fort Laramie and .5 miles from the entrance to the Fort Laramie National Historic Site. Ample space, with some tables and grills, is available for RV units or tents. 2 sites are available with electric only (20 amp). 4 Teepees sleeping from 2-3 to 6 and up are also available. Chuck wagon dinners and cattle roundups are available for groups of 20 or more as well as individual ranch experience vacation packages (with your own horses and reservations required).

Amenities – Rest rooms and showers; pool table, river fishing, yard games; common kitchen with electric range, refrigerator, and sink. *Horses okay: corrals and stalls $7.*

Rates – Electric hookups per site: $20. Tents and no hookup sites: $15. Teepees: $25-35. Reservations: phone, fax or mail.

Getting there – From the junction of Hwy 160 and US 26 in Fort Laramie, go southwest 3.2 miles on Hwy 160; then left (*just after the pavement ends at the river bridge*) .4 miles to the camp. *See map below.*

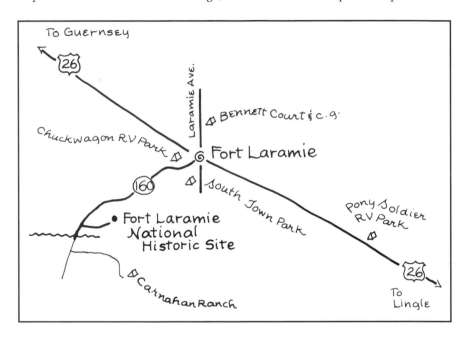

Chuckwagon RV Park

(Private, Open all year)
306 Pioneer Court, Fort Laramie, WY 82212 Ph: (307) 837-2828

About the camp – This camp at the fork of US 26 and Hwy 160 headed to the Fort Laramie Historic Site, has 13 grassy sites with full hookups (30/50 on city water). 11 sites are pull-thrus (up to 20x70) with 2 back-ins (20x35). Tent sites are available.

Amenities – Rest rooms and showers (showers only: $2).

Rates – Full hookups for 4 persons: $13. Tent sites or no hookups: $10. No credit cards. Reservations: phone or mail.

Getting there – On the west end of town turn south off of US 26 onto Hwy 160; then .1 miles to the camp on the right. *See map above.*

Fort Laramie South Town Park

(Town of Fort Laramie, Open April 15 to Oct. 31)
For more information: Ph: (307) 837-2711

About the camp – This city park is grassy and shady with rest rooms, potable water, a playground, 2 covered picnic areas and 3 grills. RVs and tenters welcome, but if setting up a tent on the grass be advised there is a buried sprinkler system and automatic watering from 12 to 3 a.m. The rest rooms are open 24 hours a day during warm weather (the open dates above indicate likely months when the water is on), but you can stay earlier or later if self-contained and not in need of the rest room facilities. Camping here is free with the singular request that you *keep it clean*! Stay limited to 3 days.

Rates – Free, with donations welcome and appreciated.

Getting there – From US 26 in downtown Fort Laramie, turn south on Laramie Ave. and follow this street about 2 blocks south to the city park on the right. *See map facing page.*

Pony Soldier RV Park

(Private, Open April 15 to Oct. 15)
PO Box 575 Lingle, WY 82227 Ph: (307) 332-3087

About the camp – This camp, located on US 26 midway between Lingle and Fort Laramie, is large, open and level. The camp has 65 gravel and native grass pull-thru sites (20x60): 35 full hookups (30/50 amp) and 30 water and electric only. Tent sites are available with some tables and portable grills. *Horses okay: free in adjacent field.*

Amenities – Rest rooms and showers, laundry; volleyball, horseshoes and rec field for team sports; snack bar, gift shop, limited groceries and RV parts, dump station and pay phone.

Rates – Full hookups per site: $15. Water and electric per site: $14. Tent site: $10. Discount for Goodsam. No credit cards. Reservations: phone or mail.

Getting there – This camp is 5 miles east of Fort Laramie and 5 miles west of Lingle on the north side of US 26. *See map facing page.*

Worth mentioning – Adjacent to this camp is the Western History Center, a museum highlighting local archaeology (modest admission).

Glendo

Glendo is a small town near the entrance to **Glendo State Park.** The state park has a 12,500-acre reservoir with fishing and water sports, as well as 165 tent or RV campsites, but no hookups. For hookups and hot showers, there is a privately-owned camp in town. Basic groceries, fishing tackle and limited hardware and sporting goods are available. The marina inside the state park has a small self-contained RVs only option. Glendo's small free museum, at 202 S. Yellowstone Ave., is open all year, 8-4, M-F.

Glendo State Park

(Wyoming State Parks, Open all year)
PO Box 398, Glendo, WY 82213 Ph: (307) 735-4433

About the camp – Glendo Dam was completed in 1957 forming a reservoir three miles long and two miles across at its widest point. This body of water, like so many in Wyoming, is a big draw for campers, water sports fans, anglers and swimmers and sun bathers, who muster on Sandy Beach. There are three boat launches at the park and a marina offering boat rentals, fuel and other supplies (see Halls Glendo Marina below). Below the dam, there is a popular launch site for a 12-mile float on the North Platte River to Guernsey State Park. There are three hiking trails within the park each about one-mile long. Two wetlands trails feature interpretive displays and are wheelchair-accessible. There is a dump station and the park has 300 RV or tent sites (no hookups) at various locations, and primitive or from-your-boat camping is allowed anywhere in the facility. All camps have vault toilets and sites have table and fire rings with grates. There is a Visitor Center, museum and gift shop. Stay limited to 14 consecutive days.

Rates – Day use fees for this park are $2 for residents and $5 for nonresidents. Camping fees for residents are $4 per night and $9 for nonresidents. An annual day use pass, good at all state parks, is available to residents for $25 and nonresidents for $40. Annual camping permits are available to residents for $30. The annual camping permit is not available for nonresidents. (For '99 rates see page 11)

Getting there – Use I-25 exit 111; then east about .2 miles to the stop sign in Glendo at Hwy 319 (*S. Yellowstone Ave.*); then right .1 miles to "C" St.; then left 1 block to Lincoln Ave.; then right 1.3 miles to the fee booth for the state park.

Hall's Glendo Marina

(Private, Open all summer)
383 Glendo Park Road, Glendo, WY 82213 Ph: (307)735-4216 Fax: (307) 735-4203

About the camp – This busy marina offers the only hookups available at Glendo State Park, with 8 sites on open ground near the marina store and office. All sites all pull-thrus (up to 20x34) and all full hookups (30 amp). No tents, but they offer 6 motel units.

Amenities – Groceries, cafe, fishing tackle, water sports equipment and boat sales, rentals on jet skis, fishing boats, pontoon boats, water skis, knee boards and tubes, propane, gas, full service marine repair and pay phone.

Rates – Full hookups per site: $15. Motel units for 2 persons: $48. V MC D Reservations: phone or mail.

Getting there – Use I-25 exit 111; then east about .2 miles to the stop sign in Glendo at Hwy 319 (*S. Yellowstone Ave.*); then right .1 miles to "C" St.; then left 1 block to Lincoln Ave.; then right 1.3 miles to the fee booth for the state park; then 1.6 miles to the marina turnoff to the left; then left .2 miles to the marina parking lot.

Lakeview Motel and Campground

(Private, Open all year)
422 6th St. (PO Box 231), Glendo, WY 82213 Ph: (307) 735-4461

About the camp – This camp on the north end of the town of Glendo is open and level. The camp has 15 RV sites: 2 pull-thrus (15x40) and 13 back-ins (up to 15x35). All RV sites are full hookups (20 amp) on native grass with some tables. Tent sites available on grass with some tables.

Amenities – Rest rooms, showers (showers only: $3), laundry.

Rates – Full hookups per site: $12. Tent sites: $10. V MC Reservations: phone or mail.

Getting there – Use I-25 exit 111; then east about .2 miles to the stop sign in Glendo at Hwy 319 (*S. Yellowstone Ave.*); then left .3 miles to 6th St.; then right into the camp.

Glenrock

Glenrock is the shortened version of **Rock in the Glen**, a landmark on which many Oregon Trail emigrants etched their monikers while pausing along the grassy banks of Deer Creek. Since those days, the town has seen seasons of prosperity through coal, oil and cattle. The **Dave Johnson Power Plant** located about 5 miles southeast of town is one of the largest coal-fired plants in the Rocky Mountains. The **Glenrock Deer Creek Museum** at 935 Birch St. is free and open daily Memorial Day to Labor Day, and the **Glenrock Paleontological Museum,** at 125 Mustang Trail, is free and open Tues., Thurs. and Sat. afternoons, Ph: (307) 436-2667. Camps are full in mid-July when Glenrock celebrates during **Deer Creek Days** with a mountain man rendezvous, carnival, parade and more, Ph: (307) 436-5652.

Camps located here include a privately-owned camp in town, a free town rec area and two free Game and Fish Areas along the North Platte River southeast of town. Groceries, sporting goods and hardware stores are available here. In the same building as the paleontological museum is the **Glenrock Recreation Center** for free workouts and showers. Swimming is also free with the pool located in town at the middle school. Ph: (307) 436-5434.

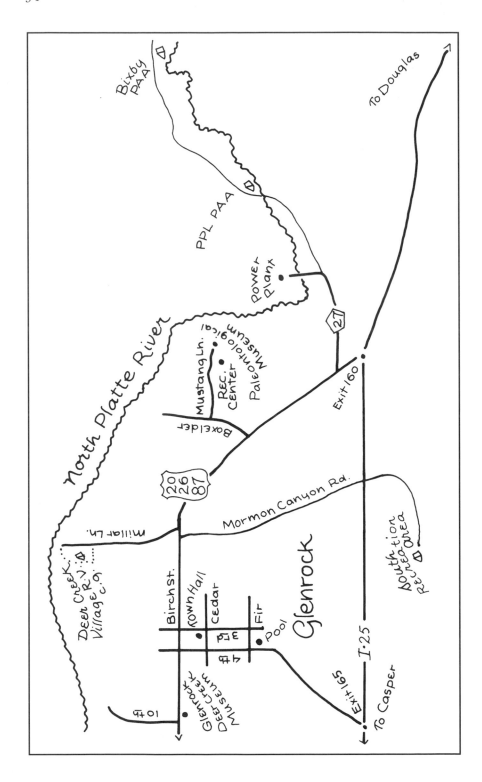

Deer Creek Village RV Campground

(Private, Open all year)

PO Box 1003, Glenrock, WY 82637 Ph: (307) 436-8121 Fax: (307) 436-5779 E-mail: LDRCREEK@aol.com

About the camp – This camp is located adjacent to the town park just northeast of downtown Glenrock in a large grassy area with lots of trees. The camp has 40 RV sites: 10 pull-thrus and 30 back-ins (all 50x100). All sites are full hookups (30/50 amp) on grass with tables. Grass tent sites are available throughout the area.

Amenities – Rest rooms and showers, laundry; cable TV (all sites: $1), use of the city park with tennis courts, volleyball and basketball; snacks and ice.

Rates – Full hookups for 2 persons: $14. Tents or no hookups for 2 persons: $12. Additional persons: $2. No credit cards. Personal checks okay. Reservations: phone, E-mail, fax or mail.

Getting there – Northbound on I-25 use exit 160; then west and north 4.7 miles on US20/26 to Millar Lane; then right .4 miles to camp.

Southbound on I-25 use exit 165; then left 2 miles to the 4-way stop in the center of Glenrock; then right .4 miles to Millar Lane; then left .4 miles to the camp. *See map page 34.*

Glenrock South Recreation Complex

(Town of Glenrock, Open all year)

About the camp – This camp is along Deer Creek in a stand of cotton-wood trees. The camp has vault toilets, potable water and is adjacent to a baseball field and rodeo arena. There are 7 sites with tables and grills and between 2 and 3 acres where dispersed camping is permitted. Stay limited to 5 days.

Rates – Free

Getting there – Northbound on I-25 use exit 160; then west and north 4.7 miles on US20/26 to Mormon Canyon Road; then left 1.9 miles to a fork just after going under I-25; then right .5 miles to another fork; then right .3 miles to the camp.

Southbound on I-25 use exit 165; then left 2 miles to the 4-way stop in the center of Glenrock; then right .4 miles to Mormon Canyon Road; then right 1.9 miles to a fork just after going under I-25; then right .5 miles; then right again .3 miles to the camp. *See map page 34.*

Bixby North Platte Access Area

(Wyoming Game and Fish, Open all year)

About the camp – This camp is located on the North Platte River below the Dave Johnson Power Plant about 12 miles south of Glenrock. The site is gravel with two nice grassy areas, one in a mature stand of cottonwood trees. There is a handicapped accessible vault toilet and one stone fire ring, but no potable water or tables. There is a nice camping spot on a grassy area beneath some cottonwoods, and the fishing can be excellent. Stay limited to 5 days.

Rates – Free

Getting there – From I-25 use exit 160: then west and north on US20/26 to CR 27 (*which goes to the power plant*); then right 8.2 miles on CR 27 (*past the power plant*) to the area on the right.

From the 4-way stop sign at Birch and S. Fourth Sts. in downtown Glenrock go east 4.6 miles on US 20/26 to CR 27 (which *goes to the power plant*); then left 8.2 miles (*past the power plant*) on CR 27 to the area on the right. *See map page 34.*

Guernsey

Guernsey, another Wyoming town with the highway as its main street, offers several good reasons for stopping. As the self-proclaimed "**Hub of the Oregon Trail**," it is near the **Oregon Trail Ruts** and **Register Cliffs State Historic Sites** as well as **Guernsey State Park**. Buildings, roads and bridges at Guernsey State Park were constructed in the 1930's by the **Civilian Conservation Corps** (CCC). The **Guernsey State Park Museum**, housed in a rock and hand-hewn log building, is open daily, 10-6 from Memorial Day to Labor Day. Ph: (307) 836-2900. The town of Guernsey has a small free museum and visitors center at the corner of S. Wyoming Ave. and Sunrise St. and behind the visitors center is an outdoor swimming pool, open summers with modest fees.

Near the historic sites the of town Guernsey has a small camp with water and electric hookups and the state park has 142 tent or RV sites, but no hookups. Guernsey you has groceries, hardware and some sporting goods.

Guernsey State Park

(Wyoming State Parks, Open all year: full service May 1 to Sept. 30)
PO 429, Guernsey, WY 82214 Ph: (307) 836-2334

About the camp – Guernsey Reservoir was formed in 1927 when an earthen dam was built by the US Bureau of Reclamation. The main purpose, then as now, is for irrigation (usually the reservoir's water level is dramatically reduced right after the 4th of July weekend and not restored until early August). The reservoir has 2,375 acres of water surface when full and there are 6,227 acres of park lands. In 1933 the **Civilian Conservation Corps** (CCC) came and in three years created the park facilities and trails, leaving for posterity some examples of their finest works. CCC projects in this park include roads, bridges, hiking trails and buildings including the Castle, a two-story overlook with stone fireplace and picnicking area; Brimmer Point lookout, and the Museum, constructed of stone, hand-hewn timbers and hand-forged iron hinges and chandeliers, with flagstone floors.

Deer, antelope, raccoon, porcupine and badger are commonly seen residents along with hundreds of species of birds. This state park is picturesque with land forms that vary from high sandstone cliffs to sandy beaches. The area is popular with water skiers as the high cliffs provide wind breaks, with still water usually found somewhere. Fishing is lackluster due to the extreme fluctuation of the water levels. Brimmer Point is the starting point for ten miles of CCC trails meandering to scenic vistas throughout the park. The park sponsors an **Annual Mountain Bike Race** during the first week in August and the **Guernsey State Park Annual Photo Contest** with a late August submission deadline.

Guernsey has 7 camps with a total of 142 RV or tent sites, a boat ramp and dock, hiking trails, public phone, Visitor Center, museum, gift shop and dump station. No hookups at campsites, but there are vault toilets, tables and fire rings with grates. Stay limited to 14 consecutive days.

Rates – Day use fees for this park are $2 for residents and $5 for nonresidents. Camping fees for residents are $4 per night and $9 for nonresidents. An annual day use pass, good at all state parks, is available to residents for $25 and nonresidents for $40. Annual camping permits are available to residents for $30. The annual camping permit is not available for nonresidents. (For '99 rates see page 11).

Getting there – From the junction of Hwy 317 and US 26 just west of the town of Guernsey go north 1 mile on Hwy 317 to the gate for the state park. *See map page 38.*

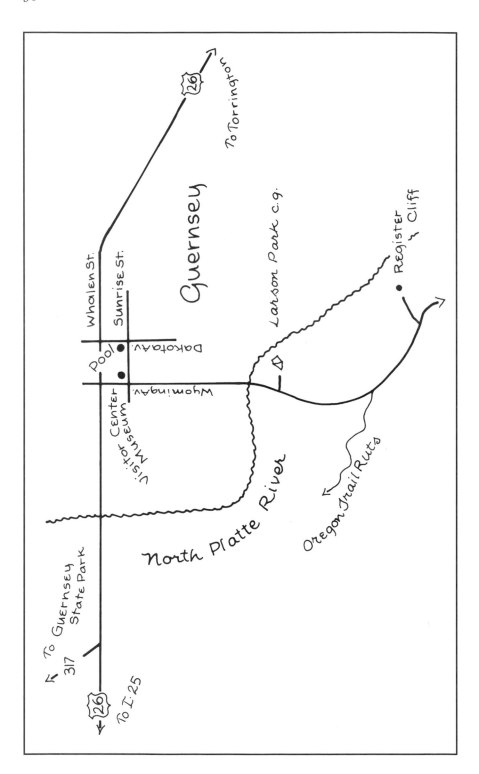

Larson Park Campground

(Town of Guernsey, Open April 15 to Oct. 15)
Ph: (307) 836-2255 E-mail: kgriffith@plt2.k12.wy.us

About the camp – Larson has 16 grass and gravel back-in RV sites (up to 20x40) with tent sites available. RV sites are water and electric only (30 amp).

Amenities – Rest rooms and showers; fishing park-side in a slough of the North Platte River, a nine-hole golf course on site; snacks in the pro shop/camp registration office.

Rates – Water and electric for 2 persons: $8.50. Tent site for 2 persons: $5. Additional persons: $1. No credit cards. Golfing is $6.25 for 9 holes and $9.25 for 18 holes weekdays and $8.25/$11.25 on weekends. Carts are $7/$11.50. Reservations: Phone, E-mail.

Getting there – From the junction of US 26 and S. Wyoming Ave. in downtown Guernsey; go south 1.5 miles on S. Wyoming Ave. to the camp on the left. *See map on facing page.*

Hawk Springs

Hawk Springs is a small community on US 85 south of Torrington which gave its name to the **Hawk Springs State Recreation Area** to the south. Supplies are at a minimum in town. The recreation site is one of the more pleasant areas in the state, popular with the locals, especially birders, due to the presence of a blue heron rookery and frequent sightings of owls and waterfowl. From the park supplies are available in Torrington about 25 miles north on US 85 or basic groceries, snacks and ice are available at LaGrange about 5 miles south on US 85.

Hawk Springs State Recreation Area

(Wyoming State Parks, Open all year)

About the camp – This is an especially nice camping option. Most of the 26 sites at this camp are located along a line of cottonwood trees just off the shore of the reservoir, where you can enjoy fishing, a cool dip, water sports, or hanging your hammock for a read or snooze. Tenters can either set up shelters by the tables, in the tree line, or on the beach area just below the trees. The camp has vault toilets, potable water, a boat ramp, trailer parking, a playground and horseshoe pits. Campsites have tables and fire rings with grates. Stay limited to 14 days.

Rates – Day use fees for this park are $2 for residents and $5 for nonresidents. Camping fees for residents are $4 per night and $9 for nonresidents. An annual day use pass, good at all state parks, is available to residents for $25 and nonresidents for $40. Annual camping permits are available to residents for $30. The annual camping permit is not available for nonresidents. (For '99 rates see page 11)

Getting there – From Hawk Springs go south about 5 miles to the turnoff on the left; then left 3.8 miles to the camp.

LaGrange

LaGrange is a crossroads community and a source for fuel, limited groceries, ice, and snacks at Bear Mountain Station, which also has an overnight camping option. It is the nearest camp to the **Hawks Springs State Recreation Area** should you be waiting for a site to be vacated on the reservoir at the state park.

Bear Mountain Station

(Private, Open May 1 to Oct. 31)
PO Box 150, LaGrange, WY 82221 Ph: (307) 834-2294

About the camp – This camp is located on an open native grass area just off of US 85 southwest of the junction of Hwy 151. The camp has 12 pull-thru RV sites with electric only (20 amp) and at least 20 undesignated tent sites. *Horses okay.*

Amenities – Rest rooms and showers; horseshoes and sheltered common area with two tables and grills; limited groceries and RV parts, gas station, potable water for fill-ups, propane and dump station.

Rates – Electric only for 2 persons: $10. Tent sites for 2 persons: $5. Additional persons: 50¢.

Getting there – LaGrange and this camp are about 32 miles south of Torrington on the west side of US 85 just south of the junction of Hwy 151.

Laramie

Like towns along the route of the railroad in southern Wyoming, Laramie arose as part of the 'Hell on Wheels' era of railroad construction. Since 1886, the **University of Wyoming** has been the focus of this city. When visiting, check UW activity schedules and get a parking pass at the **Visitors Information Center** at 1408 Ivinson, Ph: (307) 766-4075. Museums of interest on campus are the **Geological Museum**, in the east wing of the S.H. Knight Geology Building, Ph: (307) 766-4218; the **American Heritage Center** and **UW Art Museum**, at 22nd St. and Willett Dr. Ph: (307) 766-6622, (Closed Mon. Admission, but free on Thurs.); the **Rocky Mountain Herbarium**, on 3rd Floor, Aven Nelson Memorial Building, Ph: (307) 766-2236; the **Insect Gallery**, in Room 4018, Agricultural Building, Ph: (307) 766-5338, and the **Anthropology Museum**, in the Anthropology Building, Ph: (307) 766-5136. Unless noted otherwise these museums are free and open during normal university hours M-F.

In the town of Laramie, the main attractions are **The Laramie Plains Museum** housed in the restored **Ivinson Mansion**, at 603 Ivinson Ave., Ph: 742-4448 (small fee for guided tour); the **Wyoming Territorial Prison and Old West Park**, where the restored prison—once Butch Cassidy's lodgings—is the centerpiece for a **Wyoming Frontier Town** setting and the **National U.S. Marshalls Museum**. The park, at 975 Snowy Range Road, is open daily in the summer, Ph: (307) 745-6161 or 800-845-2287 (admission, Frontier Town free). Laramie celebrates during **Laramie Jubilee Days**, the first week in July, featuring rodeo, and a concert with fireworks on the night of the 4th of July.

Recreational opportunities include the **Laramie Plains Lakes** to the southwest, the **Vedauwoo Recreation Area**, a portion of the **Medicine Bow National Forest**, the **Happy Jack Recreation Area** and **Curt Gowdy State Park** (listed out of Cheyenne) to the east.

Public approaches to the Laramie Plains Lakes areas, some through private lands, were realized through the effort and commitment of the Wyoming Game and Fish Department to provide public access. These areas permit camping and are there for visitors to enjoy whether fishing, hunting, birdwatching or just trying to get out of town for a night to watch the stars. The wind is virtually constant in this area, so the unprotected bodies of water on these high plains also offer challenging wind surfing opportunities.

Vedauwoo is a unique area, where granite formations have mushroomed out of the high plains, with opportunities for light hiking; for strenuous climbing in cracks, on boulders or sheer rock faces; for the simple pleasure of viewing, or for endless photographic opportunities.

These formations are as unique as the name: **Vedauwoo** (Vee-dah-voo) comes from the Arapaho language meaning "earth born"; the Arapaho believe these rock shapes were placed there by spirits. The area is said to have been a sacred area where Indian males would make a solitary pilgrimage to fast for days in a vision quest. In the assorted array of huge hunks of granite there are balanced rocks, round rocks, square rocks and rocks of so many assorted shapes the imagination of young and old will frolic and delight.

There are four privately-owned camps in town with four free Game and Fish Access Areas to the southwest on Laramie Plains Lakes, three Forest Service camps and a private camp to the east (for camps to the west see Albany, Centennial and Woods Landing in the South Central section). Laramie has groceries, hardware, sporting goods and bicycle sales, service and rentals. **The Kourt House**, at 208 McConnell is a fitness facility with the public welcome. Day pass: $5. Ph: (307) 742-8136, There is an indoor swimming pool at the high school at 12 75 N. 11th. Ph: (307) 721-4426.

42

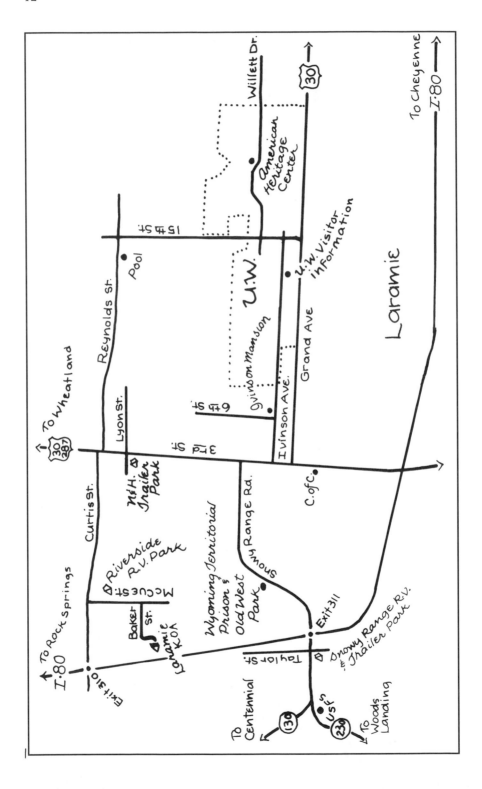

Laramie KOA

(Private, Open April 15 to Nov. 1)
1271 Baker St., Laramie, WY 82070 Ph: (307) 742-6553 Fax: (307) 742-5039

About the camp – This camp on the west end of Laramie near I-80 is large, level and grassy. The camp has 100 RV sites: all pull-thrus (12x60) on gravel with grass 'yards' and tables and some grills. All sites are full hookups (20/30/50 amp on city water). Tent sites are available on native grass with some tables. The camp has 6 one-room and 1 two-room kamper kabins. *Horses okay: free.*

Amenities – Handicapped-accessible rest rooms and showers (showers only: $5), laundry; cable at most sites ($2), game room and playground; limited groceries and RV parts, gift shop, dump station and pay phone.

Rates – Full hookups for 2 persons: $22. Water and electric only for 2 persons: $21. No hookups for 2 persons: $18. Tent sites for 2 persons: $15. Kamper kabins for 2 persons: $30-40. Additional persons: $2. V MC D Personal checks okay. Reservations: phone, fax or mail.

Getting there – From I-80 use exit 310; then east .2 miles on Curtis St. to McCue St.; then right .1 miles on McCue St.; then right and follow the road around and behind the EconoLodge Motel to the camp. *See map facing page.*

N & H Trailer Park

(Private, Open all year)
1360 North 3rd St., Laramie, WY 82070 Ph: (307) 742-3158

About the camp – This camp, on the main north/south artery in Laramie, is within easy walking distance of many city services and the closest option to downtown or the university. The camp has 20 RV sites on gravel: 10 sites are pull-thrus (12x60) and 10 are back-ins (12x40). All sites are full hookups (20/30/50 amp on city water).

Amenities – Rest rooms and showers, laundry, and pay phone.

Rates – Full hookups per site: $11.50 incl. tax. No credit cards. Personal checks okay. No reservations.

Getting there – From I-80 use exit 310; then east 1.2 miles on Curtis St. to 3rd St. (US 30/287); then south .1 miles to Lyon St. and the camp on the right. *See map facing page.*

Riverside RV Park

(Private, Open all year)
1559 McCue St., Laramie, WY 82072 Ph: (307) 721-7405

About the camp – This camp is to the rear of Handy Truck Stop just off of I-80 exit 310. The camp has gravel RV parking for 12 units at pull-thrus (15x60) with electric only (30 amp).

Amenities – Rest rooms and showers (showers only: $3), laundry; limited groceries at truck stop C-store, water, dump station and pay phone.

Rates – Full hookups per site: $12.96 incl. tax.

Getting there – From I-80 use exit 310; then east .2 miles on Curtis St. to Handy Truck Stop at McCue St.; then right on McCue St.; then left into the RV area behind truck stop. *See map page 42.*

Snowy Range RV and Trailer Park

(Private, Open all year)
208 Garfield St., Laramie, WY 82070 Ph: (307) 745-0297

About the camp – This self-service-check-in camp is located near I-80 just off the Snowy Range Road on the west end of Laramie. The camp has 15 RV sites on gravel: All sites are pull-thrus (up to 16x40) and full hookups (20/30/50 amp on city water). Tent sites are available on native grass.

Amenities – Rest rooms and showers (showers only: $3), laundry; cable included; dump station and pay phone.

Rates – Full hookups per site: $17 incl tax. Tent sites: $10 incl tax. Limited advance reservations: phone.

Getting there – From I-80 use exit 311 (*Hwys 130/230 - Snowy Range Road*); then west .2 miles to Taylor St.; then left into the camp. *See map page 42.*

—East of Laramie—

Tie City Campground

(Medicine Bow National Forest, Open May 24 to Oct. 31)

About the camp – This camp is only about 1 mile north of I-80 and in close proximity to Laramie, Vedauwoo Recreation Area, Curt Gowdy State Park and the Happy Jack Recreation area. The camp has 17 sites, vault toilets, potable water and trailheads for hiking the immediate countryside. Sites have tables, fire rings with grates and grills. 6 sites are pull-thrus. Stay limited to 14 days.

Rates – Campsite per night: $10. Rates half with Golden Age or Access Passport.

Getting there – From I-80 use exit 322; then north .1 miles to the junction of Hwy 210 at the turn to the Summit Visitors Center/Rest Area; then left .9 miles on Hwy 210 to the camp on the right. *See map page 46.*

Yellow Pine Campground

(Medicine Bow National Forest, Open May 24 to Oct. 31)

About the camp – This camp is only about 3 miles north of I-80 and in close proximity to Laramie, Vedauwoo, Curt Gowdy State Park and the Happy Jack Recreation area. The camp has 19 sites, vault toilets and potable water. Sites have tables, fire rings with grates and grills. 10 sites are pull-thrus. Stay limited to 14 days.

Rates – Campsite per night: $10. Rates half with Golden Age or Access Passport.

Getting there – From I-80 use exit 322; then north .1 miles to the junction of Hwy 210 at the turn to the Summit Visitors Center/Rest Area; then left 2 miles on Hwy 210 to the camp entrance on the right; then right .4 miles to a fork; then left .7 miles to the camp. *See map page 46.*

Curt Gowdy State Park

(State of Wyoming, Open all year)
24 miles west of Cheyenne on Hwy 210 Ph: (307) 632-7946

About the camp – This 1600-acre park has a large resident population of mule deer and is famous for birding during spring migrations, when a variety of birds, in particular the mountain bluebird visit the park by the thousands. The park has varied flora and fauna and two reservoirs that are stocked by the Wyoming Game and Fish Department. Anglers may enjoy catches of lake trout, kokanee, brown trout and perch. There are over 100 RV or tent campsites, with tables and fire rings with grates scattered throughout the park, as well as two areas designated for tents only. Many of the sites are long pull-thrus that will accommodate longer trailers and RV's. There is a boat ramp at each reservoir, but jet skis and water skis are not allowed on Crystal Reservoir and swimming is prohibited on either reservoir. For exercise or family entertainment, the park has a 6-mile Volksmarch Trail open May 1 until Oct. 1. Stay limited to 14 consecutive days.

Rates – Day use fees for this park are $2 for residents and $5 for nonresidents. Camping fees for residents are $4 per night and $9 for nonresidents. An annual day use pass, good at all state parks, is available to residents for $25 and nonresidents for $40. Annual camping permits are available to residents for $30. The annual camping pass is not available for nonresidents. (For '99 rates see page 11).

Getting there – This state park is on Hwy 210 (*Happy Jack Road*) about 28 miles west of Cheyenne. *See map page 46.*

Vedauwoo Campground

(Medicine Bow National Forest, Open June 1 to Oct. 31)

About the camp – This camp is in the heart of some of Wyoming's most unusual rock formations, with unlimited opportunities for climbing, bouldering, hiking and photography. The 28-site camp looks like new with vault toilets, potable water and paved interior roads, pullouts and

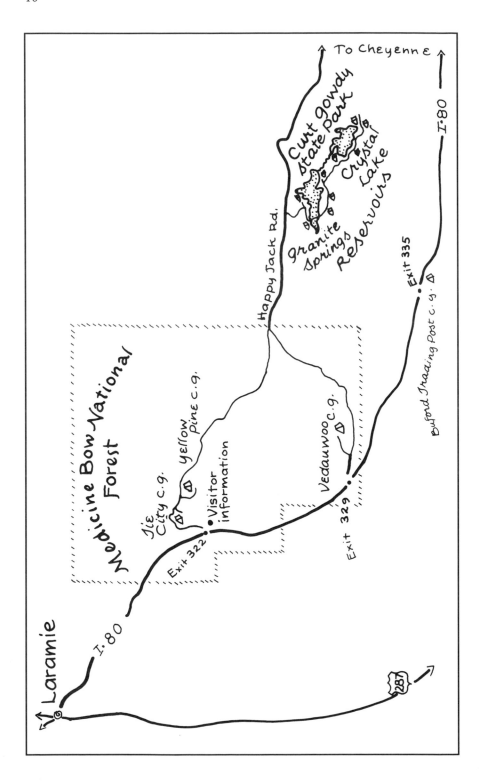

spurs. The camp has parking for 7 walk-in sites and parallel parking spurs for bigger rigs at 11 of the sites. Sites are roomy with good tenting options and have tables, fire rings with grates and grills. Stay limited to 14 days.

Rates – Campsite per night: $10. Rates half with Golden Age or Access Passport.

Getting there – From I-80 use exit 329; then north 1.2 miles into the Vedauwoo Recreation Area and a turn off to the left; then left .2 miles to the camp on the right. *See map facing page facing.*

Buford Trading Post
(Private, Open all year)
2 Buford Road, Buford, WY 82052 Ph: (307) 632-3999 Fax: (307) 632-4244

About the camp – This native grass camp offers parking for 6 electric only (20 amp) sites and up to 50 RVs with no hookups. Acres of tent sites are available on native grass. *Horses Okay: corral and water, $10.*

Amenities – Rest rooms and showers during Trading Post hours only: 7 a.m.-6 p.m. (showers only: $5 with soap and towel); cafe, limited groceries and RV supplies, camping supplies, bait and fishing tackle; gas, diesel and propane; post office, Western Union, ATM and pay phone.

Rates – Electric only per site: $10. Tent site or no hookups: $5. All major cards. Personal checks okay.

Getting there – From I-80 use exit 335; then south to the frontage road; then east .1 miles to the camp on the right. *See map page facing.*

—West of Laramie—

Meeboer Lake Public Access Area
(Wyoming Game and Fish, Open all year)

About the camp – This camping area on Meeboer Lake is gravel and native grass with a few stone fire rings and a handicapped accessible boat ramp, dock and vault toilet. Camping here is primitive: No potable water, nor tables, or grills. Stay limited to 14 days.

Rates – Free

Getting there – From I-80 and Snowy Range Road (*exit 311*), go southwest 8.9 miles on Hwy 230 to CR 422; then west 4.6 miles to the Meeboer Lake turnoff on the left; then left 1.6 miles to the camp. *See map page 48.*

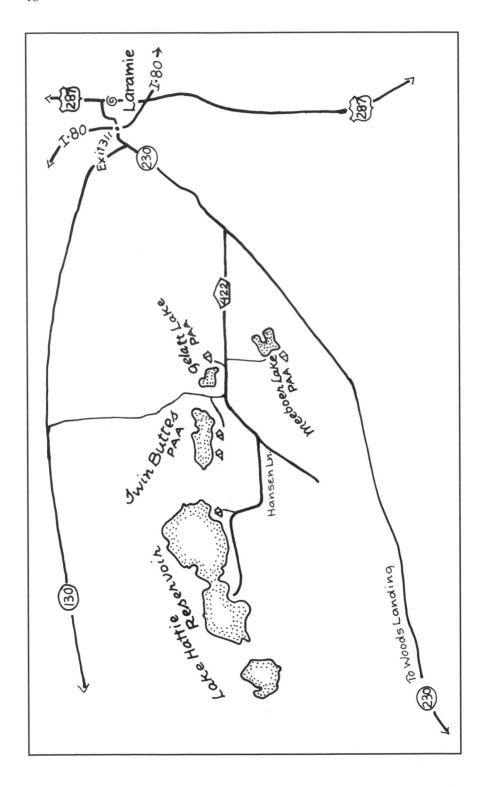

Gelatt Lake Public Access Area
(Wyoming Game and Fish, Open all year)

About the camp – This camping area on Gelatt Lake is gravel and native grass with a few stone fire rings and handicapped accessible boat ramp, dock and vault toilet. Camping here is primitive: No potable water, nor tables, or grills. Stay limited to 14 days.

Rates – Free

Getting there – From I-80 and Snowy Range Road (*exit 311*), go southwest 8.9 miles on Hwy 230 to CR 422; then west 5.2 miles to the Gelatt Lake turnoff on the right; then right 1.6 miles to the camp. *See map facing page.*

Twin Buttes Reservoir Public Access Area
(Wyoming Game and Fish, Open all year)

About the camp – There are two camping areas on this reservoir. Both are gravel and native grass with a few stone fire rings and a vault toilet. Camping here is primitive: No potable water, nor tables, or grills. Stay limited to 5 days.

Rates – Free

Getting there – From I-80 and Snowy Range Road (*exit 311*), go southwest 8.9 miles on Hwy 230 to CR 422; then west 5.6 miles to CR 44 on the right; then right 50 yards; then left on the reservoir road; then .3 miles on the reservoir road where there is a right to the first area; [*or*] continue another .7 miles to the end of the road and the second area. *See map facing page.*

Lake Hattie Public Access Area
(Wyoming Game and Fish, Open all year)

About the camp – A large camping/parking area at Lake Hattie is gravel and native grass with a few stone fire rings and handicapped accessible boat ramp, dock and vault toilet. Camping here is primitive: No potable water, nor tables, or grills. Stay limited to 5 days.

Rates – Free

Getting there – From I-80 and Snowy Range Road (*exit 311*), go southwest 8.9 miles on Hwy 230 to CR 422; then west 7.1 miles to Hansen Lane on the right; then right 2.9 miles to the camp turnoff on the right; then right .4 miles to the camp. *See map facing page.*

Lost Springs

Lost Springs is the community center for a ranching area, with a post office and secondhand store sharing space in one building, a quaint community hall and a tavern. When the post office closes, the tavern opens. Other than the free use of their nice park and the western hospitality, there isn't a lot happening here. The community hall is available for weddings, reunions, anniversaries and the like with rentals starting at $10 per day. Ph: (307) 334-3268.

Lost Springs City Park

(Town of Lost Springs, Open all year)

About the camp – This is a pleasant park in the center of the community. There is a large grassy area and adequate gravel parking for RVs and campers. No open fires and, as this is a ranching area, no loose dogs.

Amenities – Rest rooms with hot water in sinks (open all year), playground sheltered picnic area and six electric outlets (20 amp/extension cord required to reach your RV in the parking lot). Lost Springs has not justified the expense of regular testing of the water and drinking it is not advised.

Rates – No hookups: free. With electric hookup: $3.

Getting there – On the east side of the street in the center of Lost Springs. *See map page 52.*

Lusk

Historically, Lusk was a crossroads for the **Pony Express** and the **Cheyenne and Black Hills Stage Route** (1876-87), which ran nearly parallel to Hwy 85, the Main Street of Lusk. Today this is a ranching community, and for the visitor a good staging area for trips to the **Lance Creek Fossil Beds**, a 558-acre National Natural Landmark, or to the **Thunder Basin National Grasslands**. Appropriately sited along the Cheyenne-Deadwood Stage Road is the **Stagecoach Museum**, at 322 South Main St. Ph: (307) 334-3444. Lusk celebrates during the **Lusk Roundup**, a professional rodeo in June; the **Legend of Rawhide** pageant where the Indians skin a guy alive in mid-July, and the **Senior Pro Rodeo** over the Labor Day weekend.

In town there are 2 privately-owned camps and another just 2 miles east. Groceries and hardware are available. The town operates the Lusk Plunge, an outdoor pool open in the summer with modest admission on North Main St.

B.J.'s Campground

(Private, May 1 to Oct. 31)
PO Box 515, Lusk, WY 82225 Ph: (307) 334-2314

About the camp   This camp is located just southeast of downtown Lusk. Most sites are gravel parking with a concrete landing and patio-like grass area with covered picnic table. The camp has 26 RV sites: 19 pull-thrus (23x55) and 7 back-ins (up to 20x80). 25 sites have full hookups (20/30/50 amp) with one site electric only (20 amp). There is 1 grass tent site with table.

Amenities – Handicapped-accessible rest rooms and showers, laundry; cable TV (included at all sites) and pay phone.

Rates – Full hookups for 2 persons: $16. Tent sites for 2 persons: $12. Additional persons age 12 and over: $2. Under age 12: $1. No credit cards. Personal checks okay. Discount for Goodsam and seniors +60. Reservations: phone or mail.

Getting there – From the north junction in Lusk (*US 85/18 north and US 20 east*) go south .6 miles to the south junction (*US 85 south and US 18/20 west*); then south .1 miles on US 85 to 9th St.; then east 3 blocks to the camp office on the right.

From the south junction in Lusk (*US 85 south and US 18/20 west*), go south .1 miles on US 85 to 9th St.; then east 3 blocks to the camp on the right. *See map page 52.*

B-Q Corral

(Private, Open all year)
702 South Main (PO Box 1279), Lusk, WY 82225 Ph: (307) 334-3587 or 334-0128

About the camp – This camp is located on a nice grassy area behind a fast food property on US 85 in downtown Lusk. The camp has 6 RV sites: all back-ins (up to 20x40) with full hookups (30/50 amp). The parking spurs are paved with grass 'yards' and some tables. A portable grill is available.

Amenities – Rest rooms, showers; a fast food restaurant near the camp.

Rates – Full hookups per sites: $15. Water and electric only per site: $12. Tents: $10 each. No credit cards. Personal checks okay. Reservations: phone or mail.

Getting there – From the north junction in Lusk (*US 85/18 north and US 20 east*) go south .5 miles on US 85 to the camp on the right.

From the south junction in Lusk (*US 85 south and US 18/20 west*) go north .1 miles on US 85 to the camp on the left. *See map page 52.*

Prairie View Campground

(Private, Open all year)
3925 Hwy 20 (PO Box 1168), Lusk, WY 82225 Ph: (307) 334-3174 E-mail: luprview@coffey.com

About the camp – This camp is located in an open area two miles west of Lusk off of Hwys US18/20. The camp has 24 pull-thru (25x55) RV

52

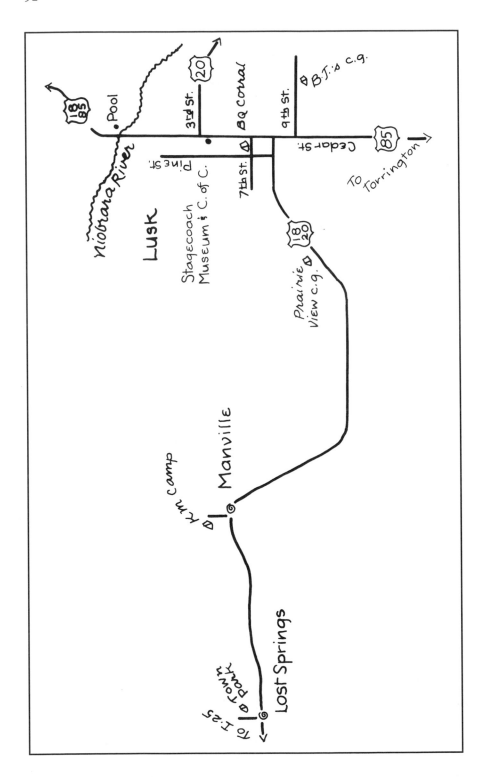

sites with full hookups (30 amp) and tables on native grass . 10 designated tent sites are available.

Amenities – Rest rooms and showers (showers only: $4), laundry; game room, playground and horseshoes; limited groceries and RV parts, modem jack in office, propane and public phone in game room for local, phone card and 800 use only.

Rates – Full hookups for 3 persons: $14. Tent sites for 3 persons: $14. Additional persons: $2. V MC D. Personal checks okay. Reservations: phone, E-mail or mail.

Getting there – Prairie View is along US18/20 about 2 miles west of Lusk and about 47 miles east of I-25. *See map facing page.*

Manville

This small community about nine miles west of Lusk has a small RV camp with hookups or tent sites. It is directly south of the **Lance Creek Fossil Beds**, a 558-acre National Natural Landmark and the **Thunder Basin National Grasslands**. Limited supplies are available at a nearby truck stop on the highway.

KM Camp

(Private, Open Memorial Day to Labor Day)
19 Lance Creek Highway, Manville, WY 82221
(PO Box 1362) Lusk, WY 82225 Ph: (307) 334-3623

About the camp – This camp is located on a nice grassy area two blocks north of US 18/20 in Manville, Wyoming, about 9 miles west of Lusk. There are 6 grass back-in sites (12x35) with full hookups (20/50 amp). Grass tent sites are available in the area. *Horse motel: portable panels, stud stall in barn with hay if needed.*

Amenities – Rest room and "cowboy" shower in pump house (the windmill here fills a holding tank and water temperature for showers depends on the weather that day); truck stop with restaurant a block away.

Rates – Full hookups per site: $15. Water and electric only per site: $10. Tent sites: $5. No credit cards. Personal checks okay. Reservations: phone or mail.

Getting there – At Manville go 1 block north to the house at 19 Lance Creek Highway (*the first house on the left*) for check-in. The turn to the camp is 2 blocks north; then left 50 yards; then left into the camp. *See map facing page.*

Pine Bluffs

Pine Bluffs is known as the "Frontier Crossroads" due to a concentration of early historic travel routes that skirted the foot of the bluffs. These trails range from Native American Indian paths thousands of years ago to modern conveyances: the bluffs are within sight and sound of I-80 and the Union Pacific Railroad. The town is home to the **University of Wyoming High Plains Archaeology Lab**, with displays at 217 W. Third St., Ph: (307) 245-9372 and a dig site near the rest area off of I-80. Check at the lab or the Chamber of Commerce, at the rest area, for information on dig site tours. The Texas Trail Museum and Park, at Third and Market Sts., is open May to Sept., Ph: (307) 245-3713. Pine Bluffs celebrates the first weekend in August during the annual **Trail Days** with a rodeo, while mountain men rendezvous on the bluffs near town. There is one privately-owned camp on the east edge of town. Groceries and hardware are available. The town operates a swimming pool in summer with modest fees.

Pine Bluffs RV Park

(Private, Open March 1 to Oct. 31)
10 Paint Brush, Pine Bluffs, WY 82082 Ph: (307) 245-3665 or 1-800-294-4968 E-mail: pbrv@aol.com

About the camp – This camp is open, level, nicely landscaped and on the northeast end of Pine Bluffs. The camp has 85 RV sites with some tables: 50 pull-thrus and 35 back-ins (all 33x75). 76 sites are full hookups (30/50amp on city water). 30 tent sites, some with tables, are available. *Horses welcome if camp is not full: Inquire.*

Amenities – Rest rooms and showers, laundry; rec area with horseshoes and basketball, near community swimming pool ($), cable TV on 20 premium sites ($1.50); dump station, propane and pay phone.

Rates – Full hookups for 2 persons: $18.90 incl. tax. Water and electric only for 2 persons: $18.40 incl. tax. Tent site for 2 persons: $10. Additional persons: $2. V MC D Reservations: phone, E-mail or mail. Discounts for Goodsam, AAA and Woodalls.

Getting there – Westbound on I-80 use Nebraska exit 1; then north .5 miles to Business I-80/US 30 loop; then west .5 miles to Butler St.; then south .1 miles to Paint Brush St. and the camp on the left.

Eastbound on I-80 use exit 401; then north and east 1.4 miles on the Business I-80/US 30 loop to Butler St.; then south .1 miles to Paint Brush St. and the camp on the left.

Torrington

Hundreds of thousands of pioneer emigrants passed through this area, which is now Wyoming's most productive agricultural county. Over 120,000 cattle are raised annually on area ranches and two livestock sale barns have located here. Visitors are welcome, with sales at noon on Fri. at the **Torrington Livestock Auction** on US 26 and at 11 a.m. at the **Stockman's Livestock Auction** on Rural Route 2. The interesting **Homesteaders Museum** is located in an old railroad depot at 495 S. Main, Ph: (307) 532-5612. In July Torrington hosts the **Cowboy State Antique and Steam Gas Reunion**, with antique tractors and farm equipment, and in August the **Goshen County Fair and Rodeo** is in full swing.

Tent and hookup sites are available at the Goshen County Fair Grounds. Free camping is available in **Torrington's Pioneer Park** and at several Game and Fish Wildlife Habitat Management Areas nearby. Groceries, hardware and limited sporting goods are available in Torrington. There is a seasonal outdoor pool with a 180-foot Aqua Slide, at East D and 25th Sts., open swim 1:30-5 daily and evenings M-Sat. Adults $1.50, children $1 with 50¢ surcharge for using the slide. Ph: (307) 532-7798. For aerobics and weights, the **Fitness Center** at Eastern Wyoming College is open to the public. Day pass: $5; weekly pass: $15. Ph: (307) 532-8243.

Goshen County Fair Grounds

(County owned, Open all year)
Drawer F, Torrington, WY 82340 Ph: (307) 532-2525

About the camp – There are 20 gravel, back-in (12x50) RV sites with full hookups (20/30 amp) and 14 grassy pull-thrus with electric only. Grass tent sites are available in several locations. There are no tables or grills at the sites, but there is a large common covered picnic area with 20 tables and 4 grills. Expect this camp to be full around Goshen County Fair week in August. *Horses okay: Stalls $10 per night, per horse.*

Amenities – Handicapped accessible rest rooms and showers.

Rates – Full hookups per site: $8. Electric only or tent site: $5. No credit cards. Personal checks okay.

Getting there – From the junction of US 85 and US 26 in downtown Torrington, go west .8 miles on US 26 to GOSHENCOSHOP (Goshen County Shop Road); then right .1 miles; then left .2 miles into the fairgrounds to the registration office located in Rendezvous Hall on the right. *See map page 56.*

Pioneer Municipal Park

(City of Torrington, Open All Year)

About the camp – The camp is open all year, but when things start to freeze, rest room facilities and water at the nearby Volunteer Fire Department are not available. The camp is in a stand of cottonwood trees, and has 14 sites, most with tables and grills, on native grass with gravel spurs (up to 40') and electric (20 amp). Tenting is available at these designated sites or elsewhere on the grassy areas. There is a sheltered picnic area with tables and a grill. In the summer rest room facilities at the nearby Volunteer Fire department building are open 24 hours a day. A block to the north is the main park: shady and grassy with picnicking and a playground. No open fires in the city limits. Charcoal only in grills. Stay limited to 10 days.

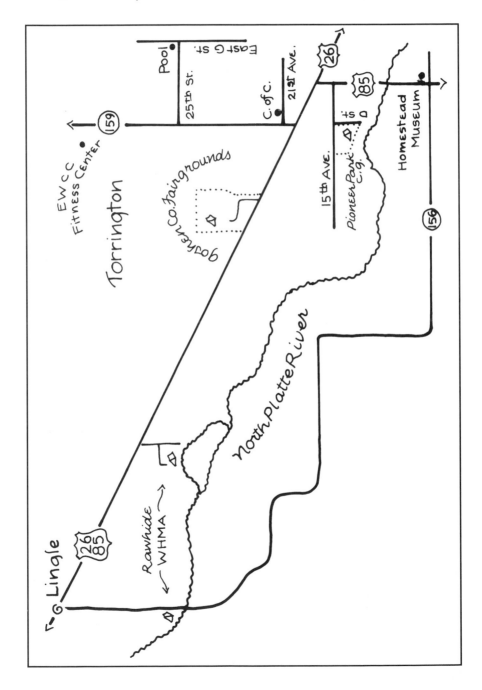

Rates – Free, with donations welcome, appreciated and expected if using electricity.

Getting there – From the junction of US 85 and US 26 in Torrington go south .1 miles on US 85 to 15th Ave.; then west 4 blocks to D St.; then south to the camp on the right. *See map facing page.*

—East of Torrington—

Rawhide Wildlife Habitat Management Area
(Wyoming Game and Fish, Open all year)

About the camp – Purchased by the Wyoming Game and Fish Commission to replace riparian habitat when Grayrocks reservoir was constructed in the late 1970's, this 740-acre area is about 8 miles northwest of Torrington and 2 miles south of Lingle along the North Platte River.

Cottonwoods and willows provide habitat diversity along these riparian zones. There are prairie grasses like sandreed, wheatgrass and blue grama. Wetlands created by fluctuations in the water levels of the North Platte River and the high water table are choked with cattails, rushes and sedges.

This diverse vegetation is used by white-tailed deer, mule deer, cottontail rabbits, red squirrels, wild turkeys, ring-necked pheasants, Canada geese, ducks and many small mammals and reptiles, including beavers, red foxes, raccoons, muskrats, turtles, toads and snakes. Optimists with the Game and Fish claim you might even spot a wood duck or a yellow-billed cuckoo, and at certain times of the year birdwatchers might also see bald and golden eagles, hawks, owls and some of more than 50 species of song birds. The area provides excellent opportunities for hiking and photography. The east parking area has a nature trail, just to get you started, and a vault toilet. The west parking area has no facilities, but is in a nice stand of trees just off the pavement on a small circle drive. No potable water. Stay limited to 14 days.

Rates – Free

Getting there – To the parking area on the east side of the WHMA: From the junction of US 85 and US 26 in downtown Torrington, go west 6.9 miles on US 26 to RD 83 F4 (*at the East Texas Station on the railroad tracks*); then left .6 miles to a turnoff to the right; then right (*staying to the right to avoid entering a lane into private property*) .7 miles to the camp.

To the parking area on the west side of the WHMA: From the bend in US 26 on the south end of downtown Lingle take Hwy 156 south 2 miles to the camp on the right. *See map facing page.*

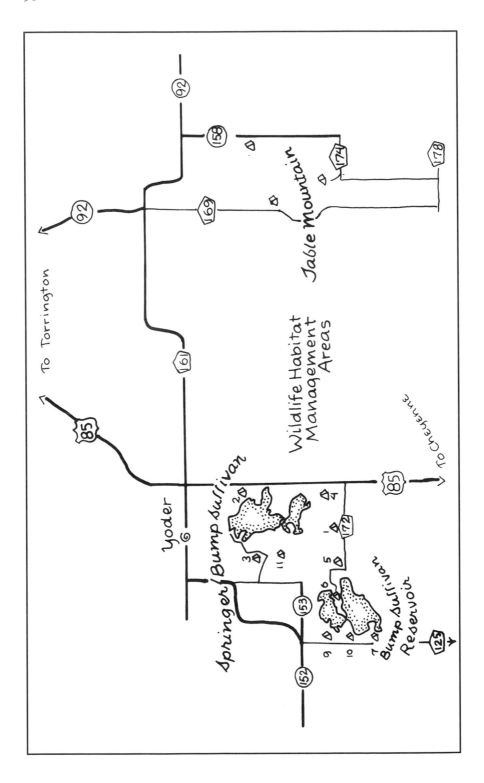

—South of Torrington—

Springer/Bump Sullivan Wildlife Habitat Management Area

(Wyoming Game & Fish, Open all year)

About the camp – The Wyoming Game and Fish Department and the Bureau of Land Management co-manage this 1,911-acre habitat area west of Hwy 85 about 15 miles south of Torrington. Now considered by many to be the best pheasant and goose hunting in the state, it was established in 1948 to provide pheasant habitat and increase hunting opportunities.

The high rolling plains surrounding the area are at an average elevation of 4200' and the vegetation is mostly sagebrush grasslands with a variety of native grasses. To improve nesting, hiding and feeding areas, various types of grasses, forbs, shrubs and trees have been planted over the years.

Current management priorities are focused on geese, ducks and pheasants. Wildlife using the area include Canada and snow geese, pheasants, many species of ducks, sandhill cranes, a variety of shorebirds, cottontail rabbits, wild turkeys, mule deer, white-tailed deer, skunks, fox squirrels, muskrats, songbirds, doves and bald eagles. During the spring and fall large numbers of waterfowl use this area as a stopover on their annual migrations.

Fishing in these waters yields catches of bullhead, carp and perch, but those opportunities are limited due to irrigation and the constant fluctuation of the water levels in these reservoirs.

When not fishing or hunting the area lends itself to wildlife observation, photography, picnicking, boating and swimming. In most of the locations, a short distance from the parking areas blinds have been built to accommodate hunters and birdwatchers when hunting is not in season. Some portions of the area will be closed to vehicles from pheasant season to Memorial Day. There are 11 designated parking/camping locations within this area. The only vault toilet is at area 1. No potable water. Stay limited to 14 days.

Rates – Free

Getting there – Directions start with site 2 which is on the highway and then 4 and 1, and directions thereafter will be in order according to their proximity to 1, but not necessarily in any numerical order:

2: From near mile marker 79 on Hwy 85 look for this parking area on the west side of the road.

4: From near mile marker 77 on Hwy 85 take RD 172W 14 west about 40 yards; then turn right and follow the ditch bank road through the Downar Bird Farm .3 miles to the parking area.

1: From near mile marker 77 on Hwy 85 take RD 172W 14 west 1.2 miles to the camp on the right, which has a large parking area, vault toilet and Springer Special Hunt Check Station.

5: From near mile marker 77 on Hwy 85 take RD 172W 14 west 1.7 miles to this parking area on the right, just after you turn to the right on RD 133 14.

6: From near mile marker 77 on Hwy 85 take RD 172W 14 west 1.7 miles to where this road turns right into RD 133 14; then .5 miles on RD 133 14 through a left hand bend in the road to the next right hand bend of the road; then straight here over the tracks and to the left .5 miles to a large open area near Bump-Sullivan Reservoir.

9, 10 and 7: From near mile marker 77 on Hwy 85 take RD 172W 14 west 1.7 miles to where this road turns right into RD 133 14; then follow Rd 133 14, through a couple of bends, 1 mile to WS 153 14 going to the left; then left 1 mile on RD 153 14 to where it joins up with RD 152 and RD 125 14; then left .6 miles on RD 125 14 to parking area 9; [or] .8 miles to parking area 10; [or] 1.1 miles to parking area 7.

3 and 11: From near mile marker 77 on Hwy 85 take RD 172W 14 west 1.7 miles to where this road turns right into RD 133 14; then follow Rd 133 14, through a couple of bends, 2 miles to a right-hand turnoff; then right about .3 miles and right to parking area 11; [or] left to parking area 3. *See map page 58.*

Table Mountain Wildlife Habitat Management Area
(Wyoming Game and Fish, Open all year)

About the camp – The Wyoming Game and Fish department and the US Bureau of Land Management have cooperatively managed this 1,716-acre area since 1962. At that time the game and fish observed only a few pairs of ducks using the area, but with extensive improvements, the area is now considered one of the most important wetlands areas in southeast Wyoming.

The land consists mainly of grasslands, sagebrush and shrub communities surrounding 8 waterfowl ponds and marsh lands occupying 590 acres. Horse Creek and Dry Creek meander through the northern and western boundaries, respectively. Both of these creeks are considered to be of archaeological significance due to the discovery of many artifacts belonging to prehistoric tribes of the Plains Indians. Visitors are asked to be respectful and help protect these archaeological areas.

Hunting opportunities here include pheasant, waterfowl, rabbits and doves, with trapping for muskrat also allowed. Coyotes and foxes also live here, along with a number of bird species including American bitterns, great blue herons, marsh and Swainson's hawks, great horned owls, American white pelicans, western grebes, white-faced ibis and bald eagles. The opportunities for wildlife observation and photography in this area are bountiful. The area is closed to vehicles from pheasant season to Memorial Day. No potable water. Stay limited to 14 days.

Rates – Free

Getting there – To the parking area on the east side of the WHMA: From the junction of US 85 and Hwy 92 south of Torrington, go east on Hwy 92 to the junction of Hwy 158; then south 2.5 miles on Hwy 158 to the parking area on the right.

To the parking area on the southerly end of the WHMA: From the junction of US 85 and Hwy 92 south of Torrington, go east on Hwy 92 to the junction of Hwy 158; then south 4 miles on Hwy 158 to RD 174 W 16; then right 1 mile to a road that takes off almost straight as RD 174 W 16 turns to the left; then straight .1 miles to the parking area and access to other interior roads open from Memorial Day until pheasant season.

To the parking area on the west side of the WHMA: From the junction of US 85 and Hwy 92 south of Torrington, go east 7 miles to RD 169 15; then south 3 miles on RD 169 15 to the parking area on the left. *See map page 58.*

Wheatland

Wheatland is the commercial hub of Platte County, where the primary crop is a plains favorite, you guessed it, wheat. The free **Laramie Peak Museum** on 16th St. is open Tues.-Sat. 11-5, Ph: (307) 322-9601. Southwest of town on Hwy 34 the **Wyoming Game and Fish Sybille Wildlife Research and Education Center and Visitor Center** is open M-F during the summer, Ph: (307) 322-2571. In July Wheatland celebrates during the **Community Fest** in Lewis Park and in August during the **Platte County Fair and Rodeo.**

In town there are two privately-owned camps (one no tents allowed) and a free city park. The surrounding area offers free camping and varied recreational opportunities at 5 Game and Fish Access Areas, four of which are on reservoirs and the fifth at the south end of the Laramie Range. Groceries, hardware and limited sporting goods are available in Wheatland. The City has an outdoor swimming pool open summers in **Lewis Park** with modest fees. Ph: (307) 322-9254.

Arrowhead RV Camp
(Private, Open all year)
2005 N. 16th St., Wheatland, WY 82201 Ph: (307) 322-3467 Fax: 322-5607

About the camp – This camp is on the north end of Wheatland and has 12 pull-thrus (12x60). All sites are full hook ups (30 amp on city water) on gravel with native grass 'yards' and tables. Tent sites with tables are also available.

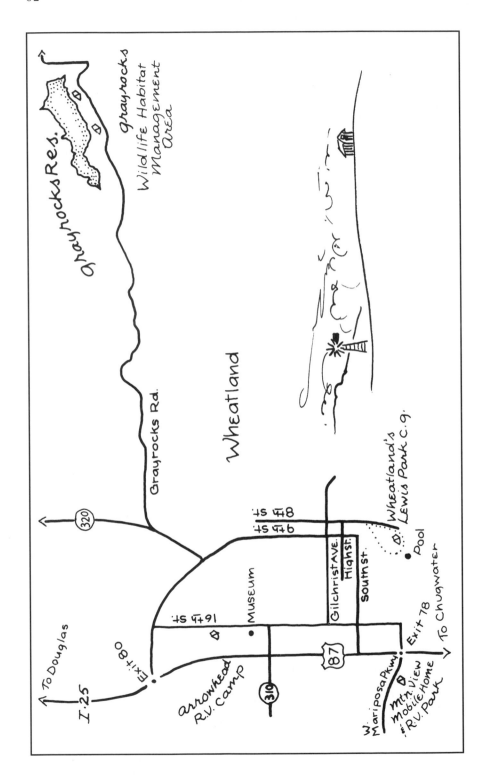

Amenities – Rest rooms, laundry; cable TV included in full hook ups, dump station and pay phone.

Rates – Full hookups per site: $10. Tents: $5.

Getting there – Use I-25 exit 80; then east about .1 mile to the first right (across from Red Fox Road); then south .5 miles to the camp on the right. *See map page 62.*

Mountain View Mobile Home and RV Park

(Private, Open May 1 to Oct. 1)
PO Box 331, Wheatland, WY Ph: (307) 322-4858 E-mail: rbutts@coffey.com

About the camp – This camp is near I-25 exit 78 on the south end of Wheatland. The camp has 36 gravel and native grass sites with full hookups (30 amp). 15 sites are pull-thrus (30x75). 21 sites have concrete patios and most have tables. No tents.

Amenities – Rest rooms, showers; laundry with television in the waiting room, and cable TV included at all sites.

Rates – Full hookups per site: $15. No credit cards. Reservations: phone, E-mail or mail.

Getting there – Use I-25 exit 78; then west .2 miles on Mariposa St. to the camp on the left. *See map facing page.*

Wheatland's Lewis Park

(City owned, Open all year)
8th St., Wheatland, WY Ph: (307) 322-2692

About the camp – This is a free, first come, first served camp, courtesy of the City of Wheatland. There are 20 gravel and grass back-ins (12x40 with 30 amp service) and a designated tenting area. Most of the sites are shaded in a stand of cottonwood trees. On the near end of the area there are rest rooms (seasonal) and a hydrant for potable water. There is a swimming pool and the rest of the park is nicely landscaped, with playground equipment, several covered picnic areas and four tennis courts. Stay limited to 3 nights in any 30 day period.

Rates – Free, with donations welcome, appreciated and expected if using electric hookups.

Getting there – Northbound on I-25 use exit 78; then go east .1 miles to the stop sign; then left .3 miles on 16th St. to the first traffic light at South St.; then right .5 miles on South St. and through the bend where it becomes 9th St.; then one block to 9th and High Sts.; then right one block on High St. to 8th St.; then right on 8th St. .3 miles to the camping area which is at the far end of the park.

Southbound on I-25 use exit 80; go east 1.8 miles on Business I-25 to the first traffic light, at 9th and Gilchrist Sts.; then left one block on Gilchrist St. to 8th St.; then right .4 miles on 8th St. to the camping area which is at the far end of the park. *See map facing page.*

Grayrocks Wildlife Habitat Management Area
(Wyoming Game and Fish, Open all year)

About the camp – Grayrocks WHMA provides quality habitat for a variety of wildlife. Many species of ducks and Canada geese use this area, especially during migration. White pelicans, pheasants, doves, wild turkey, sharp-tailed grouse, mule deer, white-tailed deer, squirrels, cottontail rabbits and pronghorn antelope also live here.

The 3,500-acre Grayrocks reservoir provides camping with recreational opportunities for all kinds of boating and water sports. Public facilities including boat ramps, 3 parking areas and handicapped accessible vault toilets are located on the south side of the reservoir where free over-night camping is permitted. Boaters may camp on the north shore. There is a convenience store and gas station catty-corner from the main entrance where supplies and ice can be replenished. No potable water. Stay limited to 14 days.

Rates – Free

Getting there – Use I-25 exit 80; then go east 1 mile on Business I-25 to Hwy 230; then left 2.3 miles to Grayrocks Road; then right 12.5 miles on Grayrocks Road to the main entrance on the left. (*If you continue 5 miles past the main entrance, you will intersect with Guernsey Road, and if going to Guernsey fits your plans, turn left on Guernsey road; then go 12.3 miles to downtown Guernsey.*)

From Guernsey: In Guernsey, at the junction of US 26 and S. Wyoming Ave., go south 12.3 miles on S. Wyoming Ave. (*which becomes Guernsey Road once you are past the Wagon Ruts and Register Cliffs historical areas*) to Grayrocks Road; then right 5 miles to the main entrance on the right. *See map page 62.*

Wheatland Reservoir #1 Public Access Area
(Wyoming Game and Fish, Open all year)

About the camp – This reservoir and access area is surrounded by private land and camping is allowed only between the reservoir's perimeter road and the shoreline. This road, from the junction of Hwy 310, is 2.1 miles long and ends as private land begins on the other side of the reservoir. Along the road there are many camping options, three vault toilets and two boat ramps. No potable water. Stay limited to 5 days.

Getting there – From Wheatland at the junction of 16th St. and Hwy 310, go west 3 miles on Hwy 310 to the junction of Hwy 310 and 311; then left 4 miles on Hwy 310 to the perimeter road at the reservoir; then right to the camping options.

From I-25 use exit 74; then go west 3.6 miles on Hwy 34 to Grange Road; then right 3 miles on Grange Road to Reservoir Road; then left .2 miles to the perimeter road; then right .8 miles (*it's private land to the left*) to the junction of Hwy 310 and straight ahead to the camping options on the 2.1 miles of perimeter road. *See map page 66.*

Wheatland Reservoir #3 Public Access Area

(Wyoming Game and Fish, Open all year)

About the camp – This reservoir and the camping options around it are completely in the open in the high plains country on the western slope of the Laramie Mountains. There is not a single tree or wind break around this reservoir making it of possible interest for wind surfing, as well as fishing.

There is a boat ramp on the northern end of the reservoir and vault toilets in three locations. Stone fire rings are in evidence, but there are no tables or potable water. To the east there is a short road that loops to the shore and back to the main road and has several camping options. For additional camping options go south on Kite Ranch Road where there is another loop road along the shore. Stay limited to 5 days.

Rates – Free

Getting there – From Wheatland at the junction of 16th St. and Hwy 310, go west 3 miles on Hwy 310 to the junction of Hwy 310 and 311; then left 1 mile on Hwy 310 to Palmer Canyon Road; then right 36.4 miles (*past Cottonwood Peak Road and Garrett Road*) to the merger of Palmer Canyon Road and Tunnel Road; then right 10.6 miles to the reservoir and boat ramp on the left. (*1.1 miles shy of the boat ramp area is the small loop road turnoff and 1 mile past the boat ramp area is the left-hand turn on Kite Ranch Road to the other loop road along the west shore with more camping options.*) *See map page 66.*

Worth mentioning – This public access area is about 16 miles from US 30 on CR 61 which turns off of US 30 a few miles north of Rock River.

Laramie Peak Wildlife Habitat Management Area

(Wyoming Game and Fish, Open May 1-7Nov. 30)

About the camp – This wildlife habitat area is cooperatively managed by the Wyoming Game and Fish, the Bureau of Land Management and the Forest Service. While there are still isolated tracts of private land within the area, Laramie Peak WHMA protects over 11,000 acres. The management plan emphasizes fisheries, bighorn sheep, elk and pronghorn antelope. Other species found here include mule deer, black bears, coyotes, wild turkeys, blue grouse, various ducks, cottontail rabbits and a variety of songbirds. Fishing for trout is permitted on Duck Creek and Cherry Creek.

The area is located where the Laramie Plains meet the southern end of the Laramie Range. Grasslands cover about one-third; ponderosa pine, limber pine and junipers cover another third; sagebrush grasslands cover a smaller area, with big sagebrush the most dominant shrub. Wet meadows make up most of the remaining area.

Duck Creek Canyon offers visitors a route to scenic Duck Creek Falls, where this creek drops 100' over a rock ledge. There are several other

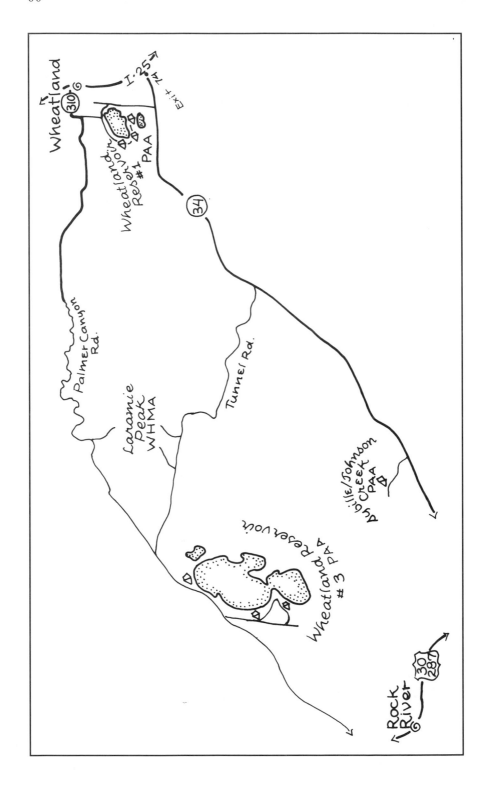

trails into the Duck Creek Falls area which are rocky and require the use of ropes and technical climbing skills.

The lands are open to the public all year excepting Hay Canyon, Tony Ridge and Duck Creek Canyon which are closed from December 1 through April 30 annually. There are no designated camping areas, but camping is allowed as long as you are not on private land. Study the map boards at entrances noting the small tracts of private land within the area. Rough terrain may make it difficult to pinpoint your location.

While camping, the area offers a variety of recreational opportunities including rock climbing, bouldering, hiking, fishing , hunting, photography and wildlife viewing. No potable water. Stay limited to 5 days (camping limits here are currently under review and may be extended to 14 days: Inquire).

Rates – Free

Getting there – From Wheatland at the junction of 16th St. and Hwy 310, go west 3 miles on Hwy 310 to the junction of Hwy 310 and 311; then left 1 mile on Hwy 310 to Palmer Canyon Road; then right 16.5 miles to the access road for this WHMA on the left.

From I-25 via Hwy 34 and Tunnel Road to the other side of the management area: Use I-25 exit 74; then southwest 16.4 miles on Hwy 34 to Tunnel Road; then right 14.5 miles; *[or]* 16.5 miles to access roads to the right for this management area. *See map facing page.*

Sybille/Johnson Creek Access Area
(Wyoming Game and Fish, Open all year)

About the camp – This rugged access area is reportedly a favorite for hardy hikers and deer hunters. There are several camping options at Johnson Creek Reservoir, which contributes to the diversity and recreational opportunities of the area and is habitat for rainbow and brook trout. No potable water. Stay limited to 5 days.

Rates – Free

Getting there – From I-25 use exit 74; then go southwest 27.5 miles on Hwy 34 to the turnoff on the right; then right 1.2 miles to an area with a vault toilet on the left, *[or]* continue another 1.4 miles to the reservoir where there is a pit toilet and several other camping options.

From US 30 about 17 miles north of Laramie go northeast 24.9 miles on Hwy 34 to the turnoff on the left; then left 1.2 miles to an area with a vault toilet on the left, *[or]* continue another 1.4 miles to the reservoir where there is a pit toilet and several other camping options. *See map facing page.*

<u>NOTES</u>

NOTES

70

Contents — South Central

South Central

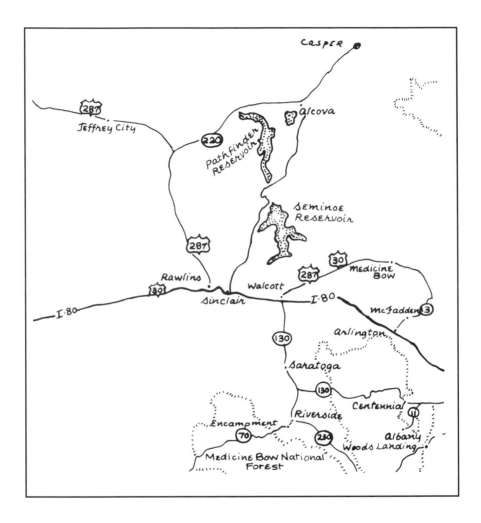

The Medicine Bow Mountains perforate the southern edge of Wyoming here, but much of this section of the state is the kind of high sagebrush plains that drove homesteaders mad or at least eccentric. In the midst of the great open vistas you find now and then a beautiful, trout-rich river like the North Platte meandering through.

This section features 87 camping options, 30 of which are in the Medicine Bow National Forest. Remaining options include 17 privately-owned camps with hookups, 14 BLM camps, 10 free Game and Fish areas, 13 county campgrounds, 2 free campgrounds and1 state park camp. These camps are under headings for 11 cities and towns, including Albany, Arlington, Casper, Centennial, Encampment, Jeffrey City, Medicine Bow, Rawlins, Riverside, Saratoga, Sinclair and Woods Landing.

Albany

Albany isn't much more than the end of the pavement, but it does provide the shortest access to five Forest Service camps and a free Fish and Game area listed here. Stock your cooler and take care of any needed supplies elsewhere along the way.

Bobbie Thompson Campground
(Medicine Bow National Forest, Open June 1 to Oct. 15)

About the camp – This camp has 12 sites on a loop road with Douglas Creek flowing past the east edge of the area. Sites are in a mature lodgepole pine forest and generally roomy with good tenting options. The camp has a vault toilet and potable water. All sites have tables and fire rings with grates and four of the sites are pull-thrus. Stay limited to 14 days.

Rates – Campsite per night: $10. Rates half with Golden Age or Access Passport.

Getting there – From Albany go west 2.8 miles on FSR 500; then left 5.6 miles on FSR 542 to 543; then left 1.3 miles on 543 to the camp turnoff on the right; then right .6 miles to the camp. *See map page 74.*

Pickaroon Campground
(Medicine Bow National Forest, Open June 15 to Oct. 15)

About the camp – This is a picturesque camp with 7 roomy sites in a stand of mature cottonwoods along the banks of the North Platte River. All sites are short walk-ins, with a central parking area. There is a vault toilet near the camp, but no potable water. All sites have tables and fire rings with grates. Stay limited to 14 days.

Rates – Free

About the camp From Albany go west 2.8 miles on FSR 500; then left 5.6 miles on FSR 542 to 543; then right 1.8 miles to the fork of 543 and 511; then left 2.6 miles on 511 to the junction of 511 and 512; then straight 10.1 miles on 512 to the North Platte River; then left 1.7 miles to the camp on the right (from this road there are several two-tracks leading to dispersed camping options along the river). See map page 74.

Pike Pole Campground
(Medicine Bow National Forest, Open June 15 to Oct. 15)

About the camp – This camp is just past Pickaroon, somewhat removed from the North Platte River and has 6 more or less remote sites. The road through this area is .8 miles long from Pickaroon to the North Platte River Trailhead. There are four well-spaced camps to the right and two more in the open, further along and on the other side of the

74

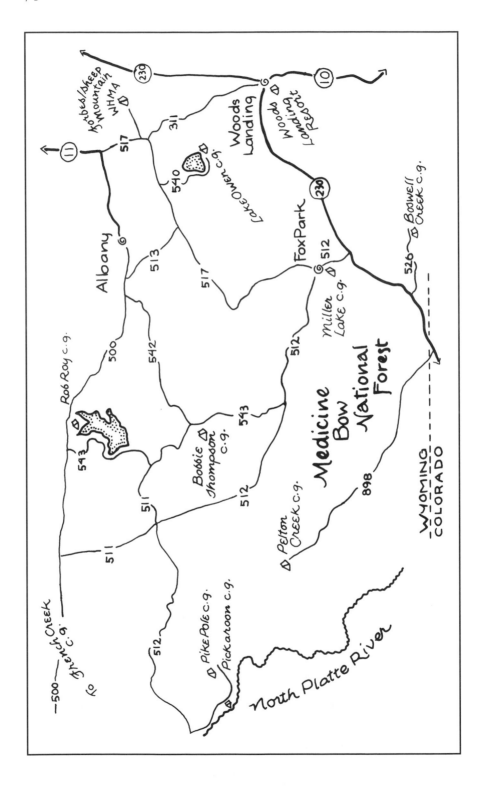

road. At the trailhead which is at the end-of-the-road loop turn around there is a pit toilet and parking. All sites have tables and fire rings with grates. No potable water. Stay limited to 14 days.

Rates – Free

Getting there – From Albany go west 2.8 miles on FSR 500; then left 5.6 miles on FSR 542 to 543; then right 1.8 miles to the fork of 543 and 511; then left 2.6 miles on 511 to the junction of 511 and 512; then straight 10.1 miles on 512 to the North Platte River; then left 1.7 miles to Pickaroon on the right and keep going. *See map page facing.*

Rob Roy Campground
(Medicine Bow National Forest, Open June 15 to Oct. 1)

About the camp – This camp, off a reservoir of the same name, has a variety of camping options from heavily timbered sites to open sites nearer the water, where there is a boat ramp. The camp has vault toilets, potable water and 65 sites. All sites have tables and fire rings with grates. Stay limited to 14 days.

Rates – Campsite per night: $10. Rates half with Golden Age or Access Passport.

Getting there – From Albany go west 2.8 miles on FSR 500; then stay right 5.6 miles on FSR 500 to the camp turnoff on the left; then left .3 miles to fee board. *See map facing page.*

Lake Owen Campground
(Medicine Bow National Forest, Open June 1 to Oct. 15)

About the camp – This camp is on a lake of the same name and has a variety of camping options at 35 shady sites on two loop roads in a mature lodgepole pine forest. There is a boat ramp and day use area. The camp has vault toilets and potable water. On the upper loop, sites 10 and 11 are lake-side options and on the lower loop, 25-30 are along the shore. All sites have tables, fire rings with grates and grills. Stay limited to 14 days.

Rates – Campsite per night: $10. Rates half with Golden Age or Access Passport.

Getting there – From Albany go west 2.3 miles on FSR 500 to FSR 513; then left 2.5 miles on 513 to 517; then left 1.5 miles on 517 to 540; then right 2.8 miles on 540 to the camp along the southeast shore of the lake. *See map facing page.*

Forbes/Sheep Mountain Wildlife Habitat Management Area
(Wyoming Game and Fish, Open July 1 to Dec. 31)

About the camp – This 950-acre Wyoming Game and Fish WHMA is on the west end of Sheep Mountain in the Sheep Mountain Game Refuge.

The Wyoming Game and Fish Commission purchased this land to provide improved public access to 20,000 acres of wild lands administered by the Forest Service on Sheep Mountain.

This location is critical winter habitat for deer and elk, but the rough and rocky terrain offers other possible wildlife sightings including mountain lions, bobcats and coyotes. Clark's nutcrackers, hairy woodpeckers, turkey vultures, pine siskins and goshawks are just a few of the bird species. Visitors can hike along a foot trail to the top of Sheep Mountain, with opportunities for remote camping, for wildlife watching and photography. No potable water. Stay limited to 14 days.

Rates – Free

Getting there – From the junction of Hwy 130 and 11 go south 8.6 miles on Hwy 11 to Fox Creek Road; then left 1.6 miles to the fork at FSR Road 517; then stay left on Fox Creek Road .5 miles to the turnoff; then left .1 miles to the parking area. *See map page 74.*

Arlington

Arlington, once a stagecoach station, is at the crossroads of Hwy 13 and I-80, with access to north end of the **Medicine Bow National Forest**. If you prefer the dirt-road approach to seeing the country, this is an excellent route through the forest from I-80 to the Snowy Range Scenic Highway (Hwy 130). Good maps are available from the USFS District Office in Laramie.

In Arlington there is a private camp with hookups. Nearby there are two Forest Service camps (one free) and eight Game and Fish options (all free). At the private camp there is a C-store with basic groceries, ice, snacks and the like.

Arlington Outpost Campground

(Private, Open May 15 to Oct. 15)
PO Box 95, Rock River, WY 82083 Ph/Fax: (307) 378-2350

About the camp – This 17-acre camp just off of I-80 is open and level. There are 50 gravel RV sites with tables and grills: all pull-thrus (up to 25x45). 20 sites are full hookups (30/50 amp) with 30 sites water and electric only. 17 designated tent sites are on native grass with tables and grills. One camper cabin is available. *Horses: Inquire.*

Amenities – Rest rooms and showers (showers only: $3), laundry; game room and playground; C-store, gas, diesel and limited RV parts, hunting and fishing licenses, gift shop, dump station, and pay phone.

Rates – Full hookups per site: $16.75. Water and electric only per site: $16. Tent sites: $11. Camper cabin (sleeps 4): $27. All major cards. Discounts: all current camper cards and seniors +55. Reservations: phone or mail.

Getting there – The camp is north of I-80 exit 272. *See map page 78.*

Deep Creek Campground

(Medicine Bow National Forest, Open June 1 to Oct. 1)

About the camp – This camp has 11 sites, water and vault toilets in dense conifer forest, but has fallen victim to funding shortages. The Forest Service provides vault toilets and potable water, but is otherwise managing this area for dispersed camping. Stay limited to 21 days.

Rates – Free, donations welcome and appreciated.

Getting there – From I-80 use exit 272; then go west 1.1 miles using the service road on the south side of the interstate; then take the left fork (FSR 111) 8.1 miles to the junction of FSR 111 and 120; then straight 5.3 miles on 111 to 101; then left 1.5 miles on 101 to the camp on the left. *See map page 94.*

Bow River Campground

(Medicine Bow National Forest, Open June 1 to Oct. 1)

About the camp – This camp, in a forest of lodgepole pine, subalpine fir and aspen, has 13 sites on a loop road. The camp has vault toilets and potable water. Sites have tables, fire rings with grates and grills. Stay limited to 14 days.

Rates – Campsite per night: $7. Rates half with Golden Age or Access Passports.

Getting there – Use I-80 exit 272; then go west 1.1 miles using the service road on the south side of the interstate; then take the left fork (FSR 111) 8.1 miles to the junction of FSR 111 and 120, then go right about 4 miles on 120 to 101; then right 2 miles on 101 to 100; then left .1 miles on 100 to the camp on the left. *See map page 94.*

Wick/Beumee Wildlife Habitat Management Area

(Wyoming Game and Fish, Open June 1 to Nov. 30)

Wick/Beumee (*Bow-May*) has two distinct areas in this 18,893-acre habitat area: One north of I-80 and one south, about five miles west of Arlington and six miles southeast of Elk Mountain.

About the camps to the south – The Wick portion, to the south of the interstate, is closed from Dec. 1 until May 31 to reduce stress on elk that winter in this area and summer in the adjacent Medicine Bow Mountains.

The Wick area has four major drainages crossing its mountainous terrain, which ranges in elevation from 7,000' to almost 9000'. Sage-brush grasslands, mountain shrubs, meadows and a mixture of conifer and deciduous forests provide habitat for the elk as well as several hundred mule deer and antelope that feed here spring, summer and fall. Other wildlife include blue and sage grouse, cottontail rabbits, waterfowl, coyotes, beavers, weasel, mink, mountain lions, bobcats, yellow-bellied marmots, black-tailed prairie dogs and black bears.

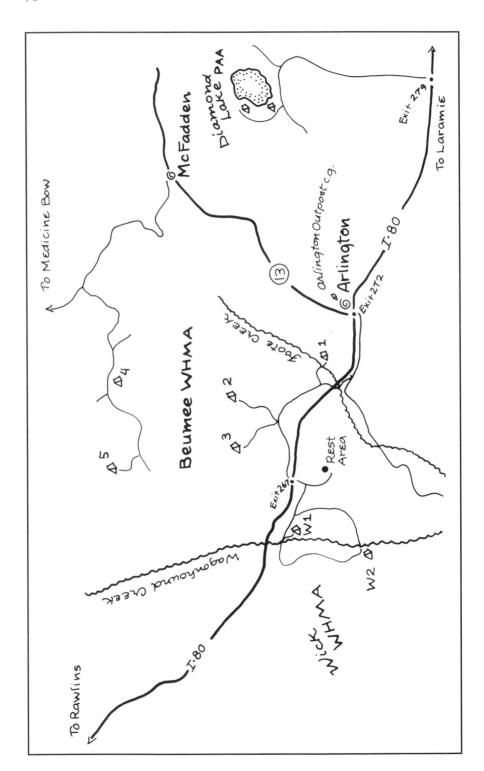

Three ponds and ten miles of stream in the Wagonhound and Foote Creek drainages provide fishing for rainbow, brook and brown trout. Wagonhound Creek provides an excellent opportunity to observe the ecology of the beaver and the benefits they provide to create a diversity of wetlands, vegetation and wildlife support system.

The recreational opportunities are bountiful and there are several roads to help you explore the area. No potable water. Stay limited to 14 days.

Rates – Free

Getting there – Wick (first parking area): From I-80 use exit 267 for the Wagonhound Rest Area; then south to a turnoff before and to the west of the rest area; then west .3 miles and go by a well-traveled fork to the left; then go 1 mile to a hard left-hand turn just before a bridge; then left .1 miles to the parking area, where there is a pit toilet on a little rise above the camp.

Wick (second parking area): Follow the above directions to the bridge over the creek; then go 3.9 miles (*keeping to the left where there are right-hand uphill forks in the road*) to the camp, which has a vault toilet and has several camping options in an open park or along Wagonhound Creek. *See map page 78.*

About the camps to the north – The Bear Creek Cattle Company public access on this management area is to the north of the interstate on high rolling plains and sagebrush grasslands. There are six designated parking/camping areas, including one that is totally in the open near a windmill; two that are by man-made impounds for water; one along the drainage of Foote Creek; one among the broken down buildings and corrals of an early homestead, and one that couldn't be found. None of the sites have vault toilets or potable water, but the homestead site does have a still-functional outhouse and aspen trees. Three of these sites are out of Arlington and three, including the mystery site, are west of McFadden.

Rates – Free

Getting there – At Arlington (to camp 1 north) use I-80 exit 272; then go west 1.1 miles using the service road on the south side of the interstate; then stay right 1.1 miles, going under the interstate to a cattle guard; then right .3 miles to the camp in the drainage of Foote Creek.

To camps 2 and 3: follow the above directions to the cattle guard; then stay left 1.3 miles on this two track, to two turnoffs to the right; then 1 mile on the right fork of this turnoff to a site by a man-made reservoir; [or] .9 miles on the left fork to the site at the old homestead.

To the camps west of McFadden: From Arlington go 6 miles north on Hwy 13 to McFadden; then left 40 yards and left again .2 miles around the town site; then down the hill behind the town staying on this road for 3.3 miles until you cross another cattle guard; then left 1.3 miles where you stay to the right for .7 miles to a parking area on the left by a man-made reservoir; [or] continue another .4 miles to another fork in the road; then left 1.4 miles and take the right fork .2 miles to a two-track on the right heading up a slight grade; then right .8 miles on this two track, past a windmill and holding tank to this wide-open site with miles of view. *See map page 78.*

Diamond Lake Public Access Area

(Wyoming Game and Fish, Open all year)

About the camp – Diamond Lake has two parking areas with vault toilets. Camping is restricted to the west shore between these two areas. The first camp has a boat ramp, but no potable water, tables or grills. Stay limited to 5 days.

Rates - Free

Getting there – From I-80 use exit 279, go north 4.2 miles on CR 15 (Cooper Cove Road) to a left fork; then left .2 miles to another fork in the road; then right . 4 miles to the first parking area with boat ramp; [or] .7 miles to the far parking area. *See map page 78.*

Casper

Casper, the second largest city in the state, is big by Wyoming standards. It sits along the banks of the North Platte River and in the shadow of Casper Mountain to the south of the city. Casper owes its growth to oil, with many signs of oil-related industry in evidence, and its central location in the state. Sites for a variety of interests here include the **Fort Caspar Museum**, at 4001 Fort Caspar Road, Ph: (307) 235-8462; the **Nicolaysen Art Museum and Discovery Center**, at 400 East Collins, Ph: (307) 235-5247; the **Casper College Tate Mineralogical Museum**, at 125 College Drive, Ph: (307) 268-2514, and the **Casper Planetarium**, at 904 North Poplar St., Ph: (307) 577-0310. Annual events in Casper include the **Mountain Man Rendezvous** in late June and the **Platte Bridge Encampment** in August, both at Fort Caspar, Ph: (307) 234-9754, and the **Central Wyoming Fair and Rodeo** in July.

In Casper there are four privately-owned camps. Nearby there are a total of 12 county camps at **Casper Mountain**, **Alcova Lake** and **Pathfinder Reservoir**, and 7 BLM camps. Casper has groceries hardware, sporting goods, bicycle sales and service and RV sales and service. Of special interest to hard sided campers is **Teton Homes**, where luxury fifth-wheel trailers are manufactured: tours weekday mornings at 10:30. In summer, Casper has 5 outdoor swimming pools scattered around the city with modest admission and workouts and showers are available at the **Casper Recreation Center** (no indoor pool here), at 1801 E. 4th St., Ph: (307) 235-8383 (Day pass: $2).

Antelope Run Campground

(Private, Open April 1 to Nov. 1)
1101 Prairieland, Bar Nunn, WY 82601 Ph: (307) 577-1664 or 800-922-1460

About the camp – This open camp, located in Bar Nunn about 3 miles north of Casper, is convenient to I-25 and adjacent to the city park with playground facilities, tennis and basketball courts. The camp has 66 RV sites: 32 pull-thrus (30x50) and 34 back-ins (20x40). 29 sites are full hookups (30 amp) and 37 water and electric only. All sites are gravel with native grass 'yards' and tables. Some grills are available. There are 8 designated tent sites with tables and grills.

Amenities - Rest rooms and showers, laundry; cable TV ($2), game room, playground, use of city park, heated indoor pool (20x50) and hot tub; limited groceries and RV parts, dump station, propane and pay phone.

Rates – Full hookups for 2 persons: $18. Water and electric for 2 persons: $17. Tent sites for 2 persons: $12. Additional persons: $2. No credit cards. Personal checks okay. Reservations: phone or mail. Discounts for Goodsam and Golden Age Passport.

Getting there – From I-25 use exit 191 about 3 miles north of Casper; then west .2 miles to the stop sign on Salt Creek Highway; then north 1 mile to the camp on the left. *See map page 82.*

Casper KOA Kampground

(Private, Open all year)
2800 East Yellowstone, Casper, WY 82609 Ph: (307) 237-5155 or 800-562-3259 Fax: (307) 266-4886

About the camp – This open camp, located near the east end of Casper, is convenient to I-25. The camp has 78 RV sites: 55 pull-thrus (30x60) and 23 back-ins (30x40). 52 sites are full hookups (30 amp and 8 sites with 50 amp) and 26 sites water and electric only. All sites are gravel with grass 'yards' and tables. 23 designated tent sites are on grass with tables and grills. There are 3 kamper kabins.

Amenities - Rest rooms and showers, laundry; cable TV at 40 sites ($1), game room, playground, heated outdoor pool and indoor spa, miniature golf ($1), nightly buffalo barbecue (summer only), and shuttle service to the Eastridge Mall; limited groceries and RV parts, dump station, propane and pay phone.

Rates – Full hookups for 2 persons: $19. Water and electric for 2 persons: $18. Tent sites for 2 persons: $14. Kamper kabins for 2 persons: $26. Additional persons 18 and under: $1. 19 and over: $2. Discounts: KOA, Goodsam, Golden Age Passport and AAA. Reservations: phone or mail.

Getting there – From I-25 use exit 185; then north (away from the mountain) .1 miles to East Yellowstone Highway; then left/west .9 miles to the camp on the right.

82

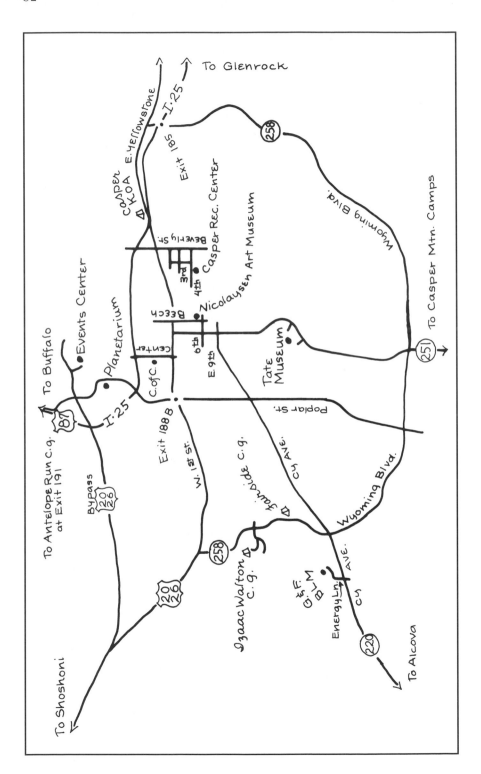

Eastbound on US 20/26 take the bypass east to I-25; then south/right to exit 185; then north (away from the mountain) .1 miles to the light at the intersection of East Yellowstone Highway; then left/west .9 miles to the camp on the right.

Eastbound on Wyoming 220 turn south/right at the junction of Hwy 258 (Wyoming Blvd.); then follow the Wyoming Blvd. bypass around the south end of the city (about 3.5 miles), go under I-25 to East Yellowstone Highway; then left/west .9 miles to the camp on the right. *See map facing page.*

Izaac Walton Fort Caspar Campground

(Private, Open all year)
4205 Fort Caspar Road, Casper, WY 82604 Ph: (307) 234-3260 Fax: (307) 473-2955

About the camp – This open camp, located behind the Fort Caspar Museum and Historic Site, is near the North Platte River in the western part of the city. The camp has 92 full hookup (30/50 amp) RV sites: 42 pull-thrus (24x60) and 50 back-ins (20x45). All sites are gravel with tables. There are 15 designated tent sites, mostly in the trees nearer the river, on grass with tables and grills.

Amenities - Rest rooms and showers (showers only: $2), laundry; playground, nature walk along the North Platte River, catch and release fishing pond (no license required); limited groceries and RV parts, dump station, and pay phone.

Rates – Full hookups for 2 persons: $16. Tent sites for 2 persons: $11. Additional persons: $1. Most major cards. Discounts: Goodsam, Woodalls, AAA and Wheelers. Reservations: phone, fax or mail.

Getting there – From I-25 use exit 188B (Poplar St.); then south (towards the mountain) 2.2 miles to the third traffic light (Collins St.); then right .5 miles where Collins merges with 13th St.; then stay on 13th St. into Fort Caspar; then follow the signs .5 miles to the camp.

Eastbound on US 20/26 turn right on Hwy 258 (Wyoming Blvd.); then 1.0 mile to the light at 13th St.; then right into Fort Caspar and follow the signs .5 miles to the camp.

Eastbound on Wyoming 220 turn left at Hwy 258 (Wyoming Blvd.); then 1.1 miles to the light at 13th St.; then left into Fort Caspar and follow the signs .5 miles to the camp. *See map facing page.*

—South of Casper—

Casper Mountain Camps

(Natrona County Parks, Open Memorial Day to Oct. 15)
528 Wyoming Blvd., Mills, WY 82644 Ph: (307) 235-9325

About the camp – Natrona County Parks operates 5 camps in the Casper Mountain Recreation Area, providing a total of 79 sites, 8 of these for tents only. The mountain is robed in lodgepole pine and camps are mostly in timbered areas. The camps — Skunk Hollow Park, Elkhorn Springs Park, Deer Haven Park, Tower Hill Park and Beartrap Meadow Park — have tables and fire rings. Vault toilets are provided, at least one in each area, and there are three group picnic shelters in the Beartrap Meadow Park area (group reservations only, no camping at the shelters). Potable water is available at all three of these shelters and in the Deer Haven Park area. Stay limited to 14 days.

Rates – Campsite per night, per vehicle: $5. Coupon books are available at the Natrona County Parks office or from caretakers at the parks: 10 nights for $35.

Getting there – From the junction of Wyoming Blvd. (Hwy 258) and Casper Mountain Road (Hwy 251) travel south 5.9 miles toward Casper Mountain to the fork of CR 505 and CR 504; then take the left fork 1 mile to a Natrona County Parks information bulletin board with maps of the area and a self-serve fee station. All camps are within .5 miles of here. *See map page 82.*

Rim Campground

(BLM, Open June 15 to Nov. 24)

About the camp – This camp on Muddy Mountain, which is to the south of Casper Mountain, has 8 open and roomy sites. The camp has a vault toilet, but no potable water (water is available at nearby Lodgepole Campground). Sites have tables and fire rings with grates and grills. Site 8 is a mini group site with 3 tables and 3 grills clustered together. There is an overlook of the Casper Mountain country near this camp and an interpretive hiking/biking trail through the area. Stay limited to 14 days in any 28 day period.

Rates – Campsite per night: $5. Rates half with Golden Age or Access Passports.

Getting there – From the junction of Wyoming Blvd. (Hwy 258) and Casper Mountain Road (Hwy 251) go south towards Casper Mountain 5.9 miles on Highway 251 to the fork of CR 504 and 505; then left 2 miles on CR 505 to the end of the pavement; then straight 2 miles more to another fork; then left 4.2 miles to a self-serve informational kiosk for the Muddy Mountain Environmental Education Center; then left .2 miles to the camp on the left. *See map page 82.*

Lodgepole Campground

(BLM, Open June 15 to Nov. 24)

About the camp – This camp has 15 sites in a mature stand of lodgepole pine on Muddy Mountain, which is south of Casper Mountain. The camp has a vault toilet, potable water and an interpretive hiking/biking trail through the area. Sites have tables, fire rings with grates and grills. Stay limited to 14 days in any 28 day period.

Rates – Campsite per night: $5.00. Rates half with Golden Age or Access Passports.

Getting there – From the junction of Wyoming Blvd. (Hwy 258) and Casper Mountain Road (Hwy 251) go south towards Casper Mountain 5.9 miles on Hwy 251 to the fork of CR 504 and 505; then left 2 miles on CR 505 to the end of the pavement; then straight 2 miles more to another fork; then left 4.2 miles to a self-serve informational kiosk for the Muddy Mountain Environmental Education Center; then right .2 miles to the camp on the left. *See map page 82.*

(Fees at the BLM camps on Muddy Mountain are new in 1999, and will include a day use/occupance fee of $3 for using the campground. Under the Receation Fee Demonstration program there will be an opportunity to make voluntary donations for using the area and trails. The voluntary funds will help maintain the trail system in the area.)

—West of Casper—

Alcova Lake and Pathfinder Reservoir Camps
(Natrona County Parks, Open Memorial Day to Oct. 15)
528 Wyoming Blvd., Mills, WY 82644 Ph: (307) 235-9325

About the camp – Natrona County Parks manages a total of 9 developed camps for tents or RVs on Alcova Lake and Pathfinder Reservoir: 5 camps including Cottonwood, Black Beach, Okie, Westside and Fremont are on Alcova Reservoir; 4 camps including Weiss, Sage, Diabase and Bishop's Point are on Pathfinder Reservoir. One other developed campground, Gray Reef, is below Alcove Dam. At these sites there are tables, fire rings, shelters, vault toilets and dumpsters. 8 of the 10 sites have boat ramps. At Alcova Lake, catty-corner across from the marina, there is a small RV camp with full hookups at 10 sites. All sites are first come, first served. Stay limited to 14 days.

Rates – RV site at Alcova Lake with hookups: $12. Campsite per night, per vehicle: $5. Coupon books are available at the Natrona County Parks office or from caretakers at the parks: 10 nights for $35.

Getting there – From Alcova there is a loop road (CR 407) which accesses side roads to camps at Cottonwood and Black Beach. After 7.2 miles there is a fork; you go right on CR 408 around and south of Alcova Lake, across Fremont Canyon and join CR 409 near Pathfinder Reservoir. A left on CR 409 takes you to Weiss, Sage and Diabase Campgrounds as well as the Pathfinder Boat Club Marina; *[or]* go right 2.7 miles to the turnoff to Bishops Point on the left; *[or]* 6.3 miles back to Hwy 220 about 4 miles west of Alcova. To get to Okie Beach, Westside, Fremont or the RV Campground from Alcova, go west 1 mile on Hwy 220; then south on this dead-end road to these camps and the RV park across from Alcova Lake Marina. The turnoff to Gray Reef is east .6 miles from CR 407 at Alcova; then right .8 miles to the camp on the right. *See map page 86.*

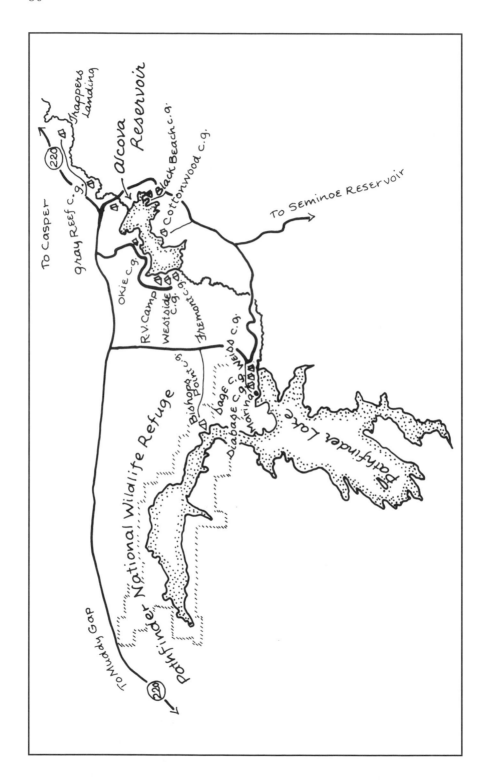

Worth Mentioning – The shore at Alcova Lake is not conducive to remote camping, but many who frequent Pathfinder Reservoir have boats and seek solitude by leaving their truck and trailer at the marina to camp from their boats at remote sites along the shore. Basic groceries, ice and snacks are available at Sloanes Store at Alcova near the junction of US 220 and CR 407, or at the Pathfinder Boat Club Marina Store.

Trapper Route Landing No. 1
(BLM, Open all year)

About the camp – This camp is on a slight rise above the North Platte River with a parking area, a vault toilet, two tables and one fire ring with grate. Walk-in tenting options are available below the parking area near the river.

Rates – Free

Getting there – From Alcova, go east .6 miles on Hwy 220 to CR 412; then right 2 miles on CR 412 to the turnoff on the right; then right .1 miles to the camp. *See map facing page.*

Prior Flat Campground
(BLM, Open June 1 to Nov. 15)

About the camp – This camp at the base of Shirley Mountain has 15 sites in a forest mix of aspen and limber and lodgepole pine. The area provides wildlife habitat for pronghorn antelope, mule deer, elk, coyotes, grouse, golden eagles and numerous smaller birds. The camp straddles BLM Road 3115 and has a vault toilet, but no potable water. Sites have tables, fire rings with grates and grills. Stay limited to 14 days in any 28 day period.

Rates – Campsite per night: $7. Rates half with Golden Age or Access Passports.

Getting there – From the junction of Hwys 220 and 487 (*southwest of Casper*) go south 26.8 miles on Hwy 487 to the junction of Hwy 487 and 77; then right 11.9 miles on Hwy 77 to the turnoff (CR 102) on the right; then right 2 miles to a fork; then right 7 miles on CR 102 to the camp and Shirley Mountain Loop Road (BLM 3115) on the left. *(Shirley Mountain Loop road is a nice drive, but it and CR 102 can easily become muddy and impassable after heavy rains or snowmelt.)*

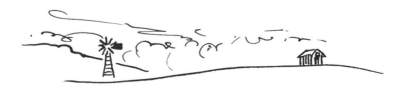

—North and West of Casper—

Buffalo Creek Campground
(BLM, Open June 15 to Oct. 31)

About the camp – This camp has 3 sites in mature forest along Buffalo Creek. The camp has a vault toilet, but no potable water. Sites are roomy with good tenting options and have tables and fire rings with grates. Stay limited to 14 days in any 28 day period.

Rates – Free.

Getting there – From Waltman and the junction of US20/26 and CR 104, go north 9.7 miles to the end of the pavement and an information kiosk for this scenic South Big Horn/Red Wall BLM National Back Country Byway; then straight 13.4 miles on CR 105 to CR 109; then left 9.1 miles on CR 109 to the camp entrance on the left; then left .1 miles to a fork; then left .1 miles to the camp (*if you go right .1 mile at this fork you will enter the trees with an opening, a stone fire ring and a secluded dispersed camping option*). *See map page 90.*

Grave Springs Campground
(BLM, Open June 15 to Oct. 31)

About the camp – This camp has 6 sites in forest overlooking a grassy open park. As you enter the park, one site is in the open on the right, two sites are up a slight rise to the left and three sites are in timber on the far side of the park. The camp has a vault toilet, but no potable water. Sites are roomy with good tenting options and have tables and fire rings with grates. Stay limited to 14 days in any 28 day period.

Rates – Free.

Getting there – From Waltman and the junction of US20/26 and CR 104 go north 9.7 miles to the end of the pavement and an information kiosk for this scenic South Big Horn/Red Wall BLM National Back Country Byway; then straight 13.4 miles on CR 105 to CR 109; then left 11 miles on CR 109 to the camp entrance on the left; then left .1 miles to a fork; then left .2 miles to the camp. *See map page 90.*

Middle Fork Campground
(BLM, Open June 15 to Oct. 31)

About the camp – This camp has 5 sites on a short road, with a small end-of-the-road turnaround, just above the Middle Fork of the Powder River. The camp has a vault toilet and a trash collection area, but no potable water. Sites have fire rings only, no tables, and one site has questionable tenting options. The preferred site is a lone walk-in site near the river and below the turnaround at the end of the road. Stay limited to 14 days.

Rates – Free.

Getting there – From Waltman and the junction of US20/26 and CR 104 go north 9.7 miles to the end of the pavement and an information kiosk about this scenic BLM South Big Horn/Red Wall National Back Country Byway; then straight 13.4 miles on CR 105 to CR 109; then left 17.4 miles on CR 109 to where this route enters Washakie County; then continue north 6.1 miles to the camp on the right. *See map page 90.*

—For the View—

South Big Horn /Red Wall BLM National Back Country Byway

(BLM, Open all year)

About this route – The Bureau of Land Management establishes National Back Country Byways as an alternative route offering new experiences with exceptional values, which can include glimpses of historic sites, scenic vistas, recreational prospects, or an individual experience with the land.

This byway takes you along the historic 33 Mile/Arminto Stock Trail into the summer pastures of the Southern Big Horn Mountains. It features high sagebrush grasslands with sweeping panoramas, several drainages that add diversity to the wildlife habitat, and the Red Wall Country: This valley is shaped by miles of red bluffs on one side of the road and gently sculptured rolling sagebrush grasslands on the other.

It is not difficult to imagine pioneer wagon trains inching along in this vast land, or early Native American hunters using the terrain for cover and concealment in their search for game.

The byway's lower loop, which follows the length of the Red Wall, is about 83 miles long, and the upper loop, which runs along the Southern Big Horn Mountains, adds 18.5 miles to the adventure. About 32 miles are paved.

Getting there – From the Casper bypass on US 20/26, go 12.5 miles west on US 20/26 to CR 125 (*.4 miles west of mile marker 18*); then right 14.7 miles on CR 125 to the information kiosk on the right where the road becomes CR 110; then 34.3 miles staying on CR 110 to the junction of CR 110 and 105.

At this junction you must make a choice: To take the upper loop go right 12.5 miles on CR 110 to a merger with CR 109; then a hard left on CR 109 and 17.4 miles back to CR 105 and the Red Wall Country; then right 13.3 miles where there is another information kiosk and CR 105 becomes CR 104; then straight 9.7 miles back to US 20/26 at Waltman; *[or]* to stay on the lower loop go straight 11.4 miles on CR 105 to the junction of CR 105 and 109; then 13.3 miles on CR 105 to another information kiosk where CR 105 becomes CR 104; then straight 9.7 miles back to US 20/26 at Waltman. *See map page 90.*

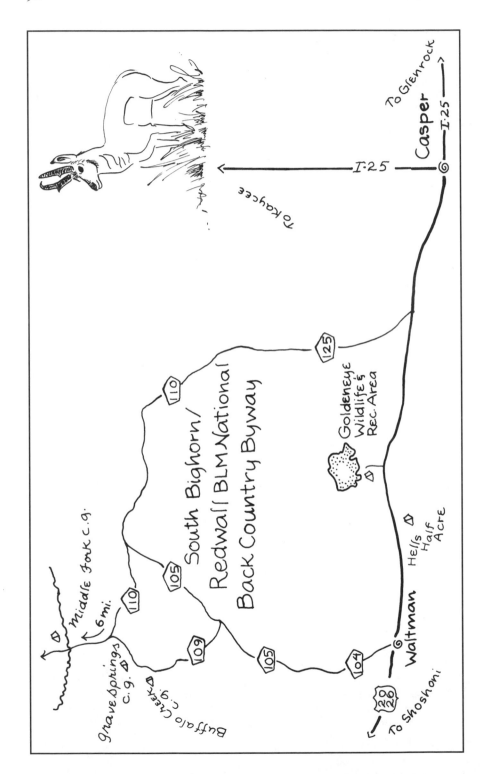

Worth Mentioning – There are three BLM campgrounds in this area. Two of the camps are off CR 109 and the third is 6.1 miles north of the merger of CR 109 and 110 which becomes a single road running north into Washakie County. While it's hard to figure out how to choose between the loop options and see it all, my opinion is that the 11.4 miles along CR 105, between the junctions of CR 109 and 110 on the lower loop, has some of the more picturesque landscape on the byway. In any event it's a win-win situation. The drive will reward the visitor with a new appreciation for the variety of Wyoming landscapes.

Hells Half Acre

(Private, Open April to Nov.)
PO 80, Powder River, WY 82648 Ph or Fax: (307) 472-0018

About the camp – This camp offers 14 full hookup (20/30/50 amp) RV sites, but they are usually taken by oil field interests in the area: Inquire. The sites (up to 12x45) are on gravel and native grass. Tent sites with some tables are available on native grass in an area overlooking these badlands which were used as location for the movie, "Starship Troopers." Hiking in the badlands of Hells Half Acre is free. *Horses okay.*

Amenities – Rest rooms and showers (showers only: $3); restaurant, lounge, limited groceries, snacks, ice and pay phone.

Rates – Full hookups per site: $15. Electric only: $10. Tent site per person: $3.

Getting there – From the Casper bypass on US 20/26 go about 39.5 miles west on US 20/26 to the turnoff on the left (at *mile marker 45*); then left into the camp. *See map facing page.*

Centennial

Centennial came to be as a result of a gold rush in the 1870's and logging interests, which are still somewhat active in the area. Today the highway is the only 'main street,' where a mishmash of 'western' architecture houses businesses catering to the needs of travelers and winter sports enthusiasts. It's located at the eastern edge of this section of the **Medicine Bow National Forest** and the **Snowy Range Scenic Byway** which goes over **Snowy Range Pass** (10,847'). **The Nici Self Museum**, located in an old railroad depot building on the east end of town is open Sat. and Sun., 1-4, July 4 to Labor Day or by appointment, Ph: (307) 742-7158. To the west, there are eight Forest Service camps, and a USFS Information Center just out of town.

Aspen Campground: Libby Creek

(Medicine Bow National Forest, Open May 24 to Sept. 30)

About the camp – This camp has 8 sites off a small cul-de-sac parking area. The camp has a vault toilet and potable water. All sites are roomy walk-ins in mixed forest, with tables and fire rings with grates. Stay limited to 14 days.

Rates – Campsite per night: $5. Rates half with Golden Age or Access Passports. Rates are reduced here due to no trash service: Pack it in, pack it out.

Getting there – From Centennial go west 2 miles on Hwy 130; then left .1 miles on Barber Lake Road to the camp on the right. *See map page 94.*

Pine Campground: Libby Creek

(Medicine Bow National Forest, Open May 24 to Sept. 30)

About the camp – Pine has 6 sites on a short loop road off of Barber Lake Road. The camp has a vault toilet and water. Sites are roomy and have tables and fire rings with grates. Stay limited to 14 days.

Rates – Campsite per night: $10.00. Rates half with Golden Age or Access Passports.

Getting there – From Centennial go west 2 miles on Hwy 130; then left .3 miles on Barber Lake Road to the camp on the right. *See map page 94.*

Willow Campground: Libby Creek

(Medicine Bow National Forest, Open May 26 to Sept. 30)

About the camp – This camp is the largest of the Libby Creek camps with 16 sites, several adjacent to Libby Creek. The first section of the road into the camp has sites 1-11 and a turnaround area from which there is another narrow .1 mile of road to camps 12-16 and another turnaround. The camp has vault toilets and potable water. Sites are roomy and have tables and fire rings with grates. Stay limited to 14 days.

Rates – Campsite per night: $10. Rates half with Golden Age or Access Passports. (Reservations are possible at this campground up to 240 days in advance and 10 days prior to arrival. Service fee per reservation: $8.65. Ph: (877) 444-6777 toll free.)

Getting there – From Centennial go west 2 miles on Hwy 130; then left .6 miles on Barber Lake Road to the camp turnoff on the right. *See map page 94.*

Spruce Campground: Libby Creek
(Medicine Bow National Forest, Open May 24 to Sept. 30)

About the camp – This camp is near Hwy 130 just past the Barber Lake Road turnoff. It is a nice camp near the river with 8 fairly open sites in light timber. The camp has a vault toilet and potable water. Sites are roomy and have tables and fire rings with grates. Stay limited to 14 days.

Rates – Campsite per night: $10. Rates half with Golden Age or Access Passports. (Reservations are possible at this campground up to 240 days in advance and 10 days prior to arrival. Service fee per reservation: $8.65. Ph: (877) 444-6777 toll free.)

Getting there – From Centennial go west 2.2 miles on Hwy 130 to the camp on the left (just past Barber Lake Road). *See map page 94.*

North Fork Campground
(Medicine Bow National Forest, Open July 1 to Sept. 10)

About the camp – This camp has 60 sites on two loop roads and is just 1.6 miles off the highway in a nice forested area. The camp has vault toilets and potable water. Sites are roomy with good tenting options and have tables and fire rings with grates. Stay limited to 14 days.

Rates – Campsite per night: $10. Rates half with Golden Age or Access Passports. (Reservations are possible at this campground up to 240 days in advance and 10 days prior to arrival. Service fee per reservation: $8.65. Ph: (877) 444-6777 toll free.)

Getting there – From Centennial go west 3.9 miles on Hwy 130 to FSR 101; then right 1.6 miles on FSR 101 (*Sand Lake Road*) to the camp on the left. *See map page 94.*

Nash Fork Campground
(Medicine Bow National Forest, Open June 15 to Sept. 10)

About the camp – This camp has 27 sites and is just off the highway in a lightly forested area. The camp has vault toilets and potable water. Sites are generally roomy with good tenting options and have tables and fire rings with grates. Stay limited to 14 days.

Rates – Campsite per night: $10. Rates half with Golden Age or Access Passports.

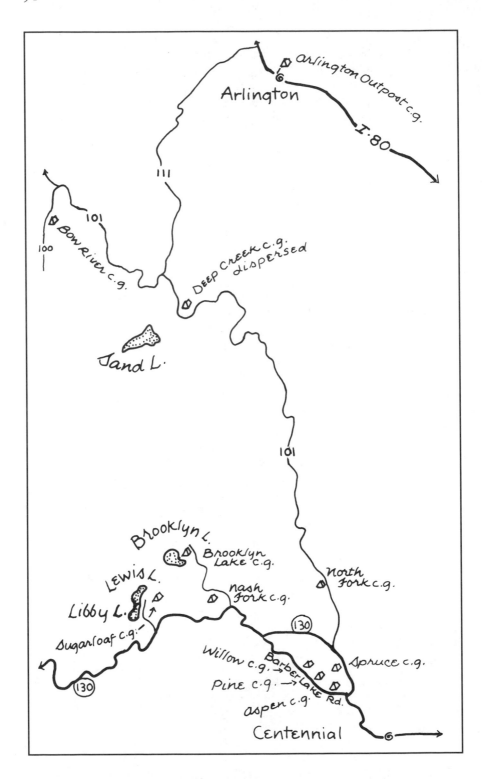

Getting there – From Centennial go west 8.1 miles on Hwy 130 to FSR 317; then right .1 miles on FSR 317 (*Brooklyn Lake Road*) to the camp on the left. *See map facing page.*

Brooklyn Lake Campground
(Medicine Bow National Forest, Open July 15 to Sept. 10)

About the camp – This camp has 19 sites (5 with pull-thrus) on two loop roads in a forested area above the lake and offers good access to the trail system in the high country of the forest. The camp has vault toilets and potable water. Sites are roomy with good tenting options and have tables and fire rings with grates. Stay limited to 14 days.

Rates – Campsite per night: $10. Rates half with Golden Age or Access Passports. (Reservations are possible at this campground up to 240 days in advance and 10 days prior to arrival. Service fee per reservation: $8.65. Ph: (877) 444-6777 toll free.)

Getting there – From Centennial go west 8.1 miles on Hwy 130 to FSR 317; then right 2.0 miles on FSR 317 (Brooklyn Lake Road) to the camp on the left. *See map facing page.*

Sugarloaf Campground
(Medicine Bow National Forest, Open July 15 to Sept. 10)

About the camp – This camp, only 1 mile off the highway, has 16 sites (2 with pull-thrus) on a loop road and is located on a rise near Libby and Lewis Lakes. It offers good access to the trail system in the high country of this national forest, and from the area there is an excellent view of Sugar Loaf Mountain (11,398') with Libby Lake in the foreground. The camp has vault toilets and potable water. Sites are roomy with good tenting options and have tables and fire rings with grates. Stay limited to 14 days.

Rates – Campsite per night: $10. Rates half with Golden Age or Access Passports. (Reservations are possible at this campground up to 240 days in advance and 10 days prior to arrival. Service fee per reservation: $8.65. Ph: (877) 444-6777 toll free.)

Getting there – From Centennial go west 14.4 miles on Hwy 130 to a right-hand turnoff; then right 1 mile to the camp on the right. *See map facing page.*

Encampment

Encampment is a small logging community on the east end of Hwy 70, which crosses the southern end of the **Medicine Bow National Forest**. For maps and information, there is a USFS Ranger District Office here. The chips and sawdust fly as hewers and sawyers compete during the **Woodchoppers Jamboree and Rodeo** on the third weekend in June. Copper mining, which also played a role in the area's history, is celebrated during **Encampment Copper Days** the weekend after Labor Day, with an antique tractor pull and displays of antique machinery. The excellent **Grand Encampment Museum**, at 817 Barnett St., Ph: 372-5308, has developed a grassy area around its main building into a frontier town with several buildings, each in its own right a mini-museum of period enterprise. Living history demonstrations are featured on Memorial Day weekend. A stretch of the Encampment River near here is becoming a favorite spring run for kayakers.

Listed here are six Forest Service camps, one BLM camp, free tent camping in a town park and a free RV park with water, electric and a dump station. Hardware and sporting goods are in short supply, but Kintzmans Cash Store offers groceries, frozen food, fresh produce and meat cut-to-order.

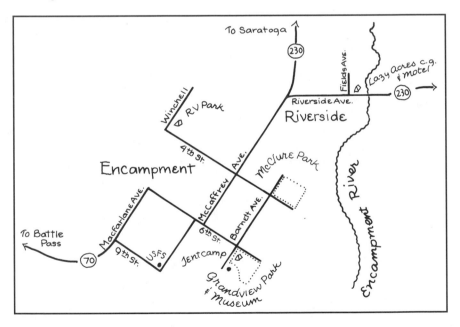

Encampment Camper Park

(Town of Encampment, Open all year)
4th and Winchell, Encampment WY 82325 Ph: 327-5501

About the camp – The Town of Encampment has an RV camp with 8 pull-thru sites (up to 15x40), water and electric (20/30 amp) only. The camp has rest rooms and a dump station (seasonal). Stay limited to 3 days.

Rates – Campsite per night: Free, with donations welcome, appreciated and expected with electric hookups.

Getting there – From McCaffrey Ave. and 4th Sts.; go northwest 3 blocks on 4th St. to Winchell St. and the camp on the right. *See map facing page.*

Grand View Park
(Town of Encampment, Open all year)
6th and Barnett, Encampment, WY 82325 Ph: 327-5501

About the camp – The town of Encampment allows tent camping at Grand View Park, at 6th and Barnett near the Grand Encampment Museum. The park has rest rooms (seasonal), a playground and a sheltered picnic area with tables and grills. Stay limited to 3 days.

Rates – Free

Getting there – From McCaffrey and 6th Sts. go southeast 3 blocks on 6th St. to Barnett St. and the park on the right. *See map facing page.*

Encampment River Campground
(BLM, Open June 1 to Nov. 15)

About the camp – This camp has 8 sites with most in a stand of cottonwoods along the Encampment River. At the easterly end of the campground a bridge over the river marks the Encampment River Trailhead which leads to Commissary Park and the Colorado State Line. The camp has a vault toilet and potable water. Sites are roomy with good tenting options and have tables, and fire rings with grates. Stay limited to 14 days in any 28 day period.

Rates – Campsite per night: $7. Rates half with Golden Age or Access Passports.

Getting there – From Encampment go southwest .5 miles on Hwy 70 to a sign stating, "Encampment River Canyon and Trail"; then left 1.7 miles, staying left at the fork about halfway in, to the camp. *See map page 98.*

Worth mentioning – In the spring this is a popular camp with kayakers who put in on the Encampment River upstream near Lakeview Campground (see Lakeview Campground page 99).

Bottle Creek Campground
(Medicine Bow National Forest, Open May 24 to Oct. 31)

About the camp – This camp has 12 sites in mixed forest very near the highway. The camp has vault toilets, potable water and a large group picnic area. Sites are roomy with good tenting options and have tables, fire rings with grates and grills. Stay limited to 14 days.

98

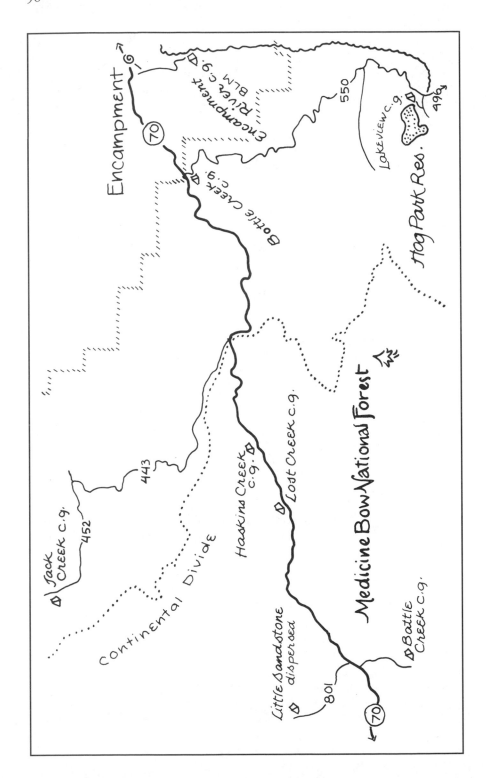

Rates – Campsite per night: $7. Rates half with Golden Age or Access Passports.

Getting there – From Encampment go west 6 miles on Hwy 70 to FSR 550; then left .1 miles to the camp on the right. *See map facing page.*

Worth mentioning – At Bottle Creek near site 4 a sign reads "Memorial Overlook 200 feet." It is a short walk to this perch overlooking a huge valley of conifers and aspen stands. The overlook is dedicated to Rev. John McClure or "Reverend John" who was the pastor at the Encampment Presbyterian Church and minister-at-large to the whole Saratoga and Encampment Valley.

Just past the entrance to this campground on FSR 550, there is a USFS informational billboard for the Sierra Madre Scenic Drive: a self-guided auto tour covering 50 miles with a recommended travel time of about 2 hours not including stops for hiking or the like. There is a box of free brochures explaining the 24 numbered stations on the route marking scenic, historic or natural points of interest. If the box is empty, brochures are available at the USFS district office in Encampment.

Lakeview (Hog Park) Campground

(Medicine Bow National Forest, Open June 10 to Oct. 31)

About the camp – This camp has 50 sites in mostly lodgepole pine near Hog Park Reservoir. There is a boat ramp with handicapped accessible dock and day use area near the camp. The camp has vault toilets, potable water and 9 pull-thru sites. Sites are roomy with good tenting options and have tables and fire rings with grates. Sites 38-40 and 42-45 are nearest the shore on a small rise above the water. Stay limited to 14 days.

Rates – Campsite per night: $10. Rates half with Golden Age or Access Passports.

Getting there – From Encampment go west 6 miles on Hwy 70 to FSR 550; then left 16.2 miles to the junction of 550 and 496; then left 1.6 miles on FSR 496 to the camp entrance road on the right; then right .7 miles to a road on the right which goes across the dam and into the camp; then right on this road .1 miles to the fee board. *See map facing page.*

Worth mentioning – About 2.4 miles south of the entrance to this camp on the left-hand side of FSR 496 is a parking lot at the trailhead for the Encampment and Commissary Park Trails. It is also the launching area for those who kayak the Encampment River in the spring of the year (see Encampment River Campground page 97).

Jack Creek Campground
(Medicine Bow National Forest, Open May 24 to Oct. 31)

About the camp – This camp has 16 sites in mixed but largely lodgepole pine forest. The camp has vault toilets, potable water and 4 pull-thru sites. Sites are roomy with good tenting options and have tables and fire rings with grates. Stay limited to 14 days.

Rates – Campsite per night: $7. Rates half with Golden Age or Access Passports.

Getting there – From Encampment go west 6.5 miles on Hwy 70 to FSR 443; then right 11.2 miles to the junction of 443 and 440; then left 9.0 miles on 443 to 452; then left 7.1 miles on 452 to the camp on the left. *See map page 98.*

Haskins Creek Campground
(Medicine Bow National Forest, Open June 15 to Oct. 31)

About the camp – This camp is just off the highway with 10 sites on a loop road in mature forest. The camp has a vault toilet and potable water. Sites are generally roomy with good tenting options and have tables, fire rings with grates and grills. Stay limited to 14 days.

Rates – Campsite per night: $7. Rates half with Golden Age or Access Passports.

Getting there – From Encampment go west 16.3 miles on Hwy 70 to the camp on the right. *See map page 98.*

Lost Creek Campground
(Medicine Bow National Forest, Open May 24 to Oct. 31)

About the camp – This camp is in mature forest and just off the highway with 13 sites on a short road with an end-of-the-road loop turnaround. The camp has a vault toilet and potable water. Sites are generally roomy with good tenting options and have tables, fire rings with grates and grills (at 5 sites). Stay limited to 14 days.

Rates – Campsite per night: $7. Rates half with Golden Age or Access Passports.

Getting there – From Encampment go west 18.6 miles on Hwy 70 to the camp on the right. *See map page 98.*

Battle Creek Campground
(Medicine Bow National Forest, Open June 15 to Oct. 31)

About the camp – This camp is a local favorite due to its scenic, aspen-dappled location and small size. It has only 4 camps and is located 2.2 miles south of Hwy 70 along FSR 807. The road into the camp goes through aspen stands and switchbacks providing grand views of the forested mountain country to the south. The camp has a pit toilet and potable water. Sites are open and roomy with good tenting options and have tables and fire rings with grates. Stay limited to 14 days.

Rates – Free

Getting there – From Encampment go west 24.1 miles on Hwy 70 to FSR 807 on the left; then left 2.2 miles to the camp on the left. *See map page 98.*

Worth mentioning – CR 401 and FSR 801 head north from Hwy 70 about .3 miles east of FSR 807 going south to the Battle Creek Campground. About 1 mile north on this route you will see "Aspen Alley" where hundreds of aspen trees form a picturesque arch over the road. Drive through, do a U turn and view it from the other direction too.

Should you elect to continue north on CR 401/FSR 801 it is about 56 miles to Rawlins and I-80. If you're looking for another camp, you will find several dispersed camping options along the first 10 miles of this road before leaving the national forest. Most notable is the former Little Sandstone Campground — which has become a dispersed camping area, with a pit toilet — about 2.5 miles north on the right.

Jeffrey City

Jeffrey City reached its height as the company town for Western Nuclear with around 3000 people, during the uranium boom in the 1970's. Today it is all but a ghost town with boarded-up bunk houses and basement foundations snaring tumbleweeds in empty fields. The oil and gas industry and a stable ranching community keep the town in business. There is a gas station with limited hours, two bars and restaurants. Stock your coolers and get your supplies elsewhere along the way. Nearby is **Green Mountain, Crooks Mountain** and **Agate Flats,** where rock hunting is a popular. Be sure you're on public land or get permission from the landowners.

There are three camps listed here: two BLM camps (one free), a free Fremont County camp on Green Mountain and two privately-owned camps, one near Muddy Gap to the east and one near the Sweetwater River to the west.

River Campground
(Private, Open May 1 to Sept. 30)

About the camp – This camp has 22 designated sites near the Sweetwater River. 5 sites are full hookup (20 amp) back-ins (up to 16 x 40). There are 4 pull-thrus and 11 back-in sites with electric only, plus 2 camps for tents or no hookups. Most sites have fire rings and tables with sun shelters. Overflow areas are available at this 10-acre camp. *Horses okay.*

Amenities – Rest rooms and showers; snacks and ice.

Rates – Full hookups for 4 adults: $11.50. Electric only for 4 adults: $10.50. Tents or no hookups for 4 adults: $9.00. Additional adults: .50¢. Bicycle campers: $4 per person.

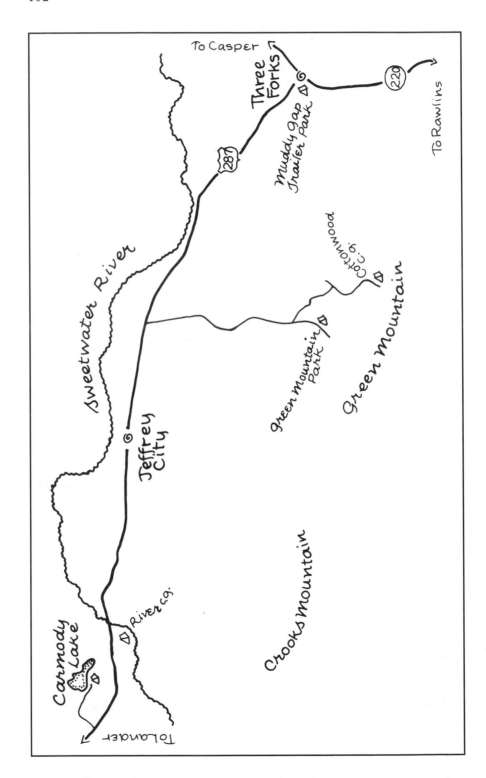

Getting there   From Jeffrey City go west 19 miles to the Sweetwater River and the camp on the left. *See map facing page.*

Carmody Lake
(BLM, Open all year)

About the camp – This camp is primitive and should be treated as a dispersed camping area while practicing 'Leave No Trace' in the area. The camp has no tables, no vault toilets or potable water.

Rates – Free. Pack it in, Pack it out.

Getting there – From Jeffrey City go west 24.3 miles on US 287 to the turnoff on the right (*BLM Road 2302/Hudson Atlantic City Road*); then north .9 miles to a fork in the road; then right 1.7 miles to the lake. *See map facing page.*

Cottonwood Campground
(BLM, Open Memorial Day to mid-Oct.)

About the camp – This camp is in a shady treed area in the lower elevations of Green Mountain. The camp has a vault toilet, potable water and 18 sites with tables and fire rings with grates. Most sites are roomy with good tenting options, with a few walk-ins. Stay limited to 14 days in any 28 day period.

Rates – Campsite per night: $6.

Getting there – From Jeffrey City, go east 6 miles on US 287 to the Green Mountain turnoff (*this is BLM 2411 and easy to miss as the sign is on the other side of the fence above the highway right-of-way*); then right 6.3 miles to a fork in the road; then left about 3 miles to the camp. *See map facing page.*

Green Mountain Park
(Fremont County, Open all year)

About the camp – This area is near the bottom of the grade going to the top of Green Mountain. There are several sites off of an open park as well as several walk-in sites across foot bridges to the other side of a small stream. There is ample room for tenting off the park, but several of the walk-ins are tight with regard to tenting options. The camp has vault toilets, but no potable water. Sites have tables and fire rings with grates. Stay limited to 14 days.

Rates – Free. Pack it in, pack it out.

Getting there – From Jeffrey City, go east 6 miles on US 287 to the Green Mountain turnoff (*this is BLM 2411 and easy to miss as the sign is on the other side of the fence above the highway right-of-way*); then right 6.3 miles to a fork in the road; then right about 2.5 miles to the camp on the left. *See map facing page.*

Muddy Gap Trailer Park
Private, Open Memorial Day to Nov. 1)

    About the camp – This camp is at Muddy Gap, about 23 miles east of Jeffrey City at the junction of US 287 and Hwy 220. The camp is on gravel with 6 full hookup (30/50 amp) RV back-ins (up to 15x60). Tenting is available and free.

    Amenities – Outhouse, potable water; fuel, propane and C-store one-quarter mile across junction, and pay phone at camp.

    Rates – Full hookups per site: $12.50. Tent site: Free.

    Getting there – From Jeffrey City go east on US 287 toward the Muddy Gap junction. The camp is on the right about .2 miles before the stop sign. *See map page 102.*

Medicine Bow

Medicine Bow is best known as the setting for Owen Wister's novel *The Virginian*. It sits along US 30/287 an east-west 'off-the beaten-path' optional route from I-80. The **Virginian Hotel**, built in 1911, is on the National Register of Historic Places. Across the street from the hotel is the **Owen Wister Cabin** and the **Medicine Bow Museum**, located in an old railroad depot. To the east is a well-known dinosaur dig site, **Como Bluff Dinosaur Graveyard**, which is a National Natural Landmark, and **Como Bluff Museum**, built entirely of dinosaurs bones — naturally they call it the "world's oldest" building. The main event here in the summertime is **Medicine Bow Days**, with rodeo, melodrama, casino, dancing and the hanging of "Dutch" Charlie, who with "Big Nose" George was suspected of killing two deputies and was hanged without benefit of a trial, Ph: 379-2571 for dates.

There is one small privately-owned camp with hookups in town and a Game and Fish area just to the south.

Bow Market Campground
(Private, Open all year)
PO Box 340, Medicine Bow, WY 82329 Ph: (307) 379-2262 Fax: (307) 379-2263

    About the camp – This camp is located in downtown Medicine Bow just behind the Bow Market. The camp has 4 full hookup (20/50 amp on city water) RV sites: all back-ins (25 x 50). Sites are gravel with concrete parking spurs at 3 sites.

    Amenities – Full service grocery store and pay phone.

    Rates – Full hookups per site: $8. V MC D Personal checks okay. Reservations: phone, fax or mail.

    Getting there – This camp is behind the Bow Market on US 30.

East Allen Lake Access Area

(Wyoming Game and Fish, Open all year)

About the camp – There are two locations at this camping option, one on the east side and one on the south side of the lake. The east shore has a parking area and a pit toilet and the south area has a vault toilet, stone fire rings and a boat ramp. Stay limited to 5 days.

Rates – Free

Getting there – From US 30 right across the highway from the Virginian Hotel, go south .8 miles to a right-hand turn on BLM Road 3157; then 1.2 miles to the shore; [or] continue south another .5 miles to BLM Road 3158; then right 1.5 miles on 3158 to the south shore site with the boat ramp.

Rawlins

This medium-sized Wyoming city is one of several that grew along the state's first railroad line, with a history in freighting as well as ranching and oil and gas development. To the north and west is the **Rawlins Uplift**, which to geologists is a thrust-faulted anticline notable as a site with exposed Precambrian rock that defines the eastern end of **The Great Divide Basin**. Further north on US 287, another example of uplift has created the "**Flat Irons**" along the southern exposure of **Ferris Mountain**. It is the site of the Wyoming State Penitentiary and the historic **Wyoming Frontier Prison**, at 5th and Walnut, Ph: (307) 324-4422, which is open from Memorial Day to Labor Day with hourly tours of the cell blocks, grounds, gallows and gas chamber ($). In contrast to the ominous stone architecture of the Frontier Prison stands **Ferris Mansion**, a three-story Victorian salute to gingerbread, which is now a Bed and Breakfast at 607 West Maple. The **Carbon County Museum**, at 9th and Walnut, Ph: (307) 328-2740, open M-F from May to Sept., is free. Rawlins celebrates in August with the **Old West Summerfest,** held in conjunction with the **Carbon County Fair and Rodeo**, Ph: (307) 324-4111.

In town there are four privately-owned camps and a BLM camp to the south (BLM has an office here for maps and information). For workouts and showers, there is the **Rawlins Family Recreation Center** ($3), at 1616 Harshman, Ph: (307) 324-7529. For a swimming pool try the Rawlins High School just around the corner at Brooks and Colorado Sts., Ph: (307) 328-9272 ($1).

American Presidents Campground

(Private, Open all year)
2346 W. Spruce St., Rawlins, WY 82301 Ph: (307) 324-3218

About the camp – This camp is open, level and located on the west end of Rawlins with an office at radio station KRAL-AM and KIQZ-FM. The camp has 72 gravel RV sites with some tables and grills: 62 pull-

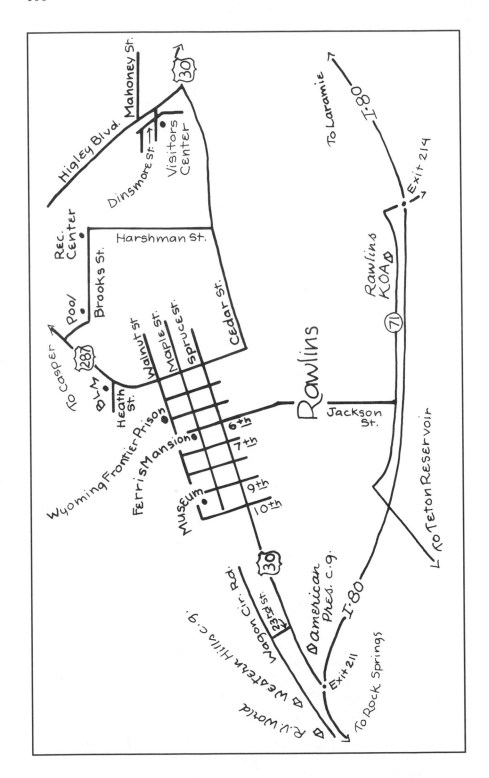

thrus (25x55) and 10 back ins (25x45). 25 sites are full hookups (20 amp on city water). Tent sites are available on grass with tables and grills.

Amenities – Rest rooms and showers (showers only $3.23), laundry; cable TV included at all full hookups, playground adjacent to camp; snacks and ice, dump station, modem jack in radio station office and pay phone.

Rates – Full hookups for 2 persons: $15.54. Water and electric for 2 persons: $13.60. Electric only for 2 persons: $11.66. Tent sites for 2 persons: $9.71. Additional persons 13 years and over: $1.94 (All prices include tax and discounts). Discounts: Goodsam, Coachman, AAA, Seniors and AARP. Most major cards. Personal checks okay. Reservations: phone or mail.

Getting there – Use I-80 exit 211; then follow Business I-80 (*Spruce St.*) .2 miles to the camp on the right. *See map facing page.*

Rawlins KOA

(Private, Open April 1 to Oct. 31)
205 E. Hwy 71, Rawlins, WY 82301 Ph: (307) 328-2021

About the camp – This camp is located south of downtown Rawlins on the I-80 frontage road. The camp has 50 gravel RV sites with tables: 36 pull-thrus (20x60) and 14 back-ins (20x40). 11 sites are full hookups (30/50 amp on city water) and 39 are electric and water only. The camp has 6 designated tent sites on pea gravel with grills and tables and kamper kabins.

Amenities – Rest rooms and showers, laundry; cable TV included at 39 sites, sheltered picnic pavilion with sinks and electric cook tops, game room and playground; limited groceries and RV parts, dump station, propane and pay phone.

Rates – Full hookups for 2 persons: $26.95, Electric and water only for 2 persons: $24.95. Tent sites for 2 persons: $17.95. Kamper Kabins for 2 persons: $34.95. Additional persons: $3. All major cards. Reservations: phone or mail.

Getting there – From I-80 use exit 214; then north to the frontage road; then west .3 miles to the camp on the right. *See map facing page.*

RV World Campground

(Private, Open April 1 to Sept. 30)
(PO Box 1282) 3101 Wagon Circle Road, Rawlins, WY 82301 Ph: (307) 328-1091 E-mail: rvwrld@coffey.com

About the camp – This camp on the west end of the city of Rawlins is open with paved interior roads. The camp has 70 RV sites on gravel, with tables: all are pull-thrus (23x60). 31 are full hookups (30/50 amp on city water). There are 5 designated grass tents sites with grills and tables.

Amenities – Rest rooms and showers, laundry; cable TV (included with full or EW hookups), game room, playground, heated pool, and miniature golf ($1); limited groceries and RV parts, modem jack in office and pay phone.

Rates – Full hookups w/cable for 2 persons: $20. Electric and water w/cable for 2 persons: $19. Electric and water only for 2 persons: $17. Electric only for 2 persons: $16. Tents or no hookups for 2 persons: $14. Additional persons: $2. Discounts: seniors, C-C, Escapee, AAA, AARP, KOA and Goodsam. All major cards. Reservations: phone, E-mail or mail.

Getting there – Use I-80 exit 211; then follow Business I-80 (*Spruce St.*) .3 miles to 23rd St.; then left/north on 23rd St. to stop sign, then left/west .5 miles to camp on the right. *See map page 106.*

Western Hills Campground

(Private, Open all year)
(PO Box 760) 2500 Wagon Circle Road, Rawlins, WY 82301 Ph: (307) 324-2596 E-mail: whctrib.com

About the camp – This camp on the west end of Rawlins is large, open and level. The camp has 171 gravel RV sites with tables: 114 full hookups (30/50 amp on city water). 96 are pull-thrus (24x65) and 75 are back-ins (24x65). The camp also has 50 tent sites on grass with tables. *Horses okay.*

Amenities – Rest rooms and showers (showers only: $3), laundry; cable TV at 114 sites ($1), game room, playground, miniature golf ($2 green fee); limited groceries and RV parts, dump station, modem jack in office and pay phone.

Rates – Full hookups for 2 persons: $17. Electric only for 2 persons: $16. Tent or no hookups for 2 persons: $12. Additional persons: $1. Discounts: Seniors, Goodsam, AAA and AARP. All major cards. Reservations: phone, E-mail or mail.

Getting there – Use I-80 exit 211; then follow Business I-80 (*Spruce St.*) .3 miles east to 23rd St.; then left/north on 23rd St. to stop sign; then left/west .2 miles to camp on the right. *See map page 106.*

Teton Reservoir Recreation Site

(BLM, Open all year)

About the camp – This camp is on a small reservoir about 15 miles south of Rawlins. There is a vault toilet, but no potable water. 5 sites are on a small loop road above the reservoir. Site 1 has a table and grill and sites 2-5 have tables, fire rings and grills. At the far end of the reservoir, where the road ends, there is a vault toilet, boat ramp and 2 tables.

Rates – Free

Getting there – From Rawlins use I-80 exit 214; then go north to Hwy 71, which here looks like a westbound frontage road on the north side of I-80; then west and south, going under the interstate, 14.8 miles to the turnoff on the left; then .8 miles to the campsites on the right; *[or]* 1.1 miles to the boat ramp at the end of the road. *See map page 106.*

Riverside

Hwy 70 and 230 mark this crossroads community with one privately-owned camp. Out-of-town there are two Forest Service and two BLM camps (one free). Basic groceries, fuel, ice and snacks are available. A unique local bathing option near here is Indian Bathtubs which consist of deep natural hollows in rock formations, usually holding rain water or snow melt. Water temperature will vary with season and time of day. The bathtubs are about a mile hike on a trail which starts off of Blackhall Mountain Road about a mile south of town . Ask locals for directions, or call the Riverside Town Hall, Ph: (307) 327-5266

Lazy Acres Campground and Motel

(Private, Open May 1 to Nov. 1)
(PO 641) Hwy 230, Riverside, WY 82325 Ph: (307) 327-5968

About the camp – This camp has lots of green space amidst a mature stand of cottonwood trees. The camp has 33 RV sites (up to 16x40) on gravel spurs with grass 'yards' and tables. 12 sites are pull-thrus, 21 are back-ins and 17 are full hookups (15/30/50 amp). Many have fire rings and portable grills are available. 6 designated tent sites are available. There is also one camper cabin and four motel units.

Amenities – Rest rooms and showers, laundry; cable TV included, rec field, and horseshoes; limited RV supplies, fishing tackle, dump station and pay phone.

Rates – Full hookups for 2 persons: $17.50. Electric only for 2 persons: $15.50. Tent site for 2 persons: $12.50. Camper cabin for 2 persons: $20. Motels units $25 to $37. Reservations: phone or mail.

Getting there – From junction of Hwys 230 and 70, go southeast .2 miles on Hwy 230 to the camp on the left. *See map page 110.*

Corral Creek Campground

(BLM, Open June 1 to Nov. 15)

About the camp – This camp has 8 sites on a rise in sight of the North Platte River, with trails to the river at the trailhead for the Willow and Boulder Gaps Trails. The camp has day-use, angler and hiker parking; and a vault toilet, but no potable water. Sites have tables, fire rings with grates and grills. Stay limited to 14 days within any 28 day period.

110

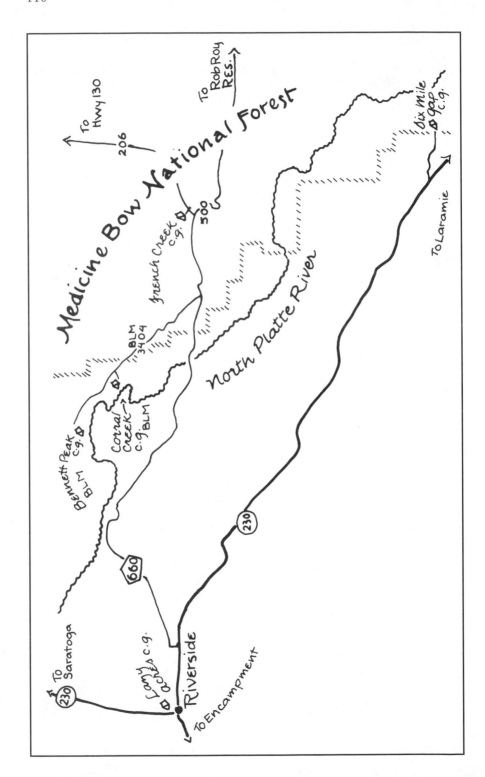

Rates – Free

Getting there – From Riverside go southeast 4.2 miles on Hwy 230 to CR 201 (French Creek Road); then left .3 miles on CR 201 to CR 660; then right 12.1 miles on CR 660 to BLM Road 3404 on the left; then left 5.5 miles on BLM Road 3404 to the turnoff on the left; then left .2 miles to the camp. *See map facing page.*

Bennett Peak Campground

(BLM, Open June 1 to Nov. 15)

About the camp – This camp has 11 sites and is located on the banks of the North Platte River just past the turnoff to Corral Creek Campground. The camp has a vault toilet and potable water. Sites are fairly well spaced on two short loop roads and have tables and fire rings with grates. A few sites have sandy tent pads. Sites 6-8 and 10 are the river-bank options. Stay limited to 14 days within any 28 day period.

Rates – Campsite per night: $7. Rates half with Golden Age or Access Passport.

Getting there – From Riverside go southeast 4.2 miles on Hwy 230 to CR 201 (French Creek Road); then left .3 miles on CR 201 to CR 660; then right 12.1 miles on CR 660 to BLM Road 3404 on the left; then left 6.9 miles on BLM Road 3404 to the camp. *See map facing page.*

French Creek Campground

(Medicine Bow National Forest, Open May 15 to Oct. 31)

About the camp – This camp has 11 grassy sites in an aspen stand, with a vault toilet and potable water. Sites have tables and fire rings with grates and are generally roomy with good tenting options and some tent pads. Stay limited to 14 days.

Rates – Campsite per night: $10. Rates half with Golden Age or Access Passport.

Getting there – From Riverside go southeast 4.2 miles on Hwy 230 to CR 201 (French Creek Road); then left .3 miles on CR 201 to CR 660; then right 14.8 miles on CR 660 to the junction of FSR 206 and 500; then left .1 mile on FSR 206 to the camp on the left. *See map facing page.*

Worth mentioning – This is a pleasant drive through open range on sagebrush grasslands and along the fertile valley of the North Platte River, highlighted by the aspen stands and hay meadows in a small valley along French Creek.

Six Mile Gap Campground
(Medicine Bow National Forest, Open May 15 to Oct. 31)

About the camp – This camp, on the edge of the Platte River Wilderness, is a favorite when river conditions dictate kayaking the North Platte River through this area. The camp has a vault toilet and potable water. There is parallel parking for six walk-in campsites, somewhat screened in a mix of aspen and conifers, creating a sense of seclusion. These sites are 50 yards up a slight rise, and have tables, fire rings with grates and good-sized tent pads. The other three sites are in the open right on the loop road and perhaps better suited to hard sided camping. Stay limited to 14 days.

Rates – Campsite per night: $10. Rates half with Golden Age or Access Passport.

Getting there – From Riverside go 23.5 miles southeast on Hwy 230; then left 2.0 miles to the camp. *See map page 110.*

Saratoga

Saratoga is known for its blue-ribbon fishing, but the town's fun-friendly wonder is its **Hobo Hot Pool**, free and open 24 hours a days seven days a week. There are clean change rooms with the basics: a sink, a stool and a shower. The locals like to hit the pool early in the morning when the east wall provides a shaded area. By afternoon, with the sun on the water all day and no shade, "it's too hot." The average temperature is posted as 104° F. There is a pleasant grass area behind the change house with two picnic tables and grills. If the spa is too hot but you want to swim and shower anyway, the **Saratoga Swimming Pool** is just in front of the Hobo Hot Pool, heated by running spa waters through a heat exchanger. The commercial pool is open 12-9 M-F and 11-9, S-S and holidays ($). Just south of town, across from the airport, is the **Saratoga Museum** which is open daily 1-5 in summer. About .5 miles south, on the same side of the road, is the Forest Service Office.

There is one privately-owned camp listed in town, a city-run camp on Saratoga Lake just to the north and out-of-town there are five USFS camps, five BLM camps. The **North Platte River** here provides 'blue-ribbon' fishing, with tackle shops and float and fishing outfitters in good supply. Groceries, sporting goods and hardware are available.

Saratoga RV Park
(Private, Open all year)
(PO Box 455) 116 Farm St., Saratoga, WY 82331 Ph: (307) 326-8870

About the camp – This camp three blocks from downtown Saratoga is on 1.5 acres with lots of shade and 250 feet of frontage on the North Platte River. The camp has 27 gravel and grass RV sites: 3 pull-thrus (up to 25x40) and 24 back-ins (up to 15x28). 17 sites are full hookups (30 amp on city water) and 10 are electric only. The camp has 6 designated grass tent sites with tables and grills as well as lodging in a furnished 28' camper trailer.

Amenities – Rest rooms and showers (showers only: $3); Cable TV included at full hookups, river fishing on private frontage; dump station and phone available in office.

Rates – Full hookups for 2 persons: $16. Electric only for 2 persons: $13. No hookups for 2 persons: $10. Camper trailer with bedding for 2 persons: $20. Additional persons: $1. MC V Personal checks okay. Reservations: phone or mail.

Getting there – From downtown Saratoga go north .2 miles on Hwy 130 to Rochester St.; then left one block to 2nd St.; then right one block to Farm St.; then right into camp. *See map below.*

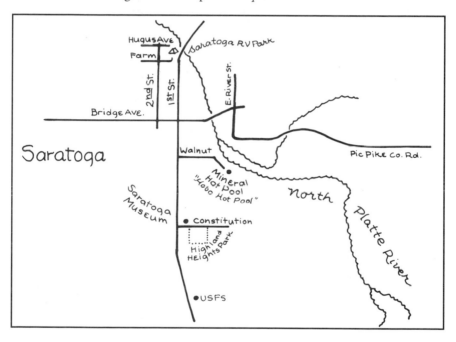

—East of Saratoga—

Pennock Mountain WHMA

(Wyoming Game and Fish, Open May 1 to Nov. 30)

About the camp – This habitat management area is open all year, but closed to vehicular traffic from Dec. 1 to April 30 to reduce disturbance to wintering wildlife.

Within the 9,800-acre area are 33 miles of roads and trails making most of the area accessible while also providing routes to adjoining Forest Service lands to the east.

There are hunting or wildlife viewing opportunities for elk, mule deer, antelope, sage grouse, blue grouse and rabbits. Numerous birds and small mammals also inhabit the area. During a brief visit there, one very pleasant camping option was located, for tent or hard sided camping (see 'getting there' for directions). No potable water. Stay limited to 14 days.

Rates – Free. Pack it in, pack it out.

Getting there – From Saratoga take Bridge St. east across the river; then right .1 miles on River St.; then left as River St. bends into Pic Pike Road; then east 1 mile to CR 205; then left 4.6 miles to the first access road going right; *[or]* straight another .8 miles to the second access road; then right 1.9 miles to a left fork that dips into a cottonwood lined riparian area with the camping option noted above. *See map page 116.*

South Brush Creek Campground
(Medicine Bow National Forest, Open May 24 to Oct. 31)

About the camp – This camp has 20 sites on two loop roads in hearty timber along Brush Creek, which flows near the back of several sites located on the south side of the road. The first loop has sites 1-10, with site 6 the lone pull through. In the second loop, sites 11,13,15,16 and 18 are pull-thrus and there is a sign between camps 18 and 19 marking the way to a bridge for fishing and hiking opportunities across the creek. The camp has vault toilets and potable water. Sites have tables and fire rings with grates. Stay limited to 14 days.

Rates – Campsite per night: $10. Rates half with Golden Age or Access Passports.

Getting there – From Saratoga go south 8.1 miles on Hwy 130 to the junction of Hwy 230; then left about 12.6 miles on Hwy 130 to Brush Creek Road/FSR 100; then left .5 miles; then right 1 mile to the camp on the right. *See map page 116.*

Lincoln Park Campground
(Medicine Bow National Forest, Open June 15 to Oct. 31)

About the camp – Lincoln Park is a wide open camp with 12 sites on 2 loop roads. The camp has vault toilets and potable water. Sites have tables and fire rings with grates. Stay limited to 14 days.

Rates – Campsite per night: $10. Rates half with Golden Age or Access Passports.

Getting there – From Saratoga go south 8.1 miles on Hwy 130 to the junction of Hwy 230; then left about 12.6 miles on Hwy 130 to Brush Creek Road/FSR 100; then left 3 miles to the camp on the right. *See map page 116.*

Bow River Campground
(Medicine Bow National Forest, Open May 24 to Oct. 31)

About the camp – This camp in a mixed forest of lodgepole pine, subalpine fir and aspen has 13 sites on a loop road. The camp has vault toilets and potable water. Sites have tables, fire rings with grates and grills. Stay limited to 14 days.

Rates – Campsite per night: $7. Rates half with Golden Age or Access Passports.

Getting there – From Saratoga go south 8.1 miles on Hwy 130; then left about 12.6 miles on Hwy 130 to Brush Creek Road/ FSR 100; then left 19.6 miles to the camp on the right. *See map page 116.*

Ryan Park Campground
(Medicine Bow National Forest, Open June 1 to Oct. 1)

About the camp – This 48-site camp is just off the highway in a mixed forest which is mostly lodgepole pine. The camp has vault toilets and potable water. Sites have tables, fire rings with grates and grills. Stay limited to 14 days.

Rates – Campsite per night: $10. Rates half with Golden Age or Access Passports. (Reservations are possible at this campground up to 240 days in advance and 10 days prior to arrival. Service fee per reservation: $8.65. Ph: (877) 444-6777 toll free.)

Getting there – From Saratoga go south 8.1 miles on Hwy 130 to the junction of Hwy 230; then left 15.4 miles on Hwy 130 to the camp on the right. *See map page 116.*

Silver Lake Campground
(Medicine Bow National Forest, Open July 1 to Sept. 15)

About the camp – This camp has 17 sites on a loop road near Silver Lake. There are a couple of pull-thrus and sites 10-15 are walk-in camps. The camp has vault toilets and potable water. Sites have tables and fire rings with grates. Stay limited to 14 days.

Rates – Campsite per night: $10. Rates half with Golden Age or Access Passports.

Getting there – From Saratoga go south 8.1 miles on Hwy 130 to the junction of Hwy 230; then left 23.9 miles on Hwy 130 to the camp on the right. *See map page 116.*

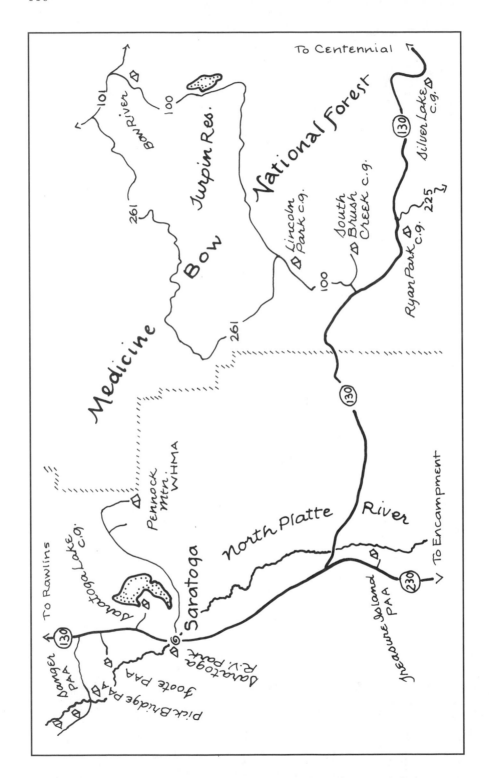

Saratoga Lake Campground
(City of Saratoga, Open all year)

About the camp – This camp is on three levels near the shore of Saratoga Lake, with a boat dock and ramp. Level B has 25 sites, all electric only (20 amp) with some tables and grills. On the end of level A there are two tables and fire rings. Level C has 4 tables with grills and C-2 has 6 sites with tables and fire rings. Behind the self-serve office there is an area designated for bicycle camping. The camp has vault toilets, potable water, a playground and horseshoes. An RV dump station is located across the highway at the sewage lagoon.

Rates – Sites with electric: $10. Sites without hookups: $7.50. Bicycle sites behind office: $1. Personal checks okay.

Getting there – From Saratoga go north 1.3 miles on Hwy 130; then right .9 miles to a fork; then left to the camp. *See map facing page.*

Worth mentioning – Storer/Saratoga Lake Wetlands border the campground and provide habitat for a variety of birds, including white-faced ibis, American white pelican, osprey, American bittern, snowy egret, marsh wren, great blue heron, Canada geese and locally common species of ducks. Muskrats, minks and raccoons use the marshes and wetlands and species such as mule deer, pronghorn and red fox can be seen in the upland areas.

The area is open all year, however, best wildlife viewing is during the spring, when the greatest number of migrant birds are visiting the area, and late summer and early fall, when young mammals and birds are old enough to become active. During your visit, cause as little disturbance as possible to the wildlife and their habitat.

Foote Public Access Area
(Wyoming Game and Fish, Open all year)

About the camp – This access area has two undeveloped camping areas, both on the North Platte and both with primitive float launch ramps. When you reach the area, go left to find camping options near the river in a stand of cottonwoods; *[or]* right to find a grassier area with several site options and a vault toilet. No potable water. Stay limited to 5 days.

Rates – Free

Getting there – From Saratoga go north 4 miles on Hwy 130 to the turnoff to the left; then left 1.8 miles to the fork; then right; *[or]* left .1 miles to the camp of your choice. *See map facing page.*

Pick Bridge Public Access Area

(Wyoming Game and Fish, Open all year)

About the camp – At this camp mature cottonwoods line the bank of the North Platte. There are a few ancient stone fire rings, a few tables, a vault toilet and a primitive float access to the river, but no potable water. Stay limited to 5 days.

Rates – Free

Getting there – From Saratoga go north 6.6 miles on Hwy 130 to Pick Bridge Road; then left 4 miles on Pick Bridge Road (CR 508) to just before the river bridge; then left into the camp on the left. *See map page 116.*

Sanger Public Access Area

(Wyoming Game and Fish, Open all year)

About the camp – There are two camps in this access area, both with float access to the river. The first is a large grassy area near the river with several stone fire rings and a vault toilet. The second is a small, pleasant and grassy camp on the banks of the North Platte River, in a stand of mature cottonwood trees, with 2 tables, a few stone fire rings and a vault toilet. The far side of the river is lined with cottonwoods and high bluffs that display tiers of steep rock faces. No potable water. Stay limited to 5 days.

Rates – Free

Getting there – From Saratoga go north 6.6 miles on Hwy 130 to Pick Bridge Road; then left 5.4 miles on Pick Bridge Road (CR 508) to a fork; then right .5 miles to another fork; then left 1 mile to the first area on the right; *[or]* another 1.2 miles to the end of the road and the second smaller camp. *See map page 116.*

—South of Saratoga—

Treasure Island Access Area

(Wyoming Game and Fish, Open May 1 to Nov. 30)

About the camp – At first glance, this camp appears to be just a gravel parking area with a float ramp, a vault toilet and a couple of stone fire rings. However, a short walk upstream through the bushes reveals a couple of suspended footbridges providing access to the island, with nice tenting options and more fishing access. Stay limited to 5 days.

Rates – Free. Pack it in, pack it out.

Getting there – From Saratoga go south on Hwy 130 to the junction of Hwy 130 and 230; then go straight 1.6 miles on Hwy 230 to a left at the Plattoga Ranch Road; then left .4 miles to a fork; then take the right fork .6 miles to the camp. *See map page 116.*

Sinclair

In the 1920's, Sinclair was built by an oil company as a showplace company town with Spanish mission-style architecture. Though largely vacant it still stands. You won't find a grocery, sporting goods store or even a motel here, but befitting the local architecture is the Su Casa Restaurant with excellent homemade Mexican fare as well as cheeseburgers and the like: It's on the west end of town, small, usually busy, but worth the wait.

Camping options near here are all to the north on either **Seminoe Reservoir** or along the **North Platte River** in the **Miracle Mile** country. Listed are two privately-owned camps with some hookups, one BLM camp, one State Park and the Game and Fish North Platte Miracle Mile Access Area with over 50 free campsites.

Dugway Campground
(BLM, Open April to Dec.)

About the camp – This camp is native grass, on the North Platte River with a vault toilet, several tables and fire rings and a primitive float ramp, but no potable water. Stay limited to 14 days in any 28 day period.

Rates – Campsite per night: $4.

Getting there – From Sinclair take 10th St. north 7.9 miles to the camp on the right *(10th St. is on the west end of Sinclair and to the north turns into CR 351). See map page 121.*

Seminoe Boat Club
(Private, Open Memorial Day to Labor Day)
PO Box 234, Sinclair, WY 82327 Ph: (307) 320-3043

About the camp – This camp is part of a marina complex at the Seminoe Boat Club, with the office at PJ's Store. The camp has 16 gravel RV sites: all pull-thrus (17x40) with tables, and all full hookups (20/30 amp). Tent sites are available.

Amenities – Rest rooms and showers, limited groceries, fishing tackle and licenses, use of boat ramp and phone at boat club ($).

Rates – Full hookups per site: $18. Tent sites: $12. No credit cards. Personal checks okay. Reservations: phone or mail.

Getting there – From Sinclair take 10th St. north 26.1 miles to the marina turnoff to the right; then right 2.6 miles to the camp office at PJ's Store *(10th St. is on the west end of Sinclair and to the north turns into CR 351). See map page 121.*

Seminoe State Park

(Wyoming State Parks, Open April 15 to Oct. 15)

About the camp – This state park has the North and South Red Hills Campgrounds with a total of 94 designated sites with tables and fire rings with grates at most sites. Sites are varied, but there are a number of pull-thru sites. There are vault toilets and potable water and there is a dump station at the North Red Hills Campground. Both campgrounds have public boat ramps. Fishing might yield catches of walleye, or brown, lake, rainbow or cutthroat trout.

Rates – Day use fees for this park are $2 for residents and $5 for nonresidents. Camping fees for residents are $4 per night and $9 for nonresidents. An annual day use pass, good at all state parks, is available to residents for $25 and nonresidents for $40. Annual camping permits are available to residents for $30. The annual camping pass is not available for nonresidents (see State Parks in 1999 - page 11).

Getting there – From Sinclair take 10th St. north about 36 miles to the camp on the right (10th St. is on the west end of Sinclair and to the north turns into CR 351). See map facing page.

Miracle Mile Ranch Campground

(Private, Open all year)
Kortes Dam, Hanna, WY 82327 Ph: (307) 325-6710

About the camp – This camp offers the only hookups in the popular Miracle Mile area. The camp has 24 gravel and native grass RV sites: all pull-thrus (12x40) and all full hookups (20 amp). Native grass tent sites are available. Cabins are available at the ranch. *Horses: Inquire*

Amenities – Porta-potty at camp. At ranch, cabins and store area: rest rooms and showers (showers only: $3 and only available when cabins are not fully booked), limited groceries, ice, fishing tackle, bait, charcoal, firewood and pay phone. (Tables, grills and playground planned for '99.)

Rates – Full hookups per site: $12. Tent sites: $6. Cabins: $29.70 per person. No credit cards. Personal checks okay. Reservations: phone or mail.

Getting there – From Sinclair take 10th St. north 42.2 miles to BLM Road 3108 (just before the bridge over the North Platte River); then left 2.3 miles to a fork in the road; then left .9 miles to the ranch, office, store and cabins (10th St. is on the west end of Sinclair and to the north turns into CR 351). See map facing page.

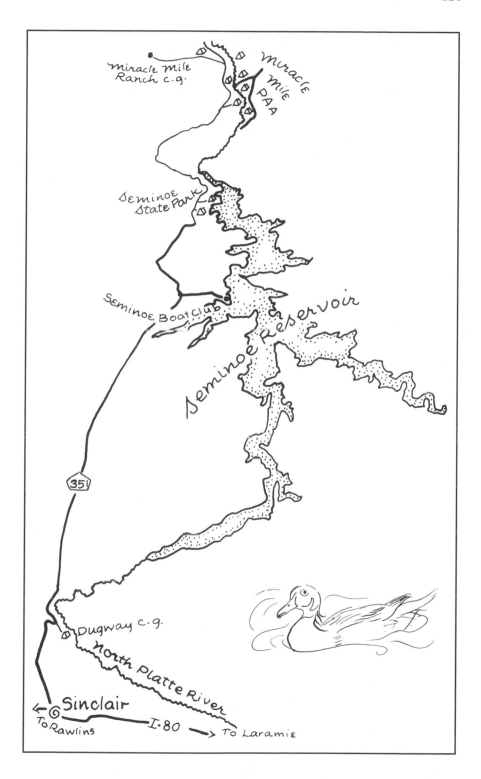

Miracle Mile
Ranch c.g.

Miracle Mile PAA

Seminoe State Park

Seminoe Boat Club

Seminoe Reservoir

351

Dugway c.g.

North Platte River

Sinclair

To Rawlins

I·80 → To Laramie

Miracle Mile Public Access Area

(Wyoming Game and Fish, Open all year)

About the camp – This stretch of the North Platte River has camping options on both sides of the river; upstream and downstream. Most of the camping areas have vault toilets — there are seven or eight in the area. For about 1.5 miles up or downstream, on both sides of the river, there are over 50 tables with fire rings and grates. No potable water.

Keep in mind this area can be crowded as it is popular with locals as well as out-of-state visitors. Stay limited to 14 days.

Rates – Free. Pack it in, pack it out.

Getting there – From Sinclair take 10th St. north 42.4 miles to the North Platte River and you're there (10th St. is on the west end of Sinclair and to the north turns into CR 351.). See Map page 121.

Woods Landing

This Wyoming crossroads community has hookups and tenting options behind the Jelm Post Office and the historic log Woods Landing Resort building. Good fishing is the mainstay, but there is also the lure of the University of Wyoming's Jelm Observatory which houses one of the world's largest infra red telescopes. The post office has a store with limited groceries, and in the Woods Landing Resort there is a restaurant and bar where live bands perform most Saturday nights during the summer. There is one privately-owned camp in Woods Landing and nearby to the south, 3 Forest Service camps.

Woods Landing Resort

(Private, Open all year)
#9 State Highway 10, Jelm, WY 82063 Ph: (307) 745-9638

About the camp – This camp, located at the junction of Hwy 10 and 230 southwest of Laramie, is behind the Jelm post office and the historic log Woods Landing Resort building on the Big Laramie River. The camp has 10 back-in sites on gravel and native grass with water and electric only (30 amp). There are two designated native grass tent sites, plus lodging options in a teepee or rustic cabins. Horses okay on limited basis: Inquire.

Amenities – Rest rooms and showers (showers only: $3); fly fishing, mountain biking and hiking on premises; limited groceries, hardware and automotive supplies, gift shop, bar and cafe (live music Saturday nights during summer), dump station, propane, gas and pay phone. Guided white water rafting and horseback trips are available.

Rates – Water and electric per site: $12. Tent sites: $10. Teepee (sleeps up to 8): $15-35. Rustic cabins with bedding: $30-45. M V D Personal checks okay. Reservations: phone or mail.

Getting there – Woods Landing is at the junction of Hwys 230 and 10 about 27 miles southwest of Laramie on Hwy 230. *See map page 74.*

Miller Lake Campground
(Medicine Bow National Forest, Open June 1 to Oct. 15)

About the camp – This camp is small, in a nice stand of lodgepole pine, and just a short distance off the highway in the southeast part of the forest. The camp has potable water, vault toilets and 7 roomy sites with good tenting options. All sites have tables, fire rings with grates and grills. Stay limited to 14 days.

Rates – Campsite per night: $10. Rates half with Golden Age or Access Passport.

Getting there – From the junction of Hwys 230 and 10, go southwest 9 miles on Hwy 230 to FSR 512 on the right; then right .8 miles to the camp turnoff on the left. *See map page 74.*

Boswell Creek Campground
(Medicine Bow National Forest, Open June 1 to Oct. 15)

About the camp – This camp is small, straddling Boswell Creek in a shady stand of lodgepole pine, and just 3 miles off the highway in the southeast part of the forest. The camp has a vault toilet, potable water and 9 roomy sites with good tenting options. All sites have tables, fire rings with grates and grills. (*Due to a lack of turnaround on the main entrance road into the camp for sites 1-4, trailers or long RVs are not recommended; sites 5-9 on the near side of the creek, as you approach this camp, have more ample parking and turnaround options.*) Stay limited to 14 days.

Rates – Campsite per night: $10. Rates half with Golden Age or Access Passport.

Getting there – From the junction of Hwy 230 and 10, go southwest 13.2 miles on Hwy 230 to FSR 526 on the left; then left 3 miles to the camp on the right. *See map page 74.*

Pelton Creek Campground
(Medicine Bow National Forest, Open June 15 to Oct. 15)

About the camp – This camp at the trailhead for the Platte Ridge and Douglas Creek trails has 15 roomy sites in lodgepole pine. The camp has vault toilets and potable water. Sites have tables, fire rings with grates, grills and good tenting options. Stay limited to 14 days.

Rates – Campsite per night: $10. Rates half with Golden Age or Access Passport.

Getting there – From the junction of Hwys 230 and 10, go southwest on Hwy 230 to the Colorado State Line; then continue .2 miles to FSR 898; then right 8.8 miles to the camp. *See map page 74.*

NOTES

<u>NOTES</u>

Contents — Southwest

Southwest Wyoming

Even after a shaky exposé by "Sixty Minutes" on gunslinging corruption in the energy boomtown of Rock Springs, most travelers on I-80 continue to speed across this corner of Wyoming with little more than a blink. You have to slow down and venture off into what appears to be flat and endless sage-brush to find the gems in the desert sands: well-preserved historic trading posts, sinuous rivers sculpting sandstone, and the Switzerland-like beauty of the Star Valley and the rarely visited Wyoming Range.

This section of Wyoming includes the southern portion of the Shoshone and the Bridger-Teton National Forests, including the Salt River and Wyoming Ranges near the Idaho border. Camps at the center of this area are

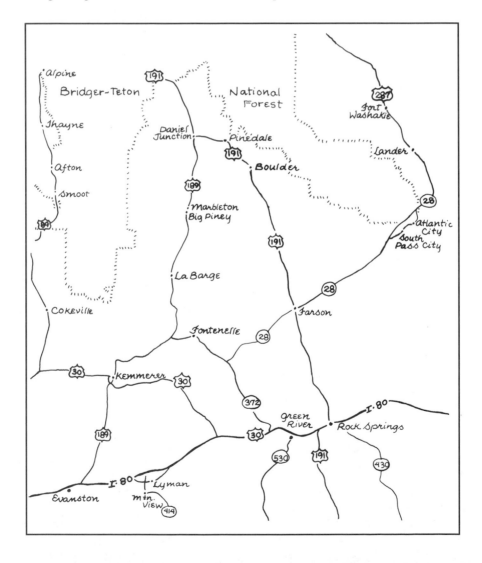

generally primitive, near water and managed by either the BLM or the US Bureau of Reclamation. This section features 105 camping options, with 26 privately-owned camps with hookups. Remaining options include 38 Forest Service camps, 19 free Game and Fish areas, 13 BLM camps (11 of these are no fee areas), 6 National Recreation Area camping areas (4 of which are free), 2 state park camps and 2 free town parks. These camps are listed under headings for 16 cities and towns including Afton, Alpine, Big Piney, Boulder, Cokeville, Evanston, Farson, Fort Bridger, Green River, Kemmerer, Lander, Lyman, Marbleton, Pinedale, Rock Springs and Thayne.

Afton

Afton is the largest commercial center in the Star Valley, a fertile enclave bordered east and west by mountains. In 1870 Mormon apostle Moses Thatcher stood on a knoll and said, "I hereby name this valley Star Valley because it is the star of all valleys." Also called the 'Swiss Alps of Wyoming,' it is prime real estate with a variety of camping and recreational opportunities.

Just east of Afton is **Periodic Springs**, one of the world's three cold water geysers and the only one in the United States. In late summer and early fall the geyser is at its best, with water gushing from an opening in a cliff for about 18 minutes; it then idles for an equal time before starting the cycle again. The geyser is reached on a three-quarter mile trail about five miles up **Swift Creek Canyon Road**. This road is very scenic and also passes **Shawnee Falls**, which drops through lush mountain greenery into Swift Creek.

Afton may be best known for its 18' **Elk Antler Arch** on its main street, consisting of over 3,000 sets of horns. There is a small, **Daughters of the Utah Pioneer Museum** at 46 East 5th Ave. and open 1-5 p.m., June-August; and the **CallAir Museum**, open daily in summer at Afton Airport, Ph: (307) 886-9881. During the first week of August, Afton celebrates with the **Lincoln County Fair**.

There is one private camp just to the north of Afton, one Forest Service camp a mile and a half east of the downtown area, and two Forest Service camps to the south. In Afton there are groceries, hardware and sporting goods. Locally made outerwear is available at the Wyoming Wear outlet store on Hwy 189 at the north end of town, Ph: (307) 886-3851. For other camps in the Star Valley area, see Alpine and Thayne.

Burton Springs Trout Ranch
(Private, Open May 1 to Sept. 30)
1515 Kennington Burton Road, Afton, WY 83110 Ph: (307) 886-3517

> About the camp – This camp is on 27 acres at Burton Springs, site of a state fish breeding facility which moved after biologists decided they needed a location with warmer water. The area is greener than green, with ponds, 30 spacious all-grass RV or tent sites and 8 designated tent sites, all with tables and fire rings.

Amenities – Flush toilets and potable water; playground, volleyball, sandbox; catch and release fee fishing in preserve (no license required), catch-out fee fishing, bait shop, paddle boat and canoe rentals, snacks, gift shop and group area.

Rates – Campsite: $8 per vehicle. No credit cards. Personal checks okay. Group area: $50.00 minimum for up to 50 persons; $1.00 per person over 50 persons. Reservations: phone or mail.

Getting there – From the Visitor Information Park on Afton's main street go north 1.4 miles on US 89; then left 1.5 miles on Kennington Burton Road (CR 136) to the first bend of the road; then left .3 miles to the camp. *See map facing page.*

Swift Creek Campground
(Bridger-Teton National Forest, open June 1 to Sept. 10)

About the camp – This camp, in a forested area along Swift Creek, is only 1.5 miles from Afton. The camp has 11 sites with tables, fire rings with grates and grills. With the exception of sites 8 and 9, which look a bit cramped in the willows, sites are in the trees and generally roomy with good tenting options. There is a vault toilet and potable water. Stay limited to 16 days.

Rates – Campsite per night: $5. Rates half with Golden Age or Access Passport.

Getting there – Go east 1.5 miles on Swift Creek Canyon Road (*directly across from Afton's Visitor Information Park*) to the camp on the right. *See map facing page.*

Worth mentioning – This road becomes more scenic as is continues through the canyon past this campground. It provides access to Shawnee Falls, which can be viewed from the road and Intermittent Springs, a cold water geyser which requires a short walk from the road to the viewing area.

Cottonwood Lake Campground
(Bridger-Teton National Forest, Open May 15 to Sept. 30)

About the camp – The eye-pleasing road to this camp follows Cotton-wood Creek through a heavily forested valley. The scenic lake near the camp is small and nestled in forested foothills. There is a picnic area at the west end of the lake and a primitive boat launch: oars and paddles only. From left of the picnic area a narrow road goes along the north shore of the lake to a turn around and an undeveloped campsite that might serve as an overflow area if the developed camp is full. In the camp there are 18 sites. Sites 1-5 appear to be primarily for use by those with horses, using tents: they have hitching posts and lie off a parking area near the corrals. Sites 6-14 have parking spurs and sites 9 and 10 are pull-thrus. Sites 15-18 are walk-ins with a common parking area. This camp is at the Trail Fork and Slide Lake Trailheads. The

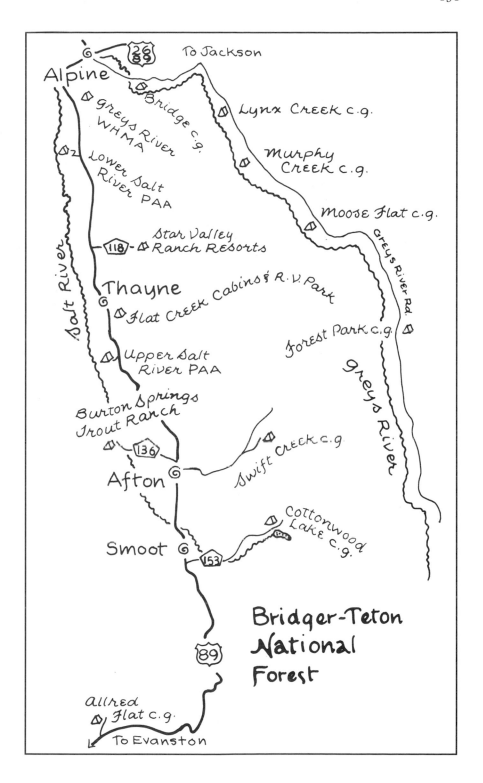

Alpine

6 · 26/89 · To Jackson

Greys River WHMA

Bridge c.g.

Lynx Creek c.g.

Murphy Creek c.g.

Salt River

2 · Lower Salt River PAA

Moose Flat c.g.

118 · Star Valley Ranch Resorts

Greys River Rd.

Thayne

6 · Flat Creek Cabins & R.V. Park

Upper Salt River PAA

Forest Park c.g.

Greys River

Burton Springs Trout Ranch

136

Afton · 6

Swift Creek c.g.

Smoot · 6 · 153

Cottonwood Lake c.g.

Bridger-Teton National Forest

89

Allred Flat c.g.

To Evanston

camp has vault toilets, potable water, and all sites have tables and fire rings with grates. Stay limited to 16 days.

Rates – Campsite per night: $5. Rates half with Golden Age or Access Passport.

Getting there – From Walton's General Store in Smoot, go south .5 miles on US 89; then left/east 6.2 miles on CR 153 to the fee board. *See map page 131.*

Allred Flat Campground
(Bridger-Teton National Forest, (Open May 25 to Oct. 31)

About the camp – This camp, in a valley near the highway, enjoys a stand of aspen at the lower end and a lodgepole forest as you move up the hill into the 32-site camp. Of the 32 sites, 12 are pull-thrus. The camp has vault toilets, potable water, and all sites have tables and fire rings with grates. There are corrals on the left a short distance before reaching the camp fee board. Stay limited to 16 days.

Rates – Campsite per night: $5. Rates half with Golden Age or Access Passport.

Getting there – From Walton's General Store in Smoot, go 12.7 miles south on US 89; then right/west .2 miles to the fee board. *See map page 131.*

Alpine

Alpine is at the northern end of the Star Valley, with Palisades reservoir for the water-sports enthusiast and the scenic Greys River Road, with access into the Bridger-Teton Forest and 400 miles of trails. Along this road, about 24 miles from Alpine, there is a roadside table and pull out to the left, with a remarkable panorama of Virginia Peak (10,141'), Visser Peak (10,015') and Man Peak (10,326'). There are several ways to enjoy the scenic beauty here and avoid backtracking by returning to the pavement elsewhere. Maps and route information are available at the **Greys River Ranger District Office,** at 125 Washington, Afton, Ph: (307) 886-3166 and district offices in Jackson, Kemmerer or Big Piney (see page 350 for USFS listings). This town celebrates annually during **Alpine's Annual Mountain Days,** held for three days every June over the Father's Day weekend.

In Alpine there are two privately-owned camps; a Forest Service camp near the highway in the Targhee National Forest just west of town; free camping at the Game and Fish Greys River Wildlife Habitat Management Area and the Lower Salt River Access Area to the south along US 89, and five developed Forest Service camps and several free dispersed camping areas to the southeast along the Greys River Road. Limited groceries, hardware and sporting goods are available. In Etna, 10 miles south of Alpine on US 89, there is Wyoming Surplus with items of possible interest to campers.

Alpen Haus Hotel Resort Campground

(Private, Open April to Nov.)
PO Box 3250, Alpine, WY 83128 Ph: (307) 654-7545 or (800) 343-6755
E-mail: alpenhau@cyberhighway.net

About the camp – This full service resort complex at Palisades Reservoir on the Snake River has 15 full hookups (20/30/50 amp) at back-in gravel sites (20x35) with cement landings and grass 'yards'. No tents.

Amenities – Rest rooms and showers in adjacent hotel (showers only: $3.50); cable TV (included), playground, spa ($3.50); restaurant, lounge, gas station, C-store, propane, dump station and pay phone. Float trips and trail rides are available.

Rates – Full hookups for 2 persons: $20. Additional persons: $7. All major cards. Discounts: AAA AARP Reservations: phone or mail.

Getting there – This camp is on the north end of Alpine at the junction of US 89/26. *See map page 131.*

Twin Pines Motel Campground

(Private, Open April to Nov.)
PO Box 3443, Alpine, WY 83128 Ph: (307) 654-7507

About the camp – This small camp is behind the Twin Pines Motel on the north end of Alpine: 8 back-in sites with water and electric (sewer lines for full hookups under construction in 1999: Inquire). Tent sites available.

Amenities – Restaurant at front of site and pay phone.

Rates – Water and electric per site: $8. Tent site: $5. All major cards. Personal checks okay. Reservations: phone or mail.

Getting there – This camp is on the north end of Alpine .5 miles south of the junction of US 89/26. *See map page 131.*

Alpine Campground

(Targhee National Forest, Open Memorial Day to Labor Day)

About the camp – This camp, in an aspen setting near the Idaho-Wyoming line, has sites designed for one- or two-family use. Double family sites are paired 5-6, 7-8, 9-10. 11-12, 13-14 and 15-16. The remaining 12 sites in the 22-site camp are single family units. All camps are off a loop road and are roomy with good options for tenting. The camp has vault toilets and potable water. Stay limited to 14 days.

Rates – Single family site per night: $8. Double family site per night: $16 (limited to 16 people and 2 vehicles). Rates half with Golden Age or Access Passport. (Reservations are possible at this campground up to 240 days in advance and 10 days prior to arrival. Service fee per reservation: $8.65. Ph: (877) 444-6777 toll free.

Getting there – From the junction of US 89/26 go west 2.1 miles on US 26 west to the camp on the left. *See map page 131.*

Bridge Campground
(Bridger-Teton National Forest, Open June 1 to Sept. 30)

About the camp – Bridge is the first of 5 campgrounds on the Greys River Road going southeast from Alpine. This camp has only five sites, but four of them are right on the banks of the river, somewhat out-of-view of the neighboring sites up or downstream. The forest is a mix of leafy stream-bank vegetation and mature conifers. The camp has vault toilets, but no potable water. Sites have tables, grills and fire rings. Stay limited to 16 days.

Rates – Campsite per night: $3. Rates half with Golden Age or Access Passport.

Getting there – From the junction of US 89/26 go south .6 miles on US 89 to Greys River Road; then left 2.5 miles to the camp on the right. *See map page 131.*

Lynx Creek Campground
(Bridger-Teton National Forest, Open June 1 to Sept. 30)

About the camp – This camp is just above the Greys River with 14 sites that didn't appear to get much use. The camp has vault toilets, but no potable water. Sites have tables, fire rings with grates and grills. Stay limited to 16 days.

Rates – Campsite per night: $3. Rates half with Golden Age or Access Passport.

Getting there – From the junction of US 89/26 go south .6 miles on US 89 to Greys River Road; then left 12.5 miles to the camp on the right. *See map page 131.*

Murphy Creek Campground
(Bridger-Teton National Forest, Open June 1 to Sept. 30)

About the camp – This camp, a little further along on the Greys River Road, has 10 sites in a stand of lodgepole pine. There are 4 pull-thrus and sites are generally roomy, but a little close to the neighboring site here and there. The camp has vault toilets, potable water and sites have tables, fire rings with grates and grills. Stay limited to 16 days.

Rates – Campsite per night: $5. Rates half with Golden Age or Access Passport.

Getting there – From the junction of US 89/26 go south .6 miles on US 89 to Greys River Road; then left 14.3 miles to the camp on the right. *See map page 131.*

Moose Flat Campground

(Bridger-Teton National Forest, Open June 1 to Sept. 30)

About the camp – This camp is along the Greys River with sites in a stand of lodgepole pine. There are several pull-thru sites in a nice forest mix and camps are roomy. The camp has a vault toilet, potable water and 10 sites with tables, fire pits with grates and grills. Stay limited to 16 days.

Rates – Campsite per night: $5. Rates half with Golden Age or Access Passport.

Getting there – From the junction of US 89/26 go south .6 miles to Greys River Road; then left 22.8 miles to the camp on the right. *See map page 131.*

Forest Park Campground

(Bridger-Teton National Forest, Open June 1 to Sept. 30)

About the camp – This camp, across the road from the river in a stand of lodgepole pine, sits in the middle of a huge open park that in winter is the Forest Park Elk Feedground. Sites are in the trees, but open, sunny and roomy with good grassy tenting options. There are 3 pull-thru sites. The camp has a vault toilet, potable water and all sites have tables, fire pits with grates and grills. Stay limited to 16 days.

Rates – Campsite per night: $5. Rates half with Golden Age or Access Passport.

Getting there – From the junction of US 89/26 go south .6 miles to Greys River Road; then left 35.1 miles to the camp on the left. *See map page 131.*

Greys River Road (Dispersed)

(Bridger-Teton National Forest, Open all year)

About this camping option – After many years of local use some areas along this road have acquired undeveloped campground status and are posted with a USFS sign designating the area as a camping option. These sites are primitive with no tables, no vault toilets, no potable water or any of the other amenities one associates with a developed campground. They usually have stone fire rings from years of use; no need to create another. Stay limited to 16 days.

Rates – Free.

Getting there – From the junction of US 89/26 go south .6 miles to Greys River Road; then about 5 miles to where dispersed camping areas are in evidence on both sides of the road; *[or]* go about 44 miles to a rather well defined dispersed area on the right with a pit toilet. *See map page 131.*

Greys River Wildlife Habitat Management Area
(Wyoming Game and Fish, Open May 1 to Oct. 31)

About the camp – This habitat area is a winter feed ground for about 1000 elk. During that time, November 1 to April 30, the area is closed, but feeding can be observed from a structure near the highway built for that purpose.

The land here has abundant natural springs on steep west-facing slopes covered with a mix of aspen, conifers and shrubs. Hunting is excellent for mule deer, ruffed grouse and elk; with elk hunting by special permit only. Other wildlife observed in this habitat area include: black bears, blue grouse, owls, hawks, a variety of songbirds and small mammals.

The area provides access to the Salt River Range of the Bridger-Teton National Forest and hiking and sight-seeing are excellent.

There is high elk fence along the highway right-of-way at this site. Access to the area is through the gate in front of the quonset hut. Stay limited to 14 days. No potable water.

Rates – Free

Getting there – From the south end of Alpine at mile marker 117 on US 89 go south .9 miles on US 89 to the gate on the left. The blind or viewing shelter is .1 miles further, also on the left. *See map page 131.*

Lower Salt River Public Access Area
(Wyoming Game and Fish, Open all year)

About the camp – This access area is gravel and native grass with some suitable tenting. The camp has a vault toilet and a couple of stone fire rings, but no potable water. Stay limited to 5 days.

Rates – Free

Getting there – From south of Alpine, at mile marker 117 on US 89 go south 5 miles on US 89 to a turnoff to the right; then right 1 mile to a left hand turn in the road; then left .5 miles (*avoid road straight ahead into private property*) to the river and the camp. *See map page 131.*

Big Piney

This small town booms during periods of oil exploration, then reverts to its more stable personality catering to the needs of local ranchers. Big Piney is home to the **Green River Valley Museum**, on US 189 (206 N. Front St.), Ph: (307) 276-5343.

Two forest service camps are located west of town in the Bridger-Teton National Forest, one on the shores of a serene mountain lake. Groceries, hardware and limited sporting goods are available. Swimming is available at the high school pool at 916 Piney Drive, Ph: (307) 279-9966 for hours ($1).

Sacajawea Campground

(Bridger-Teton National Forest, Open June 10 to Sept. 30)

About the camp – This camp is in a stand of lodgepole pine along Middle Piney Creek and has 24 roomy sites spread out along a fairly long loop road. The camp has vault toilets and potable water. Sites have tables, fire rings with grates and good tenting options. Stay limited to 16 days.

Rates – Campsite per night: $4.

Getting there – From Big Piney go west 10.7 miles on Hwy 350 to the end of the pavement and FSR 10046; then right 1.7 miles on 10046 to the junction of FSR 10024; then left 1.5 miles on 10024 to another fork; then left .1 mile to the fee board at the camp. *See map page 138.*

Middle Piney Lake Campground

(Bridger-Teton National Forest, Open June 10 to Sept. 30)

About the camp – This camp, on Middle Piney Lake, is at the end of the road and, sorry, the signs say no trailers. Boating limited to electric motors, oars and paddles. The last 2.3 miles of road into this camp is narrow, but offers delightful views as it follows Middle Piney Creek through forested mountain parks laden with wildflowers. At the lake, which is nestled in conifer-covered foothills, you find 5 campsites with tables and fire pits with grates. The camp has a vault toilet but no potable water. Stay limited to 16 days.

Rates – Campsite per night: $4.00. Rates half with Golden Age or Access Passport.

Getting there – From Big Piney go west 10.7 miles on Hwy 350 (*Middle Piney Road*) to the end of the pavement and FSR 10046; then right 1.7 miles on 10046 to the junction of FSR 10024; then left 1.5 miles on 10024 to another fork for Sacajawea Campground on the left; then right 2.3 miles to the lake and the camp. *See map page 138.*

138

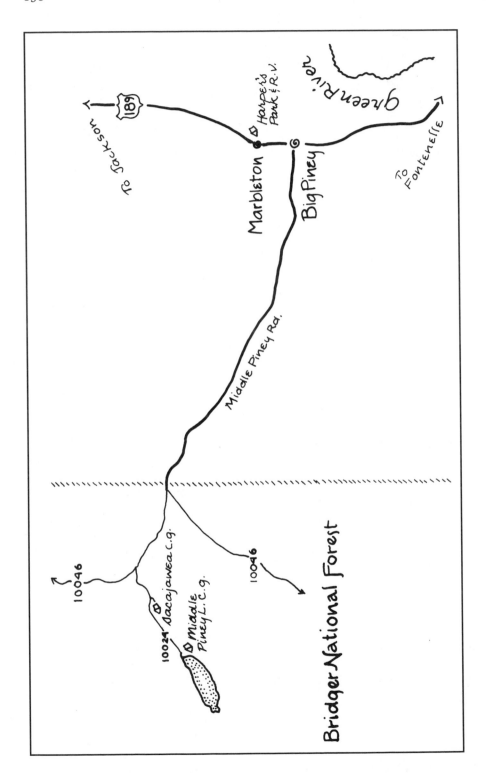

Boulder

Boulder lies in the valley of the Green River off the western slope of the **Wind River Range**. It's little more than a service station and C-store at the junction of Hwy 353 and US 191. To the north there is a private camp just off of US 191, and along Hwy 353 you access **Boulder Lake** with a Forest Service camp and free camping at this BLM recreation area, and free camping at a BLM campground in the foothills off the western slope of the Wind River Range.

Wind River View Campground
(Private, Open May 15 to Sept. 15)
8889 Hwy 191, Boulder, WY 82923 Ph: (307) 537-5453

About the camp – This is a membership camp with travelers welcome for up to 4 nights with a membership presentation. The camp is open, level and on gravel and native grass with a view of the Wind River Range. There are 29 RV sites: 7 pull-thrus (up to 30x60) and 21 back-ins (up to 30x60). Some sites have tables with sun shelters. Full hookups (30 amp) are available at 10 sites. Tent sites (members only).

Amenities – Rest rooms and showers, laundry; game room and playground; limited RV parts, gift shop, dump station and pay phone.

Rates – Overnight per RV site: $4.00. Tent sites: Current members only. Affiliations: C-C, RPI and AOR.

Getting there – From Boulder go north 1.5 miles on US 191 to the camp on the left. *See map page 140.*

Boulder Lake Recreation Area
(BLM, Open June 1 to Sept. 30)

About the camp – There are several camping options in this recreation area. All primitive, no potable water. Two locations have vault toilets: One is at the boat launch/trailer parking area and the other is near the dam where there is a table and stone fire rings. Other camping options can be found following two-tracks that lead to the edge of the lake. Stay limited to 14 days in any 28 day period.

Rates – Free

Getting there – From Boulder go east 2.4 miles on Hwy 353 to the Boulder Lake Access Road; then left 6 miles on good gravel to Boulder Dam Road; then left .7 miles to a three forks; then right .7 miles to the boat launch area, *[or]* straight on a two-track to camping options on the lake shore, *[or]* left 1.3 miles to the other vault toilet, table and stone fire ring near the dam (*along this road there are several other two-tracks going to the lake with additional camping options*). *See map page 140.*

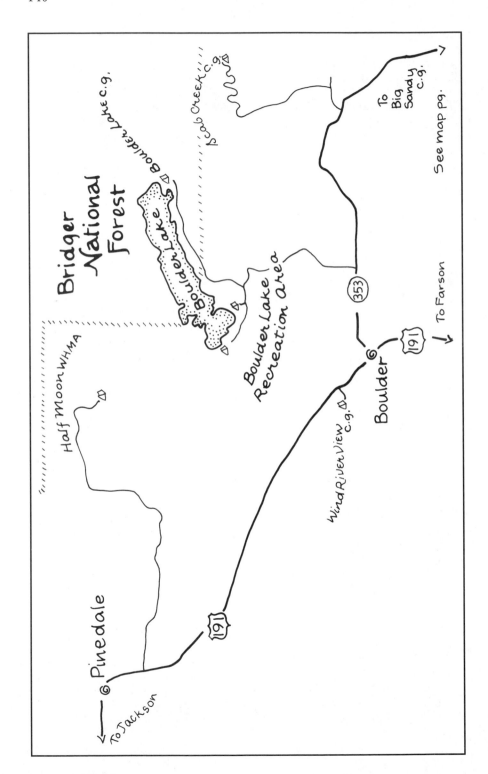

Bridger National Forest

Boulder Lake c.g.

Scab Creek c.g.

To Big Sandy c.g.

See map pg.

Boulder Lake

Boulder Lake Recreation Area

353

To Farson

191

Boulder

Wind River View c.g.

Half Moon WHMA

191

Pinedale

To Jackson

Boulder Lake Campground

(Bridger-Teton National Forest, Open June 1 to Oct. 15)

About the camp – This camp is on the upper end of Boulder Lake with campsites in a mix of aspen and conifers. The trailheads here, for Boulder Canyon and North Fork Trails, are supported with horse corrals and a pack string assembly area as well as backpacker parking and assembly area. There is a primitive boat launch nearby and an overflow area with dispersed camping options. The main camp has vault toilets, but no potable water. There are 20 sites on a loop road with tables and fire rings with grates. Stay limited to 10 days.

Rates – Campsite per night: $4.

Getting there – From Boulder go east 2.4 miles on Hwy 353 to the Boulder Lake Access Road; then left 10 miles to Boulder Lake Ranch; then left .5 miles to the camp. *See map facing page.*

Scab Creek Campground

(BLM, Open June 1 to Oct. 15)

About the camp – This camp has 9 sites on a short loop road in mostly aspen forest. There is a vault toilet, but no potable water. Several of the camps are pull-thrus and all camps have tables and fire rings with grates. Scab Creek Trailhead is nearby with horse handling facilities. Stay limited to 14 days in any 28 day period.

Rates – Free

Getting there – From Boulder go east 6.6 miles on Hwy 353 to CR 23-122; then left 1.4 miles to BLM Road 5423; then left 7.3 miles to the camp. *See map facing page.*

Cokeville

Cokeville is a small commercial center serving the ranching community in the Bear River Valley. It is on Hwy 231 just off of US 30, with Hwy 232 providing camping access in the Bridger-Teton National Forest. Listed from Cokeville are two Forest Service camps, a lone free dispersed BLM option, a free Game and Fish area and a free town park. Groceries are available.

Cokeville Town Park

(Town of Cokeville, Open May 1 to Oct. 1)
PO Box 99, Cokeville, WY 83114 Ph: (307) 279-3227

About the camp – This pleasant city park is on a grassy block bordered by mature cottonwood trees with rest rooms and potable water (*seasonal*), playground, tables and grills in a covered picnic area. RV parking is allowed along the east, west or south sides of the park or in a gravel and grass parking area across the street to the east of the main park. Tenting is not permitted in the main park due to the sprinkler system but a nice grassy area with two tables and grills is available across the street and adjacent to the RV parking area. Stay limited to 2 days.

Rates – Free

Getting there – From US 30 take Hwy 231 (East Main St.) .5 miles to the park on the left at the corner of East Main and Park Sts. *See map facing page.*

Lost Creek Wildlife Habitat Management Area
(Wyoming Game & Fish, Open all year)

About the camp – This area was recently established to provide crucial winter habitat for deer, elk and moose in the area. The area is cooperatively managed by the Rocky Mountain Elk Foundation, Bureau of Land Management, Wyoming State Land and Farm Loan Office, the Wyoming Game and Fish Commission and private landowners to improve existing habitat conditions for the benefit of wildlife and livestock. In addition to large game animals, wildlife in the area includes sage and blue grouse, cottontail rabbits, numerous raptors, coyotes, red foxes, badgers and other small mammals.

Elevations vary from 6300' to 8000'. The west half of the unit is gentle terrain with sagebrush, bitterbrush and grass meadows found at the lower elevations. To the east there is a steep west-facing aspect in the higher elevations, where there are mixed mountain shrubs, aspen and some conifers.

Several two-track roads provide public access from the main roads (*access is also currently allowed from the east on the Underwood/Dempsey Road*). The area is open to hiking, sight-seeing, photography and limited hunting and camping: State Trust land within the management area is not open to camping.

The area is currently open all year, with the recommendation that access be limited from December to May to reduce stress on wintering wildlife. Stay limited to 5 days.

Rates – Free

Getting there – From Cokeville go east 2 miles on Hwy 232 to a right-hand turnoff at the left-hand bend in the highway; then right 4.4 miles to the intersection of the BLM Stock Driveway Road; then left into the area (*On the immediate left there is a large sign with information and maps with land boundaries defined*). *See map facing page.*

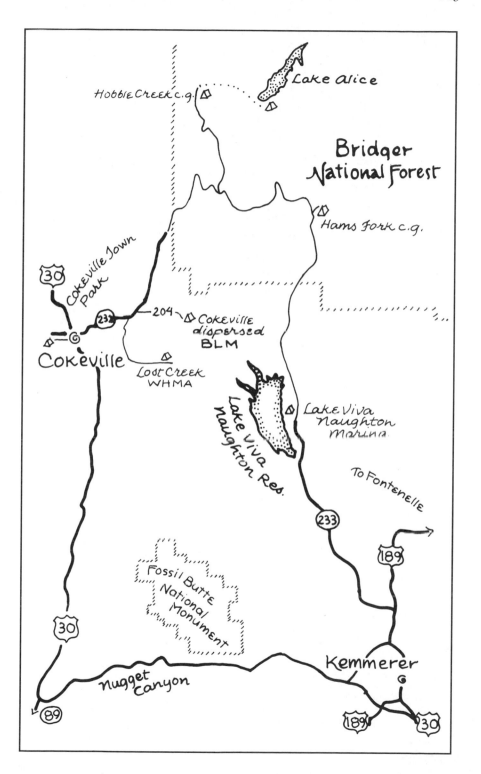

Cokeville dispersed

(BLM, Open all year)

About the camp — This area has only one campsite, but is handy, delightful, scenic and free. This camp is next to the road, on a nice grassy area near the banks of Pine Creek. It has a table and fire ring with grate.

Rates – Free

Getting there – From Cokeville go east 2.9 miles on Hwy 232 to CR 204; then right 4 miles to the parking area for the local ski area. Left of the parking area is the start of BLM Road 4215. Go .1 miles on BLM 4215 to the camp on the right. *See map page 143.*

Worth mentioning – The route is paved up to the last mile on CR 204 which is along the banks of Pine Creek with delightful views of lush greenery, flowing waters and photographic opportunities galore.

Hams Fork Campground

(Bridger-Teton National Forest, Open May 25 to Oct. 31)

About the camp — This camp, in a forest of primarily lodgepole pine with a strong population of subalpine fir seedlings and some planted Engelmann spruce, has 13 roomy sites offering good tenting options. The camp has vault toilets, potable water and all sites have tables and fire rings with grates. Opening dates are very tentative, as realistic expectations for an open camp are well into June due to snowpack. Stay limited to 16 days.

Rates – Campsite per night: $5. Rates half with Golden Age or Access Passport.

Getting there – From Cokeville go 12.5 miles on Hwy 232 to the end of the pavement; then .2 miles and take the right fork 8.5 miles to another fork signed to Hams Fork Campground; then right 1.8 miles to another fork; then left 2.0 miles to another fork; then right 2.3 miles to the camp.

From Kemmerer and the junction of US 189 and Hwy 233 go north about 19 miles on Hwy 233 to the end of the pavement where it becomes CR 305, a good gravel road; then about 20 miles to the camp on the right. *See map page 143.*

Hobble Creek Campground

(Bridger-Teton National Forest, Open July 1 to Oct. 31)

About the camp — This camp is about 40 miles north of Cokeville and, in spite of the distance, it is often full on weekends with campers from Utah and southwest Wyoming (*If you plan a stay here, it might be advisable to get there early in the week*). There are 14 sites in light timber. Sites 2 and 8 are designed as small group sites. Horse corrals are available, and there is trailhead parking for Lake Alice. The camp has vault toilets, potable water and all sites have tables and fire rings with grates. Stay limited to 16 days.

Rates – Campsite per night: $5. Rates half with Golden Age or Access Passport.

Getting there – From downtown go 12.5 miles on Hwy 232 to where pavement ends; then .2 miles and take the right fork 8.5 miles to another fork; then left 4.9 miles to another fork; then left 9.1 miles to the camp (*about 1.7 miles before getting to the camp there is a ford through Hobble Creek, which can be fairly deep in the spring of the year. In 1999, forest service plans include a concrete ford, similar to a boat ramp, in the river bottom: Inquire). See map page 143.*

Worth mentioning – While this camp is out of the way, Hobble Creek provides good fishing for cutthroat and brown trout. It is also a 1.5 mile hike to Lake Alice where the fishing is for cutthroat (no bait allowed on the lake or stream). Despite its remote location, Lake Alice has developed camps with potable water spigots tapped into area springs. The comfortable camping and short hike make it a likely choice if you're looking for a situation conducive to overnight backpacking with smaller children. There is parking at the trailhead. See Lake Alice below.

Lake Alice

(Bridger-Teton National Forest, Open July 1 to Oct. 31)

About the camp – This camp is on the largest natural lake in the western division of the Bridger-Teton National Forest and only a 1.5 mile hike from Hobble Creek Campground. The site offers a variety of recreational opportunities and a short back pack trip to semi-developed sites along the lake (*camping here is not restricted to campsites, but dispersed campers should be sure to camp at least 100' from the high water mark*). No motors or bait are allowed on the lake where fishing is for cutthroat trout: lures and flies only. There are three designated camping areas on the southwest shore of the lake: Cutthroat Point with a pit toilet, potable water, three tables and three fire rings; Huckleberry Cove with a pit toilet, potable water, four tables and two fire rings, and Fish Hawk Flat with a pit toilet, potable water, four tables and four fire rings. Stay limited to 16 days.

Rates – Free

Getting there – These directions are to the Hobble Creek Campground where you park at the trailhead for Lake Alice. From Cokeville go 12.5 miles on Hwy 232 to where pavement ends; then .2 miles and take the right fork 8.5 miles to another fork; then left 4.9 miles to another fork; then left 9.1 miles to the camp (*about 1.7 miles before getting to the camp there is a ford through Hobble Creek, which can be fairly deep in the spring of the year. In 1999, forest service plans included a concrete ford, similar to a boat ramp, in the river bottom: Inquire). See map page 143.*

Evanston

The city expanded in the 1870's when the railroad located a roundhouse and machine shop on the edge of town. A hundred years later, the area hit pay dirt when huge oil reserves were discovered nearby in the Overthrust Belt. With head waters in the Uinta Range, in sight to the south, the Bear River flows north through Evanston providing greenspace at **Bear River State Park** and wetlands in town.

Evanston is also the only place in the state with pari-mutuel betting and live racing at **Wyoming Downs** about eight miles north of town on US 89, open Memorial Day to Labor Day, Ph: 800-255-8238. Evanston's **Uinta County Museum**, at 36 10th St. (Ph: (307) 789-2757) is open all year, M-F, 8-5 and S-S, 10-4 in summer. Nearby is the **Evanston Depot**, one of the finest in its heyday, and a restored **Joss House**, sacred to the Chinese, originally built in 1870 but destroyed by fire in 1922. South of I-80 at exit 6 is a rest area and the **State of Wyoming Visitor Information Center** and **Bear River State Park**, with a small herd of Buffalo grazing there.

There are only two camping options listed out of Evanston, a private RV park in the city and a free Game and Fish site on Woodruff Narrows Reservoir to the north. Camping supplies are available in this medium-sized metropolitan area with full-service grocery, sporting goods and hardware stores, as well as outlets for a couple of the major discount chains. The **Evanston Community Recreation Center**, at 275 Saddle Ridge road, Ph: (307) 789-1770, is open to the public for swimming, workouts, steam and showers. (Adult day pass: $3. To age 18 and seniors +60: $1.50)

Evanston hosts a **Chili Cookoff** annually in late June; mountain men and traders gather in late August at the **Bear River Rendezvous** and the annual hooter of them all is **Cowboy Days,** a rodeo and more over the Labor Day weekend.

Phillips RV Park

(Private, Open April 1 to Nov. 1)
225 Bear River Drive, Evanston, WY 82930 Ph: (307) 789-3805 or (800) 349-3805

> About the camp – This camp is nicely landscaped with cottonwood, ash and aspen shading many sites. The camp has 59 RV sites: 53 pull-thrus (23x75) and 6 back-ins (23x40). All sites are gravel with grass 'yards' and tables. 56 sites are full hookups (20/30/50 amp on city water). There are 3 designated grass tent sites with tables.

> Amenities – Rest rooms and showers, laundry; cable (at 30 sites: $2), playground and horseshoes; limited gifts and RV parts, modem jack and pay phone.

> Rates – Full hookups for 2 persons: $18. Electric only for 2 persons: $16. Tent sites for 2 persons: $16. Additional persons 6 years and over: $2 (five years and under free). V MC Personal checks okay. Reservations: phone or mail.

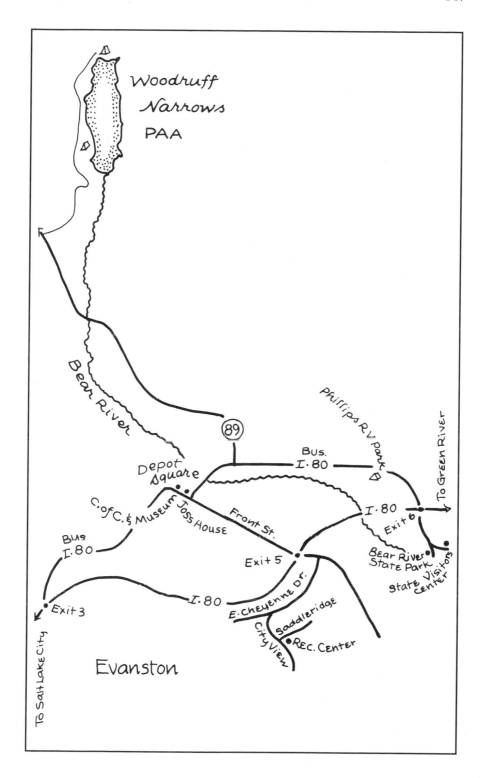

Getting there – From I-80 use exit 6; then north and west .6 miles on Business I-80 to the camp on the left. *See map page 147.*

Woodruff Narrows/Bear River Public Access Area
(Wyoming Game and Fish, Open all year)

About the camp – Woodruff Narrows is a large reservoir north of Evanston with the main camping area at the north end of the shore. This site has a vault toilet, large grassy area, stone fire rings and a boat ramp, but no potable water. Off the gravel road to this area, there are several two-tracks with options for dispersed camping, and about halfway in there is another parking area with a vault toilet and stone fire rings. Stay limited to 5 days.

Rates – Free

Getting there – From Evanston go north on US 89 to CR 101 (*just before the Utah state line*); then right .5 miles to a fork and the end of the pavement; then left 4.2 miles to the first area with a vault toilet; *[or]* 7.5 miles to the main camp at the north end of the reservoir. *See map page 147.*

Farson

Farson is located on the Pacific side of the Continental Divide in an area etched with emigrant trails from the era of westward expansion in the 1800's. Today it is a crossroads community, some distance from any city, serving the needs of travelers and the local ranching community. You will find cafes, gas, diesel, propane, snacks and ice at a couple of locations. Basic groceries are available at the **Farson Mercantile**, also an oasis for ice cream lovers and renowned state-wide as the "**home of the big cone.**"

From here you can explore the historic trails of the area; birdwatch at **Seedskadee Wildlife Refuge,** 28 miles to the west; run the dunes in the **ORV Area** or explore the **Great Divide Basin** to the south; or wind surfing at the **Big Sandy Recreation Area** to the north.

Full hookups are available at Farson and there is free primitive camping at the Big Sandy Reservoir which is becoming a popular area with local watersports enthusiasts.

Oregon Trail Campground
(Private, Open May 1 to Sept. 30)
PO Box 239, Farson, WY 82932 Ph: (307) 273-5586

About the camp – This camp is level, open, spacious and just to the rear of the Farson Mercantile. The camp has 15 sites on gravel and native grass, full hookup (30 amp on town water) RV sites: 10 pull-thrus (up to 23x100) and 5 back-ins (22x35). Tent sites are also available on grass in a shady park with common area and tables and grills.

Amenities – Rest rooms and showers.

Rates – Full hookups per site: $12. Tents: $4 per tent. Reservations: phone or mail.

Getting there – Farson is a four-corners town at the junction of Hwy 28 and US 191. The camp is located behind the mercantile on the northeast corner with registration at the Texaco station on the southeast corner. *See map page 174.*

Big Sandy Recreation Area
(Bureau of Reclamation, Open all year)

About the camp – There are two main areas near the shore of this reservoir, both with splendid views of the western slope of the Wind River Range. The west shore area has a vault toilet, a boat ramp and 7 sites with tables and fire rings with grates, but no potable water. Three of these site are sheltered near the few trees that exist on this shoreline. There are isolated ancient stone fire rings where overflow camping has been established. The south shore area has a vault toilet and 4 tables with fire pits and grates. On the way to this area, there are several two-tracks to previously used stone fire rings and isolated campsites along the shore. Stay limited to 14 days.

Rates – Free

Getting there – From the junction of Hwy 28 and US 191 in Farson go north 9.3 miles on US 191; then right 1.2 miles to a fork in the road; then right 1.6 miles over the dam to the south shore area; *[or]* left 1.3 miles to the west shore area and boat ramp. (*From the fork you will see both areas and will be able to decide which one looks more appealing or less crowded*). *See map page 174.*

Worth Mentioning – This camp seems to be minimally maintained, but has a great view. Locals note it has been 'found' by wind surfers.

150

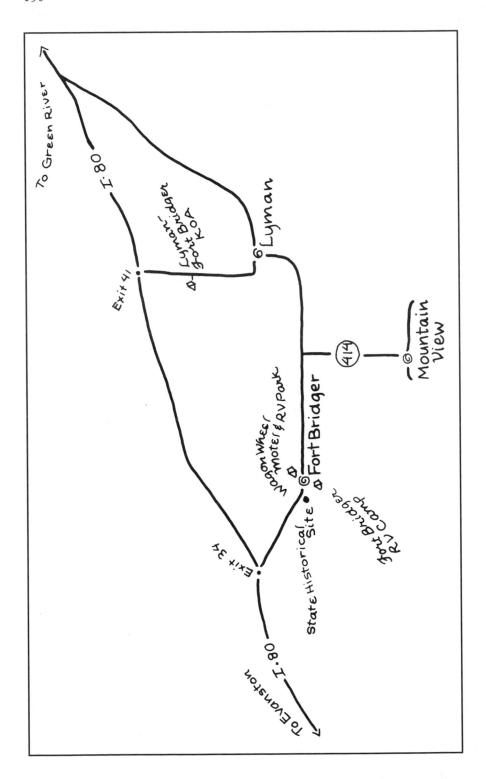

Fort Bridger

The town of Fort Bridger is a small support community for the state historic site of the same name, offering supplies and services just as Jim Bridger did 150 years ago. The **Fort Bridger State Historic Site** is impeccably restored, with grounds open all year, 8 a.m. to sunset. The site is open 9-6 weekdays (museum only in winter) and Sat., 9-4:30 summers. Ph: (307) 782-3842. In summer staff members don period dress and provide informational living history presentations. Over the Labor Day weekend the fort is the site of a teepee village, trader's row and Wyoming's grandest mountain man event, the **Fort Bridger Rendezvous**. In town there are two private RV camps, with tenting none to costly. Basic groceries are available.

Fort Bridger RV Camp

(Private, Open April 1 to Nov. 1)
PO Box 244, Fort Bridger, WY 82933 Ph: (307) 782-3150 or (800) 578-6535

About the camp – This camp is in downtown Fort Bridger behind the trading post, adjacent to the State Historic Site. The camp has 30 RV sites with cable TV: half pull-thrus and half back-ins (all 50x100). All sites are full hookups (20/30/50 amp on city water), on native grass and have tables. Tenting is available on native grass at RV sites.

Amenities – Rest rooms and showers, laundry; limited groceries at trading post and pay phone.

Rates – Full hookups per site: $16. Tent site: $16. No credit cards. Personal checks okay. Reservations: phone or mail.

Getting there – From I-80 use exit 34; then south 2.3 miles to Fort Bridger; then right (*at the trading post*) two blocks to the camp. *See map facing page.*

Wagon Wheel Motel and RV Park

(Private, Open March 1 to Oct. 1)
PO Box 47, Fort Bridger, WY 82933 Ph: (307) 782-6361 or 1-888-228-5475 Fax: (307) 782-3545

About the camp – This camp is in the heart of downtown Fort Bridger adjacent to the motel. The camp has parking for 12 self-contained RV units: all are back-ins (up to 20x35) with gravel and grass 'yards' and all are full hookups (20/30/50 amp on city water). Check in is at motel office. No tents.

Amenities – Cable included; snacks and ice, restaurant and pay phone.

Rates – Full hookups per site: $15. V Reservations: phone, fax or mail.

Getting there – From I-80 use exit 34; then south 2.3 miles to Fort Bridger and the motel and camp on the left. *See map facing page.*

Lyman-Fort Bridger KOA

(Private, Open May 15 to Oct. 1)
Star Route Box 55, Lyman, WY 82927 Ph: (307) 786-2762 or (800) 526-2762

About the camp – This camp is open, level, spacious and only a short distance from I-80. The camp has 36 pull-thru (30x90) RV sites on native grass. 18 sites are full hookups (20/30 amp). There are 17 designated tent sites as well as a large overflow area. All sites have tables and there are some grills. This camp also offers 2 kamper kabins. *Horses okay: $3 with own feed.*

Amenities – Rest rooms and showers (showers only: $3), laundry; game room, playground, heated outdoor pool, combo tennis/basketball court and horseshoes; gift shop, limited RV parts, dump station and pay phone.

Rates – Full hookups for 2 persons: $20. Water and electric only for 2 persons: $19. Tent sites for 2 persons: $16. Kamper Kabins for 2 persons: $29. Additional persons 4 years and over: $1.50. All major cards. Personal checks okay. Reservations: phone or mail.

Getting there – From I-80 use exit 41; then south 1.2 miles to the camp on the right. *See map page 150.*

Green River

'Tie hacks' cut timber on the slopes of the Wind River Range near Pinedale and used the Green River to float logs south to the railroad line, and the town of Green River grew where the wood and water met iron. Today that railroad ships ore from area mines producing two-thirds of the world's supply of trona, a substance used in everything from baking soda to glass. Of interest in town is **Expedition Island**, on the National Historic Register, where John Wesley Powell launched his exploration of the Green and Colorado Rivers in 1869; the **Sweetwater County Museum,** at 80 West Flaming Gorge Way, Ph: (307) 872-6411, open M-F all year and Sat. 1-5, June-Aug, and the **Flaming Gorge National Recreation Area Information Center** and the **Green River Chamber of Commerce,** at 1450 Uinta Drive. Ph: (307) 875-5711 open all year 8-5 M-F and 8-4, S-S in summer.

There is a private camp on the west end of town and nine other camps nearby with water-sports options. To north there are four BLM camps, three are free and on the banks of the Green River and one on the shores of Fontenelle Reservoir. To the south there are five options on the west shore of **Flaming Gorge Reservoir** in the **Flaming Gorge National Recreation Area,** two with fees and three free. To the north, enroute to the BLM camps near Fontenelle Reservoir, is **Seedskadee National Wildlife Refuge,** with good seasonal birdwatching, but no camping. Groceries, sporting goods and hardware are available. For workouts, showers, steam, sauna, hot tub or a swim, the **Green River Recreation Center,** at 1775 Hitching Post Drive, Ph: (307) 872-0511 (adult day pass: $3.25; to age 18 and seniors +60: $2).

Tex's Travel Camp

(Private, Open May 1 to Oct. 1)
Star Route 2-Box 101, Green River, WY 82935 Ph: (307) 875-2630

About the camp – This camp, located just west of Green River, is nicely landscaped with lots of trees, many shaded sites and the Green River running past the back of the camp. The camp has 70 RV sites: some gravel, some gravel with grass 'yards' and some tables and grills. 35 sites are pull-thrus (up to 25x85) and 35 are back-ins (up to 25x55). There are 36 full hookups (20/30/50 amp) with 29 of those designated premium sites with cable and other niceties. Tent sites, with tables and grills, are available on grass or riverside.

Amenities – Rest rooms and showers, laundry; cable included at premium sites, playground, river fishing with permit; limited groceries and RV parts, modem jack, dump station, C-store adjacent to camp and pay phone.

Rates – Full hookups for 2 persons: Premium site: $22-$26; Regular site: $22. Water and electric only for 2 persons: $19. Electric only for 2 persons: $17-18. Tent sites for 2 persons: $16. Additional adults: $4. Additional teens: $2. Additional 12 years and under: $1. V M Reservations: phone or mail.

Getting there — From I-80 use exit 85; then south .1 miles to stop sign at Hwy 374; then left 1.3 miles to the camp on the right. *See map page 157.*

—North of Green River—

Slate Creek Campground

(BLM, Open all year)

About the camp – This camp is on the Green River in a large grassy area with mature Cottonwoods. The camp has a primitive float ramp, a vault toilet and 6 very roomy sites with tables, fire rings and grills but no potable water. In addition, there are acres of grassy tent or trailer options with several stone fire rings in place. Stay limited to 14 days within any 28 day period.

Rates – Free

Getting there – From I-80 use exit 83 west of Green River; then north about 40 miles on Hwy 372 to the junction of Hwy 372 and Lincoln CR 311 and 316; then right .8 miles on CR 311 to the camp on the left. *See map Page 155.*

Weeping Rock Campground

(BLM, Open all year)

About the camp – This camp is on the Green River in a grassy area with a small stand of mature cottonwood trees. The camp has a primitive float ramp, vault toilet and 8 roomy sites with tables, fire rings and grills but no potable water. Stay limited to 14 days within any 28 day period.

Rates – Free

Getting there – From I-80 use exit 83 west of Green River; then north about 40 miles on Hwy 372 to the junction of Hwy 372 and CR 311 and 316; then straight 3.0 miles on CR 316; then right 1.4 miles to the camp. *See map facing page.*

Tail Race Campground

(BLM, Open all year)

About the camp – This camp has some trees and is on the Green River in a gravel area just below the Fontenelle Dam. The camp has a primitive float ramp, 2 sites with tables, fire rings and grills plus several stone fire rings but no potable water or vault toilet. Stay limited to 14 days within any 28 day period.

Rates – Free

Getting there – From I-80 use exit 83 west of Green River; then north about 40 miles on Hwy 372 to the junction of Hwy 372 and CR 311 and 316; then straight 4.7 miles on CR 316 to the dam and a road that takes off to the right and down about halfway across the dam; then to the bend in the road at the bottom of the hill; then drop off this road and onto a lower road going to the right and left; then right .3 miles to the river and the camp on the right. *See map facing page.*

Fontenelle Creek Campground

(BLM, Open Memorial Day to Labor Day)

About the camp – This camp is totally open, on the west shore of the reservoir, potentially a prime area for wind surfing. The camp has a picnic area, a boat ramp, potable water, rest rooms with sinks and flush toilets and 55 sites on two loop roads. Sites have sun shelters and wind breaks at the tables, grills and the occasional fire ring. Stay limited to 14 days within any 28 day period.

Rates – Camping per vehicle: $5. Rates half with Golden Age or Access Passports.

Getting there – From I-80 use exit 83 west of Green River; then north about 40 miles on Hwy 372 to the junction of Hwy 372 and CR 311 and 316; then straight 3.3 miles on CR 316 to the junction of CR 313; then left 4 miles to US 189; then right 3.5 miles to the camp on the right. *See map facing page.*

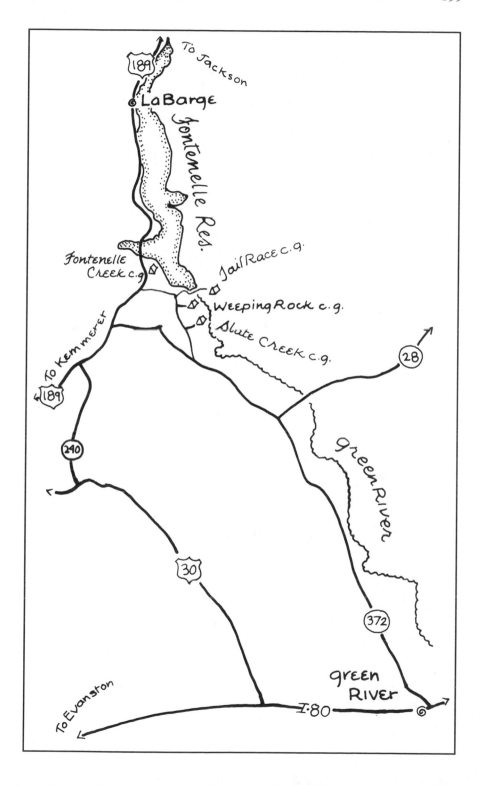

Lost Dog (dispersed)

(Flaming Gorge National Recreation Area, Open All year)

About the camp – This area offers dispersed camping on a finger of land along the northwest shore of Flaming Gorge Reservoir. There is a vault toilet and spacious camping options, but no potable water or boat ramp. Stay limited to 14 days.

Rates – Free. There are, however, fees for using the National Recreation Area (1 day: $2. 16 days: $5. Annual pass: $20.).

Getting there – From I-80 use exit 91 east of Green River; then follow the signs for Hwy 530 south which winds around town before going south over the railroad tracks; then south about 1 mile on Hwy 530 to the Flaming Gorge National Recreation Area Information Center and the Green River Chamber of Commerce on the right; then south 7.2 miles on Hwy 530 to the turnoff on the left; then left 10 miles to the vault toilet and a series of two-track roads with a variety of camping options. *See map facing page.*

Buckboard Campground

(Flaming Gorge National Recreation Area, Open May 1 to Sept. 30) 15

About the camp – This camp is open, level, grassy with a few smallish trees and very roomy sites with good tenting options. The camp has two loops with 34 sites each, rest rooms with sinks and flush toilets, potable water and a dump station. Sites have sun shelters and wind breaks at tables and grills. Below the camp is a marina, a gas dock, a fish cleaning station, a boat ramp and The Buckboard Marina Store which has boat rentals and service, fishing tackle and licenses, bait, limited groceries, firewood and ice. The marina also offers showers ($4; $5 if they provide the soap and towel). Stay limited to 14 days.

Rates – Campsite per night: $12. Rate half with golden Age or Access Passports. (Reservations are possible at this campground up to 240 days in advance and 10 days prior to arrival. Service fee per reservation: $8.65. Ph: (877) 444-6777 toll free.) There are also fees for using the National Recreation Area (1 day: $2. 16 days: $5. Annual pass: $20.).

Getting there – From I-80 use exit 91 east of Green River; then follow the signs for Hwy 530 south which winds around town before going south over the railroad tracks; then south about 1 mile on Hwy 530 to the Flaming Gorge National Recreation Area Information Center and the Green River Chamber of Commerce on the right; then 22.2 miles south on Hwy 530 to the Buckboard Recreation Area turnoff on the left; then left 1.4 miles to the camp registration office on the right. *See map facing page.*

24 sites

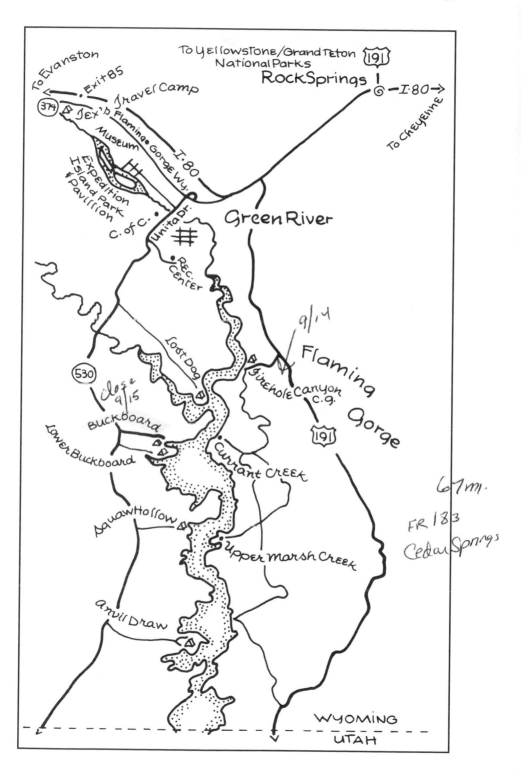

To Evanston
Exit 85
To Yellowstone/Grand Teton National Parks
191
RockSprings
I·80
To Cheyenne
374
Traver Camp
Jet'n
Flaming Gorge Wy.
Museum
I·80
Expedition Island Park & Pavillion
C. of C.
Uinta Dr.
Green River
Rec. Center
9/14
Flaming
Lodt Dog
Firehole Canyon C.g.
530
close 9/15
Buckboard
191
Gorge
Lower Buckboard
Currant Creek
Squaw Hollow
Upper Marsh Creek
67 m.
FR 183
Cedar Springs
Anvil Draw
WYOMING
UTAH

South Buckboard (dispersed)

(Flaming Gorge National Recreation Area, Open All year)

About the camp – This area offers dispersed camping on a peninsula just south of the marina at Buckboard. There are two vault toilets and spacious camping options, but no potable water or boat ramp. Stay limited to 14 days.

Rates – Free. There are, however, fees for using the National Recreation Area (1 day: $2. 16 days: $5. Annual pass: $20.).

Getting there – From I-80 use exit 91 east of Green River; then follow the signs for Hwy 530 south which winds around town before going south over the railroad tracks; then south about 1 mile on Hwy 530 to the Flaming Gorge National Recreation Area Information Center and the Green River Chamber of Commerce on the right; then south 22.9 miles on Hwy 530 to the turnoff on the left; then left 1.8 miles to the first vault toilet and a series of roads with a variety of camping options. *See map page 157.*

Squaw Hollow

(Flaming Gorge National Recreation Area, Open All year)

About the camp – This is a small area with a boat ramp and vault toilet. Stay limited to 14 days.

Rates – Free. There are, however, fees for using the National Recreation Area. (1 day: $2. 16 days: $5. Annual pass: $20.)

Getting there – From I-80 use exit 91 east of Green River; then follow the signs for Hwy 530 south which winds around town before going south over the railroad tracks; then south about 1 mile on Hwy 530 to the Flaming Gorge National Recreation Area Information Center and the Green River Chamber of Commerce on the right; then 29.5 miles south on Hwy 530 to the Squaw Hollow turnoff on the left; then left 2.6 miles to the camp. *See map page 157.*

Anvil Draw

(Flaming Gorge National Recreation Area, Open all year)

About the camp – The main area at this camp is gravel with a boat ramp and vehicle and trailer parking and a vault toilet, but no potable water. However, if you take the right fork (*see getting there*) you will find a sizeable gravel and native grass area with several two-tracks and more than a few stone fire rings from earlier campers. There are, as well, several options for launching a small boat or canoe. A small island a short distance from the shore would be a short paddle to a remote camp. Stay limited to 14 days.

Rates – Campsite: $5. There are also fees for using the National Recreation Area (1 day: $2. 16 days: $5. Annual pass: $20.).

Getting there – From I-80 use exit 91 east of Green River; then follow the signs for Hwy 530 south which winds around town before going south over the railroad tracks; then south about 1 mile on Hwy 530 to the Flaming Gorge National Recreation Area Information Center and the Green River Chamber of Commerce on the right; then 35.8 miles south on Hwy 530 to the Anvil Draw turnoff on the left; then left 2.5 miles to the fork; then left .2 miles to the main area with boat ramp; [or] right .7 miles to the dispersed camping options. *See map Page 157.*

Little America
(Private, Open All year)

About the camp – Parking for self-contained RVs in the southwest parking area or with the tractor-trailer parking. Stay limited to 1 night.

Amenities – Rest rooms and showers ($), laundry; restaurant, deli, lounge, C-store, gift shop and pay phone.

Rates – Free.

Getting there – From I-80 use exit 68 east of Green River.

Kemmerer

Kemmerer is home to the **J.C. Penny Mother Store**, founded in 1902 as the Golden Rule Store by James Cash Penny after coal was discovered in the area. The **Fossil Country Frontier Museum**, at 400 Pine Ave., Ph; 877-6551; open M-F 10-6 and Sat. 10-4 is free and eleven miles west is the **Fossil Butte National Monument** open daily 8:30-4:30 all year and 8-5:30 in summer. Kemmerer celebrates during their annual **Turn of the Century Days**, with Little Buckaroos Rodeo, parade, chili cookoff, carnival and more, usually the last weekend in July.

In town at there are two RV camps (no tents) and the Kemmerer Community Park (tents only). To the north is Lake Viva Naughton, with camping at this marina complex. Groceries and hardware are available. For showers, sauna, spa and a workout, the **Kemmerer Recreation Center** is open to the public at 1776 Del Rio Drive, Ph: (307) 828-2365. In summer the city pool at 1100 Post Pl. is open to the public for showers and a swim. (Rec center or pool adult day pass: $2. To age 18 and seniors +60: $1.

Foothills Mobile Home and RV Park
(Private, Open May 1 to Oct. 31)
(PO 408) 310 US Hwy 189, Kemmerer, WY 83101 Ph: (307) 877-6634

About the camp – This is a self-serve camp on the north edge of Kemmerer along US Hwy 189 for self-contained RV units only. The camp has a total of 40 sites with 15 pull-thrus (up to 30x100) and 25 back-ins (up to 30x60). All sites are full hookups (20/30/50 amp on city water).

Amenities – Cable TV included.

Rates – Full hookups per site: $14. Reservations: Phone or mail.

Getting there – This camp is on the east side of US 189 about .2 miles south of the junction of Hwy 233. *See map facing page.*

Riverside RV Park

(Private, Open May 1 to Oct. 31)
216 Spinel St., Kemmerer, WY 83101 Ph: (307) 877-3416

About the camp – This camp in on gravel near the Hams Fork River on the north edge of Kemmerer. There are 30 sites for self-contained RV units. 11 sites are pull-thrus (up to 16x40). All sites are full hookups (20/30/50 amp on city water). No tents.

Amenities – Cable TV included.

Rates – Full hookups for 2 persons: $13.00. Additional persons: $1.

Getting there – From the junction of US 30/189, go north .3 miles to Aspen St.; then right .3 miles on Aspen St. to the end and Spinel St.; then left on Spinel St. to the camp on the right. *See map facing page.*

Kemmerer Community Park

(City owned, Open Memorial Day to Labor Day)

About the camp – This camp, with 8 sites for tenting only, was established through the cooperative effort of the City of Kemmerer, Kemmerer Diamondville Joint Powers Board, USFS, BLM, Wyoming Department of Commerce and local citizens to make up for the lack of tenting options at any of the commercial RV parks in the city. The camp has only pit toilets, but is adjacent to city hall (Quealy Municipal Complex) where campers are welcome to use the rest rooms and get potable water during business hours. Stay limited to 3 days.

Rates – Campsite per night/per tent: $5.

Getting there – Follow US 189 north to the junction of Hwy 233; then west .5 miles on Hwy 233 to the camp on the right. *See map facing page.*

—North of Kemmerer—

Lake Viva Naughton

(Private, Open all year)
PO 111, Kemmerer, WY 83101 Ph: (307) 877-9669

About the camp – This camp is in marina complex at Lake Viva Naughton about 17 miles north of Kemmerer. The camp has 15 full hookup RV sites (20/30 amp) on gravel and native grass: 6 pull-thrus (up to 15 x 60) and 9 back-ins (up to 12x30). There is also a large native grass area for tents or no hookups on native grass. *Horses okay with own feed.*

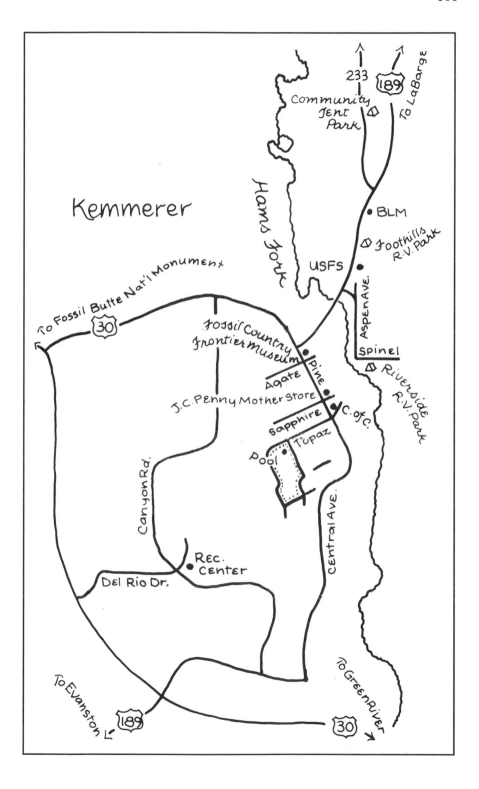

Amenities – Rest rooms and showers; restaurant and lounge, game room, horseshoes, volleyball, and shore fishing; marina, gas, pontoon boat rentals, snacks, ice, dump station and pay phone.

Rates – Full hookups per site: $15. Tents or no hookups: $5. All major credit cards. Reservations: phone or mail.

Getting there – From the junction of US 189 and Hwy 233 on the north end of Kemmerer, go north about 16 miles to the camp on the left. *See map page 161.*

Lander

Lander once known as "where the rails end and the trails begin," is located on the Popo Agie (Pa-Poh-Sha) River near the Shoshone National Forest in the foothills of the Wind River Range. The trails are still here, but the railroad has pulled up stakes. Lander now calls itself, the '**City of Bronze**,' home to **Eagle Bronze Foundry**, Ph: (307) 332-5436, with informational tours on casting and finishing of bronze sculpture, and many bronze works scattered throughout the city. The **National Outdoor Leadership School** has its headquarters offices here, and there is the small, free and interesting **Pioneer Museum,** at 630 Lincoln St., Ph: (307) 332-4137, open M-F 1-4:30 and Sat. 1-4 all year and M-F 10-6, S-S 1-4 from June to mid-Sept.

The **Loop Road** starts in **Sinks Canyon**, so named because the Popo Agie River disappears underground, reappearing at the 'Rise' about one-half mile below and on the other side of the road. Huge trout feed at the Rise; enjoy looking and feeding the fish, but fishing here is banned. The historic gold mining towns of **Atlantic City** and **South Pass City**, which is preserved as the **South Pass City Historical Site**, are near the top of the Loop Road at Hwy 28. Both communities boomed with gold fever in the late 1800's. In South Pass City, state historians and archaeologists have carefully restored stores, saloons, the hotel, the school house, the bank and assay office, the newspaper office and other buildings. Atlantic City, now a residential and 'weekend-cabin' community, is a good place to visit and stop for lunch. A lunch menu is available at either the historic **Atlantic City Mercantile**, built in 1893, or the **Sagebrush Saloon** which is right next door.

Atlantic City is three miles from Hwy 28 on good road, and along the way there are two BLM campgrounds. Off Hwy 28, on the return to Lander, there is the Wild Iris climbing area, where dispersed camping is permitted in the Shoshone National Forest (see page 172), and Red Canyon, where camping is allowed in the Game and Fish Wildlife Habitat Management Area (see page 173). If you want a more scenic and intimate route from the top of Red Canyon to Lander, take the dirt road from the top of the canyon through the wildlife management habitat area and the Red Canyon Ranch before returning to Hwy 28 about 9 miles from Lander.

Lander celebrates for three days over the Fourth of July during **Lander Pioneer Days** with rodeo, parade, street dances and more. In early June, City Park is the site of **Popo Agie Rendezvous** and in July climbers meet in town and at the Wild Iris for the annual **International Climbers Festival**. A **Pow Wow** schedule highlights the summer scene on the nearby **Wind River Indian Reservation** (Check with the Lander Chamber of Commerce for dates, Ph: (307) 332-3892). At **Fort Washakie**, about 16 miles northwest of Lander on the reservation, lie the graves of **Sacajawea**, famed guide for the Lewis and Clark expedition, and **Chief Washakie**, renowned leader of the Shoshone tribe. For Native American artifacts and authentic works by traditional artisans, visit the **Gallery of The Wind and Museum**, open daily at Fort Washakie on US 287, Ph: (307) 332-3267 or (307) 332-4231.

There are three privately-owned camping options in town and a free city park; to the northwest two private camps and a remote Forest Service camp; to the southeast two private camps; to the southwest, on the local loop road, two State Park camps, five developed and two dispersed Forest Service camps, two BLM camps and one Game and Fish Wildlife Habitat Management Area, and to the southwest over the Continental Divide four free BLM camping options and a wilderness trailhead Forest Service camp. Grocery, hardware, sporting goods (one specializing in climbing equipment), and a bicycle store are available. The National Outdoor Leadership School has an outlet store at 502 Lincoln St., and Rocky Mountain Dubbing, at 115 Poppy is a specialty store answering every need for the fly fishing enthusiast. There is a public indoor, Olympic-sized pool for lap and rec swimming, at 450 S. 9th, Ph: 332-4653 with modest admission and the **Wind River Fitness Center**, at 943 Amoretti, Ph: (307) 332-2811, for workout, sauna and shower (Day pass: $5).

Holiday Lodge Campground

(Private, Open Memorial Day to Labor Day)
210 MacFarlane Drive, Lander, WY 82520 Ph: (307) 332-2511 or (800) 624-1974

About the camp – The camp is along the Popo Agie (Pa-Poh-Sha) River on the east end of Lander. The camp offers 2 RV sites with water and electric only and has 12 tenting options. There is a large open park near the river with some tables and grills, and a concrete patio with large gas grill (you provide your own gas). RV units are limited to 16' in length.

Amenities – Rest rooms, showers, laundry and spa at motel. (Showers only: $3 with your own soap and towel or $5 with towels and toiletries furnished).

Rates – RV or tent site per night: $5 per person with $15 maximum. Hookups per night: $3. Reservations: Phone or mail.

Getting there – Check-in is at the Holiday Lodge on the hill on the east end of Lander just northeast of the junction of Hwy 789 and US 287. *See map page 164.*

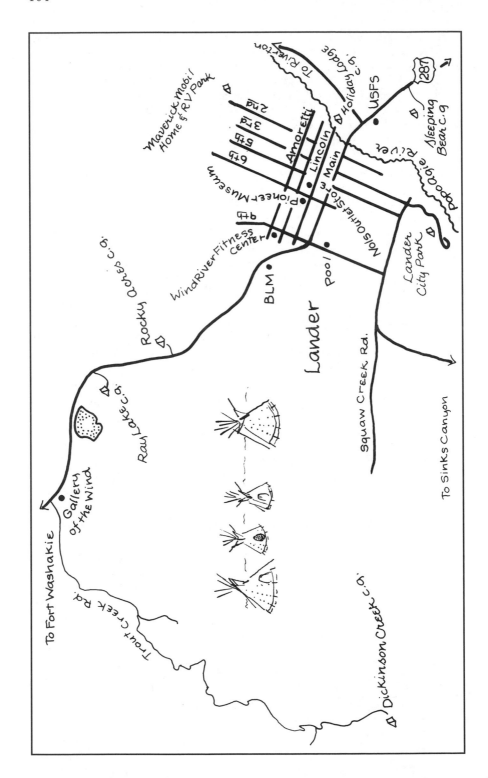

Maverick Mobil Home and RV Park

(Private, Open April 1 to Sept. 30)
1104 N. 2nd St., Lander, WY 82520 Ph: (307) 332-3142 or (800) 337-3142

About the camp – This shady camp is at the edge of rural Lander about .7 miles from the downtown area. The camp has 40 RV sites: 16 pull-thrus and 24 back-ins (all 30x65 with 20/30/50 amp on city water). Sites have gravel parking spurs with grass 'yards' and some tables and grills. Shaded tent sites are available. *Horses okay: free in adjacent pasture with camping and own feed.*

Amenities – Rest rooms and showers, laundry; fishing in 6-acre lake adjacent to property.

Rates – Full hookups per site: $15 including tax. Tent site: $8.

Getting there – From Main and 2nd Sts in downtown Lander, go north .7 miles on 2nd St. to the camp on the right. *See map facing page.*

Sleeping Bear Campground

(Private, Open all year)
715 Main St., Lander, WY 82520 Ph: (307) 332-5159 or (800) SLP-BEAR (757-2327) E-mail: slpbear@yahoo.com
Web site: www.sleeping-rv-park.com

About the camp – This camp is on a hill overlooking the entire Lander valley and the southern end of the Wind River Range and is next door to the Hitching Rack, one of the area's finest restaurants. The camp has 34 pull-thru (up to 30x70) sites and 8 back-ins (up to 25x25). All sites have gravel parking spurs and grass 'yards' with tables and grills. There are 21 full hookups (20/30/50 amp on city water) and 13 water and electric only. The camp also offers 10 tent sites, a camper cabin, a teepee and a wall tent.

Amenities – Handicapped-accessible rest rooms with showers (showers only: $3.50; with towel set rental: $4.25) and laundry; game room; RV parts, limited groceries, gifts, modem jack in office, dump station and pay phone.

Rates – Full hookups per site: $22. Water and electric per site: 18.50. Electric only per site: $16. Tent site: $13.50. Camper cabin: $30. Wall tent or teepee: $17.50. Discounts: GoodSam , AARP. V MC D Personal checks okay. Reservations: Phone, E-mail or mail.

Getting there – From the intersection of Hwy 789 and US 287 on the east end of Lander's Main St., go south .5 miles on US 287 to the camp on the right (*for an approach with less grade into this camp, large RVs should enter at the sign for the Hitching Rack Restaurant*). *See map facing page.*

Lander City Park
(City owned, Open all year)

About the camp – This city park is green with a mature stand of cotton-wood trees and allows free RV or tent camping. The park has 2 vault toilets and potable water on a seasonal basis. Stay limited to 3 days.

Rates – Free

Getting there – From Main and 3rd Sts. in downtown Lander, go south about .6 miles on 3rd St. which runs right into the park; then straight about .2 miles past the ball diamonds to where the camping areas are signed. *See map page 164.*

—North and West of Lander—

Ray Lake Campground
(Private, Open May 1 to Sept. 1)
39 Ray Lake Road, Lander, WY 82520 Ph: (307) 332-9333

About the camp – This camp has 10 pull-thru (20x50), full hook up (20/30/50 amp) sites. Tent sites are available as well as 2 teepees. All sites are native grass. *Horses okay.*

Amenities – Rest rooms and showers; horseshoes; cafe (open 8-6, reservations requested for better service).

Rates – Full hookups for 2 persons: $13. Electric only for 2 persons: $10. Additional persons: $2. Tent site per person: $3.50. Teepees: $15.

Getting there – From Lander go north 8.5 miles on US 287; then west on a well-marked gravel road .5 miles to the camp on a slight rise and visible from the highway. *See map page 164.*

Rocky Acres Campground
(Private, Open May 1 to Oct. 31)
(PO Box 1565) 5700 US Hwy 287, Lander, WY 82520 Ph: (307) 332-6953 E-mail: rockyacres@rmisp.com

About the camp – This camp has 12 pull-thru (20 x 40), full hookup RV (30 amp) sites and 28 tent sites with 4 offering electric. All sites are on grass with many of the tent sites in a tree line along flowing water. Another large grassy area (without hookups) is available for groups as needed.

Amenities – Rest rooms and showers (showers only: $2.50), laundry; swing set, rec area, horseshoes; snacks and discount cigarettes at this smoker-friendly camp.

Rates – Full hookups for two adults: $13.50. Tent sites for two adults: $10. Additional persons: $1.50. No credit cards. Reservation: phone, E-mail or mail.

Getting there – From Lander go north 5 miles on US Hwy 287 to the camp on the right. *See map page 164.*

Dickinson Creek Campground
(Shoshone National Forest, Open July 1 to Sept. 15)

About the camp – This camp is in the high country west of Lander with great views of the valley from the switchbacks on the road up to the camp. The camp has 15 sites in a mature forest on the edge of a large mountain park and near the Bears Ears Trailhead into the Popo Agie Primitive Area. There are public corrals near the camp. The camp has vault toilets, but no potable water. Sites have tables and fire rings with grates. Stay limited to 14 days.

Rates – Free

Getting there – From Lander go about 16 miles northwest on US 287 to Fort Washakie; then left on Trout Creek Road (*at the Wind River Trading Post*); then 19.5 miles (*the pavement ends at 5.1 miles*) to the fork for Moccasin Lake; then left another 3.2 miles to the camp on the right. *See map page 164.*

—East of Lander—

Hart Ranch Hideout RV Resort
(Private, Open May 1 to Oct. 31)
7192 Hwy 789-287, Lander, WY 82520 Ph: (307) 332-3836

About the camp – Campground memberships are available at this camp, located about 8 miles southeast of Lander on the Little Popo Agie River, with 55 full hookup (20/30/50 amp) RV sites and 6 water and electric or tent sites. 20 sites are pull-thrus and 41 are back-ins (all up to 25x55). All sites are on native grass with some grills and tables. The camp also offers 3 camper cabins sleeping up to 4 persons. *Horses okay, in corrals with own feed: $4 each.*

Amenities – Rest room and showers, laundry; game room, playground, and river frontage for fishing or cooling off; tackle shop and free fly fishing seminars; cafe, limited groceries and RV parts, propane and pay phone. This camp is also has its own version of a frontier town, known as Dallas, Wyoming, comprised of 12 vintage buildings with some from the 1890's.

Rates – Full hookups for 2 persons: $18.75. Tent site or water and electric only for 2 persons: $13.50. Camper cabins for 2 persons: $30. Additional persons over age 5: $2 each. (Dinner and second night of camping free with membership presentation) V MC Personal checks okay. Reservations: Phone or mail.

Getting there – From the junction of US 287 and Hwy 789 on the east end of Lander, go southeast about 8 miles on US 287 and Hwy 789 to the junction at Hwy 28; then left about one mile on US 287 and Hwy 789 to the camp on the left. *See map facing page.*

—South of Lander—

Sawmill Campground
(Wyoming State Parks, Open April 1 to Nov. 1)

About the camp – This camp has a designated handicapped camping area with a deck overlooking the Popo Agie River. There are four other sites in the camp, all with tables and fire rings with grates. The camp has a vault toilet, potable water and a playground. Stay limited to 14 days.

Rates – Resident campsite per night: $4. Nonresident campsite per night: $9. No day use fees. (Rates effective Jan. 1, 2000)

Getting there – From Main and S. 5th Sts. in Lander go south .6 miles on 5th St. to Fremont St.; then right 6.2 miles to the entrance of Sinks Canyon State Park and the camp on the left. *See map facing page.*

Popo Agie Campground
(Wyoming State Parks, Open April 1 to Nov. 1)

About the camp – This campground is about 8 miles from Lander in Sinks Canyon. The camp has a foot bridge across the river to a nature trail, vault toilets, potable water and 25 sites with tables and fire rings with grates. Sites 9-12 are short walk-ins nearer the river. Stay limited to 14 days.

Rates – Resident campsite per night: $4. Nonresidents campsite per night: $9. No day use fees. (Rates effective Jan. 1, 2000)

Getting there – From Main and S. 5th Sts. in Lander go south .6 miles on 5th St. to Fremont St.; then right 7.8 miles to the camp on the left. *See map facing page.*

Sinks Canyon Campground
(Shoshone National Forest, Open June 1 to Oct. 31)

About the camp – This camp is 9.4 miles from downtown Lander and just 1 mile above the state park campground. At this campground there is a suspended foot bridge over the river to a hiking trail or fishing access on the other side of the river. The camp has vault toilets, potable water, and 9 sites, mostly open or in very light timber, with tables and fire rings with grates. Sites 1-3 are short walk-ins nearer the river. Stay limited to 14 days.

Rates – Campsite per night: $6. Rates half with Golden Age or Access Passport.

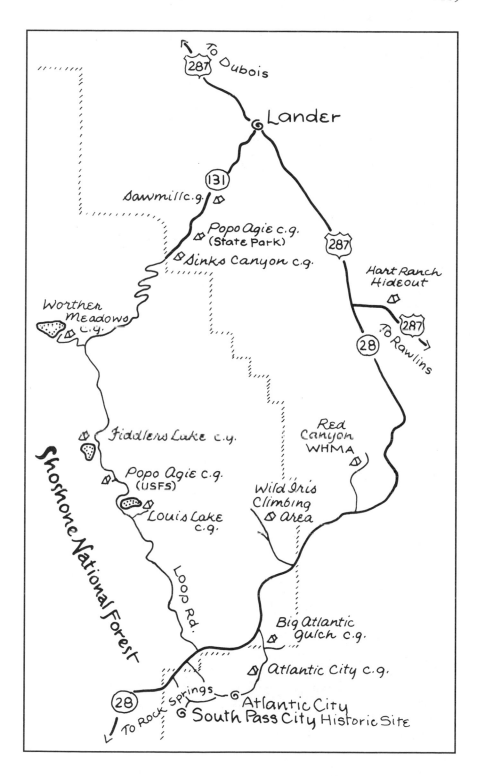

Getting there – From Main and S. 5th Sts. in Lander go south .6 miles on 5th St. to Fremont St.; then right 8.8 miles to the camp on the left. *See map page 169.*

Sinks Canyon (Dispersed)
(Shoshone National Forest, Open May to Oct.)

About the camp – Just .5 miles above the Forest Service campground, this camp has a pit toilet and some stone fire rings with camping options in the open or in very light timber. No potable water. Stay limited to 14 days.

Rates – Free

Getting there – From Main and S. 5th Sts. in Lander go south .6 miles on 5th St. to Fremont St.; then right 9.5 miles to the camp on the left. *See map page 169.*

Worthen Meadows Campground
(Shoshone National Forest, Open July 1 to Sept. 15)

About the camp – This camp is the first campground above the switchbacks alongside Worthen Meadows Reservoir, with boat ramp, picnic area and 28 campsites generally in light timber offering shade and decent tenting options. The campground is near several popular trailheads: Stough Creek Lakes Trailhead, Sheep Bridge Trailhead and Worthen Meadows Trailhead. Sites 1-8 are to the right of the fee board and near the boat ramp and picnic area. Sites 9-28 are to the left of the fee board on a loop road with sites 13, 15, 22 and 24 offering the best lake-side views. The camp has vault toilets, potable water and sites with tables and fire rings with grates. Stay limited to 14 days.

Rates – Campsite per night: $6. Rates half with Golden Age or Access Passport.

Getting there – From Main and S. 5th Sts. in Lander go south .6 miles on 5th St. to Fremont St.; then right 10.7 miles to the base of the switchbacks; then up the switchbacks 7.3 miles to the turnoff on the right; then right 2.4 miles to the camp on the right. *See map page 169.*

Fiddlers Lake Campground
(Shoshone National Forest, Open July 1 to Sept. 15)

About the camp – This camp, on Fiddlers Lake near the trailhead to Christina Lake, is the second campground above the switchbacks, with boat ramp, picnic area and 20 campsites. Generally, these sites are in light timber offering some shade and decent tenting options. The camp has vault toilets, potable water and sites with tables and fire rings with grates. Campsites 1-4 are short walk-ins on the off-lake side of the road and the remaining camps, with several on the lake-side of the road, are along a .5 mile road with end-of-the-road turn around. Stay limited to 14 days.

Rates – Campsite per night: $6. Rates half with Golden Age or Access Passport.

Getting there – From Main and S. 5th Sts. in Lander go south .6 miles on 5th St. to Fremont St.; then right 10.7 miles to base of the switchbacks; then up the switchbacks 13.0 miles to the camp on the right. *See map page 169.*

Popo Agie Campground
(Shoshone National Forest, Open July 1 to Sept. 15)

About the camp – The third campground above the switchbacks is just past the bridge over the Little Popo Agie River and close to the road in a small open area resembling a cul-de-sac. The camp has been relegated to dispersed camping: there are concrete fire rings and grates and a pit toilet, but no tables or potable water. Stay limited to 14 days.

Rates – Free

Getting there – From Main and S. 5th Sts. in Lander go south .6 miles on 5th St. to Fremont St.; then right 10.7 miles to the base of the switchbacks; then up the switchbacks 16.4 miles to the camp on the right. *See map page 169.*

Louis Lake Campground
(Shoshone National Forest, Open July 1 to Sept. 15)

About the camp – This camp is the fourth and last campground on the loop road above the switchbacks, near the southeast shore of Louis Lake. The camp has a vault toilet, potable water and 9 sites with tables and fire rings with grates. About .3 miles past the entrance to the camp is a primitive boat ramp and up the east shore of the lake from the boat ramp is a shallow and comfortable sandy beach area. (*There is a road to the parking area for the beach on the northeast side of the lake.*) Campsites are generally open in light lodgepole pine forest. Stay limited to 14 days.

Rates – Campsite per night: $6. Rates half with Golden Age or Access Passport.

Getting there – From Main and S. 5th Sts. in Lander go south .6 miles on 5th St. to Fremont St.; then right 10.7 miles to the base of the switchbacks; then up the switchbacks 19.0 miles past Louis Lake Lodge to the turnoff on the left; then left .8 miles to the camp on the left. *See map page 169.*

Big Atlantic Gulch Campground
(BLM, Open May to Oct.)

About the camp – This camp, one of two BLM campgrounds in the area of the historic and picturesque South Pass City/Atlantic City gold mining district, is located just off the Fort Stambaugh Loop Road (BLM 2324) in a stand of aspen. The camp has a vault toilet, potable water and 10 sites, several with parking spurs that would appear to accommodate the largest of RV's. Sites have tables and fire rings with grates. Stay limited to 14 days in any 28 period.

Rates – Campsite per night: $6. Rates half with Golden Age or Access Passport.

Getting there – From Lander go about 27 miles southwest on Hwy 28 to the Atlantic City Road (*near mile marker 49 and directly across from the Wyoming Highway Shop*); then left .5 miles to the Fort Stambaugh Loop Road; then left .3 miles to the camp on the left. *See map page 169.*

Atlantic City Campground
(BLM, Open May to Oct.)

About the camp – This camp, one of two BLM campgrounds in the area of the historic South Pass City/Atlantic City gold mining district, is located on the Atlantic City Road, less than a mile from Hwy 28, in a stand of aspen. The camp has vault toilets, potable water and 18 sites. Sites have tables and fire rings with grates. Stay limited to 14 days in any 28 period.

Rates – Campsite per night: $6. Rates half with Golden Age or Access Passport.

Getting there – From Lander go about 27 miles southwest on Hwy 28 to the Atlantic City Road (near *mile marker 49 and directly across from the Wyoming Highway Shop*); then left .8 miles to the camp on the right. *See map page 169.*

Wild Iris Climbing Area
(Shoshone National Forest, Open all year)

About the camp – This camp is on Limestone Mountain about 16 miles south of Lander. The climbing area is heavily used all summer and especially during Lander's International Climber's Festival held annually in July (*check with the Lander Chamber of Commerce for dates: See page 351*). There is a parking area with portable toilet at the trailhead to the climbing walls, which are about .5 miles distant. Dispersed camping options abound. No potable water. Stay limited to 16 days.

Rates – Free

Getting there – From Lander go southwest about 24 miles on Hwy 28 to the turnoff to the right near mile marker 53; then right 1.3 miles on FSR 326 to a fork; then right .7 miles on FSR 327 to the parking area on the left. Past the parking area there is a fork, with the right fork going to another climbing area known as Okay Corral and the left going to a quarry area and more camping/parking options. *See map page 169.*

Red Canyon Wildlife Management Habitat Area
(Wyoming Game and Fish, Open all year)

About the camp – This 1,785-acre area is at the top of Red Canyon just off of Hwy 28. It is a historic elk winter range as well as the site of a stagecoach station used until the late 1800's. The old stage route is still used as a county road and rejoins Hwy 28 about 9 miles from Lander. The area serves as crucial winter habitat for elk which can be seen here during hard winters. Mule deer, pronghorn antelope, blue and ruffed grouse, chukar, snowshoe hares, songbirds and sakes are common to the area. No potable water. Stay limited to 14 days.

Rates – Free

Getting there – From the junction of Hwy 28 and US 287 about 8 miles south of Lander, go south 19.5 miles on Hwy 28 to the turnoff on the right. *See map Page 169.*

—West of Lander—

Sweetwater Bridge Campground
(BLM, Open all year)

About the camp – This camp on the Sweetwater River in Sweetwater Gap country, north of South Pass in the foothills of the Wind River Range. The camp has a vault toilet, but no potable water. There are 8 sites, one on the near side of the bridge and 7 across the bridge, with two of those sites very close together on the same parking spur. Campsites, with tables and fire rings with grates, are in the open with little to no shade. Stay limited to 14 days within any 28 day period.

Rates – Free

Getting there – Turn off Hwy 28 about one mile southwest of the rest area near the Sweetwater River (*about 34 miles from Farson and about 44 miles from Lander*); then go northwest 15.1 miles on good dirt road to a turnoff to the right; then right 3.4 miles to a fork; then right 2.5 miles to a second fork; then right 2.1 miles to the camp. *See map page 174.*

Sweetwater Guard Station Campground

(BLM, Open all year)

About the camp – This camp, upstream from the Sweetwater Bridge Campground, is also along the Sweetwater River in Sweetwater Gap country in the foothills at the south end of the Wind River Range. Lodgepole pine shades the edges of a little basin with 10 sites, of which 5 are walk-ins off a short trail that follows the course of the river. All sites have fire rings with grates, but 3 of the five walk-in sites lack tables. The camp has a vault toilet, but no potable water. Stay limited to 14 days within any 28 day period.

Rates – Free

Getting there – Follow the directions above to Sweetwater Bridge Campground, but at the last fork go left 2.2 miles to the camp on the right. *See map below.*

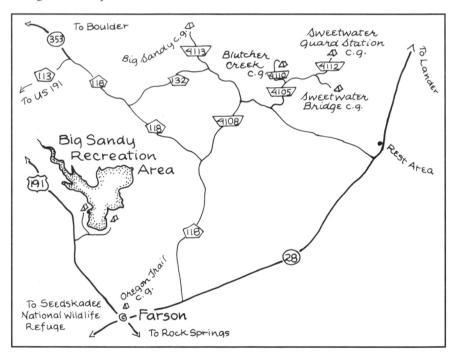

Blucher Creek (Dispersed)

(BLM, Open all year)

About the camp – This camp has numerous camping options in and at the edge of a mature stand of lodgepole pine overlooking a small mountain park. There are several well used stone fire rings along the tree line and a pit toilet located a short distance back in the trees. The camp is popular during hunting season. No potable water. Stay limited to 14 days within any 28 day period.

Rates – Free

Getting there – Turn off Hwy 28 about one mile southwest of the rest area near the Sweetwater River (*about 34 miles from Farson and about 44 miles from Lander*); then go northwest 15.1 miles on good dirt road to a turnoff to the right; then right 3.4 miles to a fork; then left 4.2 miles to another fork; then right .4 miles to the main camping area on the right (*off the last .4 miles of road, there are several other smaller dispersed areas that might appeal*). *See map facing page.*

Big Sandy Campground
(Bridger-Teton National Forest, Open June 20 to Sept. 10)

About the camp – This camp is situated at the trailhead for the Highline Trail which allows wilderness users to travel north to Green River Lakes, or access the East Fork, Washakie or Big Sandy Trails. The camp has a vault toilet and two loop roads with 12 sites that have tables and fire rings with grates. Horse handling facilities are near the camp. No potable water. Stay limited to 10 days.

Rates – Free

Getting there – Turn off Hwy 28 about one mile southwest of the rest area near the Sweetwater River (*about 34 miles from Farson and about 44 miles from Lander*); then go northwest 19.7 miles on good dirt road to a fork; then right 5.5 miles to another fork; then right 10.0 miles to the fork of FSR 859 and 850; then right .7 miles on FSR 850 to the camp. *See map facing page.*

Marbleton

The Lander Cutoff of the Oregon Trail crosses the highway just to the north of Marbleton, which has the only privately-owned camp with hookups or tenting in the area.

Harper's Park and RV
(Private, Open all year)

23 East 3rd St., Marbleton, WY 83113 Ph: (307) 276-3611

About the camp – This camp is open, level and just off the main drag (US 189) in Marbleton. There are 14 pull-thru (12x30) RV sites, all with full hookups (30 amp on city water). Sites are gravel with grass 'yards' and tables. Grass tent sites are available with some tables.

Amenities – Rest rooms and showers (showers only: $2.50), laundry; cable TV included, playground; dump station and pay phone.

Rates – Full hookups for 2 persons: $17. Tent sites for 2 persons: $10. Additional persons: $2.50 (only if using showers, otherwise no additional charge). No credit cards. Personal checks okay. Reservations: phone or mail.

Getting there – Take US 189 in downtown Marbleton to 3rd St.; then east 1/2 block to camp on right. *See map page 138.*

Pinedale

Pinedale has the Old-West look that appeals to many, as well as several lakes, the Bridger-Teton National Forest and panoramic views of the western slope of the Wind River Range. The Green River Lakes area, 45 miles north, offers spectacular views of **Square Top Mountain,** second only to the views of the Tetons in Wyoming. There is access here to the **Union Pass Road,** a gravel route going over the mountain to US 287 near Dubois. For history of the fur trapping era, Pinedale's **Museum of the Mountain Men,** at 700 E. Hennick St., Ph: (307) 367-4101, is open summers, Tues.-Sat. 9-5 and Sun. 1-5 ($). The second weekend in July marks the **Green River Rendezvous** with a host of related activities including rodeo, black powder shoots and historic demonstrations.

In town there is a private camp and the marina on Fremont Lake for RV hookups or tent camping, with 18 other primitive options in the area, and several are free. Groceries, hardware and sporting goods are available. **Nocora Inc.,** at 23 W. Pine, Ph: (307) 367-2206, which specializes in medical, first aid and safety packs and cases has an outlet store for their line of soft luggage and will custom design packs or cases for you or your company.

Pinedale Campground

(Private, Open May 1 to Oct. 31)
PO Box 246, Pinedale, WY 82941 Ph: (307) 367-4555

About the camp – This open, level camp is on the west end of Pinedale and just a long block off the main street (US 191). The camp has 38 gravel and paved RV sites with some tables: 12 pull-thrus (22x50), 26 back-ins (20x40) and 28 full hookups (20/30/50 amp on city water). 36 tent sites are available on grass with some tables and grills.

Amenities – Rest rooms and showers, laundry; cable TV, playground and pool table in laundry room; snacks, limited RV parts, dump station and pay phone.

Rates – Full hookups for two persons: $17.60. Water and electric only for 2 persons: $15.60. Electric only for 2 persons (2 sites only): $14. Tent sites for 2 persons: $11. Additional persons under age 16: $3. Age 16 and over: $4. V MC Reservations: phone or mail.

Getting there – From the east end of Pinedale on US 191 go west .7 miles through the center of town to Jackson St. (*at the Coast to Coast store*); then left, one long block, to the camp. *See map page 181.*

Lakeside Lodge Resort and Marina

(Private, Open May 15 to Oct. 15)
PO Box 1819, Pinedale, WY 82941 Ph: (307) 367-2221 Fax: (307) 367-6673 E-mail: lakesidelodge@wyoming.com Web site: www.lakesidelodge.com

About the camp – This camp is part of a marina complex on the south end of Fremont Lake. The camp offers 20 RV sites, some shaded, on native grass with tables. All sites are back-ins (up to 15x35). 10 sites are full hookups (20/30/50 amp) and 10 are electric only (20 amp). Tent sites are available on grass. *Horses okay: free with camping and own feed.*

Amenities – Rest rooms and showers (showers only: $3); restaurant, lounge, slip rentals, pontoon boat, fishing boat and canoe rentals, gas dock, dump station and pay phone.

Rates – Full hookups per site: $20. Water and electric per site: $18. Tent sites: $10. All major cards. Personal checks okay. Reservations: phone, E-mail, fax or mail.

Getting there – From the east end of Pinedale on US 191 take the Fremont Lake Road 2.8 miles, then left .2 miles to a fork; then left .4 miles to the marina on the right. *See map page 181.*

Lower Fremont Lake (Dispersed)

(Bridger-Teton National Forest, Open June 1 to Sept. 10)

About the camp – This camp is an undeveloped site on the south end of Fremont Lake and considered dispersed camping. Stay limited to 16 days.

Rates – Free

Getting there – From the east end of Pinedale on US 191 take the Fremont Lake Road 2.8 miles, then left .2 miles to a fork; then left .7 miles to a dirt road the goes straight as the main road bends to the right; then .2 miles to the camp. See map page 181.

Fremont Lake Campground

(Bridger-Teton National Forest, Open May 25 to Sept. 10)

About the camp – This large campground, on the east side of Wyoming's second largest natural lake, has a variety of camping options. The lower end of the area is primarily aspen forest, the middle range is mature conifers and several sites near the lake are more open, with light lakeside shrubbery. Interior roads are paved and there are more than a few pull-thrus. The camp has vault toilets, potable water, a boat ramp and 53 sites with tables and fire rings with grates. Stay limited to 10 days.

Rates – Campsite per night: $6. Rates half with Golden Age or Access Passport. (Reservations are possible at this campground up to 240 days in advance and 10 days prior to arrival. Service fee per reservation: $8.65. Ph: (877) 444-6777 toll free.)

Getting there – Use Fremont Lake Road off of US 191 on the east end of Pinedale; then 2.8 miles to a turnoff to the left; then left .1 miles to a fork; then right 3.2 miles to another fork; then left to the campground. *See map page 181.*

Half Moon Lake Campground

(Bridger-Teton National Forest, Open June 1 to Sept. 10)

About the camp – The camp is near a small beach area on the lake shore with somewhat private sites nestled in leafy greenery. Conifer-covered foothills rise above the lake on three sides with the fourth end opening into rolling sagebrush hills and aspen stands. The camp has vault toilets and 10 sites with tables and fire rings with grates, but no potable water. There is a boat ramp and trailer parking near this camp. Stay limited to 10 days.

Rates – Campsite per night: $4. Rates half with Golden Age or Access Passport.

Getting there – Use Fremont Lake Road off US 191 on the east end of Pinedale; then go 6.6 miles to FSR 743 where a sign marks the route to Half Moon Lake Resort; then right 1.2 miles on FSR 743 to the camp turnoff to the right. The boat ramp and trailer parking is also on the right, a short distance beyond the turnoff to the camp. *See map page 181.*

Trails End Campground

(Bridger-Teton National Forest, Open June 25 to Sept. 10)

About the camp – The road is paved all the way to this camp and the trailheads into the Bridger-Teton Wilderness. The camp is situated near parking areas for several wilderness trails and the Elkhart Park Guard Station. The road at the camp forks, with more secluded sites 6-8 on the right in a stand of lodgepole pine, and camps 1-5 closer to the sometimes busy parking area for Pine Creek Trail. The camp has vault toilets, potable water and all sites have tables and fire rings with grates. Stay limited to 10 days.

Rates – Campsite per night: $7. Rates half with Golden Age or Access Passport.

Getting there – Use Fremont Lake Road which turns off of US 191 on the east end of Pinedale; then go 11.5 miles on this paved road to the camp. *See map page 181.*

Worth mentioning – Even if you're not planning to camp here, this is a short drive that offers great views of the valley and lakes around Pinedale and a prominent section the Wind River Range.

Upper Fremont Lake Campground
(Bridger-Teton National Forest, Open June 1 to Sept. 10)

About the camp – This small campground on the upper end of Fremont Lake has only one table, one fire ring and a dock, and is only accessible by boat or trail. Most users here arrive by boat as the trail from Elkhart Park is steep and about two miles long. This camp is near the wilderness boundary and could offer solitude if that's your quest. If the single site is occupied dispersed camping is available in the area of this camp. No potable water. Stay limited to 10 days.

Rates – Free

Getting there – If going there by boat or trail, get directions at the Lakeside Marina or the Forest Service Office. *See map page 181.*

—North and West from Pinedale—

Soda Lake Wildlife Habitat Management Area
(Wyoming Game and Fish, Open May 1 to Nov. 15)

About the camp – This 3,786-acre wildlife habitat area was established in 1948 as one in a series of elk feedgrounds to provide winter forage and reduce damage to private haystacks. The area, bordered by the foothills on the western slope of the Wind River Range, is rolling sagebrush grasslands, meadows, aspen, shrubs and native plants. The management area and adjacent public lands provide feed for elk and a variety of other wildlife species. You may see elk, moose, mule deer, black bears, coyote, sage grouse, an assortment of waterfowl and many various small mammals and song birds.

Soda Lake and 370 acres of adjoining wetlands are a significant addition to the habitat diversity of the area. Just north of the lake is a developed wetlands area and viewing blind where one can watch the waterfowl using the area.

There are many camping options around Soda Lake, all with spectacular views of Fremont Peak and a portion of the Wind River Range. Camping in the area is primitive, with only scattered stone fire rings, 4 vault toilets sited around the lake and a primitive boat ramp. No potable water. Stay limited to 14 days.

Rates – Free

Getting there – From the Fremont Lake Road intersection at the east end of Pinedale on US 191 go west .7 miles on US 191 through the center of town to Jackson St. (*at the Coast to Coast store*); then right 5.2 miles to the Soda Lake area information board. *See map page 181.*

Worth mentioning – If you go up the west side of the lake, you will encounter a two-track that goes to a blind at the Soda Lake Wetlands Wildlife Viewing Area. Constructed in 1998, with three islands used primarily by nesting ducks and geese, the wetlands attracts a variety of waterfowl and shore birds, as well as osprey, non-game birds, mule deer, moose and coyote.

Willow Lake Campground

(Bridger-Teton National Forest, Open June 1 to Oct. 1)

About the camp – All camps at Willow Lake are near the shore and in at least a couple of cases there is the opportunity to pitch a tent right on the water's edge. There are only 6 camps sites here: 5 are on the main loop with a pit toilet, and a single camp is on the other side of the boat ramp/trailer parking area, with a vault toilet a little further up the road, but no potable water. All sites have tables and fire rings with grates. Stay limited to 10 days.

Rates – Campsite per night: $4. Rates half with Golden Age or Access Passport.

Getting there – From the Fremont Lake Road intersection at the east end of Pinedale on US 191 go west .7 miles on US 191 through the center of town to Jackson St. (*at the Coast to Coast store*); then right 10.9 miles to the camp. *See map facing page.*

New Fork Lake Campground

(Bridger-Teton National Forest, Open June 1 to Sept. 10)

About the camp – The camp is on a loop road in an aspen stand on a slight rise above the lake. There is a primitive boat launch and lake access by foot. The camp has vault toilets, potable water and 15 sites with tables and fire rings with grates. Stay limited to 10 days.

Rates – Campsite per night: $4. Rates half with Golden Age or Access Passport.

Getting there – From the junction of Hwy 352 and US 191 go north 14.5 miles on Hwy 352 to New Fork Lake Road; then right 3.3 miles on a good gravel road that provides nice views of the Wind River Range; then right .1 miles to camp entrance on left. *See map facing page.*

Narrows Campground

(Bridger-Teton National Forest, Open June 1 to Sept. 10)

About the camp – The camp is on a rise above the lake in an aspen stand with horse corrals and wilderness parking for the New Fork trailhead. The camp has vault toilets, potable water and 19 sites with tables and fire rings with grates. There is a boat ramp and trailer parking off the road, 1.2 miles before reaching this camp. Stay limited to 10 days.

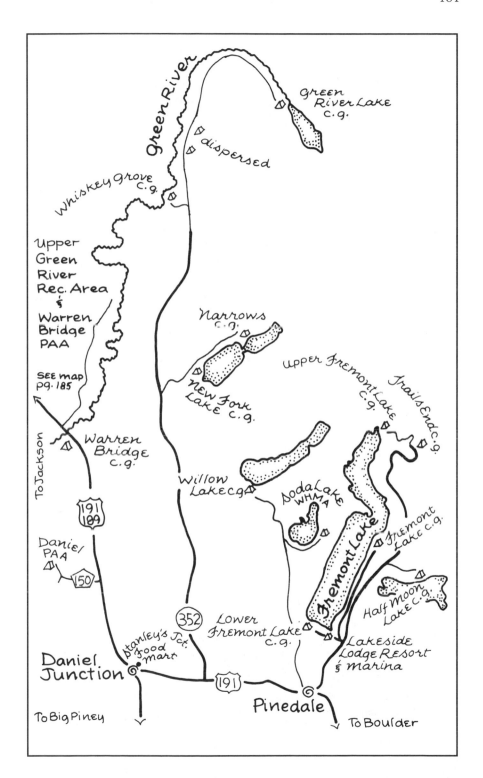

Green River

Green River Lake C.g.

dispersed

Whiskey Grove C.g.

Upper Green River Rec. Area § Warren Bridge PAA

SEE map pg. 185

To Jackson

Warren Bridge C.g.

Narrows C.g.

New Fork Lake C.g.

Upper Fremont Lake C.g.

Trails End c.g.

191 189

Daniel PAA

50

Willow Lake c.g.

Soda Lake WHMA

Fremont Lake

Fremont Lake c.g.

352

Lower Fremont Lake C.g.

Half Moon Lake c.g.

Daniel Junction

Stanley's Jct. Food Mart

191

Lakeside Lodge Resort § Marina

Pinedale

To Big Piney

To Boulder

Rates – Campsite per night: $5. Rates half with Golden Age or Access Passport. (Reservations are possible at this campground up to 240 days in advance and 10 days prior to arrival. Service fee per reservation: $8.65. (877) 444-6777).

Getting there – From the junction of Hwy 352 and US 191, take Hwy 352 north 14.5 miles to New Fork Lake Road; then right 6 miles on a good gravel road that provides nice views of the Wind River Range. *See map page 181.*

Whiskey Grove Campground
(Bridger-Teton National Forest, Open June 15 to Sept. 10)

About the camp – Driving in to this camp, all you see are the tree tops; the camp is below a bench, on the flood plain along a meander of the Green River. While this camp is small, sites are roomy with good tenting options. The camp has a vault toilet, potable water and 9 sites with tables and fire rings with grates. Stay limited to 10 days.

Rates – Campsite per night: $4. Rates half with Golden Age or Access Passport.

Getting there – From the junction of Hwy 352 and US 191 go north 28.8 miles on Hwy 352 (*the first 11 miles are paved*) to the camp turnoff on the left; then left .4 miles to the camp. *See map page 181.*

Dollar Lake (Dispersed)
(Bridger-Teton National Forest, Open all year)

About the camp – This dispersed camping area has been in use for years and a 16 day limit is posted by the Forest Service. In the trees, on the east side of the road there are several primitive sites marked with stone fire rings, but no toilet or potable water.

Rates – Free

Getting there – From the junction of Hwy 352 and US 191 go north 29.9 miles on Hwy 352 (*the first 11 miles are paved*) to the turnoff on the right; then right .1 miles to the trees and pick a spot. *See map page 181.*

Green River Lake Campground
(Bridger-Teton National Forest, Open June 15 to Sept. 10)

About the camp – The camp is on a rise over the lower Green River Lake in mixed forest that is largely lodgepole pine. Camps are roomy with good options for tenters. There are 39 sites, with 4 pull-thrus and 3 walk-ins (A, B & C) that have a common parking area. Of these, site A gets the early morning sunlight and is closest to the lakeside trail, which takes off from the main camp behind site 11. All sites have tables and fire rings with grates. There is a roadway to the lake and a primitive boat/canoe launching area. The camp also has trailhead parking for backpackers and corrals for horse packers. There are three group sites with parking, grills, tables and a fire pit. Two are rated for 35 people while the last one can accommodate 75. Stay limited to 10 days.

Rates – Campsite per night: $7. Group sites: $25. Rates half with Golden Age or Access Passport. (Reservations are possible at this campground up to 240 days in advance and 10 days prior to arrival. Service fee per reservation: $8.65. (877) 444-6777).

Getting there – From the junction of Hwy 352 and US 191 go north 40 miles on Hwy 352 (*the first 11 miles are paved*) to the camp. Allow plenty of time; this dirt road gets lots of use and little maintenance. *See map page 181.*

Worth mentioning – The wilderness boundary crosses the lower Green River Lake, which is encircled by an easy hiking trail. This trail merges with other trails heading into the wilderness or to the upper lake. Looming above Green River Lakes is Square Top Mountain, second only to the Tetons for its dramatic beauty.

Stanley's Junction Food Mart

(Private, Open all year)

About the camp – This establishment offers free overnight RV or truck parking on gravel near the store, gas station and deli.

Rates – Free

Getting there – It's at the junction of US 189 and 191 west of Pinedale. *See map page 181.*

Daniel Public Access Area

(Wyoming Game and Fish, Open all year)

About the camp – This parking/camping area is along the banks of the Green River with access for fishing, waterfowl hunting, bird watching and photography. The camp has a gravel and native grass area with a pit toilet and some stone fire rings, but no potable water. Stay limited to 5 days.

Rates – Free

Getting there – From the junction of US 189 and 191 at Daniel go north 3.6 miles on US 191/189 to the turnoff on the left (Sublette County 23-150); then left 2.4 miles to a fork; then right 1.4 miles to the camp on the left. *See map page 181.*

Warren Bridge Campground
(BLM, Open all year)

About the camp – This camp is in an open area of gravel and native grass near the banks of the Green River. There are 16 sites with large pull-thrus, tables with fire pits and grates and grills. Water hydrants have hose bibs for filling holding tanks, and well water is tested every 30 days. Free day use area with 9 tables and grills. Fishing is reportedly good along the river and there is a nice view of the western slope of the Wind River Range. Dump station is free with camping fee (dump station use only: $3.) Stay limited to 16 days in any 28 day period.

Rates – Campsite per night: $6. Rates half with Golden Age or Access Passport.

Getting there – From Daniel and the junction of Hwy 354 and US 191/189 go north 9.5 miles on US 191/189 to the camp on the left, just before the bridge over the Green River. *See map page 181.*

Warren Bridge Public Access Area
and
Upper Green River Recreation Area
(Wyoming Game and Fish and BLM, Open all year)

About the camp – This access area, a cooperative effort between the Wyoming Game and Fish Department and the U. S. Bureau of Land Management, provides access to 12 riverside camping and fishing options all accessed from an 8.6 mile-long road on the west side of the Green River. There are 13 different two-tracks off this gravel road, the longest .5 miles to a camp by the river.

There are no less than three warning signs banning trailers because the roads are considered steep. However, if you can get your boat, canoe or raft on top of your vehicle this might be an excellent opportunity to float, as well as fish. There are no designated or developed boat ramps at these sites, but it should be fairly easy to carry a small boat or canoe in and out. No potable water. Stay limited to 14 days in any 28 day period.

Rates – Free

Getting there – From Daniel and the junction of Hwy 354 and US 191/189 go north 9.7 miles on US 191/189 to the Green River and the turnoff to the right (Warren Bridge Road/BLM # 5201); then right and choose your two-track to the river. *See map page 185.* Two-track roads to the river are all to the right and are as follows:

(1) .3 miles from pavement — this goes to the river, but there are no facilities and a small turn around. Not recommended.

(2) 1 mile from pavement go to the right as the main road turns to the left; then .3 miles to the river and a nice park with river-bank greenery, two tables, fire rings and a pit toilet.

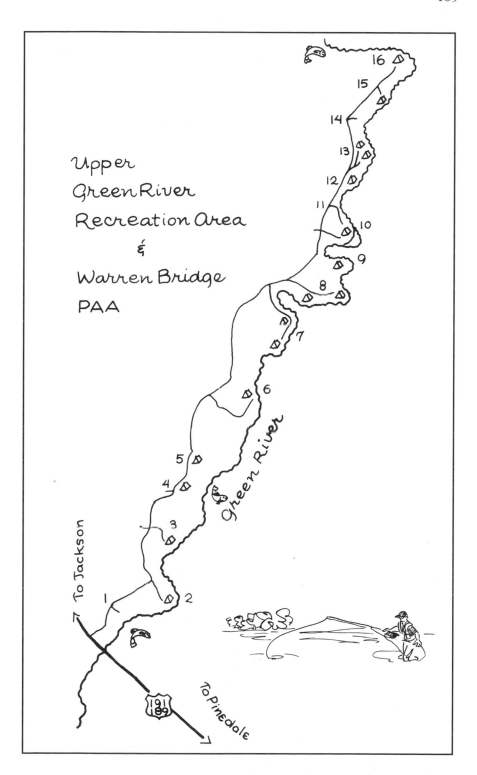

Upper
Green River
Recreation Area
&
Warren Bridge
PAA

Green River

To Jackson

To Pinedale

191
89

(3) 1.6 miles from pavement go right .4 miles to a nice green and level park with a few Engelmann spruce on the banks and aspen stands behind the camp (*these are the only trees at any of these camps*). There are two tables, fire rings and a pit toilet.

(4) 2.3 miles from pavement go right .1 miles to a parking area on a bluff with a fair hike to the river below.

(5) 2.5 miles from the pavement go to the right .2 miles to a parking area and a mile-long hike to the river below.

(6) 3.5 miles from pavement go right .5 miles to the river and a nice level grassy park with a table, fire ring and a pit toilet.

(7) 5 miles from pavement go right .4 miles to the river and a nice level grassy park with a table, fire ring and a pit toilet; *[or]* continue on another .4 miles through this camp and you will come to another nice level grassy park with a table, fire ring and a pit toilet.

(8) 5.1 miles from pavement go right .3 miles to the river and a nice level grassy park with a table, fire ring and a pit toilet; *[or]* continue on another .3 miles through this camp and you will come to another nice level grassy park with a table, fire ring and a pit toilet.

(9) 5.4 miles from pavement go right .4 miles to the river and a nice level grassy undeveloped park.

(10) 5.7 miles from pavement go right .3 miles to the river and a nice level grassy park with a table, fire ring and a pit toilet.

(11) 5.9 miles from pavement go right .4 miles to the river and to the same site as 10.

(12) 6.1 miles from pavement go right .1 miles to the river and a nice level grassy park with a table, fire ring and a pit toilet.

(13) 6.5 miles from pavement go right .2 miles to a fork in the road; then .1 miles on either fork to a nice level grassy park with a table, fire ring and a pit toilet.

(14) 7.4 miles from pavement go right following a fence line for .1 miles to the river and a tight turnaround on a hillside with no improvements.

(15) 7.7 miles from pavement take a hard right .1 miles to the river and a nice level grassy park with a table, fire ring and a pit toilet.

(16) 8.6 miles from pavement is the end of the road; there is plenty of room to turn around and another nice level grassy park with a table, fire ring and a pit toilet. *See map page 185.*

—East of Pinedale—

Half Moon Wildlife Habitat Management Area
(Wyoming Game and Fish, Open May 1 to Oct. 31)

About the camp – This wildlife management area is about 6 miles southeast of Pinedale and provides quality winter range for as many as 700 elk and a substantial population of mule deer. The area is sagebrush grasslands with conifer forests on the flanks of Half Moon Mountain, which rises 800' in elevation in less than one mile and is one of the most striking features in this area.

In addition to elk and mule deer, the area provides habitat for pronghorn antelope, moose, sage grouse, rabbits, coyotes and many songbirds. Pole Creek, where there are brook and brown trout, runs through the area. These lands offer a variety of recreational opportunities, including wildlife viewing, photography, fishing and access to adjacent Forest Service lands.

The directions take you to one primitive camping area on the tree-lined banks of Pole Creek where there is a stone fire ring. No toilet, tables or potable water. Stay limited to 14 days.

Rates – Free

Getting there – From the Fremont Lake Road intersection and US 191 on the south end of Pinedale go south .8 miles on US 191 to a left-hand turnoff; then left 5.1 miles (*the pavement ends after 4.8 miles*) to a fork in the road; then left .9 miles and left through a cattle guard; then 1.5 miles to a fork and game and fish sign; then right 2.2 miles to a two track on the right; then right .1 miles and right again following this road .6 miles to the campsite on Pole Creek. *See map page 140.*

Rock Springs

Rock Springs has a colorful, freewheeling history punctuated by diverse ethnic immigration, from Chinese coal miners to Basque sheepmen. The city is still considered the melting-pot of Wyoming. The **Rock Springs Historical Museum,** at 201 B St., Ph: (307) 362-3138, highlights the history and ethnic diversity of the area with maps for a self-guided walking tour. **Western Wyoming Community College,** at 2500 College Drive, Ph: (307) 382-1600, houses a premier dinosaur display, with life-size replica skeletons and more. In late July or early August, Rock Springs hosts the **Red Desert Round Up,** the second largest rodeo in Wyoming. The **Sweetwater County Fair** takes place in early August and in late August they kick up their heels at the **Great Wyoming Polka and Heritage Festival.**

In town there is only one camping option, a privately-owned KOA. In the area are a free undeveloped BLM camp at the sand dunes ORV area to the north, a free developed BLM camp on Aspen Mountain to the southeast, and Firehole Canyon Campground in the Flaming Gorge National Recreation Area to the southwest. There is a BLM office, at 280 US 191, Ph: 352-0256, for maps and information. Groceries, sporting goods and hardware are available. For workouts, indoor track, steam, spa, pool and showers, the **Rock Springs Family Recreation Center,** at 3900 Sweetwater Drive, Ph: (307) 352-1440, is open to the public (Day pass for adults: $3.75; youth age 6-18: $2; seniors +62: $1.25, and age 5 and under free). The city also operates a free swimming pool in the summer, at 1035 Jackson St. behind the YWCA, Ph: (307) 352-1421.

Rock Springs KOA

(Private, Open April 1 to Oct. 15)
(PO Box 2910) 86 Foothill Blvd., Rock Springs, WY 82902
Ph: (307) 362-3063 or (800) KOA-8699

About the camp – This roomy 12-acre camp, located on the west end of Rock Springs, is open, level and an easy in and easy out. There are 116 gravel pull-thrus (up to 25x60) RV sites with tables: 77 full hookups (30/50 Amp) and 39 water and electric only. The camp also has 10 designated tent sites on pea gravel with grills and tables as well as 6 Kamper Kabins. *Horses okay: free corrals with camping and own feed.*

Amenities – Rest rooms and showers (showers only $5.), laundry; cable TV (available at 30 sites: $2.50), game room, playground, heated pool and spa; limited groceries and RV parts, gift shop, modem jack in office, dump station, propane and pay phone.

Rates – Full hookups for 2 persons: $22. Electric and water for 2 persons: $20. Tent sites for 2 persons: $17. Kamper Kabins: $32. Additional persons: $3. Discounts for KOA Value Kard. MC D Reservations: phone or mail.

Getting there – From I-80 use exit 99; then go north following the paved service drive as it bends to the east on the north side of the interstate; then 1.3 miles to the camp on the left. *See map facing page.*

Firehole Campground

(Flaming Gorge National Recreation Area, Open May 1 to Oct. 31)

About the camp – This camp has a beach area, a boat ramp and trailer parking, rest rooms with sinks and flush toilets and showers. The camps here are a little different and something like a duplex in nature. Each of 40 camps has its own table and fire ring, but shares a parking spur and shelter over the tables. These are nice, fully-roofed shelters with a divider in the center and a table on each side. There is sufficient level area near each camp for tenting. Stay limited to 14 days.

Rates – Campsite per night: $12.00. Half with golden Age or Access Passports. (Reservations are possible at this campground up to 240 days in advance and 10 days prior to arrival. Service fee per reservation: $8.65. Ph: (877) 444-6777 toll free.) There are also fees for using the National Recreation Area. (1 day: $2. 16 days: $5. Annual pass: $20.)

Getting there – From I-80 use exit 99 west of Rock Springs; then south 13.8 miles on US 191 South to the Firehole Canyon turnoff on the right (CR 33); then right 10 miles to the camp on the right. *See map Page 157.*

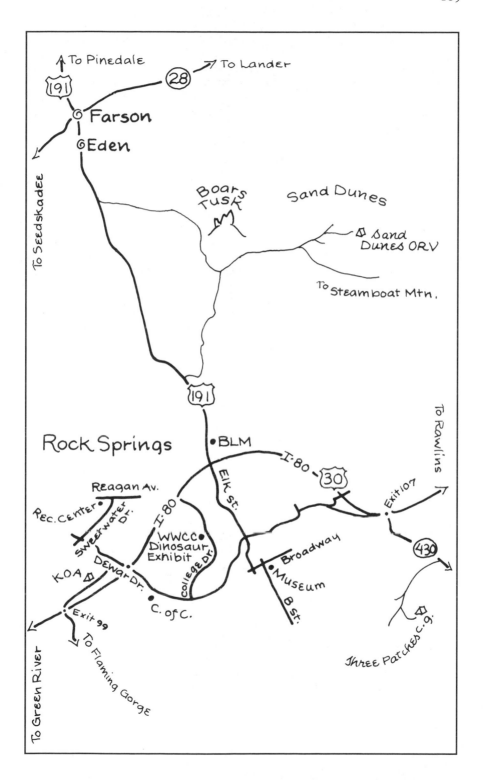

Worth mentioning – All roads to this camp are paved and the views are excellent. From Rock Springs south the bench lands of this high plains country make up the view, but once you turn toward Firehole Canyon, you will be driving through small canyons with rock walls, scrub brush and sagebrush. Chimney Rock, which comes into view here and there along the way, and other interesting formations highlight the view from this camp.

Three Patches Campground

(BLM, Open all year)

About the camp – This camp, located in an aspen stand on Aspen Mountain about 17 miles south of Rock Springs, is a local favorite. The area is fenced, with a perimeter road, making all of the sites walk-ins. Signs may suggest that this site is designated for picnicking but, camping is allowed and encouraged. The camp has several tables, fire rings with grates and two vault toilets, but no potable water. For a more secluded camp, there is a road to an undeveloped area in a stand of aspens to the front and left of this camp. Stay limited to 14 days in any 28 period.

Rates – Free

Getting there – From I-80 use exit 107; then follow Pilot Butte Ave. west to first stop light and the junction of Hwy 376 (*to 430*); then left 1.9 miles to the Hwy 430 access on the left; then left .1 miles to the stop sign at Hwy 430; then right 4.3 miles to CR 27 on the right (*across from a fertilizer plant*); then right 6.6 miles to the fork of CR 27 and CR 31; then left 3 miles on CR 27 to the junction of Radar Tower Road; then right 1.7 miles where County 27 bears right and a lesser road goes to the left: then .7 miles on this lesser road to the camp. *See map page 189.*

Sand Dunes ORV Area

(BLM, Open all year)

About the camp – This camp, located where the roads end and the sand begins, is on the western end of the Killpecker Dunes that stretch 55 miles across the Red Desert and the Great Divide Basin. Camping is a fringe benefit at this area, designated for off road vehicle use, and popular with quad runners and sand railers. The camp has a vault toilet but no potable water.

The area is habitat for pronghorn antelope, deer, elk, golden eagles, and a variety of smaller birds and small mammals. The parking area is your spot if you're staying in a hardsided unit, but if you're tenting, sand, sagebrush and native grasses are in abundance. Stay limited to 14 days in any 28 period.

Rates – Free

Getting there – From Rock Springs and I-80 (exit 104) at Elk St. go north about 9 miles to CR 17, then right 15.1 miles to a fork; then right 5.6 miles, where you take the left fork off the main road (*which bends to the right*); then .6 miles, where you take the left fork; then another .6 miles where you take the right fork; then .9 miles to the camp.

From Farson go south 7.9 miles on US 191 to the turnoff on the left, then 2.2 miles to a fork with a two-track to the right, where you stay left; then 13.6 miles past Boar's Tusk to a fork; then left 5.6 miles where you take the left fork off the main road (*which bends to the right*); then .6 miles where you take the left fork; then another .6 miles where you take the right fork; then .9 miles to the camp. *See map page 189.*

Thayne

Thayne is best known for the **Star Valley Cheese Factory.** You can watch cheese being made through a window, and it's a good place to stock up on dairy products, grab a sandwich or sample their excellent pies.

A privately-owned camp, a RV resort (with tenting) and a free Game and Fish access area are in the neighborhood. Groceries and limited hardware and sporting goods are available in the area.

Star Valley Ranch Resorts
(Private, Open May 15 to Oct. 15)
(PO Box 635) 3522 Muddy String Rd., Thayne, WY 83127 Ph: (307) 883-2670

About the camp – This camp has 50 overnight RV sites and 14 designated tent sites. The RV sites are pull-thrus and back-ins (up to 20x120) with full hookups (30/50amp). Sites have gravel parking areas with grass 'yards' and tables. Tent sites are grass with tables and some fire pits with grates.

Amenities – Rest rooms, showers, laundry; club house, playground, two heated outdoor pools, saunas and spas, 18-hole golf course; restaurant (breakfast and lunch only: closes 2 p.m.), dump station, limited groceries and RV parts and pay phones.

Rates – Full hookups per site: $20. Tents per site: $9. MC V Reservations: phone or mail.

Getting there – Southbound on US 89 turn left on CR 118, about 1 mile south of the junction of Hwy 239 and US 89; then east 2 miles on CR 118 to the camp office.

Northbound on US 89 turn right on CR 118 about 3.5 miles north of downtown Thayne; then east 2 miles on CR 118 to the camp office. *See map page 131.*

Flat Creek Cabins and RV Park

(Private, Open all year)
PO 239, Thayne, WY 83127 Ph: (307) 883-2231

About the camp – This camp is on the south end of Thayne with 23 RV sites on gravel and native grass. All sites are back-ins (30x50) with full hookups (20/30/50 amp). Grass tent sites are available. *Horses okay.*

Amenities – Rest rooms and showers (showers only: $3), laundry; pay phone.

Rates – Full hookups for 2 persons: $18. Tent sites for 2 persons: $12. Additional adults: $2. Reservations by phone or mail.

Getting there – This camp is along US 189 on the south edge of Thayne. *See map page 131.*

Upper Salt River Public Access Area

(Wyoming Game and Fish, Open all year)

About the camp – This access area is gravel and native grass with some of the area suitable for tenting. The area is large and scenic with conifer-covered hillsides on the far side of the river. There are four tables with stone fire rings and one of the sites is especially nice, on a slight rise in some aspen trees. The camp has a vault toilet, but no potable water. Stay limited to 5 days.

Rates – Free

Getting there – From south of Thayne, at mile marker 99 on US 89 go south 2.1 miles to a turnoff on the right (*about .2 miles south of a highway rest area and directly across from CR 126*); then right .3 miles to the river and the camp. *See map page 131.*

<u>NOTES</u>

<u>NOTES</u>

Contents — Northeast

Northeast Wyoming

Wyoming's northeast corner lies outside the snug circle of the State's primary settlements and transportation routes, but it was attractive enough to lure aliens for a cinematic Close Encounter, and terrestrial visitors might want to get closer, too. First, there is the stirring volcanic monolith of Devils Tower, then there are the pine-clad foothills of the Black Hills along the east border, and finally there is Gillette. This prosperous city can be hard to reach during howling winters on the plains, but it's a shiny penny, a perpetual boom town set amidst the rolling pasture-lands and gigantic strip mines of the Powder River Basin.

The northeast section of Wyoming includes privately-owned, developed and undeveloped primitive camping options at or near the Black Hills National Forest, Devils Tower National Monument, Keyhole State Park and Thunder Basin National Grassland. A total of 23 camps are listed under headings for 7 cities and towns including Beulah, Devils Tower, Gillette, Moorcroft, Newcastle, Upton and Sundance.

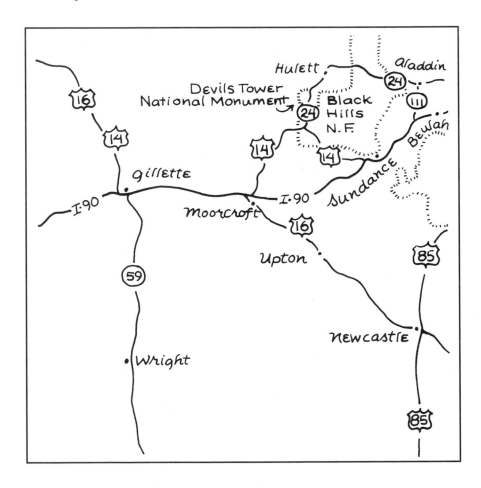

Beulah

Beulah is a popular stop for bikers on the way to and from the annual motorcycle rally at Sturgis, South Dakota in early August. Expect full camps from the end of July to mid-August. In Beulah there is a privately-owned camp for tents and RVs and 2 miles south of town there is free camping at a Wyoming Game and Fish Public Access Area along Sand Creek. At I-90 there is a service station and C-store, and in Beulah a trading post with basic groceries.

Sand Creek Campground
(Private, Open April 15 to Oct. 15)
(PO Box 333) 5879 Old Highway 14, Beulah, WY 82712 Ph: (307) 643-2277 or (888) BEULAHW (238-5249) E-mail: fun@beulah.com Web site: http://www.beulah.com

About the camp – This camp is in Beulah just off I-90 near the eastern border of Wyoming in the Black Hills. The area is a popular stopover for bikers going to and from the Sturgis Motorcycle Rally: expect the camp to be full and the rates higher from late July to mid-August. The 2 camping areas are just west of the Sand Creek Trading Post, which is the office and check-in for campers. The north area has 15 sites: five sites are pull-thrus, all have water and electric hookups (20/30 amp) with some tables. The south area is for tents only, with some tables.

Amenities – Porta-potties, shower house at north camp (showers only: $3); limited groceries, free coffee and pay phones at trading post.

Rates – North area, water and electric per site: $15. Water only per site: $10. South area tents only, per person: $5.

Getting there – Use I-90 exit 205 at Beulah; then north to the stop sign on Old Highway 14; then left .3 miles to registration at the Sand Creek Trading Post on the right. The camps are .2 miles past the trading post. *See map page 212.*

Sand Creek Public Access Area
(Wyoming Game & Fish, Open April 1 to Nov. 1)

About the camp – This camp is south of Beulah on Sand Creek, near the eastern border of Wyoming. All sites are undeveloped. There are numerous stone fire pits from previous generations of campers, but no tables, wood, or potable water. One vault toilet is centrally located within a mile-long stretch of excellent camping options in the greenery along this creek. Stay limited to 5 days.

Rates – Free

Getting there – Use I-90 exit 205 at Beulah; then go south 2 miles on this good gravel road; then for about the next mile take any of about six two-tracks on the right leading to campsites along Sand Creek. *See map page 212.*

Devils Tower

This national monument is a favorite with climbers and considered a site of religious significance to Native Americans. The landmark was formed as molten lava cooled about 50 million years ago and softer earth around it eroded away over thousands of years. Indian legend has it that seven Indian maidens, threatened by a bear, climbed onto a tree stump, which was clawed by the bear as it rose into the heavens, accounting for the deep vertical gouges on its flanks. Having foiled the bear, the maidens remained in the heavens as the stars of Ursa Major, the "Big Dipper." If you notice people lying around in the grass with cameras, they are likely trying to snap portraits of one or more of the prairie dogs that populate a large protected 'prairie-dog town' near the road about a half-mile from the entrance.

At the parking area near the base of the monument is a Visitors Center and the trailhead for the mile-long Tower Trail, a paved path circling the base of the monument. Dirt trails include the three-mile Red Beds/South Side Trail for a longer loop around the tower, or the one-and-one-half mile Joyner Ridge Trail, with hilltop views offering a different perspective of the area. For the record book, the monolith is the tallest formation of this kind in the United States, at 867 feet from the base. At Devils Tower there are two privately-owned camps and the National Park Service campground. Basic groceries, snacks and ice are available.

Devils Tower KOA

(Private, Open May 10 to Sept. 30)
PO Box 100, Devils Tower, WY 82714 Ph: (307) 467-5395 or (800) KOA-5785 E-mail: dtkoa@trib.com

About the camp – This grassy 25-acre camp, located near the entrance to Devils Tower National Monument, has oak trees bordering on the west and north and the Belle Fourche River along its north edge. The camp has 45 RV sites with tables, some with gravel and grass 'yards' and some all gravel. There are 17 full hookups (30amp/50 amp at 4 sites). 25 sites are pull-thrus (up to 15x50) with back-ins (up to 15x40). Within the sprawling grass areas of this camp there are 80 undesignated tent sites, with tables and grills. *Horses okay.*

Amenities – Rest rooms and showers, laundry (two locations); game room, playground, heated outdoor pool and nightly outdoor showings of the movie, *Close Encounters of the Third Kind* (summer); restaurant, limited RV parts, two gift shops, dump station and pay phone. Summer hay rides and trail rides are available.

Rates – Full hookups for 2 persons: $23.75. Electric and water for 2 persons: $21. Tent sites for 2 persons: $18. 7 Kamping Kabins for 2 persons: $35. Additional persons 17 and under: $2.50, over 17: $3.50. V MC D Reservations: phone, E-mail or mail. AAA rates same, but for 4 persons plus extras.

Getting there – From Devils Tower Junction (*Hwys 24/110*) go east 1.5 miles on Hwy 110 to the camp on the right. *See map page 212.*

Fort Devil's Tower Campground

(Private, open April 15 to Oct. 31)

601 Hwy 24, Devils Tower, WY 82714 Ph: (307) 467-5655

About the camp – This camp is open and in sight of Devils Tower. The camp has 12 gravel and native grass RV sites with some tables and some fire rings: all full hookups (20/30/50 amp) and all back-ins (up to 20x40). 25 tent sites are on native grass with some tables and some fire rings.

Amenities – Rest rooms and showers($) (showers only: $4); limited groceries, propane and pay phone.

Rates – Full hookups for 2 persons: $14.95. Tent sites for 2 persons: $12. Additional persons: $2. V MC D Personal checks okay. Reservations: phone or mail.

Getting there – From Devils Tower Junction (*Hwys 24/110*) the camp is .1 miles east on Hwy 24. *See map page 212.*

Devils Tower National Monument

(National Park Service, Open May 1 to Oct. 1)

About the camp – Devils Tower has a National Park Service campground with 50 sites. All sites are gravel with tables and grills. Rest rooms have flush toilets and cold water to the sinks. Stay limited to 14 days.

Rates – Campsites per night: $12.

Getting there – From the entrance follow the road past the prairie dog town to a left hand turn at the administration building; then left .1 miles to a fork; then left to the camp. *See map page 212.*

Gillette

The ranching community here has enjoyed prosperity in coal and oil discoveries. Gillette, the self-proclaimed "energy capital of the nation," pumps 25 million barrels of crude oil annually and has numerous open pit mines in the area which account for 90 per cent of Wyoming's coal production. Tours can be scheduled at several of the area coal mines through the **Gillette Convention and Visitors Bureau**, at 1810-A South Douglas Hwy, Ph: (800) 544-6136 or (307) 686-0040. **Gillette's Cam-Plex** is one of the world's largest multipurpose events facilities, hosting everything from conventions and concerts to the National High School Finals Rodeo, on Garner Lake Road, Ph: (307) 682-8802. Near the Cam-Plex is the **High Plains Energy and Technology Center**, displaying vintage mining and earth moving equipment. Just west of downtown, at 900 W. Second St., Ph: (307) 682-5723, is the **Campbell County Rockpile Museum.** For less earthy pursuits, the Campbell County School District has a **Planetarium**, at 1000 Lakeview, Ph: (307) 682-2225, with free public events. Gillette hosts the **Campbell County Fair** in early August and the **Annual Cat Show and Judging** in early September.

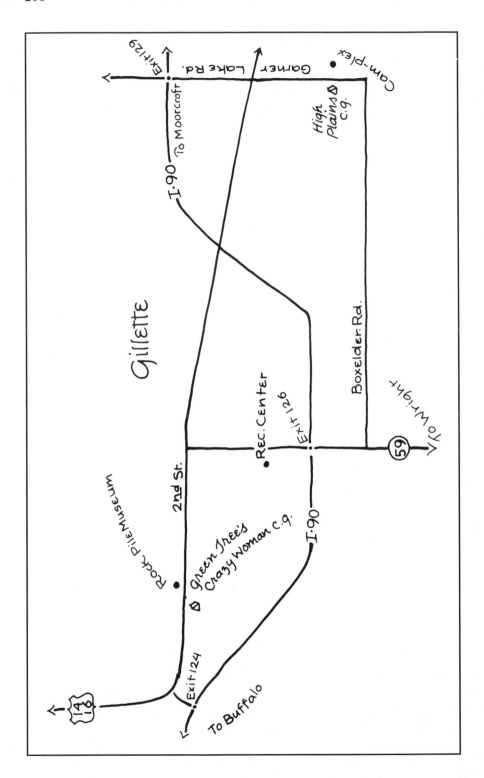

In town there are two fairly large privately-owned camps. Groceries, hardware and sporting goods are available. Gillette also has a bicycle shop and RV sales and service. For workouts, swims, saunas and showers, and, in summer, an outdoor water slide, the **Campbell County Recreation Center**, at 1000 S. Douglas Hwy, Ph: (307) 682-5470, is open daily (Day pass for adults: $2.50; children: $1.50-$1.00, family: $5.00 and seniors +62 free).

Green Tree's Crazy Woman Campground
(Private, Open April 15 to Oct.)
1001 West 2nd St., Gillette, WY 82718 Ph: (307) 682-3665 Fax: (307) 682-3750 E-mail: crazywoman@newwaveis.com

About the camp – This camp, just off the main drag on the west end of Gillette, is nicely landscaped with lots of shade. The camp has 93 RV sites: 23 pull-thrus (25x60) and 70 pull-ins (25x35). Some parking spurs are paved, most are gravel and sites have grass 'yards' with tables and grills. 48 sites are full hookups (20/30/50 amp on city water). 40 sites are water and electric only. There are 16 designated tent sites with tables and some grills plus a grassy area for additional tenting. The camp also offers lodging in 2 motor homes, 1 tent trailer, 6 tents and 4 fully furnished trailers. *Horses okay.*

Amenities – Rest rooms and showers (showers only: $3; with towel and soap: $5), laundry; video games room with pool table and TV, pool and spa, playground; gift shop, limited groceries and RV parts, modem jack in office, dump station and pay phone.

Rates – Full hookups for 2 persons: $19-30. Water and Electric only for 2 persons: $19-30. Tents for 2 persons: $16-25. Additional persons 18 and over: $2. Under 18: $1. V MC Reservations: phone, E-mail or mail.

Getting there – From I-90 exit 124, go about .2 miles north to the traffic light on Business I-90/US14; then right .6 miles to the camp on the right. *See map facing page.*

From the intersection of Hwy 59 (*Douglas Highway*) and Second St., go west 1.1 miles on Second St. to the camp on the left. *See map page 200.*

High Plains Campground
(Private, Open all year)
1600 S. Garner Lake Road, Gillette, WY 82818 Ph: (307) 687-7339

About the camp – This camp is east of downtown, directly across from the city's Cam-Plex Center which is Gillette's Convention and events facility. The camp has 64 RV sites: 23 pull-thrus (up to 25x75) and 41 back-ins (up to 25x40). All sites are full hookups (20/30/50amp on city water). Sites are gravel and have native grass 'yards' with some tables and grills. Tent sites are native grass with some tables and grills.

Amenities – Rest rooms and showers (showers only: $2), laundry; 2 playgrounds; gift shop, limited groceries and RV parts, dump station, propane, gas and pay phone.

Rates – Full hookups for 4 persons: $15. Electric only for 4 persons: $13. Tent sites for 4 persons: $11. Additional persons age 10 and over: $1. MC V D Reservations: phone or mail.

Getting there – From I-90 use exit 129 (Garner Lake Road); then south 1 mile to the camp on the right, directly across from the Cam-Plex Center.

From Hwy 59 North to Gillette and Boxelder (*the last intersection before I-90 on ramp*), go right/east 2.3 miles to the four-way stop sign at Garner Lake Road; then left/north .2 miles to the camp on the left, directly across from the Cam-Plex Center. *See map page 200.*

Moorcroft

The Texas Trail passed through Moorcroft and until the Second World War it was a large railroad cattle shipping center. Today it is just a small town and a good place to exit I-90 for supplies and the trip to Devils Tower or Keyhole State Park. There is the free Helen Robinson Zimmerschied Museum, at 200 Big Horn Ave., Ph: (307) 756-9300, open summers.

The only camping option in town is a small RVs only camp at a local motel and that is frequently reserved by construction crews for the entire summer: Inquire. Groceries, hardware and sporting goods are available. The outdoor pool on the east end of town by the elementary school is open summers with modest admission.

Wyoming Motel and RV Campground

(Private, Open July 1 to Oct. 1)
PO 7, Moorcroft, WY 82721 Ph: (307) 756-3452

About the camp – Check-in for this small camp is at the Wyoming Motel. The camp has 5 full hookup (20/30/50 amp) RV sites. All sites are back-ins (up to 20x60) on gravel. No tents. *Horses okay: free with own feed.*

Amenities – Convenient to services in Moorcroft.

Rates – Full hookups per site: $20.

Getting there – Use I-90 exit 154, then go east into Moorcroft to the motel office on the left. *See map page 204.*

Keyhole State Park

(State of Wyoming, Open all year)
353 McKean Road, Moorcroft, WY 82721 Ph: (307) 756-3596

About the camp – This state park is popular with water-sports enthusiasts in northeast Wyoming. The elevation at Keyhole is about 4100' with generally mild seasonal weather and delightful summers. Warm summer waters attract jet skiers and spring winds across these plains delight the wind surfing crowd. A local favorite swimming area is the "cliffs," accessed from Coulter Bay. Fishing here is for northern pike, walleye, bass, drum bass and perch.

Over 200 species of birds can be observed at the park during migrations (ask at park headquarters for a complete list). The most common species using the area in summer are white pelican, osprey, common yellowthroat and Savannah sparrow. Small herds of deer and antelope make the area home, as well as a population of turkey, fox, coyote, rabbit and sharp-tailed grouse (wildlife may be on the roads in the early morning and evening hours: Drive carefully). In the water, there are beaver and muskrat.

The park has vault toilets, potable water (at all camps except Wind Creek). There are a total of 140 campsites with tables and fire rings. For campers with boats seeking seclusion, there is a boat-in area on the north side of the lake (these areas have no facilities and are roadless: pack it in, pack it out.) Four camps are more isolated and away from the headquarters area: Wind Creek and Coulter Bay to the west are off points of land near the town of Pine Haven, and Cottonwood and Rocky Point are to the north (good maps are provided with fees). The park has playgrounds, horseshoe pits, boat ramps and docks, a sandy beach and hiking trails, including a three-mile-long Volksmarch Trail. A dump station and filtered water is available at the park entrance. Stay limited to 14 consecutive days.

Rates – Day use fees for this park are $2 for residents and $5 for nonresidents. Camping fees for residents are $4 per night and $9 for nonresidents. An annual day use pass, good at all state parks, is available to residents for $25 and nonresidents for $40. Annual camping permits are available to residents for $30. The annual camping pass is not available for nonresidents. (For '99 rates see page 11).

Getting there – Use I-90 exit 165; then north about 6 miles on Pine Ridge Road to the Keyhole State Park turnoff on the left; then left to the fee booth. See map page 204.

Keyhole Marina

(Private, Open April 1 to Oct. 1)
PO 617, Moorcroft, WY 82721 Ph: (307) 756-9529

About the camp – This marina has 10 electric only hookups (30 amp). All are back-ins (up to 20x40) on a mix of gravel and native grass with tables and fire rings. 10 available tent sites have tables and fire rings.

204

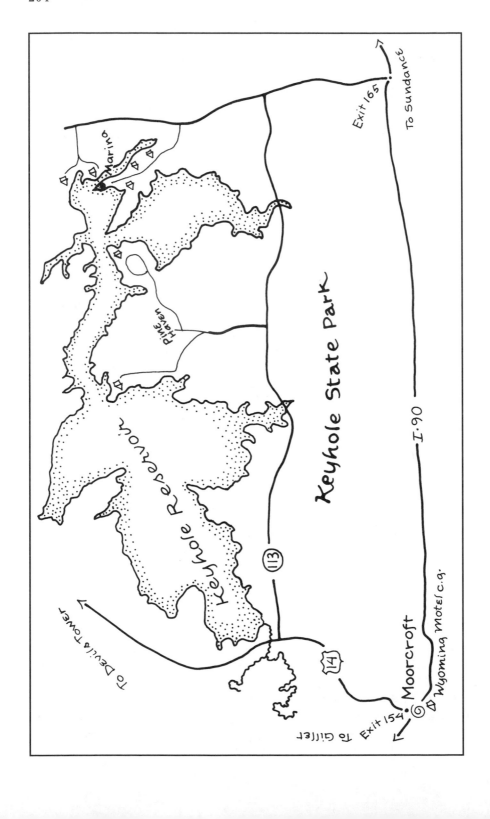

Amenities – Rest rooms (for marina campers only) and coin operated showers for marina campers and public use; cafe, limited groceries, boat ramp, gas dock, boat rentals, water-sports equipment sales and rental, boat parts and accessories, fishing tackle, propane and pay phone.

Rates – Electric hookups per site: $10. Tent site: $6. V MC Reservation: phone or mail.

Getting there – Use I-90 exit 165; then north about 6 miles on Pine Ridge Road to the Keyhole State Park turnoff on the left; then left to the fee booth; then straight 1.8 miles to the marina parking lot. *See map facing page.*

Newcastle

In the 1880's coal was discovered in Cambria Canyon, and Newcastle, named for the English coal port of Newcastle-upon-Tyne, was sited here by the railroad. The mine closed in 1928 and Newcastle, with boom and bust cycles, manages today with an economy based on oil, logging and ranching. Area memorabilia is on display at the free **Anna Miller Museum**, open M-F 9a.m.-7p.m. and Sat. 1-5, at 401 Delaware St., Ph: (307) 746-4188.

In town there are three privately-owned camps and along Hwy 85 to the north there are two small camps. Groceries, hardware and limited sporting goods are available. The indoor high school swimming pool, at 15 Stampede St., Ph: (307) 746-4850, is open to the public with modest admission.

Camp in the Trees

(Private, Open all year)
2993 West Main, Newcastle, WY 82701 Ph: (307) 746-4955 E-mail: helmut@trib.com

About the camp – This camp is located on the west edge of Newcastle amidst 15 acres of ponderosa pine with mostly shady sites. The camp has 18 back-ins (up to 30x50), all with full hookups (20/30/50 amp) on gravel with native grass 'yards' and tables. Grass tent sites are available. *Horses: free in adjacent pasture.*

Amenities – Rest room and shower, washing machine; rec room with TV and pool table.

Rates – Full hookups for 4 persons: $15. Tent sites for 4 persons: $5. Additional persons: $2. V MC Reservations: phone, E-mail or mail.

Getting there – From the junction of US 16 and Hwy 450, go east 1.1 miles on US 16 to the camp on the left.

From the junction of US 85 and 16, go west 2.2 miles on US 16, using the truck route bypass until it rejoins US 16 Business; then left .6 miles to the camp on the right. *See map page 206.*

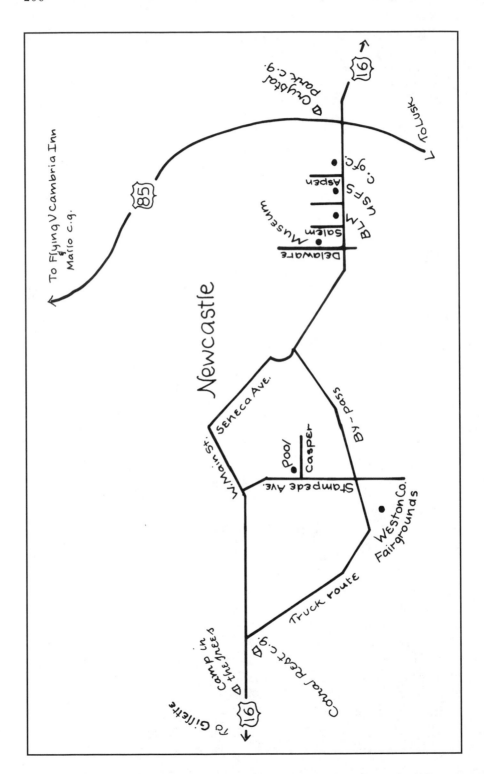

Corral Rest RV Camp

(Private, Open all year)
2206 W. Main, Newcastle, WY 82701 Ph: (307) 746-2207 Fax: (307) 746-4273 E-mail: lhsuccess@yahoo.com

About the camp – This camp is located in an open area on the west end of Newcastle. The camp has 45 RV sites: 8 pulls thrus (25x50) and 37 back-ins (29 x 60). 36 sites have full hookups (30 amp) and 9 are water and electric only. Most sites are gravel with grass 'yards' and tables. Grass tent sites are available throughout the area.

Amenities – Rest rooms and showers, laundry; snacks and ice.

Rates – Full hookups per site: $15. Tents or no hookups: $5. V MC Reservations: phone, E-mail or mail.

Getting there – From the junction of US 16 and Hwy 450, go east 1.5 miles on US 16 to the camp on the right.

From the junction of US 85 and 16, go west 2.2 miles on US 16 using the truck route bypass until it rejoins US 16 Business; then left .2 miles to the camp on the left. *See map facing page.*

Crystal Park Campground

(Private, Open April to Nov.)
2 Fountain Plaza, Newcastle, WY 82701 Ph: (307) 746-3339 Fax: (307) 746-4426

About the camp –This camp is located in an open area below the Fountain Motor Inn on the east end of Newcastle near the junction of US 16 and US 85. The camp has 60 RV sites: 40 full hookups (30 amp) and 20 electric only. 40 sites are pull-thrus (up to 25x50). Most sites are gravel with native grass 'yards' and some tables. Tent sites are available in a large grassy area with some tables and grills. There are four camper cabins, with electricity and half bath, sleeping up to six.

Amenities – Rest rooms and showers, laundry; complimentary use of heated outdoor pool and game room at the adjacent motel; modem jack and pay phone at motel office.

Rates – Full hookups for 2 persons: $13. Electric only for 2 persons: $11. Tent or no hookups for 2 persons: $9. Additional persons 12 and over: $2. Camper cabins are $24.95 (bedding packages with sheets, blankets and towels available: $5.) All major cards. No Reservations.

Getting there – From the junction of US 16/85 go north .1 miles on US 85; then right into the camp. *See map facing page.*

Flying V Cambria Inn

(Private, Open June through August)
23726 Hwy 85 North, Newcastle, WY 82701 Ph: (307) 746-2096

About the camp – This small camp is located in the shadow of the historic Cambria Casino, which was originally built in 1928 as an employee resort retreat by Cambria Coal Company. The camp has 5

208

grass back-in sites with water and electric only (20/30 amp). Grass tent sites are available throughout the area.

Amenities – Rest rooms and showers; horseshoes and volleyball; restaurant and lounge, game room and pool table.

Rates – Water and electric only per site: $10. Tent sites: Free. V MC Reservations: phone or mail.

Getting there – Southbound on US 85 from the junction of Hwy 585 and US 85 go south 9.3 miles to the camp on the left.

Northbound on US 85 from the junction of US 16/85 in Newcastle go north 8.5 miles to the camp on the right. *See map page 206.*

Mallo Campground
(Weston County, Open June through August)
Mallo Road, Newcastle, WY 82701 Ph: (307) 746-3692 or 746-4094

About the camp – This small camp is located .3 miles past the Weston County owned Mallo Resort Lodge and Motel and .2 miles from the South Dakota state line. The camp has three tables, three fire rings and a porta-potty, but no potable water. There is a pond halfway between the camp and the state line and the little stream of Beaver Creek flows below the camp. Facilities at the resort are not available to campers.

Rates – Campsite per night: $5.

Getting there – From the junction of Hwy 585 and US 85 go south .2 miles on US 85; then left on FSR 810; then 4.5 miles to Mallo Road on the right; then right .6 miles to the lodge; then keep left .3 miles to the camp on the right. *See map page 206.*

Upton

Upton is another town in northeast Wyoming that came to be largely due to railroad interests in the 1890's Today it survives in a mixed economy of ranching and the energy industry. It is along US 16 at the junction of Hwy 116, which takes you south into areas of the **Thunder Basin National Grasslands**. Dispersed camping is allowed in the grasslands, but there are lots of private lands scattered throughout the area: Be sure to get a good map and respect private property. The free **Red Onion Museum**, at Second and Pine Sts., is open M-F, 9-5, Ph: (307) 468-2672. Upton celebrates the third weekend in July during **Upton Fun Days** with rodeo, parade, dance, free barbecue in the town park and more.

In town there is a small privately-owned camp behind the C-Mart. Groceries and hardware are available. There is a public outdoor swimming pool open summers at 4th and Willow, Ph: (307) 468-2461 ($).

C-Mart RV

(Private, Open May to Oct.)
PO 905, Upton, WY 82730 Ph: (307) 468-2551

About the camp – This small camp offers six pull-thru (up to 20x50) sites with full hookups (20/30 amp on town water). All sites have gravel parking spurs with grass 'yards' and covered tables. Self-contained only: No tents.

Amenities – C-store immediately to front of camp.

Rates – Full hookups: $10.

Getting there – At corner Birch and 2nd Sts. in downtown Upton.

Sundance

Sundance is a small Wyoming town near the **Black Hills National Forest** with an economic base in logging and ranching. Some believe the town was named after Harry Longabough, the **"Sundance Kid,"** but the opposite is true. Longabough, after spending 18 months in the Crook County Jail for horse stealing, started calling himself the Sundance Kid. Memorabilia of Longabough's visit to the town and other artifacts are found at the **Crook County Museum** and **Art Gallery**, in the basement of the Crook County Courthouse on Cleveland St., Ph: (307) 283-3666, open M-F, 8-5. Sundance hosts the **Crook County Fair** with rodeo, parade and more in August.

On the east end of Sundance there is a privately-owned camp and nearby there are four Forest Service camps (one free). Groceries, hardware and limited sporting goods are available. There is a public outdoor swimming pool south of downtown, along Hwy 85 near I-90, with modest admission.

From here there are several routes to Devils Tower: for the most direct route go northwest on Hwy 14 and then north on Hwy 24; *[or]* for the best feeling for the lush lands in the Blacks Hills of Wyoming go east to Hwy 111 and then north to Aladdin; then west on Hwy 24; *[or]* for a tour on dirt roads take one of several options through the national forest (maps of the **Black Hills National Forest** are available at the district office on the east edge of town). If you choose the Aladdin route be sure to check out the picturesque and interesting **Aladdin General Store**, where you find everything from antiques to outdoor equipment and camping supplies.

210

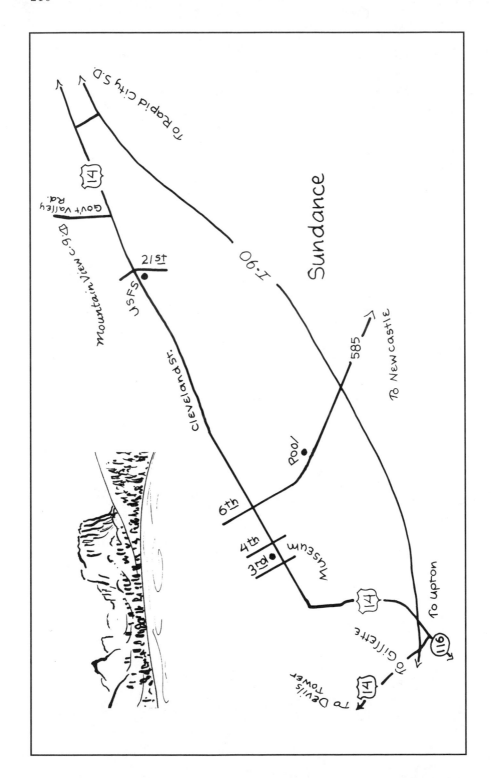

Mountain View Campground

(Private, Open April 1 to Nov. 1)
PO Box 903, Sundance, WY 82729 Ph: (307) 283-2270

About the camp – This camp is in an open area on the east end of Sundance. The camp has 36 RV sites: 20 pull-thrus (30x60) with full hookups (30/50 amp) and 16 back-ins (30x35) with water and electric. Pull-thrus are gravel with native grass 'yards', back-ins are all native grass. All sites have tables. There are 26 tent or no hookup sites, all with tables and some grills.

Amenities – Rest rooms and showers, laundry; game room, playground, basketball, volleyball, heated outdoor pool and spa, horseshoes; snacks and ice, limited RV parts, dump station and pay phone.

Rates – Full hookups for 2 persons: $18. Water and electric only for 2 persons: $16. Tent sites for 2 persons: $13. Additional persons over age 5 : $1.50. V MC Reservations: phone or mail.

Getting there – Use I-90 exit 189; then north to stop sign on the frontage road (Cleveland St.); then left/west .4 miles to Government Valley Road; then right/north .2 miles to the camp on the left.

From the junction of US 14 and Hwy 585 in downtown Sundance go east 1.3 miles to Government Valley Road; then left/north .2 miles to camp on left. *See map facing page.*

Sundance Trailhead and Campground

(Black Hills National Forest, Open mid-May to Dec. 1)

About the camp – This is a trailhead camp with horse corrals northeast of downtown Sundance, but you do not have to bring your horse along to camp there. The camp has a handicapped accessible vault toilet, but no potable water. There are 10 designated campsites with additional camper and horse trailer parking in the spaces across from the 5 corrals. Of the 10 sites, 3 are back-ins and the other 7 have parallel parking long enough for your pickup and horse trailer. Sites have tables and fire rings with grates. Stay limited to 14 days.

Rates – Campsite per night: $10. Rates half with Golden Age or Access Passport. (Reservations are possible at this campground up to 240 days in advance and 10 days prior to arrival. Service fee per reservation: $8.65. Ph: (877) 444 6777.

Getting there – Using I-90 exit 189, go north to the stop sign on the frontage road (Cleveland St.); then left/west .4 miles to Government Valley Road; then right/north 2.1 miles to the camp on the left.

From the junction of US 14 and Hwy 585 in downtown Sundance go east 1.3 miles to Government Valley road; then left/north 2.1 miles to camp on left. *See map page 212.*

212

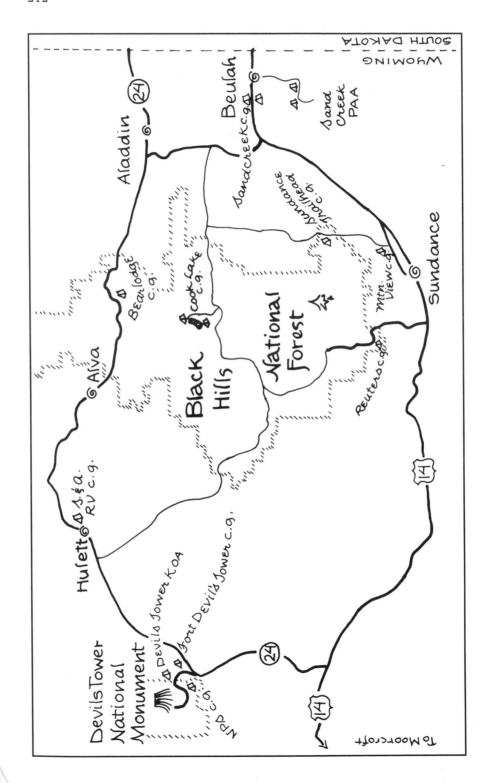

Reuters Campground

(Black Hills National Forest, Open mid-May to Dec. 1)

About the camp – This camp is located in a nice stand of ponderosa pine just inside the Black Hills National Forest west of Sundance. The camp has a vault toilet and potable water. There are 24 campsites with tables and fire rings with grates. Site 12 is a pull-thru and site 20 offers a large parallel parking area. Stay limited to 14 days.

Rates – Campsite per night: $8. Rates half with Golden Age or Access Passport. (Reservations are possible at this campground up to 240 days in advance and 10 days prior to arrival. Service fee per reservation: $8.65. Ph: (877) 444-6777.)

Getting there – Use I-90 exit 185; then go west 1 mile on US 14 to FSR 838 (*signed: Cook Lake Recreation Area*); then north 2.6 miles on paved road to the camp on the left. *See map facing page.*

Cook Lake Campground

(Black Hills National Forest, Open mid-May to Dec. 1)

About the camp – This camp is located next to a small mountain lake in the Black Hills National Forest north of Sundance. As you enter this camp, Loop A is first and near the lake with 18 camps, 8 of which are walk-ins at a reduced rate. Loop B is on a slight rise past the far end of the lake in a nice stand of ponderosa pine. The camp has vault toilets and potable water. All sites have tables and fire rings with grates. Along the northeast side of the lake, from loop A to Loop B, there are tables and grills (charcoal only) provided for picnicking and angler day use. No internal combustion motors are allowed on the lake: oars, paddles and electric motors only. Fishing offers bull heads, blue gills/green sunfish and brook, rainbow and brown trout. The area is known for white-tailed deer and wild turkey, but one might also see elk, coyote, osprey, great blue heron and the occasional bald eagle. The camp is also the trailhead for the 3.5 mile Cliff Swallow Trail loop for mountain bikers and hikers only: no motors or horses. Stay limited to 10 days.

Rates – Regular campsite per night: $11. Walk-in site per night: $7. Rates half with Golden Age or Access Passports. (Reservations are possible at this campground up to 240 days in advance and 10 days prior to arrival. Service fee per reservation: $8.65. Ph: (877) 444-6777.)

Getting there – From I-90 use exit 199, go north 4.4 miles on Hwy 111 to FSR 843; then west 10.5 miles on FSR 843 to the Cook Lake turnoff on the right; then right 1.2 miles to fee board for camp; *[or]* from Hwy 24 go south 4.4 miles on Hwy 111 to FSR 843; then west 10.5 miles on FSR 843 to the Cook Lake turnoff on the right; then right 1.2 miles to fee board for camp. *See map facing page.*

Bear Lodge Campground

(Black Hills National Forest, Open all year)

About the camp – This camp is in mature forest of ponderosa pine in the Bear Lodge Mountains of the scenic Black Hills of Wyoming along Hwy 24. The camp has a vault toilet, but no potable water. 8 sites have tables and fire rings with grates. Sites are roomy with good tenting options. Stay limited to 14 days.

Rates – Free

Getting there – From the junction of Hwy 24 and 111 near Aladdin, go west 7.5 miles on Hwy 24 to the camp on the left; *[or]* from Devils Tower at the junction of Hwy 24 and 110 go 26. 6 miles east on Hwy 24 to the camp on the right. *See map page 212.*

S & A RV Campground

(Private, Open May 1 to Nov. 30)
209 Hwy 24 East, Hulett, WY 82720 Ph: (307) 467-5652

About the camp – This camp is a small camp on the main highway through the small town of Hulett. The camp has 6 back-in (up to 15x35) gravel RV sites with full hookups (20/30 amp). Some tables are available and as well as 2 tent sites.

Amenities – Rest rooms and showers ($) (showers only: $1 for meter); Cable TV: $1.

Rates – Full hookups per site: $12. Tent site: $5.

Getting there – This camp is on the south side of Hwy 24 on the east edge of Hulett. *See map page 212.*

Wright

Wright, at the junction of Hwy 59 and 387 (known as Reno Junction) about 37 miles south of Gillette, was established in 1976 to provide housing and services for coal miners in southern Campbell County. It now has a school, small mall, golf course and is prospering. To the north along Hwy 59, the largest private bison herd, some 3500 head, roam on the 55,000-acre Durham Buffalo Ranch.

There is only one camp there, a privately-owned RV camp. Groceries, hardware and limited sporting goods are available. **Wright Recreation Center**, at 225 Wright Blvd., Ph: (307) 464-0198, is open to the public for workouts and swimming (Day pass for adults: $2.50; children: $1.50-$1.00, family: $5.00 and seniors +62 free).

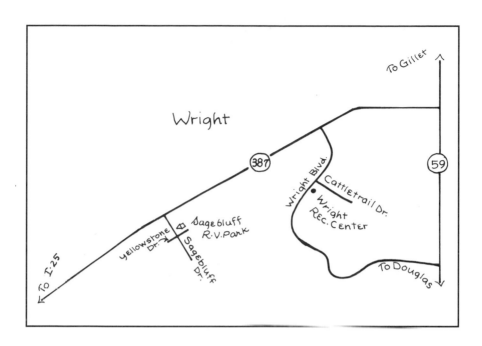

Sagebluff RV Campground

(Private, Open all year)
PO 286, Wright, WY 82732 Ph: (307) 464-1305

About the camp – This camp has 65 gravel RV sites: 25 pull-thrus and 40 Back-ins (up to 18x40). 62 sites are full hookups (20/30/50 amp on city water). Tenting is available on native grass.

Amenities – Rest rooms and showers, laundry; propane and pay phone.

Rates – Full hookups per site: $15. Tent site: $9.

Getting there – From the junction of Hwys 59 and 387, go west 1.6 miles on Hwy 387 to Sagebluff Drive; then left one block to Yellowstone Drive and the camp on the left. *See map above.*

<u>NOTES</u>

Contents — North Central

North Central Wyoming

The Big Horn Mountains may be less steep and tall than the mountains to the west, but the wilderness around Cloud Peak cannot be overshadowed. The mountains drain west into the beet-growing Big Horn Basin, while on the west slopes lie some of Wyoming's oldest and most peacefully pastoral ranchlands.

This area is one of Wyoming's truly scenic areas, with remarkable geology at every bend in the road. It is crossed by three scenic highways: the **Cloud Peak Skyway**, **Big Horn Scenic Byway** and the **Medicine Wheel Passage**; as well as the **BLM Red Gulch/Alkali** and **South Big Horn Mountains/Red Wall National Back Country Byways**. This section features 108 camping options, with 32 listings for privately-owned camps and 37 listings for For-

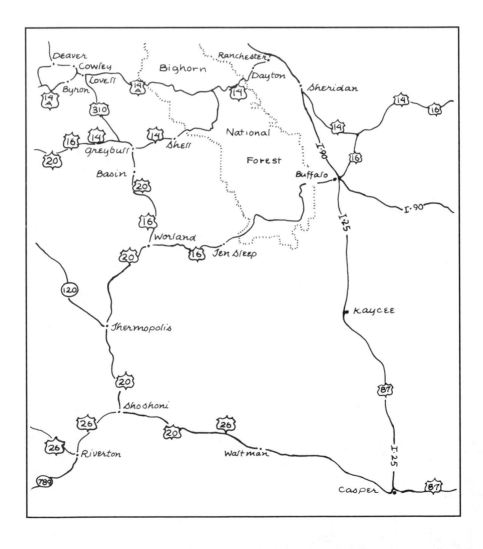

est Service camps. Remaining options include 20 free Wyoming Game and Fish Areas, 4 free BLM camps, 11 State Park campgrounds, 3 free town parks and a county-owned camp. These camps are listed under headings for 17 cities and towns, including Basin, Buffalo, Burgess Junction, Casper, Dayton, Greybull, Kaycee, Lovell, Ranchester, Riverton, Shell, Sheridan, Shoshoni, Story, Ten Sleep, Thermopolis and Worland.

Basin

For years Basin was a commercial center for area farmers and ranchers, but businesses are deserting Basin for the larger town of Greybull about eight miles to the north. In Basin there is a privately-owned camp with hookups and a shady town park with free tent and RV camping but no hookups. Groceries, hardware and basic supplies are available here. The swimming pool at the high school, at 9th and A Sts., is open to the public for a small admission fee, Ph: (307) 568-2416. The gala annual event for Basin is the **Big Horn County Fair and Bean Festival** in August.

Basin Town Park

(Town of Basin, Open all year)
D St., Basin, WY 82410 Ph: (307) 568-3333

About the camp – This camp is in a mature stand of cottonwood trees at the north end of downtown Basin. There are 6 gravel RV sites in the trees, all pull-thrus (about 25x35). Tent sites are on a hedge-lined grassy area south of the RV location. Stay limited to 7 days.

Amenities – Rest rooms and potable water (seasonal); covered table and grills between the RV and tenting areas, a playground at city park a short walk to the west, and tennis courts between the RV area and the main street of the town (US 20).

Rates – Free, donations welcome and appreciated.

Getting there – On the north end of Basin, turn west on D St. (by the tennis courts); then west one-half block to the camp on the left. *See map page 222.*

Rose Garden RV Park

(Private, Open all year)
(PO 849) 703 S. 4th St., Basin, WY 82410 Ph: (307) 568-2943 E-mail: rosegrrv@tctwest.net

About the camp – This is a self-serve camp located along US 20 on the south end of the town of Basin. The camp has 9 full hookup (30 amp on city water) RV sites. All sites are pull-thrus (up to 20x60) on gravel and native grass, with some tables. 5 sites have cable TV available.

Amenities – Rest rooms and showers (showers only: $3); Cable TV included at 5 sites and dump station.

Rates – Full hookups: $15. Reservations: Phone, E-mail or mail.

Getting there – This park is on the east side of US 20 on the south end of Basin. *See map below.*

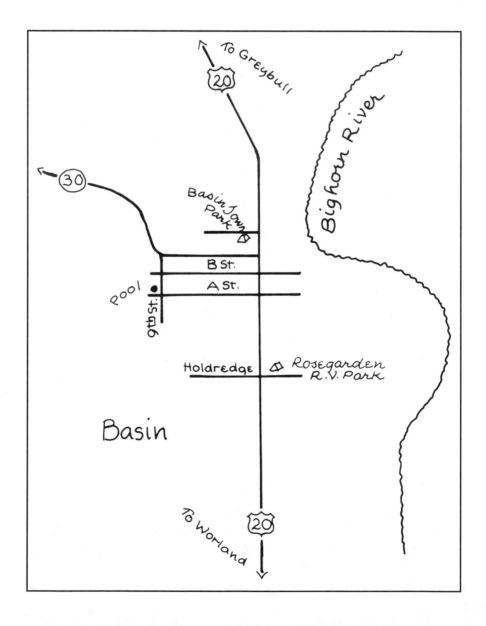

Buffalo

Buffalo is a friendly little town with a less friendly history—it was nearby that stockmen fought the Johnson County War in 1892. Now it's a favorite stop—at the junction of I-90 and I-25— for travelers visiting Wyoming and the Big Horn Mountains. Buffalo's unique historic downtown area is located on a winding street which followed an old trail on Clear Creek. Downtown you find the **Occidental Hotel**, made famous in Owen Wister's novel *The Virginian*; the **Busy Bee Diner**, a lunch counter famous for good food and homemade pies, and walking trails with self-guided history tour from the Chamber of Commerce. For an overview of the area's colorful history visit the **Jim Gatchell Museum of the West**, also in the downtown area, at 100 Fort St., Ph: (307) 684-9331. Buffalo hosts annual **Living History Days** in July, the **Johnson County Fair and Rodeo** in August and the **American Triker's Association Trike Parade** which takes place in late July or early August.

In town there are five privately-owned camps and in the area there are a free Game and Fish Wildlife Habitat Management Area, private and county camps at Lake DeSmet and five Forest Service camps along US 16 to the summit of **Powder River Pass** west of town on the **Cloud Peak Skyway**. The city has grocery, sporting goods and hardware stores. Also of interest is **Rhondele's Excess Baggage**, at 68 Fetterman, Ph: (307) 684-5152, which specializes is custom design of soft luggage for you or your company. In summer, there is a free outdoor pool in Washington Park and rec facilities for workouts and showers at the local YMCA ($) at 101 Klondike St., Ph: (307) 684-9558. Forest Service and BLM offices here provide maps and information.

Big Horn Mountains Campground

(Private, Open all year)
8935 Hwy 16 West #108, Buffalo, WY 82834 Ph: (307) 684-2307

About the camp – This camp, located on 8 open acres, is 2.8 miles west of downtown Buffalo along US 16. There are 69 RV sites: all pull-thrus (up to 35x70 big rig sites). 40 sites are full hookups (30/50 amp) with 29 sites water and electric only. Sites are mixed gravel and grass with tables and portable grills available. 14 designated tent sites are grass. This camp also offers a group area as needed.

Amenities – Rest rooms and showers, laundry; game room with pool table and card tables, playground, outdoor heated pool, and basketball; limited groceries and RV parts, firewood, gift shop, dump station and pay phone.

Rates – Full hookups for 2 persons: $18. Water and electric for 2 persons: $16.50. Tent sites for 2 persons: $14. Up to 2 additional children free. Other additional persons: $2. Discounts: All current camping cards. MC V Reservations: phone or mail.

Getting there – From I-25 use exit 298; then north on Main St. to US 16 west; then left 2.8 miles to the camp on the left. *See map page 224.*

224

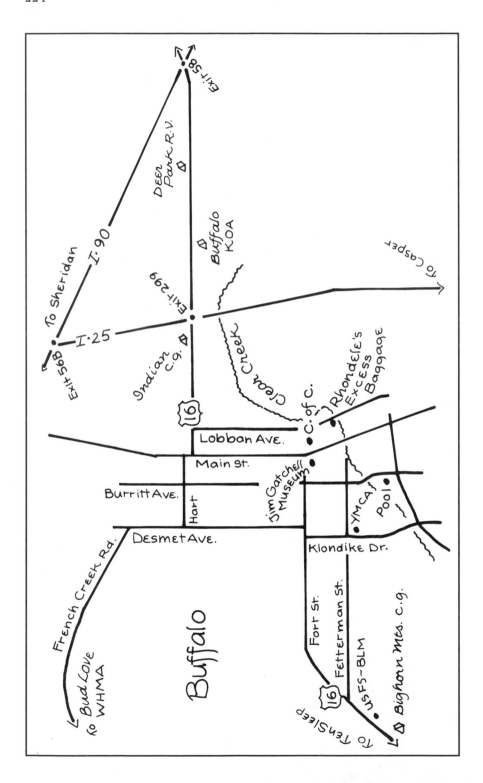

From I-90 use exit 56A; then south to US 16 west; then west 2.8 miles to the camp on the left.

East bound on US 16 from Powder River Pass to Buffalo, this is the first campground in Buffalo located on the south side of the highway, 2.8 miles west of downtown. *See map facing page.*

Buffalo KOA Kampground

(Private, Open April 15 to Oct. 15)
PO Box 189, Buffalo, WY 82834 Ph: (307) 684-5423

About the camp – This camp is located on 13 open acres bisected by French Creek just east of downtown Buffalo. There are 63 RV sites: 37 pull-thrus (13 big-rig sites) and 26 back-ins (30x40). 39 sites are full hookups (20/30 amp with 50 amp at selected big-rig sites). All sites have gravel parking areas with grass 'yards' and tables. 23 designated tent sites, strategically placed in pleasant areas on the grounds and along French Creek, are grass with grills and tables. New for 1999: a "deluxe" site with gazebo, patio and hot tub.

Amenities – Handicapped-accessible rest rooms and showers, laundry; game room, playground, heated pool and spa; limited groceries and RV parts, camping supplies, firewood and gifts, modem jack outside office, dump station, propane and pay phones. The KOA also has a Kamper Kitchen with electric stove tops and sinks and 5 Kamper Kabins sleeping 4 to 6. All-you-can-eat pancake breakfast June 1 to Aug. 31 (7:30 to 9 a.m. at $1.59 to $2.29).

Rates – Full Hookups for 2 persons: $20.95-26.95. Water and electric for 2 persons: $18.95-22.95. Tent sites for 2 persons: $14.95-18.95. Additional persons age 6 and older: $3. Kamper Kabins: $36.95-$44.95. MC V D Reservations: phone or mail.

Getting there – From I-25 use exit 299; then east .2 miles on US 16 to the camp on the right.

From I-90 use exit 58; then west 1.2 miles on US 16 to the camp on the left. *See map facing page.*

Deer Park Campground

(Private, Open May 1 to Oct. 10)
PO Box 568, Buffalo, WY 82834 Ph: (307) 684-5722 E-mail: information@deerparkrv.com Web site: www.deerparkrv.com

About the camp – This camp, off US 16 just east of downtown Buffalo, is on 40 tree-covered acres with a private 1-mile walking path through the trees on the grounds. There are 75 RV sites : 50 pull-thrus (up to 35x85, big rig sites) and 25 back-ins (30x32). 35 sites are full hookups (30/50amp), with 40 sites water and electric only. All sites have gravel parking areas and grass 'yards' with tables and grills. 25 designated tent sites, grass with tables and grills, are strategically placed in pleasant areas away from the main RV parking area.

Amenities – Rest rooms and showers, laundry; game room, playground, and pool with spa; modem jack outside office, limited groceries and RV parts, gift shop, dump station and coffee service. Affiliations include Goodsam, AAA, FCMA and Family Campers.

Rates – Full hookups for 2 persons: $21. Water and electric for 2 persons: $19. Tent sites for 2 persons: $14.50. Additional persons: $2. MC V Reservations: phone, E-mail or mail.

Getting there – From I-25 use exit 299; then go east .7 miles on US 16 to the camp on the left.

From I-90 use exit 58; then go west .7 miles on US 16 to the camp on the right. *See map page 224.*

Indian Campground

(Private, Open April 10 to Oct. 31)
660 East Hart St., Buffalo, WY 82834 Ph: (307) 684-9601 E-mail: steveng@trib.com

About the camp – This camp is located on 12 tree-covered acres just east of downtown Buffalo. The camp has 80 RV sites: 35 pull-thrus (23x65) and 45 back-ins (23x32). All sites are full hookups (30 amp with 50 amp on five sites) and have gravel parking areas with grass 'yards' and tables. Tent sites are grass with grills and tables and are situated along French Creek which runs through the back edge of the camp. This camp has one camper cabin.

Amenities – Rest rooms and showers, laundry; game room, playground, heated pool, recreation field, badminton, horseshoes, volleyball, and stream fishing; limited RV parts and groceries, modem jack in office, dump station, propane, gift shop, coffee service, and pay phone.

Rates – Full hookups for 2 persons: $20.50. Water and electric for 2 persons: $18.50. Tent sites for 2 persons $15.50. Camper cabin for 2 persons: $32. Additional persons over 6 years: $2. MC V D Discounts: Goodsam, AAA and all current camping cards. Reservations: phone, E-mail or mail.

Getting there – From I-25 use exit 299; then west .1 miles on US 16 to the camp on the right.

From I-90 use exit 56B; then south on I-25 to exit 299; then west .1 miles on US 16 to the camp on the right. *See map page 224.*

—To The North—

Lake DeSmet RV Park

(Private, Open all year)
PO Box 578, Buffalo, WY 82834 Ph: (307) 684-9051

About the camp – This camp, near Lake DeSmet, offers lots of services for the water sports enthusiast. There are 18 full hookup (30 amp) RV sites: 3 pull-thrus and 15 back-ins (up to 22x35). All sites are on native grass with some tables. Tent sites are available with some tables. There is a large common barbecue pit for camper use.

Amenities – Rest rooms and showers (showers only: $5), laundry; pool table, basketball hoops, swimming pool, playground; limited groceries and RV parts, cafe and diner, fishing tackle, boat rentals, jet ski rentals, boat service and storage, scuba sales, service and instruction, dump station, propane, and pay phone.

Rates – Full hookups per site: $15. Tent sites per tent: $10. V MC Reservations: phone or mail.

Getting there – Use I-90 exit 51; then go .7 miles east and north on the frontage road (*Monument Road*) to DeSmet Road; then right on DeSmet Road to the camp on the right.

Johnson County Lake DeSmet Recreation Area

(Johnson County Parks, Open May 15 to Sept. 15)

About the camp – This camp is near the edge of Lake DeSmet with camping and a boat ramp. The camp has a vault toilet and 28 sites on gravel with native grass 'yards.' Most sites have stone fire rings, but there is the occasional site with a metal fire ring with grate. Several sheltered tables with fire rings are scattered throughout the area. No potable water. Stay limited to 14 days.

Rates – Campsite per night, per vehicle: $5. Boat ramp day use: $3; annual permit for boat ramp: $20.

Getting there – Use I-90 exit 51, then go .7 miles east and north on the frontage road (*Monument Road*) to DeSmet Road; then right .6 miles to fork in road; then left .3 miles to the camp and the lake.

—Northwest—

Bud Love Wildlife Habitat Management Area

(Wyoming Game and Fish, Open May 15 to Nov. 22)

About the camp – Bud Love is an area of scenic beauty in the foothills of the Big Horn Mountains. The 8,000 acre Wildlife Habitat Management Area is closed from Nov. 23 to May 14 to provide crucial winter habitat for about 500 elk and 200 mule deer. Hunting for big game is allowed here as well as for blue and ruffed grouse, wild turkey, pheasant, chukar, Hungarian partridge, rabbit, black bear and mountain lion. The Game and Fish Department stock brook and rainbow trout in the North Fork of Sayles Creek and three of five man-made ponds where fishing is allowed. There are a variety of plant communities, 300 acres of grassy meadows and steep canyon walls along Rock and Sayles Creeks. It provides and excellent area for bird watching, photography, backpacking and picnicking. Stay limited to 14 days.

Rates – Free

Getting there – From the junction of US 16 west and Main St. in Buffalo, go 4 blocks west on US 16 to N. DeSmet Ave.; then right .8 miles to French Creek Road which bears to the left; then left 10.1 miles on French Creek Road to the access/camping area on the left (this road is paved for the first 7.4 miles). *See map page 224.*

—To the West—

Hunter Corrals Campground
(Bighorn National Forest, Open May 15 to Oct. 31)

About the camp – Hunter Corral is a horse camp and assembly area for people with pack strings headed into the high country of the Big Horn Mountains. The camp has a pit toilet and 9 primitive sites with no tables or potable water. Stay limited to 14 days.

Rates – Campsite per night: $10. Rates half with Golden Age or Access Passport. (Reservations are possible at this campground up to 240 days in advance and 10 days prior to arrival. Service fee per reservation: $8.65. Ph: (877) 444-6777 toll free.)

Getting there – From the junction of US 16 west and Main St. in Buffalo, go west 12.8 miles on US 16 to the camp turnoff; then right 2.4 miles to the fee board. *See map page 231.*

Middle Fork Campground
(Bighorn National Forest, Open May 15 to Sept. 21)

About the camp – The middle fork of Clear Creek runs through this pleasant little camp with sites along a short road leading to an end-of-the-road loop turnaround. The camp has vault toilets, potable water and 10 roomy sites with tables and fire pits with grates. Site 2 is a pull-thru and there is angler parking just outside the camp. Stay limited to 14 days.

Rates – Campsite per night: $10. Rates half with Golden Age or Access Passport. (Reservations are possible at this campground up to 240 days in advance and 10 days prior to arrival. Service fee per reservation: $8.65. Ph: (877) 444-6777 toll free.)

Getting there – From the junction of US 16 west and Main St. in Buffalo, go west 14 miles on US 16 to the turnoff on the right; then right .3 miles to the fee board. *See map page 231.*

Circle Park Campground
(Bighorn National Forest, Open May 22 to Sept. 21)

About the camp – The location of this camp is excellent for views of the Big Horn Mountains. The camps are well spaced along a .3 mile long road with an end-of-the-road loop turn around. The camp has vault toilets, potable water and 10 sites with tables and fire pits with grates. Stay limited to 14 days.

Rates – Campsite per night: $9. Rates half with Golden Age or Access Passport.

Getting there – From the junction of US 16 west and Main St. in Buffalo, go west 15.2 miles on US 16 to the turnoff on the right; then right 2.1 miles on Circle Park Road to a fork; then right to the fee board. *See map page 231.*

Worth mentioning – While getting to the camp on Circle Park Road you pass through two open mountain parks with great views of some of the Big Horn Mountains.

Tie Hack

(Bighorn National Forest)

About the camp – While there used to be a campground here and Forest Service officials say there will be again, this camp was closed in 1998. Tie Hack Reservoir was recently developed, and at that time the area was designated day use only with picnicking and a boat ramp. If you're camping in the area, it's a nice body of water to visit. Check with forest service on the future of camping here.

Rates – Day use: $4. Rates half with Golden Age or Access Passport.

Getting there – From the junction of US 16 west and Main St. in Buffalo, go west 15.6 miles on US 16 to the turnoff on the left; then left 1.6 miles to the lake. *See map page 231.*

South Fork Campground

(Bighorn National Forest, Open May 15 to Sept. 21)

About the camp – This camp is located in a forested area on the south fork of Clear Creek. The camp has vault toilets, potable water and 15 sites with tables and fire pits with grates. Sites 11 thru 15 are good looking walk-ins with parking off the end-of-the-road loop turn around. Stay limited to 14 days.

Rates – Campsite per night: $10. Rates half with Golden Age or Access Passport. (Reservations are possible at this campground up to 240 days in advance and 10 days prior to arrival. Service fee per reservation: $8.65. Ph: (877) 444-6777 toll free.)

Getting there – From the junction of US 16 west and Main St. in Buffalo, go west 16 miles on US 16 to the turnoff on the left; then left .1 miles to the fee board. *See map page 231.*

Crazy Woman Campground
(Bighorn National Forest, Open May 22 to Sept. 8)

About the camp – This camp along the north fork of Crazy Woman Creek is small with only 6 sites on a short road leading to an end-of-the-road loop turn. The camp has a vault toilet, potable water and 6 sites with tables and fire pits with grates. Stay limited to 14 days.

Rates – Campsite per night: $9. Rates half with Golden Age or Access Passport.

Getting there – From the junction of US 16 west and Main St. in Buffalo, go west 25.6 miles on US 16 to the turnoff; then right .3 miles to the fee board. *See map facing page.*

Doyle Campground
(Bighorn National Forest, Open June 12 to Sept. 21)

About the camp – This sprawling camp has 19 roomy sites on a .4 mile loop road. The camp has a vault toilet and 19 sites with tables and fire pits with grates, but no potable water. Stay limited to 14 days.

Rates – Campsite per night: $6. Rates half with Golden Age or Access Passport.

Getting there – From the junction of US 16 west and Main St. in Buffalo, go west 27.3 miles on US 16 to Hazelton Road (CR 3); then left 6.2 miles on Hazelton Road to the turnoff; then left .2 miles to the fee board. *See map facing page.*

Lost Cabin Campground
(Bighorn National Forest, Open June 12 to Sept. 8)

About the camp – This camp has 20 good looking camps on a half-mile-long loop road. Sites are roomy with good tenting options and 9 sites are pull-thrus. The camp has vault toilets, potable water and sites with tables and fire pits with grates. Stay limited to 14 days.

Rates – Campsite per night: $9. Rates half with Golden Age or Access Passport.

Getting there – From the junction of US 16 west and Main St. in Buffalo, go west 28.2 miles on US 16 to the turnoff; then right .3 miles to the fee board. *See map facing page.*

USFS Dump Station
(Bighorn National Forest, Open May to Oct.)

Getting there – From the junction of US 16 west at Main St. in Buffalo; go 37.4 miles west on US 16 to the dump station on the left. *See map facing page.*

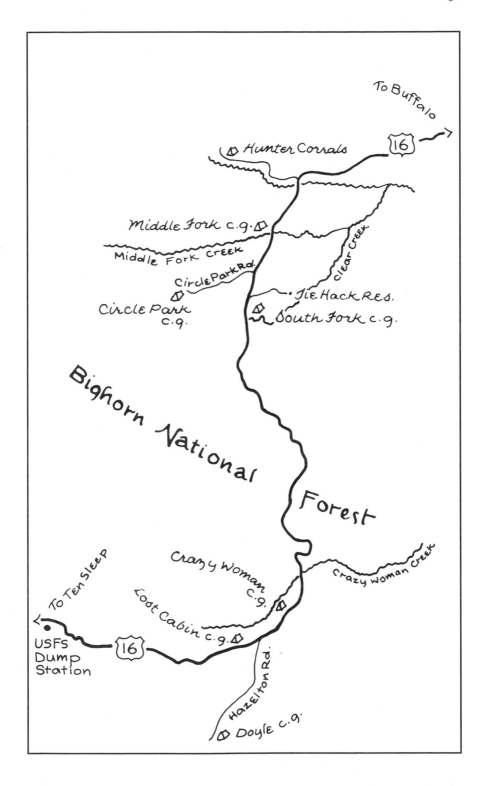

To Buffalo

16

◇ Hunter Corrals

Middle Fork c.g. ◇

Middle Fork Creek

Clear Creek

Circle Park Rd.

· Jie Hack Res.

Circle Park
c.g. ◇

◇ South Fork c.g.

Bighorn National

Forest

Crazy Woman
c.g.

Crazy Woman Creek

To Ten Sleep

Lost Cabin c.g. ◇

◇

USFS
Dump
Station

16

Hazelton Rd.

◇ Doyle c.g.

Burgess Junction

This is the junction of Hwy 14 and 14A on the crest of the Big Horn Mountains at the north end of the Bighorn National Forest. RV hookups and tent camping are available at the privately-owned Bear Lodge Resort and there are 4 developed Forest Service camps in the area. Basic groceries, fuel, ice, snacks, some sporting goods and fishing tackle are available at Bear Lodge Resort. Maps and information are available at the Bighorn National Forest's **Burgess Junction Visitors Center** about 1 mile to the east; **Shell Falls** is to the southwest on the **Big Horn Scenic Byway** (US 14), and the **Medicine Wheel National Landmark**—a mysterious prehistoric array of rocks forming a spoked wheel—is along the **Medicine Wheel Passage** (14A) to the west.

Bear Lodge Resort

(Private, Open all year)
(US 14A just west of Burgess Junction) PO Box 159, Dayton, WY 82836
Ph: (307) 655-2444 or (307) 672-4194 Voice mail: (307) 751-2444

About the camp – The lodge sits on 44 acres within the Bighorn National Forest and offers 10 overnight RV sites: 2 are pull-thrus and 8 are back-ins (all 20/30 amp and up to 35'). Sites are gravel with grass 'yards' and fire rings. There are also various tenting options by the lodge's fish pond or on other grassy areas. The lodge offers rustic cabins with electricity and wood stove (no bedding packages). *Horses okay.*

Amenities – Rest rooms and showers (showers only: $3; $2 with your own soap and towel), laundry; game room, indoor pool with spa and second spa outside, volleyball, horseshoes, fishing pond (12 and under no license required); limited groceries, restaurant, lounge, tackle, gift shop and USFS dump station one mile east.

Rates – Full hookups per site: $18.50. Water and electric per site: $12.50. Electric only per site: $7.50. Tent sites: $5. Rustic cabins: $30. All major cards. Personal checks okay. Reservations: phone or mail.

Getting there – This camp is .3 miles west of Burgess Junction (*US 14/ 14A*) on US 14A. *See map page 266.*

North Tongue Campground

(Bighorn National Forest, Open June 12 to Sept. 21)

About the camp – This camp is near Burgess Junction (US 14 and 14 A) and, for this area, pretty much on top of the world. The camp has a vault toilet, potable water and 12 sites with tables and fire pits with grates. Stay limited to 14 days.

Rates – Campsite per night: $9. Rates half with Golden Age or Access Passport.

Getting there – From Burgess Junction (*US14/14A*), go west on US 14 A to the first gravel road to the right (*FSR 15*); then right 1.1 miles on FSR 15 to the camp on the left. *See map page 266.*

Owen Creek Campground

(Bighorn National Forest, Open June 12 to Sept. 21)

About the camp – This is a small campground on Owen Creek in a shady forested area with roomy sites along an end-of the-loop turn around road. The camp has vault toilets, potable water and sites with tables and fire rings with grates.

Rates – Campsite per night: $9. Rates half with Golden Age or Access Passport.

Getting there – From Burgess Junction (*US14/14A*), go south 4.9 miles on US 14 to the camp on the right. *See map page 266.*

Tie Flume Campground

(Bighorn National Forest, Open June 12 to Sept. 21)

About the camp – This camp is on the South Tongue River with sites 1-15 on a road with an end-of-the-road turnaround and sites 16-25 on a loop road. Most sites are roomy with nice options for tenters. The camp has vault toilets, potable water and sites with tables and fire rings with grates. Stay limited to 14 days.

Rates – Campsite per night: $9. Rates half with Golden Age or Access Passport.

Getting there – From Burgess Junction (*US14/14A*), go south 5.1 miles on US 14 to the turnoff on the left (*FSR 26*); then 2.6 miles on FSR 26 to a fork; then left .1 miles to the fee board. *See map page 266.*

Dead Swede Campground

(Bighorn National Forest, Open June 12 to Sept. 21)

About the camp – In this camp the road forks near the fee board and delivers you to two distinctly different camping options. Going right you have sites 1-10 in cool and shady forest on a short loop road. The left fork takes you off the hill to sites 11-22, where the camps are open and sunnier, as well as nearer the South Tongue River. The camp has vault toilets, potable water and sites with tables and fire rings with grates.

Rates – Campsite per night: $9. Rates half with Golden Age or Access Passport.

Getting there – From Burgess Junction (*US14/14A*), go south 5.1 miles on US 14 to the turnoff on the left (*FSR 26*); then left 2.6 miles on FSR 26 to a fork; then right 2.0 miles to camp on the left. *See map page 266.*

Dayton

Dayton is a small community northwest of Sheridan on the eastern boundary of the **Bighorn National Forest** amidst fertile hilly grasslands that have always been attractive to ranchers and wildlife. Going west from here you are on the **Big Horn Scenic Byway** (US14) to **Burgess Junction** (US14/ 14A). About 10 miles west of Dayton on US 14 is **Sand Turn,** which is gaining fame in the hang-gliding world. For more information, lessons or sales and service contact Johann Nield at Eagle Air Sports, PO 312, Dayton, WY 82836, Ph: (307) 655-2562 (information is also available here for Whiskey Peak, near Baroil, Wyoming, considered a premier site worldwide where distance records are made and broken). Spelunkers may want to visit the Tongue River Cave in Tongue River Canyon. Information is available locally or at the USFS office in Sheridan. The town celebrates in late-July during **Dayton Days,** with rodeo, parade and street dancing and more.

In Dayton there is a privately-owned camp and nearby there are two exceptionally scenic free Game and Fish areas and two developed Forest Service camps are to the west along the Big Horn Scenic Byway. Dayton has groceries, snacks and ice and there is public swimming pool midtown on US 14 open summers with modest admission.

Foothills Motel and Campground

(Private, Open May 1 to Nov. 1)
PO Box 174, Dayton, WY 82836 Ph: (307) 655-2547 E-mail:
MHoodFHill@aol.com

About the camp – This camp is on 5 shady acres located on the west bank of the Tongue River near the east edge of Dayton. There are 26 RV sites: 4 pull-thrus (up to 25x50) and 22 back-ins (up to 20x35). 15 sites are full hookups (20/30/50amp on city water). Sites are grass with tables and some portable grills. 25 tent or no hookup sites are grass, have tables, and are set in the tree line along the river. There is also a vintage log camper cabin.

Amenities – Rest rooms and showers ($) (showers only: $1.50), laundry; cable TV included at full hookup sites, adjacent to city park with playground, tennis court, volleyball, basketball and walking path; modem jack in office and dump station.

Rates – Full hookups per site: $16.25 incl. tax. Water and electric per site: $14.25 incl. tax. Tent sites: $11.25 incl. tax. No credit cards. Personal checks okay. Reservations: phone, E-mail or mail.

Getting there – From I-90 use exit 9: then 6.4 miles west on US 14 to camp on the left (*just after you cross over the bridge on Tongue River on the east edge of Dayton*). *See map Page 266.*

—North of Dayton—

Amsden Creek Wildlife Habitat Management Area
(Wyoming Game and Fish, Open May 1 to Nov. 15)

About the camp – Of all the Game and Fish Wildlife Habitat Management Areas where camping is allowed, this area gets the five-pine-cone rating for scenic beauty (Even if you do not plan to camp, it's a short drive and worth a look-see).

There are two primitive camping areas: Tongue River Campground and Tongue Canyon Campground. Tongue River Campground has a large open area for RV parking on the off-river side of the road. There are several tracks, on the river side of the road, to well-seasoned stone fire rings from ancestral campers.

There is no vault toilet here, but back up the road — on the off-river side, near the Game and Fish sign for the area — there is an easy-to-miss cut in the greenery that opens into a small park with a stone fire ring and a pit toilet.

From the Tongue River Campground the road continues along the river with spectacular views of the cataract flowing through the forested and rock-walled canyon. The Tongue River Canyon Campground has a vault toilet in the center of the loop turnaround, where there is also parking, and, off the loop, several fire rings, some with elaborate grates built by former campers. Deadfall for campfires looks scarce; you might want to bring your own wood. No potable water. Stay limited to 14 days.

Rates – Free

Getting there – From I-90 use exit 9; then about 6.3 miles west on US 14 to CR 92 (*just east of the bridge over the Tongue River on the east edge of Dayton*); then 2.3 mile on CR 92 to a fork; then left 1.4 miles to the Tongue River Campground area; [or] continue on another 1.5 miles to the end of the road and the Tongue River Canyon Campground. *See map page 266.*

—West of Dayton—

Sibley Lake Campground
(Bighorn National Forest, Open May 22 to Sept. 21)

About the camp – This camp is in a peaceful forested area on a hillside above the lake. Many sites seem better suited for RVs, but some sites offer nice tenting options. The camp has vault toilets and potable water and all sites have tables, fire rings with grates and grills. There are two loops with a total of 25 sites. About 15 of these sites have 20/30 amp electric service and are $3 more per site. The main road through the camp continues on down the hill .2 miles to the lake where there is a picnic area, boat ramp (no motors) and a handicapped-accessible dock and fishing pier. Stay limited to 14 days.

Rates – Campsite per night: $10. Campsite with electric hookups: $13. Rates half with Golden Age or Access Passport.

Getting there – From the west end of Dayton (*at the Tongue River High School*), go 20.7 miles on US 14 west to the Sibley Lake Recreation Area on the left. *See map page 266.*

Prune Creek Campground
(Bighorn National Forest, Open June 12 to Sept. 21)

About the camp – This camp is in a forested area with 21 spacious sites on two loops. Sites appear to be well suited for tents as well as RV's and trailers. The camp has vault toilets, potable water and all sites have tables with lantern hooks, fire rings with grates and grills. Stay limited to 14 days.

Rates – Campsite per night: $10. Rates half with Golden Age or Access Passport. (Reservations are possible at this campground up to 240 days in advance and 10 days prior to arrival. Service fee per reservation: $8.65. Ph: (877) 444-6777 toll free.)

Getting there – From the west end of Dayton (*at the Tongue River High School*); go 22.2 miles on US 14 west to the camp on the left. *See map page 266.*

Burgess Junction Visitors Center
(Bighorn National Forest, Open May 18 to Sept. 20 • 8:30a.m.-5p.m.)

About the Visitors Center – The center provides general information, a .4 mile interpretive trail, short films on topics related to the area, maps, exhibits, rest rooms, books and gifts.

Getting there – From the west end of Dayton (*at the Tongue River High School*), go 24.7 miles on US 14 west to the center on the right. *See map page 266.*

Greybull

Greybull, a patch of green farmland where Shell Creek joins the Greybull River, was named after an albino buffalo sacred to Native Americans. The free **Greybull Museum**, at 325 Greybull Ave., Ph: (307) 765-2444, is open summers M-F 10 a.m. to 8 p.m. and on Sat. 10-6. West of town at the airport is the **Museum of Flight and Aerial Firefighting**, with World War II aircraft and several P84Y-2 planes that were used in the South Pacific during the war with Japan($). About 10 miles east of town on US 14 is the turnoff on the north end of the **Red Gulch/Alkali BLM National Back Country Byway**, and past the town of Shell US 14 becomes the **Big Horn Scenic Byway**, with a Visitors Center at **Shell Falls**. Summer here is highlighted the second weekend in June at the **Days of '49**, with parade, rodeo, barbecue, demolition derby and more.

In the town of Greybull there are two privately-owned camps. For out-of-town camps in the general area see listings under Shell, Lovell and Cody. If you're heading east on US 14, this is the place to find groceries and supplies. The town has a public swimming pool at 6th Ave. No. and No. 7th St., across from the high school ($). Maps and information are available at the **Paint Rock Ranger District Office**, at 1220 N. 8th St. Ph: (307) 765-4435.

Greybull KOA

(Private, Open March 1 to Oct. 31)
333 N. 2nd St., Greybull, WY 82426 Ph: (307) 765-2555

About the camp – This camp is off a quiet residential section of Greybull. The camp has 40 gravel and grass RV sites with grills and tables: 19 pull-thrus (up to 23x45) and 21 back-ins (up to 20x28). 31 sites are full hookups (30amp on city water). Water is included at the 22 grass tent sites which also have tables and grills.

Amenities – Rest rooms and showers (showers only: $5), laundry; cable TV ($1.50), game room, playground, volleyball, and heated outdoor pool; limited groceries and RV parts, gift shop, fishing tackle, cafe, dump station, propane, and pay phone.

Rates – Full hookups for 2 persons: $22. Water and electric only for 2 persons: $21. Tent sites for 2 persons: $17. Additional persons: $3. All major cards. Reservations: phone or mail.

Getting there – From the junction of US 14/16/20 and Hwy 789 in downtown Greybull, go east to 2nd St.; then north four blocks to the camp on the right; *[or]* go north from the junction to 4th Ave. North; then east until you reach the camp (*when going east on 4th Ave. North you drive right through the gate to the camp*). *See map page 238.*

238

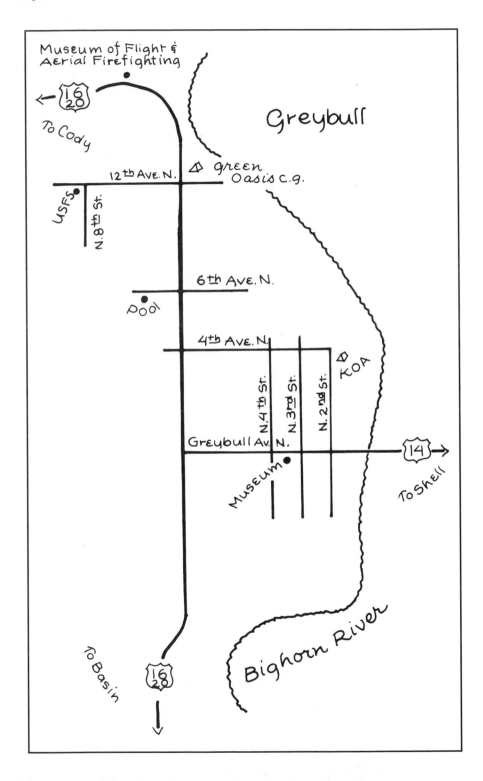

Museum of Flight &
Aerial Firefighting

← 16 20

To Cody

Greybull

12th Ave. N.   △ green
              Oasis C.g.

USFS ●

N. 8th St.

6th Ave. N.

Pool ●

4th Ave. N.

△ KOA

N. 4th St.

N. 3rd St.

N. 2nd St.

Greybull Av. N.   14 →

Museum ●

To Shell

Bighorn River

To Basin

16 28

Green Oasis Campground

(Private, Open April 1 to Oct. 31)
540 12th Ave. North, Greybull, WY 82426 Ph: (307) 765-2856 E-mail:
greenoasis@tctwest.net

About the camp – This camp is at the northern end of downtown
Greybull on 4 green, shady acres. The camp has 10 grass pull-thru RV
sites (up to 23x40): all are full hookups (30amp on city water) with
tables. 15 grass tent sites with tables are also available.

Amenities – Rest rooms and showers, laundry; game room with TV,
dump station and pay phone.

Rates – Full hookups for 4 persons: $20. Tent sites for 2 persons:
$12. Additional persons: $2. MC V Discounts: Goodsam. Reservations: phone, E-mail or mail.

Getting there – From the intersection of US 14/16/20 and Hwy 789 go
north to 12th Ave. North and the camp on the right. *See map facing
page.*

Kaycee

Kaycee is the jumping off point for visiting the **Hole-in-the-Wall** country
and **Outlaw Cave** where tracks were made by the likes of Butch Cassidy,
"Flat-Nose" George, the Sundance Kid and other loose-living characters in
the **Hole-in-the-Wall Gang.** In Kaycee there are two privately-owned camps
and a free town park. In the Hole-in-the-Wall country, west of town, there
is a privately-owned camp with water and electric hookups, a free developed
BLM camp at Outlaw Cave and a free Game and Fish Wildlife Habitat Management Area. Basic groceries, ice, snacks and the like are available in Kaycee,
where you also find the **Hoofprints of the Past Museum** on Main St., Ph:
(307) 738-2381. Two events highlight activities in Kaycee, the **Sheep Herd-
ers Rodeo and Parade** in July and a **Pro Rodeo** with **Cowboy Poetry** in
September.

KC RV Park #1

(Private, Open all year)
PO Box 11, Kaycee, WY 82639 Ph: (307) 738-2233

About the camp – This camp, located along the Middle Fork of the
Powder River where it runs by the south edge of Kaycee, is convenient
to downtown Kaycee and the fairgrounds. The camp has 9 back-in sites
(25x50): all are full hookups (20/50 amp on city water). Some sites are
shady, all have gravel spurs and grass 'yards' with tables and some grills.
Tent sites are available on grass with some tables and grills. This camp
also offers lodging in three 10x50 trailer homes each of which sleep up
to 8 persons. *Horses okay.*

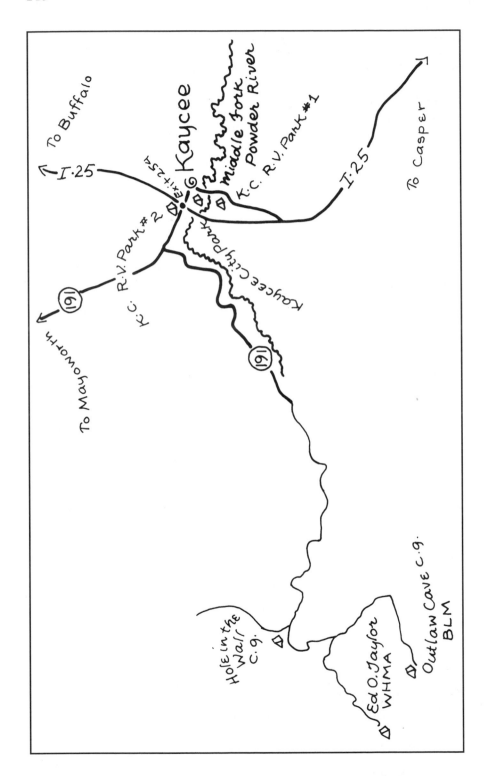

Amenities – Rest rooms and showers (showers only: $3), Cable TV (2 sites), walking distance to downtown Kaycee and free horse and buggy rides during the summer, weather permitting.

Rates – Full hookups per site: $15. Water and electric only per site: $10. Tent sites: $5. Trailer lodging: $15. per person. No cards. Personal checks okay.

Getting there – Use exit 254 off I-25; then go east to the stop sign; then go right .5 miles through Kaycee and across the river bridge; then right to the camp on the right. *See map facing page.*

KC RV Park #2
(Private, Open all year)
PO Box 11, Kaycee, WY 82639 Ph: (307) 738-2233

About the camp – This camp is located near I-25 and just west and north of Kaycee. The camp has 17 RV sites: 15 pull-thrus (25x70) and 2 back-ins (25x50). All are full hookups (20/30/50 amp on city water) and all have gravel spurs and native grass 'yards' with tables and some grills. Tent sites available on native grass with some tables and grills or tenters can hike out on the acreage. *Horses okay.*

Amenities – Free horse and buggy rides during the summer, weather permitting; C-store and gas station across road.

Rates – Full hookups per site: $15. Water and electric only per site: $10. Tents: $5. No cards. Personal checks okay.

Getting there – Use exit 254 off I-25; then go west .2 miles to the camp on the right. *See map facing page.*

Kaycee Town Park
(Town of Kaycee, Open all year)

About the camp – This camp is located a block west of the main drag in downtown Kaycee. The camp has several tables and grills in a level grassy area with a nice stand of cottonwood trees. The camp has water and rest rooms (seasonal), a conservation education nature trail, two group picnic shelters with grills, a playground and a combo tennis and basketball court. Stay limited to no more than 5 days per month.

Rates – Free, with donations welcome and appreciated.

Getting there – Use exit 254 off I-25; then go east to the stop sign; then go right .3 miles into downtown Kaycee; then right just past the Post Office and .1 miles into the camp. *See map facing page.*

Hole in the Wall Campground
(Private, Open May to Oct. 31)
1773 Barnum Road, Kaycee, WY 82639

About the camp – This camp has the nearest hookups to the Hole in the Wall country and the owner is knowledgeable about local history. The camp has 11 pull-thru (up to 20x40) sites on native grass with water and electric hookups (20/30 and one 50 amp). Tent sites with use of water are available on native grass. *Horses okay: $5 with own feed.*

Amenities – Outhouse nearby.

Rates – Water and electric per site: $10. Tent site: $5.

Getting there – From Kaycee use exit 254 off I-25; then go west .9 miles on Hwys 190 and 191; then go left 16.1 miles on Hwy 190 to a fork and the end of the pavement. The camp is about 200 yards distant, between the forks of the road. *See map page 240.*

Outlaw Cave Campground
(BLM, Open April 15 to Nov. 15)

About the camp – The camp sits on a grassy flat near the rim of the canyon on the Middle Fork of the Powder River and at the trailhead to "Outlaw Cave," where the steep canyon walls that offered shelter and security to Butch Cassidy and his men still provide protection for a variety of wildlife species. Swifts and swallows use the canyon walls for nesting and wintering deer and elk find refuge along the south-facing slopes that provide food and solar warmth. The camp has a vault toilet and 5 sites with tables and fire rings, a few isolated fire rings without tables as well as dispersed camping options near this area. No potable water. Stay limited to 14 days in any 28 period.

Rates – Free

Getting there – From Kaycee use exit 254 off I-25; then go west .9 miles on Hwys 190 and 191; then go left 16.1 miles on Hwy 190 to a fork and the end of the pavement; then go left 8.4 miles to another fork and a sign for the 'Outlaw Cave Trail'; then go right .2 miles to the camp. *(About 5.5 miles from the end of the pavement you will be on the Outlaw Cave Road, which is not recommended for motor homes, camper trailers or low clearance vehicles. It is closed annually from Nov. 16 to April 15 and is always subject to emergency closure due to snowpack or muddy conditions.) See map page 240.*

Ed O. Taylor Wildlife Habitat Management Area
(Wyoming Game and Fish, Open May 1 to Nov. 15)

About the camp – This wildlife habitat management area consists of 10,158 acres, acquired to ensure protection of winter range for elk that summer in the Bighorn National Forest, as well as year-around habitat for mule deer. Straddling the Middle Fork of the Powder River, the area blends spectacular geology and substantial wildlife populations, rewarding the effort of the visitors who venture to this special out-of-the-way camping and recreation option.

The elevation varies from 6,000 to 7,000 feet, with steep canyon walls framing the Middle Fork of the Powder River, Bachus and Blue Creeks. Anglers may find rainbow, brown, cutthroat and brook trout in these waters. There is hiking, biking, photography and wildlife watching for many game species living in the area. Blue grouse, sage grouse, Hungarian partridge, wild turkeys, doves and cottontail rabbits are plentiful and pronghorn antelope can be seen feeding peacefully on the open rangeland.

Sagebrush, mountain shrubs and grasslands account for most of the habitat, with conifers, wet meadows and rock outcrops on most of the remaining lands. No potable water. Stay is limited to 14 days.

Rates – Free

Getting there – From Kaycee use exit 254 off I-25; then go west .9 miles on Hwys 190 and 191; then go left 16.1 miles on Hwy 190 to a fork and the end of the pavement; then go left 1.7 miles to the turnoff on the right; then go right .7 miles to a fork; then go left 5 miles to the boundary fence for the habitat area. *See map page 240.*

Lovell

Lovell is the nearest commercial center to the **Bighorn Canyon National Recreation Area**, and the **Medicine Wheel National Historic Landmark** in the **Bighorn National Forest** along the **Medicine Wheel Passage** (US14A). The main event here is **Mustang Days**, with a rodeo and all the trimmings, the third week in June.

In town, there is a privately-owned camp with hookups and a free town park. To the east, camping options include the Bighorn Canyon National Recreation Area, the Game and Fish Yellowtail Wildlife Habitat Management Area, a BLM camp and two Forest Service camps. Groceries and hardware stores are available in Lovell. For workouts and showers, visit the **Lovell Recreation Center**, at 502 Hampshire Ave, Ph: (307) 548-6466.

Super 8 Motel and RV Park

(Private, Open all year)
595 East Main St., Lovell, WY 82421 Ph or Fax: (307) 548-2725

About the camp – This camp covers a large grassy area to the rear of the Super 8 Motel on the east end of Lovell. The camp has 18 RV sites on gravel spurs with grass 'yards' and some tables. All sites are back-ins (up to 25x60) with full hookups (20/30/50 amp on city water). Tent sites are available.

Amenities – Rest rooms and showers (showers only: $3), laundry; restaurant adjacent to camp, and dump station.

Rates – Full hookups per site: $12. Tent sites: $ 7. All major cards. No reservations.

Getting there – This camp is behind the Super 8 Motel on the east end of Lovell. Check-in is at the motel office. *See map page 244.*

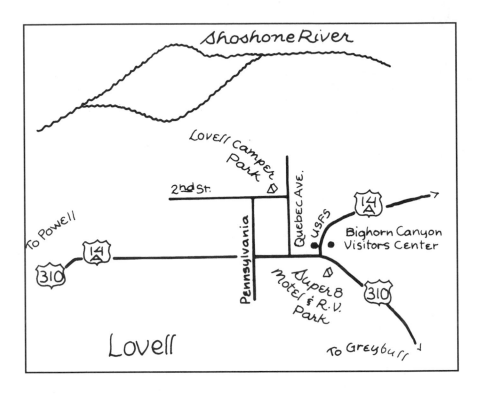

Lovell Camper Park

(City of Lovell, Open all year)
40 Quebec Ave., Lovell, WY 82421

About the camp – This a pleasant city park with lots of trees, plenty of grass and a deep water canal that borders the park. There are 7 tables with grills on concrete pads and several pull-thru options. Tenting options look best on the grass along the canal, where there are also a few tables. The camp has rest rooms and showers, potable water and dump station (seasonal), courtesy of the Town of Lovell. Stay limited to 3 days.

Rates – Free

Getting there – Near the "Welcome to Lovell" sign on the east end of town turn north on Pennsylvania St. and go 2 blocks to the 'T' at the baseball diamonds; then right one block to Quebec; then left on Quebec, across bridge to the park on the left. *See map above.*

Horseshoe Bend Campground
(Big Horn Canyon National Recreation Area, Open May 1 to Oct. 15)

About the camp – This native grass camp is open and spacious. The camp has potable water and rest rooms with flush toilets. Sites have tables and fire rings with grates. There are 61 sites in loops A and B, where there are several pull-thrus and big rig sites. Stay limited to 14 days.

Rates – The Big Horn Canyon Recreation Area has a 24-hour-user fee of $5 which includes camping. Annual permits are $30. (*Golden Eagle passes are not valid in this area*). Rates half with Golden Age or Access Passport.

Getting there – From the Big Horn Canyon Visitors Center on the east edge of Lovell go east 2.3 miles on US 14 A to Hwy 37; then left 9 miles to the boundary sign, another .5 miles to the ATM type self-service fee booth, and then .1 miles to the Horseshoe Bend turnoff on the right; then .3 miles to the right and the campground turnoff on the left; then left up a little rise .3 miles to the camp loop roads. *See map page 247.*

Worth mentioning – Straight about .3 miles past the turnoff to the camp is the marina. This facility offers a store, restaurant, boat rentals, docks, boat launch, gas, propane and a pay phone. Also available at the marina for your use and included in your entrance/camping fee are playground, beach/swimming, volleyball, horseshoes, and picnic areas near the water.

Yellowtail Wildlife Habitat Management Area
(Wyoming Game and Fish - Open all year)

The 19,424-acre Yellowtail Wildlife Habitat Area, six miles east of Lovell, was established through a cooperative agreement between the Wyoming Game and Fish Commission, the National Park Service, the U.S. Bureau of Reclamation and the U.S. Bureau of Land Management in the early 1960's to enhance waterfowl habitat. Yellowtail has one of the largest cottonwood river bottom areas in Wyoming and supports one of the richest concentrations of wildlife species in the state.

While Yellowtail may be best recognized for the area's superb pheasant hunting, there are also whitetail deer, mule deer, ducks, geese, cottontail rabbits, wild turkeys and mourning doves for hunting, wildlife watching and photography. Great blue herons and white pelicans are common during the summer months. Red-tailed hawks and the occasional trumpeter swan might also be seen among the 160 species of birds that frequent the area. Fishing in Big Horn Lake might net a walleye, trout, catfish, black crappie or perch.

There are 35 miles of roads and many trails to get you where you want to go. The game and fish information on this area suggests: "Spring is probably the best time to observe wildlife. Birds are engaged in their breeding displays and insects are not yet meddlesome."

The nine areas below were deemed the best options of 12 areas noted by area managers. The areas are listed in sequence according to where you turn off the highway east of Lovell.

Classroom Pond

(Wyoming Game and Fish, Open all year)

About the camp – This is a delightful area, but there is little parking with no handy turnaround area should another vehicle already be parked there. At the camp there is an elevated and covered deck (22x22) with built-in perimeter benches, an ancient stone fire ring and a pit toilet, but no potable water. Just across the two-track from the camp is the serene and picturesque Classroom Pond. Stay limited to 14 days.

Rates – Free

Getting there – From the Big Horn Canyon Visitors Center on the east edge of Lovell, go east 2.3 miles on US 14A to Hwy 37; then left 4 miles to the turnoff to the right; then right .8 miles to a fork; then right .9 miles to a right turn (*just a little bit past a large pond on the left*); then right .6 miles to camp on the left. *See map facing page.*

Cemetery Pond

(Wyoming Game and Fish, Open all year)

About the camp – Cemetery Pond is appropriately named, with its small parking area next to a cemetery. You will notice a two-track taking off to the left of the game and fish sign. If you wander down this road about .8 miles you will find several camping options, with stone fire rings and primitive boat ramps on the shore of Big Horn Lake. If you're putting a small boat or canoe in the water, this is a good option for a site. (Large boats can be put in at the marina and then anchored off your camp.) No toilet or potable water. Stay limited to 14 days.

Rates – Free

Getting there – From the Big Horn Canyon Visitors Center on the east edge of Lovell go east 2.3 miles on US 14A to Hwy 37; then left 4 miles to the turnoff to the right; then right .8 miles to a fork, then right 2.4 miles to a right turn (*just below bluff and rise to the left*); then right 1 mile to the Cemetery Pond parking area on the right. (*Half way down this lane there is a left hand turn where there is a vault toilet and grassy camping options, albeit removed from the water.*) *See map facing page.*

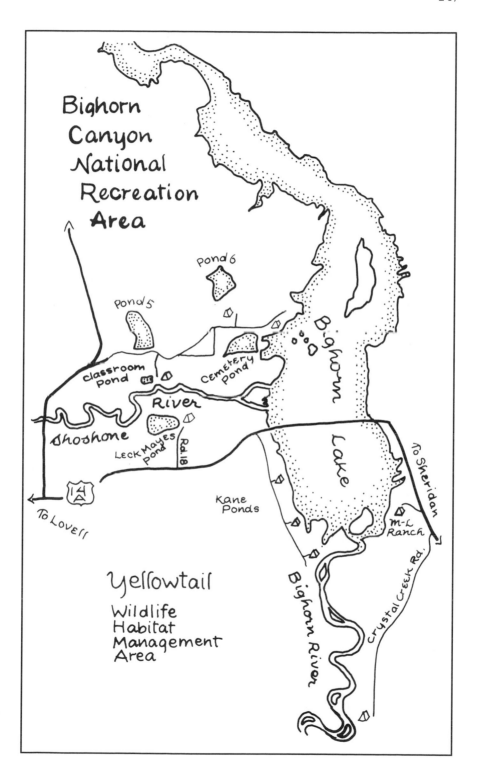

Leck Mays Pond Wetlands Viewing Area
(Wyoming Game and Fish, Open all year)

About the camp – This area has a viewing shelter on a hill above a large wetlands area. Camping is allowed to facilitate early morning and evening observations on the ponds. No toilet, potable water or fire rings. Stay limited to 14 days.

Rates – Free

Getting there – From the Big Horn Canyon Visitors Center on the east edge of Lovell go east 6.7 miles on US 14A to CR 18; then left .9 miles, past the game warden station on the right, to the blind overlooking this wetland. *See map page 247.*

Kane Ponds
(Wyoming Game and Fish, Open all year)

About the camp – There are three location off this road. The camping is bare bones but if you are an active and avid bird watcher, and self-contained, you might find these sites appealing. The native grasses in the parking areas at each of these sites had been mowed and a green metal gate shuts off further reconnoitering to all but foot traffic. No toilet or potable water. Stay limited to 14 days.

Rates – Free

Getting there – From the Big Horn Canyon Visitors Center on the east edge of Lovell go east 8.7 miles on US 14A to a right hand turn just beyond the railroad tracks; then right .9 miles to the first camp; *[or]* 1.9 miles to the second camp; *[or]* 2.4 miles to the last camp (*all camps are on the left*). *See map page 247.*

Mason-Lovell Ranch
(Wyoming Game and Fish, Open all year)

About the camp – This location, across the road from the historic buildings at the Mason-Lovell Ranch (1883-1902), offers a nostalgic atmosphere for this camping option. No camp fires allowed here due to the proximity of the historic buildings. There are a couple of two tracks in evidence that would allow you to explore the area. No toilet or potable water. Stay limited to 14 days.

Rates – Free

Getting there – From the Big Horn Canyon Visitors Center on the east edge of Lovell go east 12.5 miles on US 14A to a well-marked right hand turn; then right .3 miles to the ranch and game and fish sign. *See map page 247.*

Crystal Creek Road
(Wyoming Game and Fish, Open all year)

About the camp – This location is just off Crystal Creek Road (*BLM*

Road 1129) and gives you access to the east side of the Big Horn River. At the turnoff from Crystal Creek Road, there is a fork and a choice of two-tracks. A short way along the right fork there is a rock bluff and a cottonwood tree leaning into the rock face forming a picturesque arch over the road. No toilet or potable water. Stay limited to 14 days.

Rates – Free

Getting there – From the Big Horn Canyon Visitors Center on the east edge of Lovell go east 13.5 miles on US 14A to a well-marked right hand turn; then right 3.2 miles to the turnoff on the right. *See map page 247.*

Five Springs Falls Campground
(BLM, Open May to Oct.)

About the camp – This camp has 8 lovely sites along Five Springs Creek in a mature stand of ponderosa pine. From the camp a short trail leads to Five Springs Falls. The camp has a vault toilet, but no potable water. Sites have tables, grills and fire rings with grates. One camp is visible from the lower loop, while the others are tucked into this enchanting forest, a short hike across the creek from the upper parking area. Stay limited to 14 days in any 28 day period.

Rates – Campsite per night: $6.

Getting there – From the Big Horn Canyon Visitors Center on the east edge of Lovell, go east 18.3 miles on US 14A to a well-marked left hand turn; then left 2.2 miles to the camp on the right. (*The road sign was not encouraging: "Severe road damage, steep grade, hairpin turns, soft shoulder and falling rocks."*) That's over stated. The original surfacing is gone in many places, but the potholes aren't bad. Even damaged, the pavement is far better than any gravel road which, on this sort of grade, would be wash-boarded to bone-jarring proportions. There are also warnings about trailers and longer vehicles: It's your call. If you continue on the road past the campground you will dead end in a little over a mile, but there is a great view of the Bighorn Basin and more opportunities to hike and explore. *See map page 250.*

Medicine Wheel National Historic Landmark

About the site – This prehistoric landmark, perched on a mountain-side with a panoramic view of the Big Horn Basin, is worth a visit. The stones forming the spokes of the wheel and its perimeter were placed by ancient people with mysterious ways. Today, Native Americans are drawn to the wheel during vision quests. (You'll see their medicine bags tied to a nearby tree — don't touch!)

Getting there – From the Big Horn Canyon Visitors Center on the east edge of Lovell go east 27.6 miles on US 14A to a well-marked left hand turn and parking area (*from the parking area one must walk 1.5 miles each way to the site. If you want to see this, be sure to plan some extra time in your schedule*). *See map page 250.*

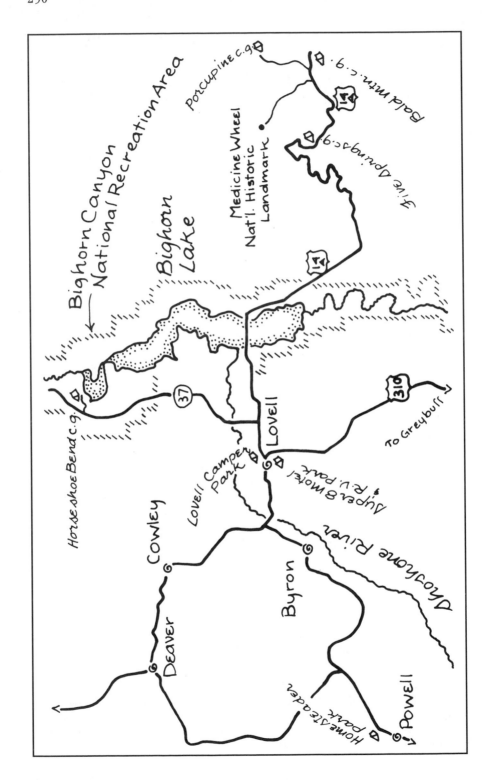

Porcupine Campground

(Bighorn National Forest, Open June 19 to Sept. 21)

About the camp – This camp is in timber, but open and sunny. There are vault toilets, potable water and 16 sites. All sites have tables with lantern hooks, fire pits with grates and grills. Sites appear to be roomy with nice tenting options. Site 14 is a pull-thru and there is a common parking area for walk-in camps 8 and 9. Stay limited to 14 days.

Rates – Campsite per night: $10. Rates half with Golden Age or Access Passport.

Getting there – From the Big Horn Canyon Visitors Center on the east edge of Lovell go east 28 miles on US 14A to a well-marked left hand turn; then left 1.8 miles to the camp on the left. *See map facing page.*

Bald Mountain Campground

(Bighorn National Forest, Open June 19 to Sept. 8)

About the camp – This camp seemed to have tighter tenting options than its near neighbor (Porcupine Campground) but offered some interesting sites. The camp has vault toilets, potable water and 15 sites. All sites have tables with lantern hooks, fire rings with grates and about half the sites have grills. Sites 11-12 and 14-15 share a common parking area. Stay limited to 14 days.

Rates – Campsite per night: $10. Rates half with Golden Age or Access Passport. (Reservations are possible at this campground up to 240 days in advance and 10 days prior to arrival. Service fee per reservation: $8.65. Ph: (877) 444-6777 toll free.)

Getting there – From the Big Horn Canyon Visitors Center on the east edge of Lovell go east 28.5 miles on US 14A to a well-marked right hand turn; then right .2 miles to the camp. *See map facing page.*

Ranchester

The name says it all; a ranching community with some old English bloodlines. This community is northwest of Sheridan along I-90 and to the east of Dayton on US 14. The **Connor Battlefield State Historical Site** is located here, just one part of the area's wealth of western American history. The **T-Rex Natural History Museum**, at the corner of US 14 and Big Horn Dr. on the west end of town, offers informative lectures on dinosaurs. Early in August the town hosts **Celebration Days**, with street dancing and more.

In Ranchester there is a privately-owned camp, camping at the Connor Battlefield commemorating the 1865 Battle on Tongue River and a free Game and Fish area to the north in the foothills of the Big Horn Mountains. Groceries, hardware and sporting goods are available. River swimming is an option at the state historical site and the **Tongue River Creative Playground**, on the east end of town, is open to the public in summer.

Lazy R Campground

(Private, Open all year)
(PO Box 286) 652 Hwy 14, Ranchester, WY 82839 Ph: (307) 655-9284
or (888) 655-9284 E-mail: lazyr-rv@wavecom.net

About the camp – This camp is on the main street in downtown
Ranchester with 22 full hookup (20/30/50 amp on town water) RV
sites (up to 23x60). 14 sites are pull-thrus and all sites are on gravel
spurs with native grass 'yards' and tables. No tents.

Amenities – Cable TV ($1.25); art gallery and gift shop, close to
downtown services, and pay phone.

Rates – Full hookups per site: $12-14. Personal checks okay. Reserva-
tions: phone, E-mail or mail.

Getting there – Use exit 9 off I-90, then go west .9 miles on US 14 into
Ranchester and the camp on the left at 1st Ave. West. *See map page
266.*

Connor Battlefield Historic Site

(Wyoming State Parks, Open April 1 to Nov. 1)

About the camp – This site is located within a meander of the Tongue
River and is grassy with lots of trees on two sides. The camp has vault
toilets, potable water, about 20 sites with tables and fire rings with
grates and several additional tables scattered in the trees near the river
where local children enjoy swimming. There are three pull-thrus, two
of which have two sites off the same pull-thru. Stay limited to 14 days.

Rates – This state park has no day use fee. The camping fee, as in all
of the other state parks, is $4 per night for residents and $9 per night
for nonresidents. Annual camping permits are available to residents for
$30. (For '99 rates see page 11).

Getting there – Use exit 9 off I-90; then go west .9 miles on US 14 west
to Ranchester and Gillette St.; then left .4 miles on Gillette St. to the
left hand turn into the site. *See map page 266.*

Kerns Wildlife Habitat Management Area

(Wyoming Game and Fish, Open June 1 to Nov. 15)

About the camp – This area consists of foothill benches separated by
deep canyons on 4,995 acres, which provide winter range for about 800
head of elk. Higher grass-covered benches are accented with pine-
covered ridges and canyons. Lower areas produce dense stands of
shrubs, including chokecherry and serviceberry. Wild turkeys, grouse,
black bears, mountain lions and a variety of small mammals live here.
Small numbers of elk and mule deer summer in the area.

Hiking opportunities, with photography and bird watching a plus, are
vast. Established trails lead to the Little Bighorn River, which flows
through a cool canyon and offers fishing for whitefish, brown and
rainbow trout. Check game and fish maps posted at the parking areas.

Getting there – From exit 9 off I-90, go west .3 miles to Hwy 345 to the right; then right 12.1 miles to CR 144 to the left; then left 10.2 miles to the first parking area on the left; *[or]* 10.9 miles to the second parking area on the left. *See map page 266.*

Riverton

Riverton is centrally located in a huge valley between the Wind River Range and the Owl Creek Mountains. It is a commercial center for farming and ranching families and much of the Wind River Indian Reservation. The free **Riverton Museum** is at 700 East Park St., Ph: (307) 856-2665, and just southwest of town is the **St. Stephen's Indian Mission**, with an especially interesting chapel. On the first weekend in July Riverton hosts the **Mountain Man Encampment**; on the second weekend in July, the **Riverton Rendezvous**, and the third weekend is highlighted by the **Riverton's Hot Air Balloon Rally**. In October, Central Wyoming College is the site of the jam-packed **Cowboy Poetry Roundup**.

In the city there are two privately-owned camps, two others in rural Riverton and 5 free camps on the Game and Fish Ocean Lake Wildlife Management Habitat Area nearby. The city has three full-service grocery stores, major chain discount outlets, sporting goods and bicycle sales and service. For a swim and shower visit the **Riverton High School Aquatic Center**, at West Sunset drive, Ph: (307) 856-4230, or in summer the outdoor pool in City Park.

Fort Rendezvous Campground

(Private, Open all year)
PO Box 1705, Riverton, WY 82501 Ph: (307) 856-1144

About the camp – This 12-acre camp with some shady sites is grassy, open and on meanders of the Little Wind River just south of town in rural Riverton. The camp has 25 full hookup (30/50 amp) sites (up to 25x60) and some tables. 12 sites are pull-thrus. Some sites are gravel with native grass 'yards' and some are all native grass. No tents.

Amenities – River fishing, game room and playground; C-store and pay phone across highway.

Rates – Full hookups per site: $15. No cards. Personal checks okay.

Getting there – From the intersection of US 26 and Hwy 789 in Riverton, go 2 miles south on Hwy 789 to the camp on the left. *See map page 254.*

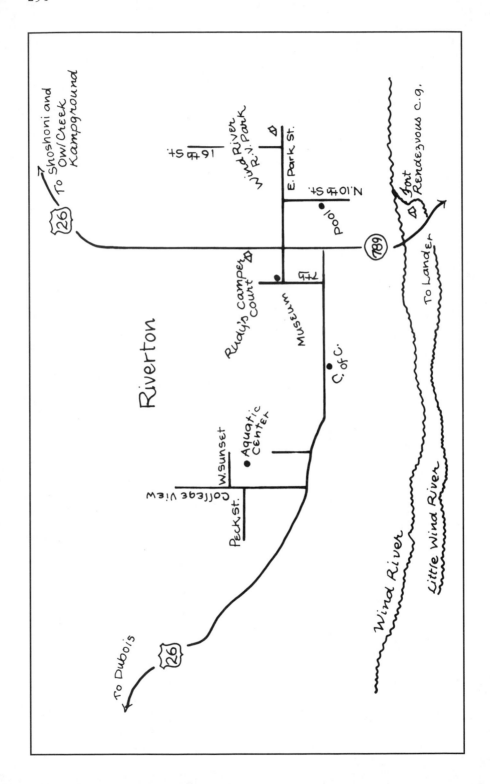

Wind River RV Park

(Private, Open all year)
1618 E. Park Ave., Riverton, WY 82501 Ph: (307) 857-3000 or out of state: (800) 528-3913 Fax: (307) 856-9559 E-mail:jpepper@wyoming.com

About the camp – This 4-acre camp is neat, landscaped and located on the east edge of Riverton, where a quiet residential area ends and the open space of agricultural lands begin. There are 60 RV sites, some shaded, all with gravel spurs and grass 'yards' with tables and grills. 38 sites are pull-thrus (15x70) and 22 back-ins (15x45). All sites are full hookups (20/30/50 amp on city water). The camp also has teepees and tent sites are available on grass using back-in sites. *Horses okay: free with camping.*

Amenities – Handicapped-accessible rest rooms and showers($) (showers only: $2), commercial laundry; cable at all sites ($2), meeting/card room with cable TV; gift shop, pop and snacks, limited RV parts, modem jack in office, dump station and pay phone.

Rates – Full hookups at all pull-thru sites for 2 persons: $23.50. Full hookups at all back-in sites for 2 persons: $21.50. Tent sites for 2 persons: $21.50. Additional persons: $2. Teepees (sleeping up to 6 persons): $21.50 V MC D Reservations: phone, E-mail, fax or mail.

Getting there – From the intersection of US 26 and Hwy 789 in Riverton; go north two blocks on US 26/Hwy 789 (Federal Blvd.) to E. Park St.; then east/right (*at Pizza Hut*) 6 bocks to the RV park on the left. *See map facing page.*

Owl Creek Kampground

(Private, Open all year)
11124 US Hwy 26 East-789, Riverton, WY 82501 Ph: (307) 856-2869

About the camp – This 5-acre camp is located in rural Riverton, secluded in a large stand of cottonwood trees. The camp has 20 RV sites, mostly shaded: 17 pull-thrus (up to 20x40) and 3 back-ins (20x20). 7 sites are full hookups (20/30 amp), 10 are water and electric only and 3 are electric only. The RV sites are paved with grass 'yards' or all grass. All sites have tables and there are some grills. The camp has 20 tent sites on grass with tables and grills. *Horses okay at neighbor's corrals: free with camping.*

Amenities – Rest rooms and showers (showers only: $3), laundry; game room and playground; limited groceries, ice, charcoal, gift shop, limited RV parts, dump station and pay phone.

Rates – All RV or tent sites for 2 persons: $16.50. Additional persons: $2. No cards. Personal checks okay. Reservations: phone or mail.

Getting there – From the intersection of US 26 and Hwy 789 in Riverton; go north about 6 miles on US 26/Hwy 789 (*Federal Blvd.*) to the camp on the right. *See map facing page.*

Rudy's Camper Court

(Private, Open all year)
622 E Lincoln, Riverton, WY 82501 Ph: (307) 856-9764

About the camp – This urban camp, close to many city services, is located across the street from one of Riverton's key shopping districts. The camp has 21 RV sites: 9 pull-thrus and 3 back-ins (all up to 12x35). All sites are full hookups (30 amp on city water) with tables on demand. The camp has 3 tent sites on grass with tables.

Amenities – Rest rooms and showers (showers only: $3); limited RV parts and dump station (grocery stores, sporting goods, restaurants, laundromat, gas/propane, pay phone, etc. nearby within easy walking distance).

Rates – Full hookups for 2 persons: $16.50. Tent sites for 2 persons: $10.50. Additional persons: $1. No cards. Personal checks okay. Reservations: phone or mail.

Getting there – From the intersection of US 26 and Hwy 789 in Riverton; go north five blocks on US 26/Hwy 789 (*Federal Blvd.*) to Roosevelt St.; then left 1/2 block to the camp on the left. *See map page 254.*

Ocean Lake Wildlife Habitat Management Area

(Wyoming Game and Fish, Open all year)

In the early 1920's, the Riverton Reclamation Project created Ocean Lake, 17 miles west of Riverton by diverting irrigation flows to a natural sump. The 12,725-acre Ocean Lake Wildlife Habitat Area, a cooperative agreement with the U.S. Bureau of Reclamation, was created in 1940 and completed in 1974.

There is a variety of habitat, from arid sagebrush grass lands and cultivated crop lands to marsh and open water. The lake is situated between the Owl Creek Mountains and the Wind River Range, and is classified as a warm water lake, with depths to 31 feet.

The area is best known for waterfowl and pheasant hunting. Between 1,500 and 2,000 pheasant are released annually to supplement native bird populations. Most of the area is classified as critical breeding and nesting range for Canada geese, and the southeastern portion provides habitat for whooping cranes. During migration, up to 3,000 geese, 400 sandhill cranes and 10,000 ducks visit the area.

Wildlife viewing and photography opportunities include grebes, terns, pelicans, snipes and avocets, mourning doves, mule deer, red fox, cottontail rabbits, muskrats, raccoons, mink and skunks. Anglers catch walleye, trout, bass, crappie, perch, bullhead and ling. In addition to power boaters, the area is a favorite with local wind surfers.

There are seven areas around the lake, maintained by the Bureau of Reclamation. No potable water. The perimeter roads to the area are US 26, Eight Mile Road, Hwys 134 and 133 and K Spur Road.

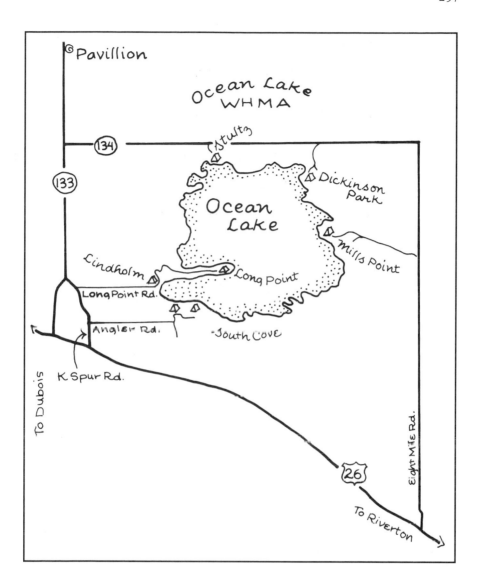

South Cove

(Game and Fish, Open all year)

About the camp – This camp is on the south shore of the lake nearest the small town of Kinnear. The camp has a vault toilet, a sheltered table with grill and a primitive boat ramp, but no potable water. If you follow a two-track east along the shore, you will find another vault toilet, two more tables with grills and acres of parking. Stay limited to 14 days.

Rates – Free

Getting there – From US 26 in downtown Kinnear, go north .8 miles on K Spur Road to Angler Road; then right 2 miles on Angler Road to a left turnoff; then left .1 miles to the camp and the lake. *See map page 257.*

Longpoint - Lindholm
(Game and Fish, Open all year)

About the camp – The main camping area here is on a long point of land on the southwest shore of the lake near Kinnear. This camp has a vault toilet, 12 sheltered tables with grills and a boat ramp, but no potable water. The Lindholm area is at the turnoff on Longpoint Road, and has only a vault toilet. Stay limited to 14 days.

Rates – Free

Getting there – From US 26 in downtown Kinnear, go north 1.4 miles on K Spur Road to Longpoint Road; then right 1.9 miles on Longpoint Road to a left turnoff; then left into the first area with vault toilet; then straight through this area 1.9 miles on a two track to the main camp. *See map page 257.*

Stultz
(Game and Fish, Open all year)

About the camp – This camp is on the northeast shore of the lake and has a small parking area, a vault toilet and a boat ramp, but no potable water. Stay limited to 14 days.

Rates – Free

Getting there – From Riverton go west on US 26 about 8 miles to Eight Mile Road; then north 9 miles to Hwy 134 at Midvale; then west 5 miles to the turnoff to the camp on the left; then left .3 miles to the shore and the camp. *See map page 257.*

Dickinson Park
(Game and Fish, Open all year)

About the camp – This camp is on the northeast shore of the lake and has one common knee-walled and covered picnic area with 3 tables and grills. No potable water. Stay limited to 14 days.

Rates – Free

Getting there – From Riverton go west on US 26 about 8 miles to Eight Mile Road; then north 9 miles to Hwy 134 at Midvale; then west 2.5 miles to the turnoff to the camp on the left; then left .7 miles to a fork in the road; then right .3 miles to the shore and the camp. *See map page 257.*

Mills Point
(Game and Fish, Open all year)

About the camp – This camp is on the east shore of the lake and has a vault toilet, one table, one stone fire ring and a primitive launch site, but no potable water. Stay limited to 14 days.

Rates – Free

Getting there – From Riverton go west on US 26 about 8 miles to Eight Mile Road; then north 6.6 miles to N. Irishman Road; then left .7 miles on N. Irishman Rd. to a fork in the road; then right 2 miles to the shore and the camp. *See map page 257.*

Shell

Shell is a very small town, with US 14 as its main street, in an area of interesting geology and paleontology. Popular dinosaur dig sites are located north of town on BLM land and open to the public (check locally for directions and road conditions). Shell is the western gateway to **Big Horn Scenic Byway (US14)**, with **Shell Falls** and the **Bighorn National Forest** along the route. In town there is a privately-owned camp with hookups and seven developed Forest Service camps nearby. Stock your coolers and take care of any equipment needs elsewhere along the way.

Shell Campground
(Private, Open April 1 to Nov. 15)
PO Box 16, Shell, WY 82441 Ph: (307) 765-2342

About the camp – This cozy camp is located on the south edge of Shell on US 14. The camp has 25 gravel and grass RV sites with tables and grills: 7 pull-thrus (up to 23x40) and 7 back-ins (up to 23x60). 14 sites are full hookups (20 amp on city water). Grass tent sites are available.

Amenities – Rest rooms and showers (showers only: $2), laundry; ice, dump station and pay phone.

Rates – Full hookups for 2 persons: $15. Water and electric only for 2 persons: $14. Electric only for 2 persons: $12. Tent sites for 2 persons: $10. Additional persons: $1. No credit cards. Personal checks okay. Reservations: phone or mail.

Getting there – This camp is on 1st St., just west of the highway, on the south end of Shell, Wyoming. *See map page 260.*

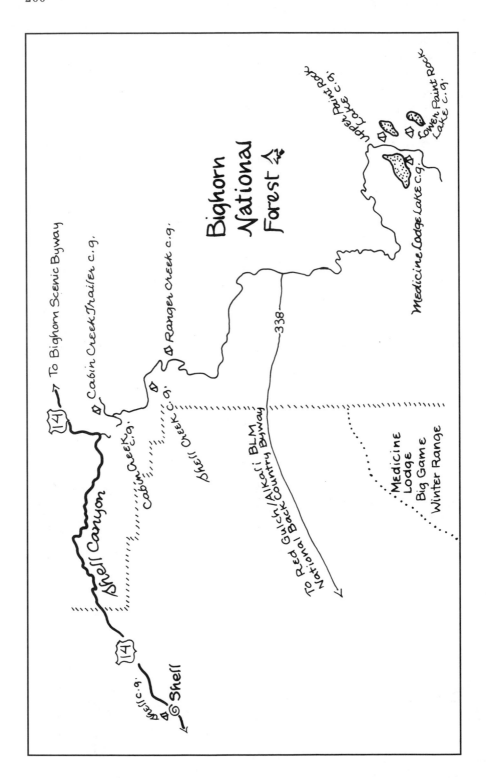

To Bighorn Scenic Byway

14

Shell Canyon

14

Shell

Shell c.g.

Cabin Creek Trailer c.g.

Ranger Creek c.g.

Cabin Creek c.g.

Shell Creek c.g.

To Red Gulch/Alkali BLM National Back Country Byway

338

Bighorn National Forest

Medicine Lodge Big Game Winter Range

Medicine Lodge Lake c.g.

Medicine Lodge

Upper Paint Rock c.g.

Lower Paint Rock Lake c.g.

Cabin Creek Trailer Campground
(Bighorn National Forest, Open May 22 to Sept. 8)

About the camp – This camp has 26 sites in an open park, most sites with fire rings. The camp has vault toilets and potable water. Stay limited to nightly or by the month.

Rates – Campsite per night: $6. Campsite per month: $105. Rates half with Golden Age or Access Passport. (Reservations are possible up to 240 days in advance and 10 days prior to arrival. Service fee per reservation: $8.65. Ph: (877) 444-6777 toll free.)

Getting there – From Shell go east 15.9 miles on US 14 to Paintrock Road (FSR 17); then right .1 miles to the camp road on the left; then left .1 miles to the fee board. *See map facing page.*

Cabin Creek Campground
(Bighorn National Forest, Open May 15 to Sept. 8)

About the camp – This camp is close to the highway and has 4 sites off of a cul-de-sac in an open park. The camp has a pit toilet but no potable water. Sites have tables and fire rings. Stay limited to 14 days.

Rates – Campsite per night: $8. Rates half with Golden Age or Access Passport.

Getting there – From Shell go east 15.9 miles on US 14 to Paintrock Road (FSR 17); then right .2 miles to the camp turnoff on the right; then right .1 miles to the camp. *See map facing page.*

Shell Creek Campground
(Bighorn National Forest, Open May 15 to Sept. 21)

About the camp – This camp is only 1.6 miles off the highway with pleasant sites, well spaced along Shell Creek. Most sites are very short walk-ins, to the tables between the road and the stream. The camp has vault toilets, potable water and sites with tables and fire rings with grates. Stay limited to 14 days.

Rates – Campsite per night: $8. Rates half with Golden Age or Access Passport.

Getting there – From Shell go east 15.9 miles on US 14 to Paintrock Road (FSR 17); then right 1.6 miles to the camp turnoff on the right; then right .2 miles into the camp. *See map facing page.*

Ranger Creek Campground
(Bighorn National Forest, Open May 15 to Sept. 21)

About the camp – This camp is 3.6 miles off the highway and has sites on both sides of the road with several cozy sites near the stream, down and off the road to the right. The camp has vault toilets, potable water and a group area that can be reserved. Sites have tables and fire rings with grates. Stay limited to 14 days.

Rates – Campsite per night: $9. Rates half with Golden Age or Access Passport. (Reservations are possible at this campground up to 240 days in advance and 10 days prior to arrival. Service fee per reservation: $8.65. Ph: (877) 444-6777 toll free.)

Getting there – From Shell go east 15.9 miles on US 14 to Paintrock Road (FSR 17); then right 3.6 miles to the camp which straddles the road. *See map page 260.*

Medicine Lodge Campground
(Bighorn National Forest, Open July 1 to Sept. 8)

About the camp – This camp on Upper Medicine Lodge Lake has 8 sites in a mixed conifer forest, and a primitive boat ramp with angler parking. The camp has vault toilets and potable water. Sites are roomy with good tenting options and have tables and fire rings with grates. Stay limited to 14 days.

Rates – Campsite per night: $8. Rates half with Golden Age or Access Passport.

Getting there – From Shell go east 15.9 miles on US 14 to Paintrock Road (FSR 17); then right 11.6 miles to the junction of FSR 17 and 338; then stay left 10.6 miles on FSR 17 to the camp on the right. *See map page 260.*

Upper Paint Rock Lake Campground
(Bighorn National Forest, Open July 1 to Sept. 8)

About the camp – The entrance to this camp is on the left, just beyond Medicine Lodge Campground. The camp has a vault toilet, potable water and 4 sites with tables and fire rings with grates. Stay limited to 14 days.

Rates – Campsite per night: $8. Rates half with Golden Age or Access Passport.

Getting there – From Shell go east 15.9 miles on US 14 to Paintrock Road (FSR 17); then right 11.6 miles to the junction of FSR 17 and 338; then stay left 10.8 miles on FSR 17 to the camp entrance on the left. *See map page 260.*

Lower Paint Rock Lake Campground
(Bighorn National Forest, Open July 1 to Sept. 8)

About the camp – This camp is on a slight rise on the off-lake side of the road at Lower Paint Rock Lake. The camp has a primitive boat ramp, horse handling facilities for the Paint Rock Trailheads, a vault toilet and potable water. Sites have tables and fire rings with grates. Stay limited to 14 days.

Rates – Campsite per night: $8. Rates half with Golden Age or Access Passport.

Getting there – From Shell go east 15.9 miles on US 14 to Paintrock Road (FSR 17); then right 11.6 miles to the junction of FSR 17 and 338; then stay left 11.3 miles on FSR 17 to the camp at the end of the road. *See map page 260.*

Sheridan

Sheridan, another town on the trail of western history, has seen good times as a ranching district. The tasteful, handsome 19th century architecture in downtown and the older residential areas reflects a prosperous past. **King's Ropes and Saddlery** in downtown Sheridan has a large free museum which heralds the function, craftsmanship and design of western tack. Real cowboys shop here for gear. **Trail End State Historic Site,** at 400 E. Clarendon Ave., Ph: (307) 674-4589, and the **Bradford Brinton Memorial Museum,** in Big Horn at 239 Brinton Road, Ph: (307) 672-3173, are museums set up in what were once palatial residences ($). In July, Sheridan hosts the **Sheridan Wyo Rodeo,** a Professional Rodeo Cowboy event and early in September, they kick up their heels during **Big Horn Mountains Polka Days.**

In town there are three privately-owned camps with hookups and nearby six Forest Service camps. Sheridan has groceries, hardware and sporting goods. Sheridan Tent and Awning for wall tents, teepees or any custom canvas products is at 128 North Brooks St., Ph: (307) 674-6313. Recreation and workout facilities are available at the **Sheridan YMCA,** at 417 North Jefferson, Ph: (307) 674-7488. In summer there is an outdoor swimming pool at Kendrick Park open to the public with modest admission. The pool is near the lower end of Sheridan's elk and bison pasture and you may see elk and bison grazing nearby as you swim.

Big Horn Mountain KOA
(Private, Open May 25 to Sept. 15)
63 Decker Road (PO Box 35A), Sheridan, WY 82801 Ph: (307) 674-8766 or (800) 562-7621

About the camp – This large clean and green camp with some 30 species of trees is located on the north end of Sheridan. There are 90 RV sites: 80 pull-thrus (up to 30x75) and 10 back-ins (up to 30x50). 35 sites are full hookups (30/50 amp on city water). Sites have gravel parking areas and grass 'yards' with sheltered tables and grills at most sites. Tent sites are grass with tables and grills. This KOA also has Kamper Kabins.

Amenities – Rest rooms and showers (showers only: $4 and only until 4 p.m.), laundry; game room, horseshoes, basketball, playground, pool and spa (adults only); gift shop, limited groceries and RV parts, dump station, propane, pay phone and all-you-can-eat pancake breakfast in summer ($2.95/and children age 11 and under, 25¢ per year of age).

Rates – Full hookups for two persons: $20. Water and electric only for two persons: $18. Tent sites for two persons: $16. Kamper Kabins for two persons: $27. Additional persons: age 17 and under $2; over age 17 $2.50. MC V D Reservations: phone or mail.

Getting there – From I-90 use exit 20, go to first intersection on Business I-90; then right on Hwy 338 north; then north .5 miles to the camp on the right. *See map facing page.*

Sheridan RV Park

(Private, Open April 1 to Oct. 15)
807 Avoca Ave., Sheridan, WY 82801 Ph: (307) 674-0722

About the camp – This clean, green, urban 3-acre camp, with Little Goose Greek flowing along the east edge, has many shaded sites in a setting of cottonwood, black walnut and ash trees. There are 32 RV sites: 20 pull-thrus (up to 30x100) and 12 back-ins (up to 30x50). 15 sites are full hookups (20/30/50 amp) on city water. Sites have gravel parking areas and grass 'yards' with tables and chairs. Tent sites are grass with tables and chairs. This camp caters to quiet couples.

Amenities – Rest rooms and showers, laundry; small museum in office, knowledgeable help on area history and sites (owner is great-grand-daughter of Wm. F. "Buffalo Bill" Cody).

Rates – Full hookups for 2 persons incl. tax: $15. Water and electric only for 2 persons incl. tax: $14. Tent sites for 2 persons incl. tax: $12. Additional persons: $3. No credit cards. Reservations: phone or mail.

Getting there – Use exit 25 off I-90; then west .2 miles to US 14/87 (*Coffeen Ave.*); then right .6 miles to Avoca Ave. (*an angle street that only goes to left at the Little Big Man Pizza Restaurant*); then left .1 miles to the camp on the right. *See map facing page.*

Bramble Motel and RV Park

(Private, Open all year)
2366 N. Main St., Sheridan, WY 82801 Ph: (307) 674-4902

About the camp – This camp has 7 full hookup sites on gravel (20/30 amp, on city water, up to 12x40) . The camp caters to long-term needs especially in winter when other area camps are closed. No tents.

Amenities – Rest room and shower.

Rates – Full hookups per site: $20. Reservations: phone or mail.

Getting there – From I-90 use exit 20, follow business I-90 south on North Main St. to the camp on the right. *See map facing page.*

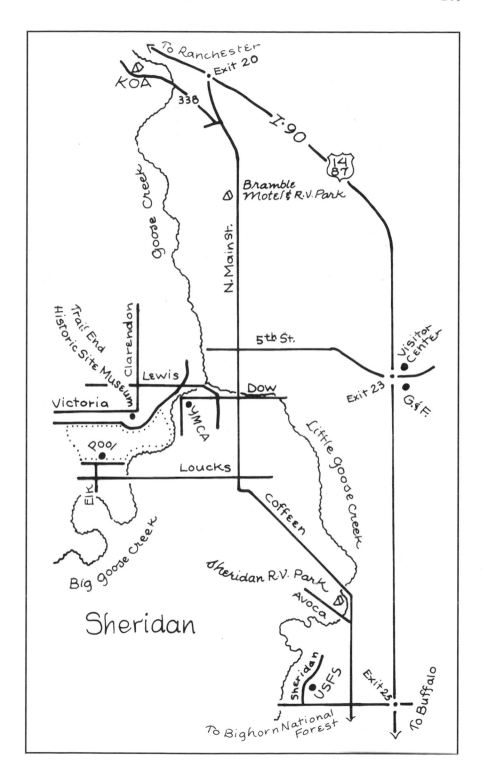

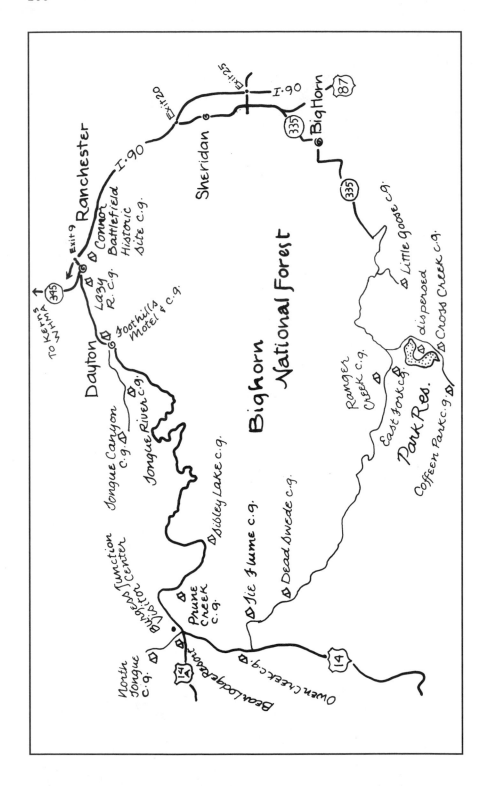

—West of Sheridan—

Little Goose Campground

(Bighorn National Forest, Open late June to Oct.)

About the camp – Little Goose is a splendid camp. It is fenced and has a vault toilet and three walk-in sites with tables and fire rings. Going in the road is downhill all the way and you may be able to get there in just about anything, but getting back up the hill will most likely require 4-wheel-drive. No potable water. Stay limited to 14 days.

Rates – Free

Getting there – From Sheridan go south on US 87 to the junction of Hwy 335; then 14.5 miles on Hwy 335 (*which becomes FSR 26*) through the edge of the town of Big Horn and up the Red Grade to the camp turnoff on the left; then left about 2 miles downhill on a some-times rough, rocky and gully-washed road to the camp. *See map facing page.*

Park Reservoir (Dispersed)

(Bighorn National Forest, Open late June to Oct.)

About the camp – This undeveloped camp has sites in the trees on a point of land on the south end of Park Reservoir. Near this area there is a primitive boat ramp and a large open park. No toilet or potable water. Stay limited to 16 days.

Rates – Free

Getting there – From Sheridan go south on US 87 to the junction of Hwy 335; then 20.9 miles on Hwy 335 (*which becomes FSR 26*) through the edge of the town of Big Horn and up the Red Grade to the camp turnoff on the left; then left about 2.5 miles on FSR 293 to the east shore of Park Reservoir and a road to the left with a sign to Spear O Wigwam, a private camp; then left about .1 miles to the fork of FSR 292; then right about .2 miles on FSR 292 to the dispersed area and the shore of the reservoir. *See map facing page.*

Cross Creek Campground

(Bighorn National Forest, Open late June to Oct.)

About the camp – Cross Creek has only three sites with tables and fire rings. It is near the south end of Park Reservoir and the East Fork of Big Goose Creek. No toilet or potable water. Stay limited to 14 days.

Rates – Free

Getting there – From Sheridan go south on US 87 to the junction of Hwy 335; then 20.9 miles on Hwy 335 (*which becomes FSR 26*) through the edge of the town of Big Horn and up the Red Grade to the camp turnoff on the left; then left about 2.5 miles on FSR 293 to the east shore of Park Reservoir and a road to the left with a sign to Spear

O Wigwam, a private camp; then left about .3 miles to the gate at Spear O Wigwam; then through the gate and 1.3 miles (*keeping this private camp to the left*) to the camp. *See map page 266.*

Coffeen Park Campground
(Bighorn National Forest, Open late June to Oct.)

About the camp – This camp has 5 sites just in the trees off a large open park, with the East Fork of Big Goose Creek a little behind and below most of the campsites. A trailhead for the Cloud Peak Wilderness leaves from the south end of the park. The camp has a vault toilet, but no potable water. Sites have tables and fire rings. Stay limited to 14 days.

Rates – Free

Getting there – From Sheridan go south on US 87 to the junction of Hwy 335; then 20.9 miles on Hwy 335 (*which becomes FSR 26*) through the edge of the town of Big Horn and up the Red Grade to the camp turnoff on the left; then left about 2.5 miles on FSR 293 to the east shore of Park Reservoir and a road to the left with a sign to Spear O Wigwam, a private camp; then left about .3 miles to the gate at Spear O Wigwam; then through the gate and 4.0 miles (*keeping this private camp to the left, and through the Cross Creek Campground*) to the camp (*the road into Coffeen Park is rough and rocky. From Cross Creek on you will want a 4-wheel-drive or at the minimum a vehicle with high clearance and a good low gear*). *See map page 266.*

East Fork Campground
(Bighorn National Forest, Open June 12 to Sept. 8)

About the camp – This camp has 12 roomy sites with good tenting options in a mixed forest. The camp has a vault toilet, potable water and sites with tables and fire rings with grates. Stay limited to 14 days.

Rates – Campsite per night: $12. Rates half with Golden Age or Access Passport.

Getting there – From Sheridan go south on US 87 to the junction of Hwy 335; then 21 miles on Hwy 335 (*which becomes FSR 26*) through the edge of the town of Big Horn and up the Red Grade to the camp turnoff on the left; then left .5 miles to the camp. *See map page 266.*

Ranger Creek Campground
(Bighorn National Forest, Open June 12 to Sept. 8)

About the camp – This camp has 11 roomy sites with good tenting options in a nice forest mix. The camp has a vault toilet, potable water and sites with tables, fire rings with grates and grills. Stay limited to 14 days.

Rates – Campsite per night: $8. Rates half with Golden Age or Access Passport.

Getting there – From Sheridan go south on US 87 to the junction of Hwy 335; then 21.6 miles on Hwy 335 (*which becomes FSR 26*) through the edge of the town of Big Horn and up the Red Grade to the camp turnoff on the right; then right .1 miles to the camp. *See map page 266.*

—For the View—

Back Country: Sheridan to US 14

The road into the Bighorn National Forest from Sheridan — the main access to the next six camps — is paved for the first 9.8 miles. From the end of the pavement, it is 46 miles on good gravel road, returning to the pavement on US 14 near Burgess Junction (*along the way back to the pavement, you pass two other camps, Dead Swede Campground and Tie Flume Campground, on FSR 26 before reaching US 14. See Burgess Junction on page 232 and map on page 266*). This could make a nice day trip from Sheridan with a right on US 14 to Burgess Junction; then to Dayton, Ranchester and I-90 back to the city; *[or]* with a left on US 14, you are heading through scenic Shell Canyon after a nice drive through the forest on an alternative back-country route.

Shoshoni

Shoshoni, situated on the plains east of the Owl Creek Mountains, is the nearest community to Boysen State Park. At Boysen there are 12 state park camps scattered around the reservoir and free Game and Fish camping areas on Lake Cameahwait (Bass Lake), off the northwest boundary of the state park. North from Shoshoni on US 20 is scenic **Wind River Canyon.** In town is the **Yellowstone Drug Store**, with an old-fashioned soda fountain atmosphere and a reputation for the best malts and ice cream sodas. Basic groceries are available at two C-stores in Shoshoni.

Boysen State Park
(Wyoming State Parks, Open all year)
15 Ash, Shoshoni, WY 82649 Ph: (307) 876-2796

About the camp – Boysen State Park is about 35,000 acres, about half of that comprising Boysen Reservoir. While the park is open to camping all year, services are reduced in the off-season: some water lines are not frost free and some lights are switched off. There are 30 vault toilets scattered around the lake with potable water facilities limited to the east shore. With the exception of Upper and Lower Wind River Canyon Campgrounds, camping here is not designated per se, but around the lake you will find 360 tables and 247 have grills.

For those who are camping with some form of watercraft, there are remote camping options on several islands within the reservoir and several have sites with tables and grills (check at park headquarters for island information).

The landscape is largely sagebrush grasslands around the reservoir with the steep-walled Wind River Canyon below the dam on the north end of the reservoir. The occasional bighorn sheep can be seen in the canyon, and on the state park lands one is likely to see mule deer, white-tailed deer, antelope, bald and golden eagles, coyotes, fox, numerous waterfowl and songbirds and the occasional moose, elk, bobcat or mountain lion.

For those interested in fishing, the reservoir holds several species of trout, walleye, sauger, ling, catfish, largemouth bass, perch and crappie. Throughout the park, stay limited to 14 days.

Rates at all campgrounds in the park – Day use fees for this park are $2 for residents and $5 for nonresidents. Camping fees for residents are $4 per night and $9 for nonresidents. An annual day use pass, good at all state parks, is available to residents for $25 and nonresidents for $40. Annual camping permits are available to residents for $30. The annual camping pass is not available for nonresidents. (For '99 rates see page 11).

The area's campgrounds are individually noted below, with directions. State park facilities and campground listings start with Lower Wind River Campground in the northeast part of this park and go clockwise down the east shore and up the west shore.

Lower Wind River Campground

About the camp – This camp has lots of trees, many shady sites and is right off of the highway near the banks of the Wind River and the mouth of Wind River Canyon. The camp has vault toilets, potable water, a playground and a group area that can be reserved. There are 32 roomy campsites with good tenting options, tables, fire rings with grates and some grills.

Getting there – From Shoshoni go north 15.8 miles on US 20/Hwy 789 to the camp on the left. *See map page 273.*

Upper Wind River Campground

About the camp – This camp, just .5 miles upstream from the Lower Wind River Campground, also has lots of trees, shady sites and is right off the highway near the banks of the Wind River at the mouth of Wind River Canyon. The camp has vault toilets, potable water, a playground and horseshoe pits. There are 50 roomy campsites with good tenting options, tables, fire rings with grates and a few grills. Two sites are walk-ins along the river on the downstream end of the camp.

Getting there – From Shoshoni go north 15.3 miles on US 20/Hwy 789 to the camp on the left. *See map page 273.*

Brannon Campground

About the camp – This camp is on the northeast shore of the reservoir, with a boat ramp on one end and a picnic area, swimming beach and change house on the other. The are two camping options: A lower gravel area with a vault toilet and 7 tables; 6 with fire rings and grates and one with a grill, and a top-side camp that has a grassy area with 15 tables and grills, and 3 tables with fire rings and grates with camper parking on the perimeter. Tent camping is allowed on this grassy area, but only on the weekends due to a watering schedule Monday through Friday. The upper area has a vault toilet, potable water and a pay phone.

Getting there – From Shoshoni go north 13.2 miles on US 20/Hwy 789 to the camp turnoff on the left; then left .2 miles to the camp on the right. *See map page 273.*

Boysen Marina

(Private, Open all year)
827 Brannon Road, Shoshoni, WY 82649 Ph: (307) 876-2772

About the camp – The marina has two electric (15/30 amp) hookups and the only hookups of any kind for over-nighters within Boysen State Park.

Amenities – Restaurant, C-store, tackle, bait, gas dock, marine mechanic on staff, vault toilet, and pay phone.

Rates – Electric only per site: $12.50. V MC Personal checks okay. Reservations: phone or mail.

Getting there – From Shoshoni go north 13.2 miles on US 20/Hwy 789 to the camp turnoff on the left; then .6 miles to the marina on the right. *See map page 273.*

Tamarask Campground

About the camp – This camp is just south of Brannon Campground and the marina on the northeast side of the reservoir, with sites on three peninsula-like protrusions of land along the shore line. The camp has a vault toilet, potable water, playground, 25 tables with fire rings and grates and a couple of grills.

Getting there – From Shoshoni go north 13.2 miles on US 20/Hwy 789 to the camp turnoff on the left; then left .8 miles to the camp. *See map page 273.*

Boysen State Park Headquarters

About the headquarters – This office offers information and maps for this and other state parks in Wyoming, and a dump station. If the office is closed, campground hosts at the Upper and Lower Wind River Campground should have area maps and information.

Getting there – From Shoshoni go north 13 miles on US 20/Hwy 789 to the turnoff on the right; then right .3 miles to the office; *[or]* .1 miles to the dump station on the right. *See map facing page.*

Tough Creek Campground

About the camp – This camp is on the edge of the reservoir with about 60 sites, a boat ramp, dock and picnic area. The camp has vault toilets and potable water. Camps have tables, fire rings with grates and there are some grills. This area is open, with light lake-side greenery, few trees and little shade. Many sites are close to the water, offering the possibility of anchoring your boat near your camp.

Getting there – From Shoshoni go north 6.2 miles on US 20/Hwy 789 to the camp turnoff on the left; then left 1.1 miles to the camp. *See map facing page.*

Poison Creek Campground

About the camp – This camp is on the edge of a small inlet on the southeastern end of the reservoir. There is a primitive boat launch, vault toilet and several stone fire rings, but no potable water.

Getting there – From Shoshoni go west 1.5 miles on US 20/Hwy 789 to the camp turnoff on the right; then right .3 miles to a fork; then left 1 mile and right at the cattle guard; then .5 miles to the camp. *See map facing page.*

Fremont Bay Campground

About the camp – This camp is on the edge of the west shore of the reservoir, with a boat ramp, vault toilet, playground and group area which can be reserved. Beyond the group area and playground there are 3 tables with fire rings and grates . No potable water.

Getting there – From Shoshoni go west 5.5 miles on US 20/Hwy 789 to the turnoff on the right; then right .4 miles to a fork; then right 3 miles on State Park Loop #1 to the camp turnoff on the right; then right .3 miles to the camp. *See map facing page.*

South Muddy Campground

About the camp – This camp on the south shore of an inlet along the west side of the reservoir has 2 tables with sun and wind shelters and fire rings with grates and a vault toilet, but no potable water.

Getting there – From Shoshoni go west 5.5 miles on US 20/Hwy 789 to the turnoff on the right; then right .4 miles to a fork; then right 4.8 miles on State Park Loop #1 to the camp turnoff on the right; then right .1 miles to the camp. *See map facing page.*

North Muddy Campground

About the camp – This camp is on the north shore of an inlet on the west shore of the reservoir, with a vault toilet, but no potable water.

Getting there – From Shoshoni go west 5.5 miles on US 20/Hwy 789 to the turnoff on the right; then right .4 miles to a fork; then left 8.3 miles to State Park Loop #2; then right 4.2 miles (*past Lake Cameahwait and camps that will be noted following the state park listings*), to the camp turnoff on the right; then right .7 miles to the camp.

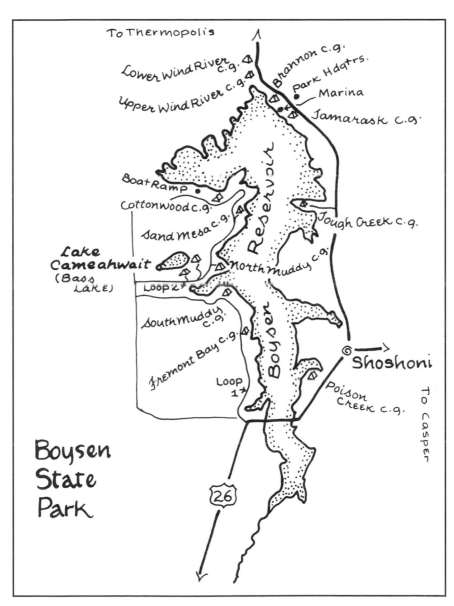

Sand Mesa Campground

About the camp – This camp is on the west shore of the reservoir and has a vault toilet, 2 tables with sun and wind shelters and fire rings with grates. No potable water.

Getting there – From Shoshoni go west 5.5 miles on US 20/Hwy 789 to the turnoff on the right; then right .4 miles to a fork; then left 8.3 miles to State Park Loop #2; then right 6.0 miles (*past Lake Cameahwait and camps that will be noted following the state park listings*), to the camp turnoff on the right; then right .3 miles to the camp. *See map page 273.*

Cottonwood Campground

About the camp – This camp is on the south shore of a bay along the west side of the reservoir, and has a boat ramp and trailer parking near the camp. The camp has some trees, a smooth beach area, a vault toilet and small group area with tables and a large grill. There are several sites with tables, some with fire rings and shelters as well as other camping options. No potable water.

Getting there – From Shoshoni go west 5.5 miles on US 20/Hwy 789 to the turnoff on the right; then right .4 miles to the fork; then left 11.1 miles to the upper end of State Park Loop #2; then right 3.0 miles to the boat ramp; *[or]* 3.3 miles to the camp on the left. *See map page 273.*

Lake Cameahwait Campgrounds
(Wyoming Game and Fish, Open all year)

About the camp – These camps on Lake Cameahwait (Bass Lake) are managed by Wyoming Game and Fish Department and are not within the boundaries of Boysen State Park. There are 2 camping areas on the lake with vault toilets, but no potable water. Each area has several sites with shelters, tables and fire rings.

Rates – Free

Getting there – From Shoshoni go west 5.5 miles on US 20/Hwy 789 to the turnoff on the right; then right .4 miles to the fork; then left 8.3 miles to State Park Loop #2; then right 2.5 miles to the lake on the left. *See map page 273.*

Story

Story is in the heart of an area with many historic sites and the nearest town to the **Fort Phil Kearney State Historic Site Museum and Visitors Center** ($) Ph: (307) 684-7629. In Story there is one privately-owned camp with electric only hookups and tenting. Groceries are available in Story.

Wagon Box Campground

(Private, Open Memorial Day to Sept. 30)
PO Box 494 Story, WY 82842 Ph: (307) 683-2491

About the camp – This lush shady camp is on Spring Creek on the north edge of Story behind the Wagon Box Inn. The camp has 7 grass, electric only (20 amp) RV sites. All sites are back-ins (up to 20x40) with some tables and some fire rings. Grass tent sites with some tables and some fire rings are available throughout the area. *Horses okay.*

Amenities – Rest rooms and showers; meeting/card room, horseshoes, volleyball and fishing.

Rates – Electric only per site: $15. Tent sites: $10. No cards. Personal checks okay. Reservations: phone or mail.

Getting there – From I-90 use exit 33 (*Meade Creek Road*); then west 1.1 miles on Hwy 342 to the stop sign at US 87; then south 5 miles on US 87 to Hwy 193; then right 2.3 miles to Hwy 194; then right .5 miles to Hwy 340; then right 1 mile through downtown Story and right to the Wagon Box Inn; then right through the parking lot; then left to the camp office.

Ten Sleep

Ten Sleep is another of those Wyoming towns where the highway serves as a long main street. The community's name is a Native American way of measuring distance as 'ten sleeps' from there to here. In town there is one privately-owned camp with hookups and tenting. In the area there are nine developed Forest Service camps, one free BLM camp, three free Game and Fish areas and camping at the Medicine Lodge State Archaeological Site. Groceries and basic supplies are available here.

East from Ten Sleep on US 16 is the **Cloud Peak Skyway** crossing **Powder River Pass,** on the way to Buffalo. Going north you find the **BLM Red Gulch/Alkali National Back Country Byway.** In town look for the **Vista Park Museum.** Ten Sleep puts on **Ten Sleep Celebration Days** in July, with rodeo, chili cookoff and more.

Ten Broek R.V. Park and Cabins

(Private, Open April 1 to Nov. 1)

PO Box 10, Ten Sleep, WY 82442 Ph: (307) 366-2250

About the camp – This camp, on the west end of Ten Sleep, is on 4 grassy acres with lots of trees and mostly shaded sites. The camp has 75 sites: 50 RV sites are grass pull-thrus (20x60) with tables, portable grills, and full hookups (30 amp on city water). 25 grass tent sites with tables round out the camp. Camper cabins are available. *Horses okay.*

Amenities – Rest rooms and showers, laundry; cable TV included at all RV sites, game room, basketball, volleyball, badminton and horseshoes; antique and gift shop, snacks and ice, limited RV parts, dump station, propane and pay phone.

Rates – Full hookups for 2 persons: $12. Tent sites for 2 persons: $11. Additional persons age 10 and over: $2; under 10: $1 and under 3: free. Camper cabins: $22-31.

Getting there – This camp is on the south side of US 16 on the west edge of Ten Sleep. *See map facing page.*

—Northwest of Ten Sleep—

Wigwam Rearing Station Access Area

(Wyoming Game & Fish, Open April 1 to Nov. 1)

About the camp – There are two areas to this camp which is on Tensleep Creek about five miles east of Ten Sleep: both are primitive. There are several stone fire pits from previous generations of campers, but there is little available wood, no potable water, no tables and only one pit toilet, which is located in the first camping area. In the first area there are several stone fire rings that mark campsites and a pit toilet. In the second area there is only one fire pit in a roomy, open area on the bank of Tensleep Creek. Stay limited to 14 days.

Rates – Free

Getting there – From Ten Sleep go east 5 miles on US 16 to the first turnoff to the left; *[or]* 5.1 miles to the second turnoff to the left. *See map facing page.*

Leigh Creek Campground

(Bighorn National Forest, Open May 15 to Oct. 31)

About the camp – This small camp is along Leigh Creek with mostly cozy sites partially hidden in the creek-side greenery. The camp has a vault toilet, potable water and 11 sites with tables and fire rings with grates. Stay limited to 14 days.

Rates – Campsite per night: $9. Rates half with Golden Age or Access Passport.

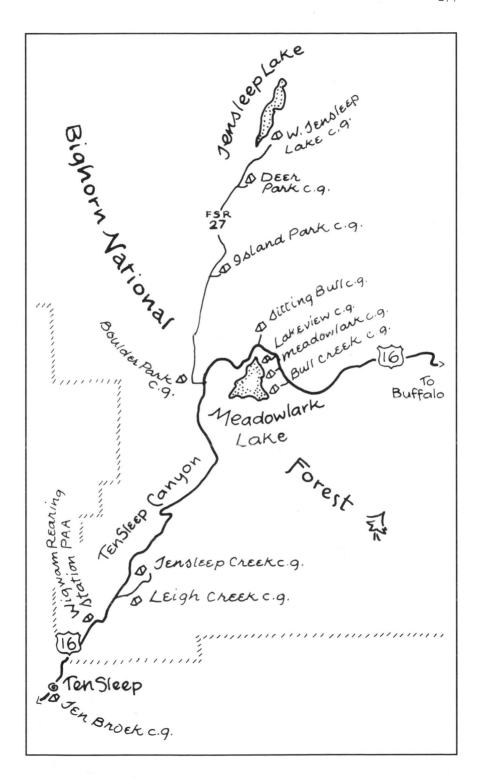

Jensleep Lake

W. Jensleep Lake c.g.

Deer Park c.g.

FSR 27

Bighorn National

Island Park c.g.

Sitting Bull c.g.

Lakeview c.g.

Meadowlark c.g.

Bull Creek c.g.

16

To Buffalo

Boulder Park c.g.

Meadowlark Lake

Forest

TenSleep Canyon

Wigwam Rearing Station PAA

Jensleep Creek c.g.

Leigh Creek c.g.

16

TenSleep

Ten Broek c.g.

Getting there – From Ten Sleep go east 7.5 miles on US 16 to the junction of US 16 and Hwy 435; then right .9 miles on Hwy 435 to the camp on the right. *See map page 277.*

Tensleep Creek Campground
(Bighorn National Forest, Open May 15 to Oct. 31)

About the camp – This small camp, designated for tents only, is along Tensleep Creek with most sites nicely tucked away on the off-river side of the road. The camp has a vault toilet, potable water and 5 sites with tables and fire pits with grates. Stay limited to 14 days.

Rates – Campsite per night: $9. Rates half with Golden Age or Access Passport.

Getting there – From Ten Sleep go east 7.5 miles on US 16 to the junction of US 16 and Hwy 435; then right 1.3 miles on Hwy 435 to the camp. *See map page 277.*

Boulder Park Campground
(Bighorn National Forest, Open June 1 to Sept. 30)

About the camp – This campground has 34 sites, and month-long reservations are possible. The camp has vault toilets, potable water and sites with tables and fire rings with grates. Stay limited to 5 days and 30 days.

Rates – Campsite per night: $9. Campsite for 30 days: $170. Rates half with Golden Age or Access Passport. (Reservations are possible at this campground up to 240 days in advance and 10 days prior to arrival. Service fee per reservation: $8.65. Ph: (877) 444-6777 toll free.)

Getting there – From Ten Sleep go east 17.7 miles on US 16 to the Deer Haven Lodge turnoff (FSR 27); then left .2 miles to the camp on the left. *See map page 277.*

Island Park Campground
(Bighorn National Forest, Open June 15 to Sept. 30)

About the camp – This camp has 10 sites on a short road with an end-of-the-road loop turnaround. West Tensleep Creek flows behind the camp. Site 10 is a pull through. The camp has a vault toilet and potable water. Sites have tables and fire rings with grates. Stay limited to 14 days.

Rates – Campsite per night: $8. Rates half with Golden Age or Access Passport.

Getting there – From Ten Sleep go east 17.7 miles on US 16 to the Deer Haven Lodge turnoff (FSR 27); then left 3 miles to the camp on the right. *See map page 277.*

Deer Park Campground

(Bighorn National Forest, Open June 15 to Sept. 30)

About the camp – This small camp lies just off the Forest Service road near West Tensleep Creek. The camp has a vault toilet, potable water and 7 sites with tables and fire rings with grates. Stay limited to 14 days.

Rates – Campsite per night: $8. Rates half with Golden Age or Access Passport.

Getting there – From Ten Sleep go east 17.7 miles on US 16 to the Deer Haven Lodge turnoff (FSR 27); then left 6.2 miles to the camp on the right. *See map page 277.*

West Tensleep Lake Campground

(Bighorn National Forest, Open June 15 to Sept. 30)

About the camp – This small camp is near West Tensleep Lake, which is closed to all motorboats: oars and paddles only. The camp has a vault toilet, potable water and 10 roomy sites with tables and fire rings with grates. Stay limited to 14 days.

Rates – Campsite per night: $9. Rates half with Golden Age or Access Passport. (Reservations are possible at this campground up to 240 days in advance and 10 days prior to arrival. Service fee per reservation: $8.65. Ph: (877) 444-6777 toll free.)

Getting there – From Ten Sleep go east 17.7 miles on US 16 to the Deer Haven Lodge turnoff (FSR 27); then left 7.4 miles to the camp. *See map page 277.*

Sitting Bull Campground

(Bighorn National Forest, Open June 15 to Sept. 30)

About the camp – This camp is large with several interior loop roads and mostly roomy sites in mixed forest. Sites 3-10 overlook a large open forest park ringed with timbered hillsides. The camp has vault toilets, potable water and 43 sites with tables and fire rings with grates. Stay limited to 14 days.

Rates – Campsite per night: $10. Rates half with Golden Age or Access Passport. (Reservations are possible at this campground up to 240 days in advance and 10 days prior to arrival. Service fee per reservation: $8.65. Ph: (877) 444-6777 toll free.)

Getting there – From Ten Sleep go east 20.1 miles on US 16 to the turnoff on the left; then left to the fee board. *See map page 277.*

Lakeview Campground

(Bighorn National Forest, Open June 15 to Sept. 30)

About the camp – This camp has sites on two small loop roads above the lake. Table locations for sites 9 and 10 on first loop offer the best views of the lake. Sites 4 and 5, the last sites on the other road have a fair view of the lake, albeit from the far side of the road. The camp has vault toilets, potable water and 11 sites with tables and fire rings with grates. Stay limited to 14 days.

Rates – Campsite per night: $10. Rates half with Golden Age or Access Passport. (Reservations are possible at this campground up to 240 days in advance and 10 days prior to arrival. Service fee per reservation: $8.65. Ph: (877) 444-6777 toll free.)

Getting there – From Ten Sleep go east 20.5 miles on US 16 to the turnoff on the right; then right to the fee board. *See map page 277.*

Meadow Lark Resort

(Private, Open June to Sept. 30)
PO Box 86, Ten Sleep, WY 82442 Ph: (307) 366-2424 or (800) 858-5672
Fax: (307) 366-2477

About the camp – The resort offers 12 full hookup (20 amp) sites near Meadowlark Lake. Sites are on gravel and native grass with tables and fire rings.

Amenities – Rest rooms and showers; cafe, limited groceries, gas, ice, snacks, and pay phone. Rentals available for canoes, paddle boats, row boats, boats with motors and mountain bikes.

Rates – Full hookups per site: $15. All major credit cards. Personal checks okay. Reservation: Phone or mail.

Getting there – From Ten Sleep go east 20.7 miles on US 16 to the turnoff on the right. *See map page 277.*

Bull Creek Campground

(Bighorn National Forest, Open June 15 to Sept. 30)

About the camp – The road to this camp goes 1 mile down the hill with no turn around at the end. You either turn around in a campsite parking spur (all of which may be full) or back out: Trailers are not advised. The camp has a vault toilet and 10 sites with tables and fire rings with grates. At the bottom of the camp there is a footpath leading to Veterans Cove Day Use Area where there is another vault toilet and beach access to the water. No potable water. Stay limited to 14 days.

Rates – Campsite per night: $7. Rates half with Golden Age or Access Passport.

Getting there – From Ten Sleep go east 21.3 miles on US 16 to the turnoff on the right. *See map page 277.*

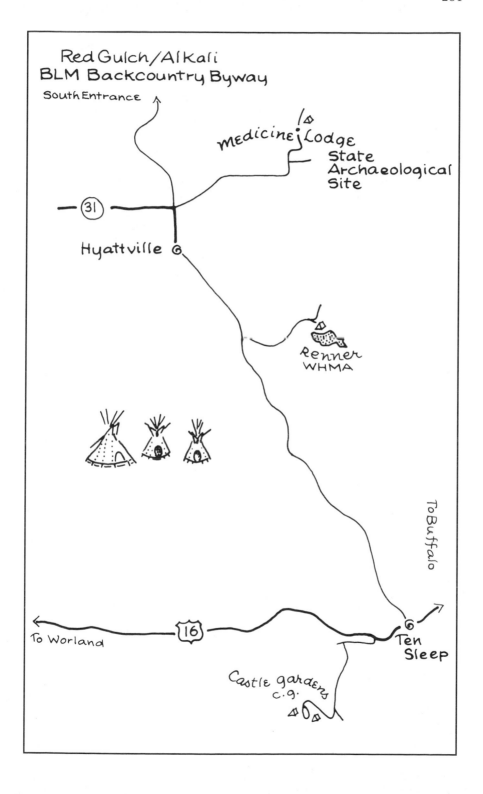

Red Gulch/Alkali
BLM Backcountry Byway

South Entrance

Medicine Lodge
State
Archaeological
Site

(31)

Hyattville

Renner
WHMA

To Buffalo

To Worland   (16)

Ten
Sleep

Castle gardens
c.g.

North of Ten Sleep

Renner Wildlife Habitat Management Area
(Wyoming Game & Fish, Open all year)

About the camp – Much of this area is open all year, but the upper portion, which is critical winter habitat for a herd of about 350 mule deer and 80 elk, is closed from Dec. 1 to May 31.

On 16,548 acres you will find sagebrush grasslands, mountain shrub and ponderosa pine forests. Wildlife of interest to hunters includes deer and elk, chukar, cottontail rabbits and blue grouse. Canada Geese, ducks, shore birds, song birds and many small mammals share the turf. Renner Reservoir, a 72-acre man-made impoundment, is stocked with largemouth bass. There is a small boat ramp at the reservoir, but no motors over 15 horse power are permitted.

Ziesman Canyon, a small but scenic area with lots of hiking opportunities, runs partly along the road into this reservoir. There are a few dispersed camping options as you travel through this red-, grey- and yellow-walled canyon along Buffalo Creek. No potable water. Camping limited to 14 days.

Rates – Free

Getting there – From the west end of Ten Sleep go north 9.1 miles on Cottonwood St. to the junction of CR 83; then bear right 2.2 miles to the Washakie County line and a turnoff to the right; then right 2.5 miles to a fork in the road; then right .6 miles to the reservoir. *See map page 281.*

Medicine Lodge State Archaeological Site
(State of Wyoming, Open May 4 to Nov. 4)

About the camp – This is one of the most interesting areas of the state: It is one of the oldest homestead ranches in the area; locals tell stories about skeletons wearing Spanish armor found in the cracks of the cliffs, and Native Americans left behind a wall of petroglyphs. With a more everyday note on the site, one state official said, "this has to be counted as a heaven for birdwatchers, botanists, wildlife viewers, geologists, fishermen, and hunters, not to mention kids who have more fun catching snakes and lizards than any place I know."

The State Parks Site is within the Wyoming Game and Fish Medicine Lodge Habitat Management Area which is 12, 700 acres including steep walled canyons along Wet and Dry Medicine Lodge Creeks. Hiking opportunities, combined with photography and wildlife viewing abound.

The camp is in the lush green vegetation along Medicine Lodge Creek and a stunning contrast to the stark red sandstone buttes and yellow and grey sandstone canyon cliffs that nearly surround the area. The camp has vault toilets, potable water, 26 sites with tables and fire rings and a group site. The group site may be reserved for 40 or more by calling the park superintendent, as early as the first working day of the year in which you wish to reserve the site, Ph: (307) 469-2234.

Rates – Campsite per night for resident: $4. Campsite per night for nonresident: $9. Residents may purchase an annual camping permit good for camping at all state parks for $30. The annual camping permit is not available to nonresidents. Group site per day: $35 with $35 damage deposit. (For '99 rates see page 11).

Getting there – From Ten Sleep go west .5 miles on US 16 to Washakie CR 47; then right 20.0 miles to Hwy 31; then right 6.8 miles to Alkali/Cold Springs Road (just north of Hyattville); then left .2 miles; then right 3.8 miles to the entrance on the left, off a right hand bend of the pavement; then left (*straight off the bend*) 1.4 miles to the camp. *See map page 281.*

—East of Ten Sleep—

Castle Gardens

(BLM, Open all year)

About the camp – This area is ringed with exotic sandstone rock formations which seemly change shape from morning to night as the sun's angle alters light and shadow on the landscape. The camp has a vault toilet and two sites with tables and fire rings with grates. One site offers some shade, on a slight rise amidst junipers. Hikers will be attracted to other interesting formations and opportunities for dispersed camping within sight of this area. No potable water. Stay limited to 14 days in any 28 day period.

Rates – Free

Getting there – From the west end of Ten Sleep go west 2 miles on US 16 to a left-hand turnoff on the top of the hill; then left .3 miles; then right 1 mile (*on what looks like old highway*) to a turnoff to the left; then left .5 miles to a fork; then left 2.5 miles to a fork; then right .8 miles to the camp. *See map page 281.*

— For the View —

Red Gulch/Alkali BLM National Back Country Byway

This road heads north from near the historic town of Hyattville and the Medicine Lodge State Archaeological site. It is about 35 miles long and returns to the pavement, US 14, between Greybull and Shell. The southern portion of the route is marked by long, deep sagebrush-covered draws and valleys; in the northern portion there are dramatic red bluffs and buttes, and grey and red mesas overlooking arroyos; all with red ribbons of dry creek beds nestled deep in the terrain and the Big Horn Mountains as backdrop. If you wanted a full day of sight-seeing this road could fit into a loop: Ten Sleep to Shell on the back country byway; Shell to Sheridan through the Big Horn Scenic Byway; Sheridan to Buffalo, and Buffalo to Ten Sleep over Powder River Pass and the Cloud Peak Skyway.

Getting there – From Ten Sleep go west .5 miles on US 16 to CR 47; then right 20 miles to Hwy 31; then right 6.8 miles to Alkali/Cold Springs Road (*just north of Hyattville*); then left .2 miles to the south end of the byway. North end of the byway joins US 14 about 10.6 miles east of Greybull and 4.6 miles west of Shell. *See map page 281.*

Worth mentioning – This road can be a miserable experience if wet and muddy. Keep your visits here to dry weather, which in Wyoming is most of the time.

Thermopolis

Thermopolis is home to **Hot Springs State Park** and what claims to be the world's largest single mineral hot spring. Swimming or soaking are available at two privately-owned plunges ($) as well as the free soaking at **Hot Springs State Park Bath House** (no soap allowed here even in showers), Ph: (307) 864-3765. This park maintains a free-roaming breeding herd of bison which rely primarily on natural feed in the area, but enjoy a daily "cake" supplement with essential minerals to help insure good health. Feeding occurs daily between 8 and 9 a.m. offering visitors a unique opportunity to view these animals at close range, but from their vehicles. Of interest are **The Hot Springs Historical Museum**, at 700 Broadway, Ph: (307) 864-5183 ($2), and **The Wyoming Dinosaur Center & Dig Sites**, 110 Carter Ranch Road, Ph: (307) 864-2997 or (800) 455-3466 ($). In early August, the grounds at the state park become a teepee village while celebrating the **Gift of the Waters Pageant. Legend Rock State Petroglyph Site** is eight miles off of Hwy 120 and 21.5 miles northwest of Thermopolis. The gate to the site is locked, but keys are available at the **Hot Springs State Park Bath House.** Keys can be returned or mailed in a free self-addressed stamped envelope provided by the state park.

In town there are four privately-owned camps all with hookups and three with tenting. On the outskirts of town are two other private camps with hookups and tenting. Groceries, hardware and limited sporting goods are available.

Country Campin' R.V. & Tent Park

(Private, Open April 1 to Nov.)
710 E. Sunnyside Lane, Thermopolis, WY 82443 Ph: (307) 864-2416 or (800) 609-2244 E-mail: camp@trib.com

About the camp – This grassy camp bordered by mature cottonwood trees is located on 5 acres of a 150-acre ranch property about 6 miles north of Thermopolis. There are 42 RV sites: all pull-thrus (up to 30x70) and all full hookups (20/30/50 amp). Sites have gravel parking areas with grass 'yards' and tables. Tenting is available with fire rings along the tree line. Teepees, with fire rings, are available. *Horses okay.*

Amenities – Rest rooms and showers, laundry; playground, horseshoes, volleyball, petting zoo, river fishing; fishing licenses, limited groceries, firewood, gift shop, propane, modem jack in office, dump station and pay phone.

Rates – Full hookups for 2 persons: $18. Tent sites for 2 persons: $13.50. Additional persons: $1.50. Teepees: $25 per unit. Discounts: Goodsam, Escapees , and AAA. MC V D Reservations: phone, E-mail or mail.

Getting there – From the junction of Hwy 120 and US 20 in Thermopolis, go north 5.6 miles on US 20 to East Sunnyside Lane; then right 1.6 miles to the camp on the left. *See map page 287.*

Eagle RV Park

(Private, Open April 15 to Nov. 30)
204 Hwy 20 South, Thermopolis, WY 82443 Ph/Fax: (307) 864-5262 E-mail: eaglerv@wyoming.com Web site: interbasin.com/eagle/

About the camp – This shady 7-acre camp is on the south edge of Thermopolis. There are 33 RV sites: 27 pull-thrus (up to 20x45) and 6 pull-ins (up to 18x50). 15 sites are full hookups, 18 water and electric only (all 30 amp on city water). Sites have gravel parking areas with grass 'yards' and tables. Tent sites with tables are available as well as some portable grills. This camp offers 2 camping cabins. *Horses okay.*

Amenities – Rest rooms and showers (showers only: $3), laundry; cable TV at 15 sites (included at 9 full hookup sites and $1 at 6 water and electric only sites), playground, game room and volleyball; snacks and ice, gift shop, limited RV parts, modem jack in office, propane, dump station and pay phone.

Rates – Full hookups for 2 persons: $18. Water and Electric for 2 persons: $15. Tent sites for 2 persons: $12.50. Camper cabins for 2 persons: $20. Additional persons over five years: $1.50. Discounts: Goodsam. All major cards. Reservations: phone, E-mail, fax or mail.

Getting there   From the junction of Hwy 120 and US 20 in Thermopolis go south 1.9 miles on US 20 to the camp on the right. *See map page 287.*

Fountain of Youth R.V. Park

(Private, Open April 1 to Oct. 31)
Box 711, Thermopolis, WY 82443 Ph: (307) 864-3265 Fax: (307) 864-3388

About the camp – This shady park, located on 14 riverside acres with its own mineral pool, is about 2 miles north of Thermopolis on US 20.

The park has 47 RV sites: all pull-thrus (up to 25x50) and all full hookups (15/30/50 amp). Sites have gravel parking areas, concrete pads with table and grills and grass 'yards.' Tenting available at RV sites.

Amenities – Rest rooms and showers($), laundry; mineral pool, horse-shoes, holey board; limited RV parts, limited gifts, dump station and pay phone. *Horses okay.*

Rates – Full hookups for 2 persons: $18.50. Tent sites for 2 persons: $18.50. Additional persons: $2. MC V Reservations: phone, fax or mail.

Getting there – From the junction of Hwy 120 and US 20 in Thermopolis go north 2.5 miles on US 20 to the camp on the right. *See map facing page.*

Grandview RV Park

(Private, open May to Oct.)
122 Hwy 20 South, Thermopolis, WY 82443 Ph/Fax: (307) 864-3463

About the camp – This 2.5-acre RV park, located about 1 mile south of downtown Thermopolis, is grassy with lots of shade. The park has 21 RV sites: 17 pull-thrus (up to 20x88) and 4 pull-ins (up to 20x55). All sites are full hookups (30 amp on city water). Sites have gravel parking areas with grass 'yards' and tables. Grass tent sites are available as well as portable charcoal grills.

Amenities – Rest rooms and showers, laundry; cable TV (at 8 sites: $1), propane, dump station and pay phone.

Rates – Full hookups for 2 persons: $16 for units over 20 feet; $14 for units under 20 feet or pickup campers. Tent sites for 2 persons: $13. Additional persons over age 5: $1.50. Discounts: All current camper cards. MC V Reservations: phone, fax or mail.

Getting there – From the junction of Hwy 120 and US 20 in Thermopolis, go south 1.1 on US 20 to the camp on the right. *See map facing page.*

M-K RV Park

(Private, Open May 1 to Sept. 10)
720 Shoshone St., Thermopolis, WY 82443 Ph: (307) 864-2778

About the camp – This camp has 13 sites on the west end of Thermopolis: 10 pull-thrus (12x38) with full hookups (20/30 amp on city water) and 3 sites with water only for tents or campers. All sites have gravel parking spurs and grass 'yards' with tables and grills.

Amenities – Rest rooms and showers (showers only: $3); cable TV included at full hookup sites, and close to laundromat, grocery store and cafes.

Rates – Full Hookups for two persons: $12.50. Water only, tent or camper for 2 persons: $10. Additional persons over age 4: $1.25. No credit cards. Personal checks okay. Reservations: Phone or mail.

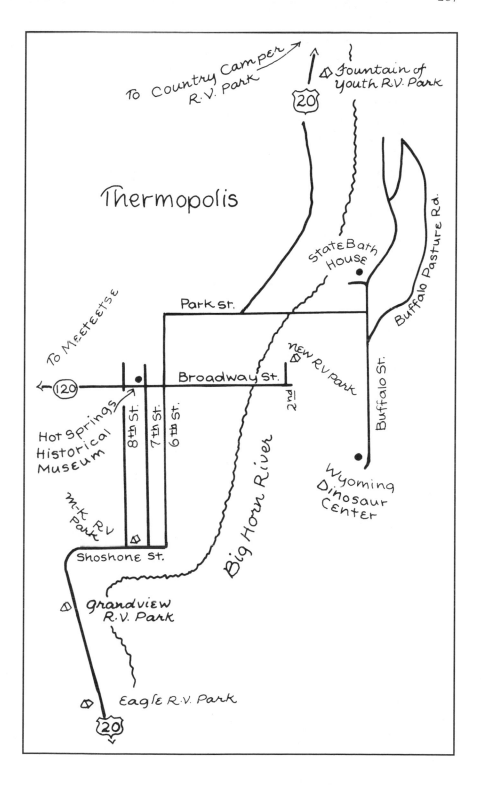

Getting there – From the junction of Hwy 120 and US 20 in Thermopolis, go south .6 miles on US 20 to the camp on the right. *See map page 287.*

New RV Park

(Private, Open April 1 to Nov. 1)
113 N. 2nd St., Thermopolis, WY 82443 Ph: (307) 864-3926

About the camp – This small RV parking option offers some shade and is a short distance from downtown or Hot Springs State Park. There are 6 RV sites: all pull-thrus (12x40) and all full hookups (20/30/50 amp on city water). Sites are gravel with a common area that has a table and charcoal grill. No tents.

Rates – Full hookups per site: $9.50.

Getting there – From the junction of Hwy 120 and US 20 go east .3 miles through the downtown area to 2nd St.; then left one block on N. 2nd St. to the camp on the right. *See map page 287.*

Worland

Worland is a sizeable agricultural town at the crossroads of Hwy 16 east going to Ten Sleep on the way through the **Bighorn National Forest** to Buffalo, and US 16/20 west going north and west through the **Big Horn Basin**. The **Washakie County Museum and Cultural Center** is at 1115 Obie Sue Ave., Ph: (307) 347-4102. Worland celebrates in mid-August during the **Washakie County Fair**.

One privately-owned camp in Worland has hookups and tenting. Near here to the west is an interesting free BLM dispersed camping area in a badlands area along Hwy 431. Groceries, hardware, sporting goods and a bicycle shop are available.

Worland Cowboy Campground

(Private, Open all year)
2311 Big Horn Ave., Worland, WY 82401 Ph: (307) 347-2329 or (307) 347-8804

About the camp – This spacious campground, on the east end of downtown Worland, has lots of trees and many shady sites. The camp has 35 RV sites: 25 pull-thrus (18x45) and 10 back-ins (16x25). Sites are gravel with grass 'yards' and tables. All site are full hookups (30/50 amp on city water). Grass tent sites are available with tables and grills. *Horses okay.*

Amenities – Rest rooms and showers (showers only: $5), laundry; playground, volleyball and horseshoes; snacks and ice, dump station and pay phone.

Rates – Full hookups for 2 persons: $20. Tent sites for 2 persons: $16. Additional persons: $2. V MC Reservations: phone or mail.

Getting there – From the junction of US 16/20 and Hwy 789 in downtown Worland go east .9 miles on US 16 to the camp on the left.

Fifteen Mile Badlands (BLM dispersed)
(BLM, Open all year)

About the camp – This is a striking area of badlands and is accessible by foot from a highway parking area or off of dirt roads just to the east or west of the parking area. It offers a scenic hike—a little or a lot, near or far—and a dry camp in a geologically intriguing area where the angle of light and shadow near sunset and sunrise will highlight the intriguing shapes and colors in these formations. Stay limited to 14 days in any 28 day period.

Rates – Free

Getting there – From the junction of US 20 and Hwy 431 about 9 miles south of Worland, go west 22.7 miles on Hwy 430 to the first road on the right; [or] 23.4 miles to the parking area on the right; [or] 24.5 miles to the second road to the right.

NOTES

<u>NOTES</u>

Contents — Northwest

Northwest Wyoming

This is the Wyoming you see on post cards: towering, snow-clad peaks, moose browsing among the willows, whitewater rivers loaded with native cutthroat trout. The towns offer visitors a rustic 'cowboy' look, but the prices can rise to Grand Teton scale. Still there is plenty of real wilderness here, and few regions can match a wildlife trove that includes elk, wolves, bison and grizzly bears.

This section features 84 camping options, with 26 listings for privately-owned camps and 49 listings for Forest Service camps. Remaining options include 5 free Wyoming Game and Fish Areas, 1 BLM camp, 2 Wyoming State Park campgrounds, and 1 free town park. The camps are listed under headings for 7 cities and towns including Cody, Dubois, Hoback Junction, Jackson, Meeteetse, Moran Junction and Powell. Scenic roads include the Wyoming Centennial scenic byway over Togwotee Pass; the Buffalo Bill Scenic

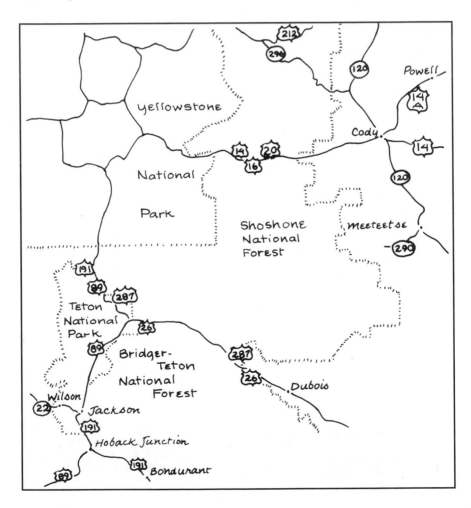

Byway from Cody to Yellowstone National Park; the Chief Joseph scenic highway through Sunlight Basin, a portion of the Beartooth Scenic Highway on the way to the northeast entrance of Yellowstone Park, US 189 through Hoback Canyon and US 89 through Snake River Canyon, famous for adventurous whitewater rafting.

Cody

Cody is second only to Jackson as a mecca for tourists going to and from **Yellowstone National Park**. The city has beautiful mountains to the west and north, with a choice of two scenic driving options to the park. The traditional route is west on **Buffalo Bill Scenic Byway** through the **Wapiti Valley**, where you'll review a parade of rock formations on the canyon walls. Northwest along the recently-paved **Chief Joseph Scenic Highway** through **Sunlight Basin** you'll see less traffic and more varied landscape. The view of Sunlight Basin from the **Dead Indian Pass Overlook** is remarkable as is **Sunlight Creek Bridge**, spanning **Sunlight Gorge** 280 feet above the stream. For light, photography and the scenery, take the Sunlight Basin route with the early morning light and return through the Wapiti Valley with the evening light.

In Cody, the main attraction is the **Buffalo Bill Historical Center**, one of the country's top museums, frequently referred to as the 'Smithsonian of the West.' It includes the **Buffalo Bill Museum**, the **Cody Firearms Museum**, the **Plains Indian Museum** and the **Whitney Gallery of Western Art**, as well as the Harold McCracken Research Library. Open daily, admission is good for two consecutive days, Ph: (307) 587-4771. Featured in Cody's downtown area is the stately Irma Hotel, built by Buffalo Bill in 1902 to accommodate tourists and named for his daughter. On the west end of Cody lies **Trail Town,** an assembled collection of 20-odd buildings dating from as early as 1849, with assorted wagons and other western artifacts.

During the summer there are nightly rodeos at Cody's rodeo grounds and 'shoot outs' near the Irma Hotel. Main events are the **Cody Stampede**, a professional rodeo held July 2-4; the **Frontier Festival** in mid-July, featuring living history and turn-of-the-century skills; the **Plains Indian Powwow** in June at the Buffalo Bill Historical Center; the **Yellowstone Jazz Festival** in mid-July, and the **Wild West Balloon Fest** in mid-Aug.

There are 8 privately-owned camps in town, two private camps, two state park campgrounds and 9 Forest Service camps on the way to the east entrance. Northwest there are two other private camps, one free BLM camp, one free Game and Fish camp, one free Forest Service camp and 10 other Forest Service camps. There are BLM and Forest Service offices here for maps and information.

Groceries, hardware and sporting goods outlets as well as RV sales and service are available. An outdoor swimming pool is open daily in summer at 1234 Beck Ave. and the **Stock Natatorium** at 8th St. and Beck Ave. has an indoor pool open to the public Tues. and Thurs. evenings 7-9.

Ponderosa Campground

(Private, Open April 1 to Nov. 1)
1815 8th St., Cody, WY 82414 Ph: (307) 587-9203

About the camp – This 14-acre camp with a nice stand of cottonwood trees is just off the main route through Cody and only three blocks from the Buffalo Bill Historical Center. The camp has 133 full hookup (30/50 amp on city water) RV sites: 28 pull-thrus (up to 20x75) and 105 back-ins (up to 20x65). Sites have gravel parking areas with grass 'yards' and tables . Portable grills are available with a refundable-on-return fee. Tent sites are grass with tables, in pleasant areas away from the main RV areas. There are 6 rustic tent sites below the bluff in trees along flowing water away from the city lights. Teepees and kabins are also available.

Amenities – Rest rooms and showers in two locations, laundry; cable TV included and available at most sites, game room and playground; limited groceries and RV parts, gift shop, dump station and pay phone. Management provides shuttle service for Cody's summer-long nightly rodeos and will arrange for float trips and trail rides.

Rates – Full hookups for 2 persons: $17. Tent sites for 2 persons: $15. Teepees for 2 persons: $20. Kabins for 2 persons: $29. Additional persons age 7 and over: $2. Discounts: Goodsam. No credit cards. Personal checks okay. Reservations: phone or mail.

Getting there – From the junction of US 14/16/20 and Hwy 120 in downtown Cody, go west 1.3 miles on US 14 to the camp on the right, three blocks past the Buffalo Bill Historical Center. *See map page 298.*

Camp Cody

(Private, Open all year)
415 Yellowstone Ave., Cody, WY 82414 Ph: (307) 587-9730 or (888) 231-CAMP E-mail: ccody@adventuresoutdoors.com

About the camp – This camp is west of Cody's downtown area on the main route to Yellowstone National Park. There are 63 RV sites: 4 pull-thrus (up to 24x50) and 59 back-ins (up to 20x35). 50 sites are full hookups (20/30/50 amp on city water). Sites have gravel parking areas with grass 'yards' and tables. Tent sites and portable grills are available.

Amenities – Rest rooms and showers (showers only: $5), laundry; pool, cable TV included with hookups, game room; ice, dump station and pay phone. Affiliations: AAA.

Rates – Full hookups for two persons: $12-15. Tent sites for two persons: $10-12. Additional persons age four and over: $2. V MC Personal checks okay. Reservations: phone, E-mail or mail.

Getting there – From the junction of US 14/16/20 and Hwy 120 in downtown Cody, go west 2 miles on US 14 to the camp on the right. *See map page 298.*

Buffalo Bill Village

(Private, Open May 1 to Oct. 1)

1701 Sheridan Ave., Cody, WY 82414 Ph: (307) 587-5555 or (800) 527-5544

About the camp – This camp on the east end of downtown Cody has parking for self-contained units only. The camp has 30 RV sites, all back-ins (up to 25x40). Sites are gravel, some with grass 'yards' and tables. All sites are full hookups (20/30/50 amp on city water). No rest rooms or showers.

Amenities – Cable TV included, complimentary use of the pool and spa at adjoining motel; gift shop and pay phone.

Rates – Full hookups per site: $15. Reservations: phone or mail.

Getting there – From the junction of US 14/16/20 and Hwy 120 in downtown Cody, go east 2 blocks on US 14 to the camp on the left. *See map page 298.*

Absaroka Bay RV Campground

(Private, Open May to Sept.)

(PO Box 953) 2001 Hwy 14/16/20, Cody, WY 82414 Ph: (307) 527-/440 E-mail: campground@wyoming.com

About the camp – This camp on the east edge of Cody is spacious, open and level providing easy in and out for the overnight camper. The camp has 99 RV sites: 82 pull-thrus (up to 23x65) and 17 back-ins (23x25). Sites are gravel with grass 'yards' and tables. All sites are full hookups (30/50 amp on city water). 20 grass tent sites are available with tables and some grills.

Amenities – Rest rooms and showers (showers only: $2.50), laundry; modem jack in office and pay phone.

Rates – Full hookups per site: $15. Tent site per tent: $10. Reservations: phone, E-mail or mail.

Getting there – From the junction of US 14/16/20 and Hwy 120 in downtown Cody, go east 1 mile on US 14/16/20 to the camp on the left.

From the junction of US 14 and Hwy 120 on the east edge of Cody, go west 1.2 miles on US 14/16/20 to the camp on the right. *See map page 298.*

Cody KOA

(Private, May 1 to Oct. 1)

5561 Greybull Highway, Cody, WY 82414 Ph: (800) 562-8507 Ph/Fax: (307) 587-2369 E-mail: codykoa@aol.com

About the camp – This 10-acre camp with many shaded sites is east of downtown Cody. The camp has 128 RV sites: 54 pull-thrus (up to 21x50) and 70 back-ins (21x40). 64 sites are full hookups (20/30/50 amp on city water). Sites are gravel with grass 'yards'. Tent sites are

298

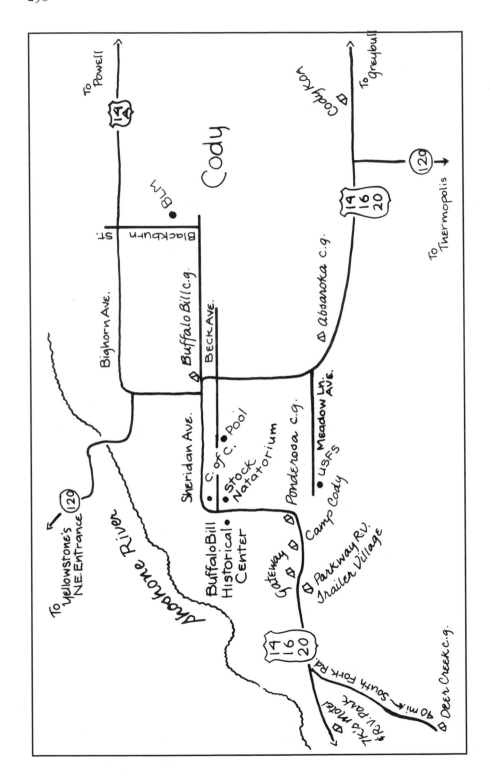

designated. KOA also offers 20 Kamping Kabins and a full-service Kamping Kottage with kitchenette.

Amenities – Rest rooms and showers, laundry; playground, game room, heated pool and spa, horseback riding, free shuttle to summer nightly rodeo and free pancake breakfast; gift shop, limited groceries and RV parts, dump station, propane, modem jack in office and pay phones.

Rates – Full hookups for 2 persons: $26.95. Water and electric for 2 persons: $24.95. Tent sites for 2 persons: $18.95. Additional persons: $2.95. Kamping Kabins: $34.95-40.95. Kamping Kottage: $99.95. Day use: $3.50. MC V D Reservations: phone, E-mail, fax or mail.

Getting there – From the junction of US 14/16/20 and Hwy 120 in downtown Cody, go east 3.1 miles on US 14/16/20 to the camp on the left.

From the junction of US 14 and Hwy 120 south on the east edge of Cody, go east .9 miles on US 14 to the camp on the left. *See map facing page*.

Gateway Motel and Campground

(Private, Open May 1 to Oct. 1)
203 Yellowstone Ave., Cody, WY 82414 Ph: (307) 587-2561 Fax: (307) 587-4862 E-mail: gateway@wyoming.com

About the camp – This 5-acre camp on the west side of Cody just off the main route to Yellowstone National Park is grassy and offers lots of shade. The camp has 41 RV sites: 12 pull-thrus (up to 20x50) and 29 back-ins (up to 20x45). 12 sites are full hookups (20/30 amp on city water) and 29 are electric only. Sites have gravel parking areas with grass 'yards' and tables . Portable grills are available. Tent sites have tables and are located in pleasant grass areas. *Horses okay: corrals and boarding $6 per night*.

Amenities – Rest rooms and showers (showers only: $4), laundry; cable TV included at full hookups, playground; gifts, ice, complimentary coffee, dump station and pay phone. Trail rides and float trips arranged with shuttle from/to campground.

Rates – Full hookups for 2 persons: $18. Electric only for 2 persons: $14. Tent sites for 2 persons: $12. Additional persons age 7 and over: $2. All major cards. Reservations: phone, E-mail, fax, or mail.

Getting there – From the junction of US 14/16/20 and Hwy 120 in downtown Cody, go west 2.4 miles on US 14 to the camp on the right. *See map facing page*.

Parkway RV Campground & Trailer Village

(Private, Open all year)
132 Yellowstone Ave., Cody, WY 82414 Ph: (307) 527-5927

About the camp – This campground is located west of downtown Cody on the main route to Yellowstone National Park. The camp offers 25

RV sites: 8 pull-thrus (up to 20x120) and 17 back-ins (up to 20x50). 23 sites are full hookups (20/30/50 amp on city water) and 2 electric only. Sites have gravel parking areas with grass 'yards' and tables. Grass tent sites are available.

Amenities – Rest rooms and showers (showers only: $3), laundry; C-store adjacent to camp, dump station and pay phone.

Rates – Full hookups per site: $14. Electric only per site: $12. Tents per site: $10. MC V Personal checks okay. Reservations: phone or mail.

Getting there – From the junction of US 14/16/20 and Hwy 120 in downtown Cody, go west on US 14 for 2.4 miles to the camp on the left. *See map page 298.*

7 K's Motel and RV Park

(Private, Open May 1 to Oct. 1)
232 W. Yellowstone Highway, Cody, WY 82414 Ph: (307) 587-5890 or (800) 223-9204

About the camp – This 6-acre property, with a stand of mature native cottonwood trees, is on the route to Yellowstone National Park at the west end of Cody. The camp has 39 RV sites: all back-ins (up to 23x45) and all full hookups (20/30 amp on city water). Sites have gravel parking areas with grass 'yards' and tables. 15 grass tent sites are in the trees, shaded and have tables.

Amenities – Rest rooms and showers (showers only: $3), laundry; heated pool, dump station and pay phone.

Rates – Full hookups for 2 persons: $15-20. Tent sites for 2 persons: $10 and up. Additional persons: $2. Discounts: Goodsam and AAA special value rate. MC V Reservations: phone or mail.

Getting there – From the junction of US 14/16/20 and Hwy 120 in downtown Cody, go west 2.9 miles on US 14 to the camp on the left. *See map page 298.*

Deer Creek Campground

(Shoshone National Forest, Open June 15 to Sept. 3)

About the camp – This camp is about 40 miles from Cody on the South Fork Road. The camp has 7 sites with tables and fire rings with grates. Bear rules apply. Stay limited to 16 days.

Rates – Free. No potable water. Pack it in, pack it out.

Getting there – From the junction of South Fork Road and US 14/16/20 on the west end of Cody, go southwest about 40 miles on South Fork Road to the camp. *See map page 298.*

—West of Cody—

Buffalo Bill State Park

In summer, when the reservoir is full, this state park consists of 8500 water acres and 3500 lands acres. Only about 500 acres of this park are developed and wildlife sightings are numerous with the early morning and late evening providing the optimum viewing hours. Mule deer are the most common, with white-tailed deer seen less frequently and usually along the river. Red fox, coyotes, golden and bald eagles, osprey, great horned owls and numerous hawks are common to the area. Canada geese, American white pelicans, numerous ducks and other water fowl also use the reservoir.

As Buffalo Bill is a cold water reservoir, wind surfers, water-skiers and jet-skiers will want wet suits. Boaters using the area are usually fishing or sailing. The Wyoming Game and Fish Department presides over boating and fishing here, so check the regulations and be sure you have a valid fishing license.

There are two well-maintained campgrounds in this state park. With this country setting—near the water, with a view of the mountains and only about 9 miles from Cody—the park is gaining in popularity for those staying overnight in the area. Camps are listed below.

North Shore

(Wyoming State Parks, Open May 1 to Oct. 1)

About the camp – Going west from Cody, this is the first campground in this state park. It is located on the shoreline of the reservoir, with a total of 35 sites. These campsites are well spaced and roomy. 32 sites are for tents or RVs and most have parallel pull-thrus. The remaining 3 sites, for tents only, are short walk-ins to grassy areas with large sandy tent pads. The camp has vault toilets and potable water. All sites have tables and grills. Stay limited to 14 days.

Rates – Day use fees for this park are $2 for residents and $5 for nonresidents. Camping fees for residents are $4 per night and $9 for nonresidents. An annual day use pass, good at all state parks, is available to residents for $25 and nonresidents for $40. Annual camping permits are available to residents for $30. The annual camping pass is not available for nonresidents. (For '99 rates see page 11).

Getting there – From the junction of US 14/16/20 and Hwy 120 in downtown Cody, go 10.4 miles west on US 14 to the camp on the left. *See map page 304.*

North Fork Campground
(Wyoming State Parks, Open May 1 to Oct. 1)

About the camp – This camp is open, level and while more distant from the reservoir is near the North Fork of the Shoshone River which flows into the reservoir. It is the larger of the two camps at this state park, with 65 total sites. These campsites are well spaced and roomy. 56 sites are for tents or RVs and most have parallel pull-thrus. The remaining 6 sites, for tents only, are short walk-ins to grassy areas with large sandy tent pads. The camp has vault toilets and potable water. All sites have tables and grills. Stay limited to 14 days.

Rates – Day use fees for this park are $2 for residents and $5 for nonresidents. Camping fees for residents are $4 per night and $9 for nonresidents. An annual day use pass, good at all state parks, is available to residents for $25 and nonresidents for $40. Annual camping permits are available to residents for $30. The annual camping pass is not available for nonresidents. (For '99 rates see page 11).

Getting there – From the junction of US 14/16/20 and Hwy 120 in downtown Cody, go 15.1 miles west on US 14 to CR 6KV; then left to the camp on the right. *See map page 304.*

Yellowstone Valley Inn
(Private, Open all year)
3324 Yellowstone Park Highway, Cody, WY 82414 Ph: (307) 587-3961 or (888) 705-7703

About the camp – This camp is on 12.8 acres in the scenic Wapiti Valley west of Cody. The camp has 75 pull-thru (up to 20x60) RV sites: 25 sites are full hookups (20/30 amp) and 50 are water and electric only. Sites are grass with tables. Grass tent sites are available with water and electric. *Horses okay.*

Amenities – Rest rooms and showers (showers only: $3), laundry; restaurant, lounge, playground, horseshoes, badminton, volleyball and video games in office; dump station and pay phone.

Rates – Full hookups per site: $20. Water and electric only per site: $15. Tent sites (water and electric included): $15. MC V D Personal checks okay. Discounts: AAA, AARP & Military. Reservations recommended by phone or mail.

Getting there – From the junction of US 14/16/20 and Hwy 120 in downtown Cody, go west 19.2 miles on US 14 to the camp on the left. *See map page 304.*

Elk Valley Inn
(Private, Open May to Oct.)
3356 North Fork Hwy, Cody, WY 82414 Ph: (307) 587-4149

About the camp – This camp is about 18 miles west of Cody in the Wapiti Valley. The camp has 35 RV sites: 17 pull-thrus (11x30) and 18 back-ins (20x30). 24 sites are full hookups (20/30/50 amp) and 11 water and electric only. RV sites are gravel with tables. Grass tent sites (some along the Shoshone River) are available with tables and some grills. Motels and cabins available. *Horses: Inquire.*

Amenities – Rest rooms and showers (showers only: $3), laundry; playground, basketball, petting zoo, fishing pond and paddle boat rentals; pay phone and homemade brick oven pizza, a house specialty.

Rates – Full hookups for 2 persons: $21.50. Water and electric for 2 persons: $19.50. Electric only for 2 persons: $17.50. Tent sites for 2 persons: $12-$15. Additional persons: $2. Reservations: Phone or mail

Getting there – From the junction of US 14/16 20 and Hwy 120 in downtown Cody, go west 18 miles on US 14 to the camp on the left. *See map page 304.*

Big Game Campground
(Shoshone National Forest, Open May 15 to Sept. 30)

About the camp – This camp is in the lower end of the canyon of the North Fork of the Shoshone River, where there are interesting sandstone formations on the canyon wall with names like Holy City, Slipper Rock, Goose Rock and Camel Rock. The camp has 15 sites on a loop road in a nicely forested area along the river, vault toilets, potable water, and 6 pull-thru sites. Campsites are generally roomy with good tenting options and have tables and fire rings with grates. Stay limited to 14 days.

Rates – Campsite per night: $9. Rates half with Golden Age or Access Passport.

Getting there – From the junction of US 14/16/20 and Hwy 120 in downtown Cody, go west 29.7 miles on US 14 to the camp on the right. *See map page 304.*

Wapiti Campground
(Shoshone National Forest, Open May 15 to Oct. 30)

About the camp – Just west of Big Game Campground, this camp is also in the lower end of the canyon of the North Fork of the Shoshone River, with interesting rock formations on the canyon walls (see Big Game Campground). There are 41 sites on two loop roads in a nicely forested area along the river. The camp has vault toilets and potable water. Campsites are generally roomy with good tenting options and have tables and fire rings with grates. Stay limited to 14 days.

Rates – Campsite per night: $9. Rates half with Golden Age or Access Passport.

Getting there – From the junction of US 14/16/20 and Hwy 120 in downtown Cody, go west 30.1 miles on US 14 to the camp on the right. *See map page 304.*

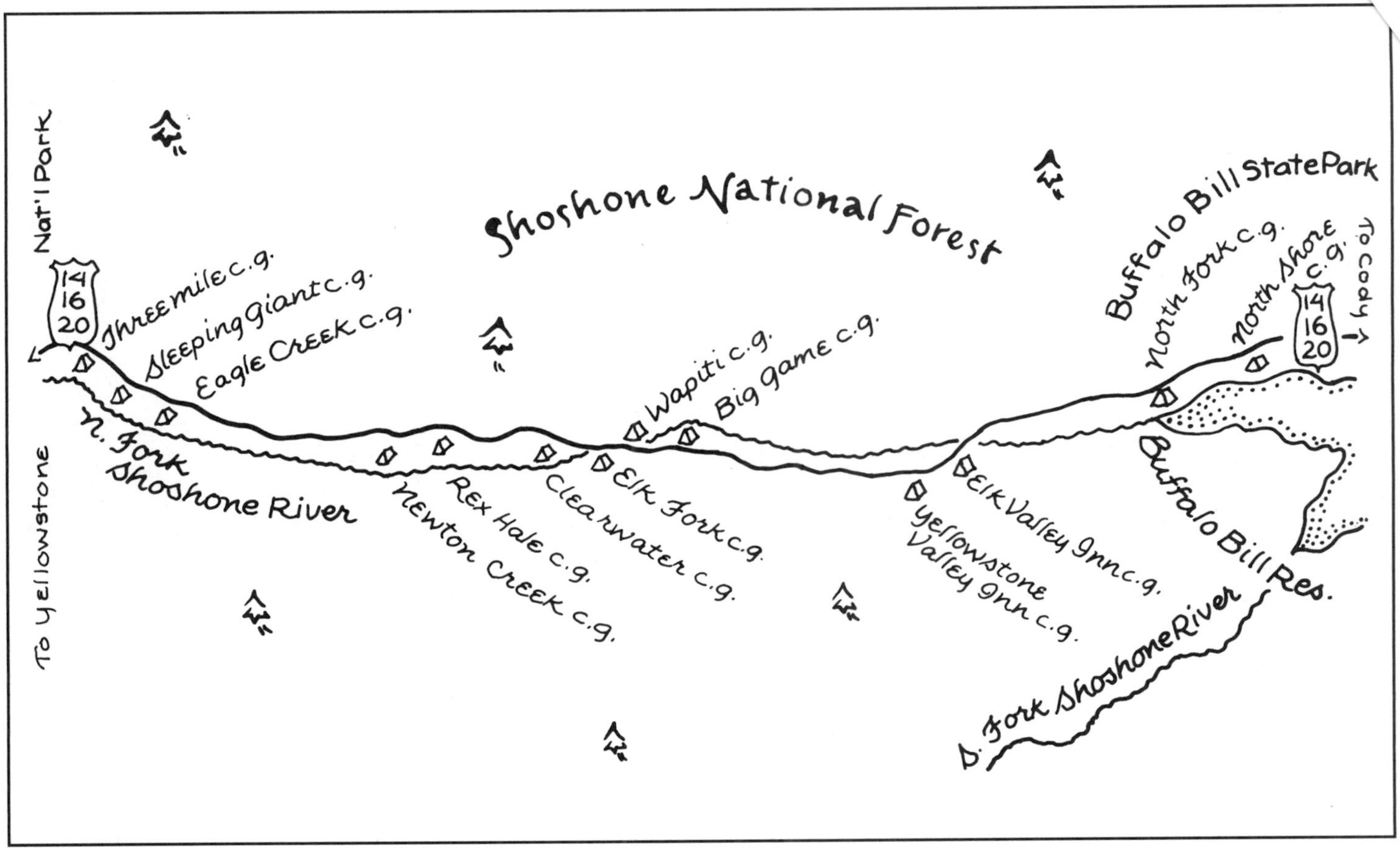
Shoshone National Forest
Buffalo Bill State Park
To Cody
North Shore c.g.
North Fork c.g.
14
16
20
Buffalo Bill Res.
S. Fork Shoshone River
Elk Valley Inn c.g.
Yellowstone Valley Inn c.g.
Wapiti c.g.
Big Game c.g.
Elk Fork c.g.
Clearwater c.g.
Rex Hale c.g.
Newton Creek c.g.
Threemile c.g.
Sleeping Giant c.g.
Eagle Creek c.g.
N. Fork Shoshone River
Nat'l Park
To Yellowstone

Elk Fork Campground
(Shoshone National Forest, Open May 15 to Oct. 30)

About the camp – This camp, only about .1 mile west of Wapiti Camp-ground on the other side of the road, has the Elk Fork River running at the edge of the camp on its way to feed into the North Fork of the Shoshone River. This camp is also in the lower end of the canyon with interesting rock formations on the canyon walls (see Big Game Camp-ground). There are 13 forested sites on a lane with an end-of-the-road loop turnaround. The camp has vault toilets and potable water. Camp-sites are generally roomy with good tenting options and have tables and fire rings with grates. Stay limited to 14 days.

Rates – Campsite per night: $9. Rates half with Golden Age or Access Passport.

Getting there – From the junction of US 14/16/20 and Hwy 120 in downtown Cody, go west 30.2 miles on US 14 to the camp on the left. *See map facing page.*

Clearwater Campground
(Shoshone National Forest, Open May 15 to Sept. 30)

About the camp – This 32-site camp is located in an area of sheer canyon walls on the North Fork of the Shoshone River. There is a semicircular parking area for 19 walk-in sites located in grassy and mostly shaded areas. The camp has vault toilets and potable water. Campsites are generally roomy with good tenting options, have tables and fire rings with grates, and several are located near the river bank. Stay limited to 14 days.

Rates – Campsite per night: $9. Rates half with Golden Age or Access Passport.

Getting there – From the junction of US 14/16/20 and Hwy 120 in downtown Cody, go west 33.3 miles on US 14 to the camp on the left. *See map facing page.*

Rex Hale Campground
(Shoshone National Forest, Open May 15 to Sept. 30)

About the camp – This camp has 5 sites on a little loop road off the highway, with access from the east or west end of the facility. The camp has vault toilets and potable water. Campsites are generally roomy with good tenting options and have tables and fire rings with grates. Stay limited to 14 days.

Rates – Campsite per night: $9. Rates half with Golden Age or Access Passport.

Getting there – From the junction of US 14/16/20 and Hwy 120 in downtown Cody, go west 37.5 miles on US 14 to the camp on the left. *See map facing page.*

Newton Creek Campground

(Shoshone National Forest, Open May 15 to Sept. 30)

About the camp – In this camp bear rules apply and it is restricted to hard-sided camping only (no tents) due to the proximity to Yellowstone National Park and possible bear activity. The camp is in mature forest and has 31 sites on two loop roads. The west loop holds sites 1-11 and the east loop, with an end-of-the-road loop turnaround, has sites 12-31, with most sites on the river side of the road. The camp has vault toilets and potable water. All sites have tables, fire rings with grates and bear boxes (see page 8). Stay limited to 14 days.

Rates – Campsite per night: $9. Rates half with Golden Age or Access Passport.

Getting there – From the junction of US 14/16/20 and Hwy 120 in downtown Cody, go west 38.9 miles on US 14 to the camp on the left. *See map page 304.*

Eagle Creek Campground

(Shoshone National Forest, Open May 15 to Oct. 30)

About the camp – This camp is in a nice forest display of Colorado blue spruce, douglas fir, white pine, cedar, cottonwood and mountain ash. The camp has 20 sites and is hard-sided camping only (no tents) due to the proximity to Yellowstone National Park and possible bear activity. The sites are on two loops with sites 5-7 on the west loop offering river bank options. The camp has vault toilets and potable water. All sites have tables, fire rings with grates and bear boxes (see page 8). Stay limited to 14 days.

Rates – Campsite per night: $9. Rates half with Golden Age or Access Passport.

Getting there – From the junction of US 14/16/20 and Hwy 120 in downtown Cody, go west 46.5 miles on US 14 to the camp on the left. *See map page 304.*

Sleeping Giant Campground

(Shoshone National Forest, Open May 15 to Oct. 30)

About the camp – This camp has 6 sites in a mature forest with a good mix of trees and is hard-sided camping only (no tents) due to the proximity to Yellowstone National Park and possible bear activity. Sites 1, 5 and 6 are on the river side of the camp. The camp has vault toilets and potable water. All sites have tables, fire rings with grates and bear boxes (see page 8). Stay limited to 14 days.

Rates – Campsite per night: $9. Rates half with Golden Age or Access Passport.

Getting there – From the junction of US 14/16/20 and Hwy 120 in downtown Cody, go west 49.4 miles on US 14 to the camp on the left. *See map page 304.*

Three Mile Campground
(Shoshone National Forest, Open May 15 to Oct. 30)

About the camp – This densely forested camp has 33 sites and is hard-sided camping only due to the proximity to Yellowstone National Park and possible bear activity. The camp has vault toilets and potable water. All sites have tables, fire rings with grates and bear boxes (see page 8). Stay limited to 14 days.

Rates – Campsite per night: $9. Rates half with Golden Age or Access Passport.

Getting there – From the junction of US 14/16/20 and Hwy 120 in downtown Cody, go west 50.4 miles on US 14 west to the camp on the left. *See map page 304.*

—Northwest of Cody—

Hogan Reservoir
(BLM, Open all year)

About the camp – This camp is on Hogan Reservoir and at the Hogan Trailhead to Bald Ridge Trail, with 5 camps and horse facilities in the form of stalls and hitching racks. The camp is also the trailhead for Luce Reservoir, the larger of these two reservoirs and only about 250 yards distant: no motorized vehicles on this little trail. The camp has a vault toilet, but no potable water. All sites have tables and fire rings with grates. Hogan Reservoir holds brown and cutthroat trout with Kamloops rainbow trout in Luce where special fishing rules apply. Waterfowl and raptors are frequent visitors around these bodies of water and trail users might well encounter antelope, mule deer, elk, moose or bear. The lands beyond the campground are closed to all visitors and uses from Dec. 15 to April 30 each year to protect crucial winter habitat for area deer and elk. Stay limited to 14 days within any 28 day period.

Rates – Free

Getting there – From the junction of US 14 and Hwy 120 in downtown Cody, go north .4 miles on Hwy 120 and US 14A; then left 18.7 miles on Hwy 120 west *(towards Belfry, Montana)* to the turnoff to the left *(1.5 miles past the turnoff to the Chief Joseph Scenic Highway)*; then left 4.7 miles to a turnoff to the left; then left 1 mile to the camp. *See map page 310.*

Dead Indian Campground
(Shoshone National Forest, Open all year)

About the camp – This camp is in a basin on Dead Indian Creek with a view of high hillsides with sheer rock faces on three sides and an opening downstream toward Clarks Fork Canyon. The camp straddles

Dead Indian Creek, with two entrances off the highway, one on each side of the bridge. The camp has a total of 10 roomy sites with tables, fire rings with grills and vault toilets, but no potable water. Camps 2 and 3, on the west side, share a common parking area for walk-in camps. Stay limited to 14 days.

Rates – Campsite per night: $7. Rates half with Golden Age or Access Passport.

Getting there – From the junction of US 14 and Hwy 120 in downtown Cody, go north .4 miles on Hwy 120 and US 14A; then left 17.2 miles on Hwy 120 west (*towards Belfry, Montana*) to Hwy 295 (*Chief Joseph Scenic Highway*); then left 21.1 miles to the camp on the right. *See map page 310.*

Sunlight Wildlife Habitat Management Area

(Wyoming Game and Fish, Open May 1 to Dec. 15)

About the camp – This pleasant undeveloped camp is in one of the more special areas of the state. As you turn into the area, you enter a large parking area with a vault toilet. Camping is allowed here, but the better, although more primitive, sites are 1.9 miles along a gravel road that leaves this area just to the right of the vault toilet. Follow this road, staying to the left all the way and you will find a stand of cottonwoods and several stone fire rings at sprawling campsites near Little Sunlight Creek. This camp has only a pit toilet, but is easy to get to and is one of the best Game and Fish camping options in the state. No potable water. Stay limited to 14 days.

Rates – Free

Getting there – From the junction of US 14 and Hwy 120 in downtown Cody, go north .4 miles on Hwy 120 and US 14A; then left 17.2 miles on Hwy 120 west (*towards Belfry, Montana*) to Hwy 295 (*Chief Joseph Scenic Highway*); then left 22.7 miles to Sunlight Road; then left 6.1 miles to the camp on the right. *See map page 310.*

Little Sunlight Campground

(Shoshone National Forest, Open June 1 to Nov. 30)

About the camp – This camp has 4 roomy sites with tables and fire rings with grills. There are several stone fire rings and a vault toilet but, no potable water. Stay limited to 16 days.

Rates – No fees, but donations for upkeep and maintenance are requested and appreciated.

Getting there – From the junction of US 14 and Hwy 120 in downtown Cody, go north .4 miles on Hwy 120 and US 14A; then left 17.2 miles on Hwy 120 west (*towards Belfry, Montana*) to Hwy 295 (*Chief Joseph Scenic Highway*); then left 22.7 miles to Sunlight Road; then left 10.7 miles to the camp on the right. Sign at turnoff reads: Little Sunlight Trailhead. *See map page 310.*

Painter Store RV Resort

(Private, Open May 1 to Dec. 31)
PO Box 1931, Cody, WY 82414 Ph: (307) 527-5248

About the camp – This camp is nearly 60 miles northwest of Cody in scenic Crandall Creek country on the west end of the Chief Joseph Scenic Highway. The camp has 16 short-term RV sites for over-nighters: all pull-thrus (15x100) on native grass with electric only (20 amp). Tenting is available on native grass. *Horses okay: $2.*

Amenities – Rest rooms and showers (showers only: $2), laundry; limited groceries, river swimming and fishing from private land, fishing licenses and restaurant; potable water, gas, dump station and pay phone.

Rates – Electric only per site: $20. Tent sites per person: $5. No cards, no checks. Reservations: phone or mail.

Getting there – From the junction of US 14 and Hwy 120 in downtown Cody, go north .4 miles on Hwy 120 and US 14A; then left 17.2 miles on Hwy 120 west (*towards Belfry, Montana*) to Hwy 295 (*Chief Joseph Scenic Highway*); then left 40.5 miles to the camp on the right. *See map page 310.*

Hunter Peak Campground

(Shoshone National Forest, Open all year)

About the camp – This camp is in a mature mixed forest and has 9 sites: 1 and 2 in a cul-de-sac and 3 - 9 on a short loop road. The camp has a vault toilet and potable water. Campsites are generally roomy with good tenting options and have tables and fire rings with grates. Bear rules apply. Stay limited to 14 days.

Rates – Campsite per night: $9. Rates half with Golden Age or Access Passport.

Getting there – From the junction of US 14 and Hwy 120 in downtown Cody, go north .4 miles on Hwy 120 and US 14A; then left 17.2 miles on Hwy 120 west (*towards Belfry, Montana*) to Hwy 295 (*Chief Joseph Scenic Highway*); then left 41.8 miles to the camp on the left. *See map page 310.*

Lake Creek Campground

(Shoshone National Forest, Open June 1 to Sept. 30)

About the camp – This camp has 7 sites in a mature stand of lodgepole pine. The camp has a vault toilet and potable water. Campsites are generally roomy with good tenting options and have tables and fire rings with grates. Bear rules apply. Stay limited to 14 days.

Rates – Campsite per night: $9. Rates half with Golden Age or Access Passport.

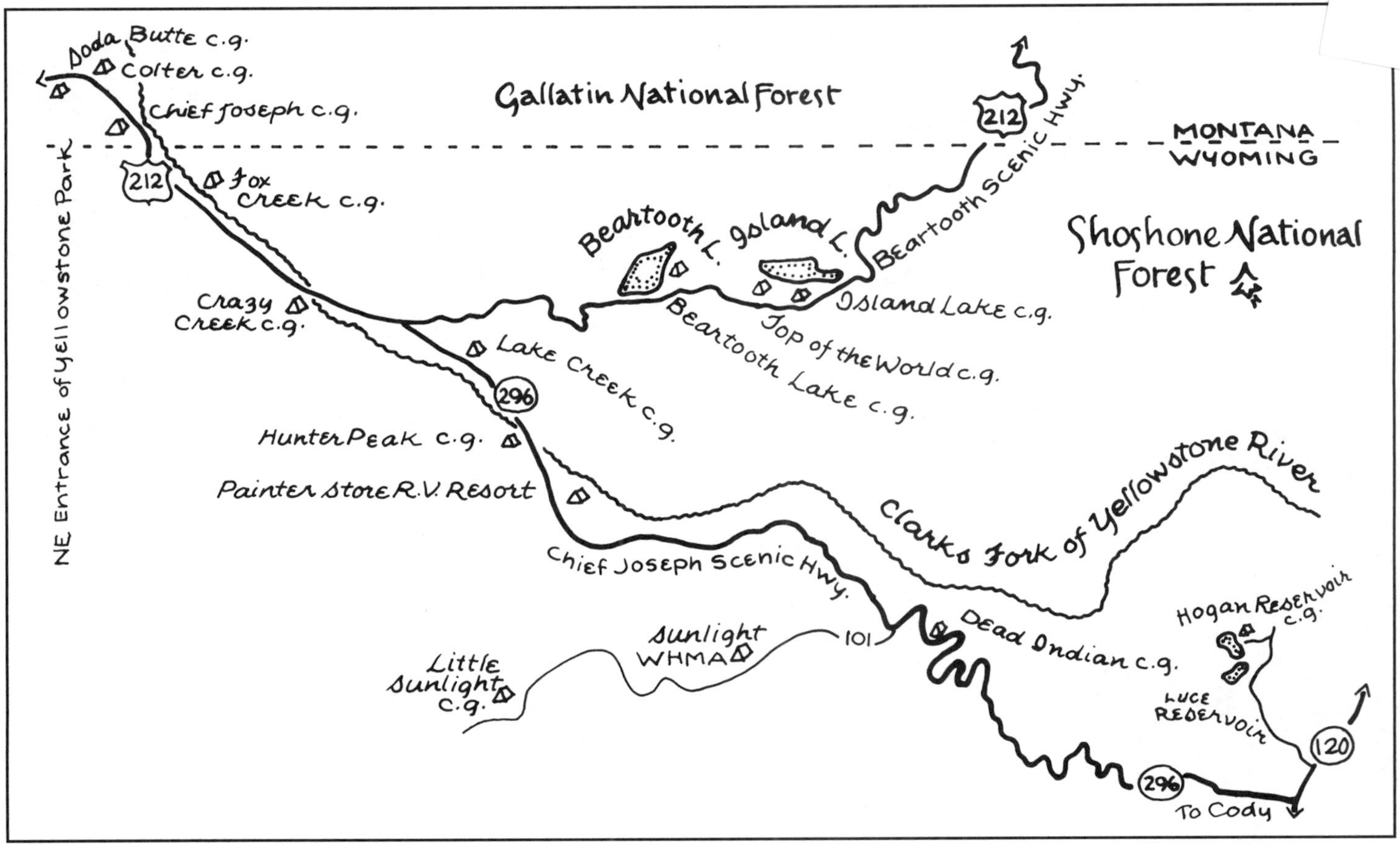
Soda Butte c.g.
Colter c.g.
Chief Joseph c.g.
Gallatin National Forest
212
MONTANA
WYOMING
NE Entrance of Yellowstone Park
Fox Creek c.g.
Beartooth L.
Island L.
Beartooth Scenic Hwy.
Shoshone National Forest
Crazy Creek c.g.
Island Lake c.g.
Top of the World c.g.
Beartooth Lake c.g.
Lake Creek c.g.
296
Hunter Peak c.g.
Painter Store R.V. Resort
Clarks Fork of Yellowstone River
Chief Joseph Scenic Hwy.
Dead Indian c.g.
Hogan Reservoir c.g.
Sunlight WHMA
101
Little Sunlight c.g.
Luce Reservoir
120
To Cody

Getting there – From the junction of US 14 and Hwy 120 in downtown Cody, go north .4 miles on Hwy 120 and US 14A; then left 17.2 miles on Hwy 120 west (*towards Belfry, Montana*) to Hwy 295 (*Chief Joseph Scenic Highway*); then left 45.5 miles to the camp on the right. *See map facing page.*

Beartooth Lake Campground

(Shoshone National Forest, Open July 1 to Sept. 7)

About the camp – This camp has 21 sites on three loops in a mature forest mix above Beartooth Lake. Sites 1-17 on loops A and B are in heavy timber above the lake. Sites 18-21 on loop C are in lighter timber and more removed from the lake. Most sites offer good tenting options and have tables and fire rings with grates. The camp has vault toilets and potable water. Just before getting to the camp there is a boat ramp and picnic area to the left. Bear rules apply. Stay limited to 14 days.

Rates – Campsite per night: $9. Rates half with Golden Age or Access Passport.

Getting there – From the junction of Hwys 212 and 296, go east 9.3 miles on US 212 (*Beartooth Scenic Highway*) to the camp on the left. *See map facing page.*

Top of the World Store

(Private, Open July to Oct.)
(PO Box 684) Beartooth Highway US 212, Red Lodge, MT 59068 Cell Phone (June-Nov.): (307) 899-2482 Radio Phone (May-Nov.): (307) 587-9043 Unit 7248

About the camp – This camp is a forest service inholding with 10 RV sites and the only hookups of any kind in the immediate area. All sites are back-ins (up to 15x35) with sewer and water only, on native grass with some tables and grills. (The generator is in place and basic electric hookups are on the drawing board: inquire). No tents, but 3 motel units are available at this site. *Horses okay.*

Amenities – Rest rooms; limited groceries, gifts, fishing tackle, Wyoming and Montana fishing licenses; ice, firewood, and gas.

Rates – Water and sewer per site: $9. Motel for 2 persons: $30.

Getting there – From the junction of Hwys 212 and 296, go east 11.1 miles on US 212 (*Beartooth Scenic Highway*) to the camp on the left. *See map facing page.*

Island Lake Campground

(Shoshone National Forest, Open July 1 to Sept. 7)

About the camp – This camp has 20 sites with all but one site on three loop roads in mature forest. The lone site, 12, has a good view of the lake from an area across the road from the rest of the camps. Most sites are roomy with good tenting options. The camp has vault toilets and potable water. Bear rules apply. Stay limited to 14 days.

Rates – Campsite per night: $9. Rates half with Golden Age or Access Passport.

Getting there – From the junction of Hwys 212 and 296, go east 12.4 miles on US 212 (*Beartooth Scenic Highway*) to the camp on the left. *See map page 310.*

Crazy Creek Campground
(Shoshone National Forest, Open June 1 to Oct. 20)

About the camp – This camp is in a forest of mature lodgepole pine and Engelmann spruce. The camp has 16 sites with tables and fire rings with grates. Sites are roomy with good tenting options. The camp has vault toilets and potable water. Bear rules apply. Stay limited to 14 days.

Rates – Campsite per night: $9. Rates half with Golden Age or Access Passport.

Getting there – From the junction of Hwys 212 and 296, go west 2.6 miles on Hwy 212 to the camp on the left. *See map page 310.*

Fox Creek Campground
(Shoshone National Forest, Open June 1 to Sept. 30)

About the camp – This camp has shaded forest sites in mature lodge pole pine and Engelmann spruce. The camp has two loops with a total of 27 sites with tables and fire rings with grates. Most sites are roomy with good tenting options. The camp has vault toilets and potable water; bear rules apply. Stay limited to 14 days.

Rates – Campsite per night: $9. Rates half with Golden Age or Access Passport.

Getting there – From the junction of Hwys 212 and 296, go west 6.5 miles on Hwy 212 to the camp on the right; then right .1 miles to the loop A fee board; [or] .2 miles to the loop B fee board. *See map page 310.*

Chief Joseph Campground
(Gallatin National Forest, Open June 1 to Sept. 30)

About the camp – This small camp is close to the highway, with 6 sites on a short loop road. All sites have tables and fire rings with grates. Only a couple of these sites are roomy with good tenting options. The camp has a vault toilet and potable water. Bear rules apply. Stay limited to 14 days.

Rates – Campsite per night: $8. Rates half with Golden Age or Access Passport.

Getting there – From the junction of Hwys 212 and 296, go west 10.5 miles on Hwy 212 to the camp on the left. *See map page 310.*

Colter Campground

(Gallatin National Forest, Open June 1 to Sept. 30)

About the camp – This camp has 23 largely open sites on an interior loop road and another road that circles back to the highway. All sites have tables and fire rings with grates. Many sites are roomy, but some are cramped or on inclines with questionable tenting options. The camp has vault toilets and potable water. Bear rules apply. Stay limited to 14 days.

Rates – Campsite per night: $8. Rates half with Golden Age or Access Passport.

Getting there – From the junction of Hwys 212 and 296, go west 11.8 miles on Hwy 212 to the camp on the right. *See map page 310.*

Soda Butte Campground

(Gallatin National Forest, Open June 1 to Sept. 30)

About the camp – In this camp most sites are open and sunny or in light timber with good tenting options. The camp has 21 sites spaced out along a half-mile road with an end-of-the-road loop turnaround. All sites have tables and fire rings with grates. The camp has vault toilets and potable water. Bear rules apply. Stay limited to 14 days.

Rates – Campsite per night: $8. Rates half with Golden Age or Access Passport.

Getting there – From the junction of Hwys 212 and 296, go west 13.1 miles on Hwy 212 to the camp on the left. *See map page 310.*

Dubois

Dubois (Dew-boys) is sited along the Wind River, partly bounded by picturesque red sandstone badlands at the edge of the Absaroka (Ab-sore-kah) Range with Ramshorn Peak (11,635') within sight to the northwest. This scenic town gained a foothold in the era of logging and tie hacking, but has made a successful transition to recreation and retirement living. Dubois is known for mild winters and frequent warm Chinook winds which add to its charm for retirees and tourists. Numerous petroglyphs found near Trail Lake in the Whiskey Basin WHMA and the archaeological areas found in the Inberg/Roy WHMA suggest prehistoric people found it alluring as well.

In Dubois you find the free **Dubois Museum**, at 909 Ramshorn, Ph: (307) 455-2284, open 9-5 May to Sept., and the **National Bighorn Sheep Interpretive Center**, at 907 Ramshorn, Ph: (307) 455-3429, open daily in summer, admission. Dubois hosts the **Pack Horse Races** in May and the **Whiskey Mountain Buckskinners Wind River Rendezvous** in August.

There are three privately-owned camps: one in town, one in rural Dubois and one 20 miles west on the way to Togwotee Pass along the **Wyoming Centennial Scenic Byway.** Seven Forest Service camps (including two free dispersed camping options) and 11 free Game and Fish areas are listed in the Dubois area. Groceries, hardware and limited sporting goods are available.

Circle up Camper Court
(Private, Open all year)
PO Box 1520, Dubois, WY 82513 Ph: (307) 455-2238

About the camp – Within walking distance of downtown Dubois, this camp is open and level on 8 acres with frontage along the Wind River at the back of the camp. The camp has 80 RV sites: 24 pull-thrus (up to 25x35) and 56 back-ins (up to 30x45). 51 sites are full hookups (20/30/50amp) on city water, 29 are water and electric only. Sites have gravel parking areas with native grass 'yards' and tables. Grass tent sites with tables are available. Portable grills are available. The camp has 2 camping cabins and 6 teepees.

Amenities – Rest rooms and showers ($), laundry; cable available at 18 premium sites, heated indoor pool, game room and playground; limited groceries and RV parts, bakery, snacks, ice, gifts, dump station and pay phone.

Rates – Full hookups for 2 persons: $18.50-22.50. Water and electric for 2 persons: $17. Tent sites for 2 persons: $14. Additional persons age five and over $1. Teepees per unit: $17. Camper cabins: $25. MC V Reservations: phone or mail.

Getting there – In downtown Dubois, turn south between the Conoco Station and the Catholic Church; then straight .1 miles to the camp. *See map page 318.*

—Southeast of Dubois—

Riverside Inn and Campground
(Private, Open May 1 to Oct. 31)
(PO Box 642) 5810 US 26, Dubois, WY 82513 Ph: (307) 455-2337

About the camp – This is a quiet camp with 10 shady full hookup (30/50 amp) sites in a stand of mature cottonwood trees. Sites (up to 25x60) have gravel parking spurs between the trees and grass 'yards' with tables and fire rings. 5 sites are pull-thrus. The camp has 10 designated grass tent sites with tables and fire rings. *Horses okay.*

Amenities – Rest rooms and showers (showers only: $5); playground, 2500 feet of private riverbank fishing access on the Wind River, and trail rides (summer); snacks, and pay phone.

Rates – Full hookups per site: $20. Water and electric per site: $18. Electric only per site: $16. Tent sites: $15. MC V D Reservations: phone or mail.

Getting there – From the junction at the corner on the east end of Dubois, go 2.6 miles east on US 26/287 to the camp on the left. *See map page 318.*

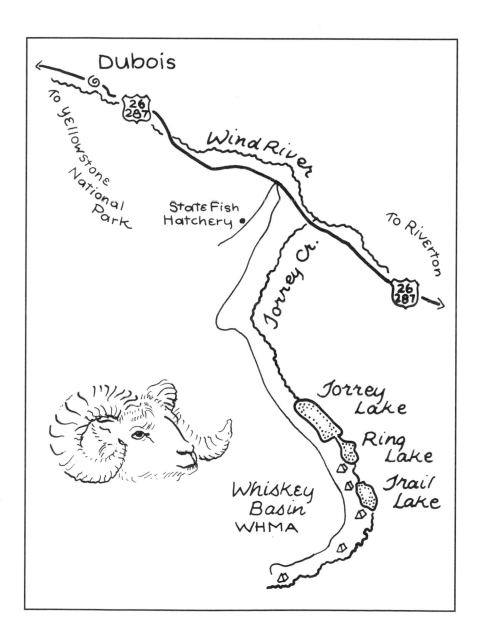

Whiskey Basin Wildlife Habitat Management Areas
(Wyoming Game & Fish, Open all year: Some areas restricted)

About the camp – There are four primitive camping areas along Ring and Trail Lakes and another below the Glacier and Whiskey Mountain Trailhead parking area. The first camping option is at the south edge of Ring Lake, where there is a nice level park, one table, stone fire rings, a primitive boat ramp and a handicapped accessible vault toilet. The second is on a rise at the north end of Trail Lake with stone fire rings and a pit toilet. The third area is on a rise at the south end of Trail Lake with stone fire rings, a table and vault toilet. The fourth is just a parking area, designated by stones on three sides and a fence just outside the entrance to the Audubon Camp in the West. The fifth and last is near the trailhead at the end of the road; here the vault toilet and a couple of tables are located by the trailhead registration board, but camping is off a loop road just to the east. There is plenty of room, but no more than a couple of stone fire rings. No potable water. Stay limited to 14 days.

Rates – Free

Getting there – From Dubois go east 3.8 miles on US 26/287 to Trail Lake Road; then go right on this road 2.4 miles to the Whiskey Mt. Big Horn Sheep Winter Range *(where there is an information kiosk and a spotting scope to view the sheep in winter)*; then left 3.7 miles to the first area; *[or]* continue a total of 4.1 miles to the second area; *[or]* continue a total of 5 miles to the third area; *[or]* continue a total of 6.6 miles to the fourth area; *[or]* continue a total of 9 miles to the last area and the trailhead parking lot. *See map page 315.*

Worth mentioning – Petroglyphs in the area indicate the presence of prehistoric people, whose art works decorate many rocks on the off-lake side of the road. These can be found from about a half-mile from the turnoff to first camping area to about a half-mile past the third camping area, a stretch of about 1 mile. In many cases, posts have been set along the west side of the roadway to indicate the presence of a petroglyph, some of which are near the road, and some a good distance up on the hillside.

Spence/Moriarity Wildlife Habitat Management Area
(Wyoming Game & Fish, Open all year: Some areas restricted)

About the camp – This WHMA is managed primarily for elk, but with the exception of mountain goat, all species of big game animals in Wyoming use the habitat. The 37,469 acres are mainly sagebrush grasslands with stands of mixed conifers and river bottom areas with cottonwood stands. The Wiggins Fork River, Bear Creek and the East Fork River flow through, adding to the diversity as well as providing fishing opportunities for cutthroat, brook, brown and rainbow trout. At the three designated camping/parking areas, there is no potable water, but two areas have vault toilets. Stay limited to 14 days.

Rates – Free

Getting there – From the junction at the corner on the east end of Dubois, go southeast 10.6 miles on US 26/287 to East Fork Road; then left 3.9 miles on the East Fork Road to a right-hand turn; then right .7 miles to the first area (with a vault toilet) near the East Fork River and a stand of cottonwoods; *[or]* continue a total of 7.4 miles on the East Fork Road to a left-hand turn; then left 1.4 miles to the second area near the Wiggins Fork River in a stand of cottonwoods; *[or]* continue a total of 9.9 miles on the East Fork Road (just past the fork at the Bear Creek Road) to a large open roadside area on the left with a vault toilet. *See map page 318.*

Inberg/Roy Wildlife Habitat Management Area
(Wyoming Game & Fish, Open May 16 to Dec. 15)

About the camp – Previously known as the East Fork Wildlife Habitat Management Area, this preserve is now named after two Wyoming Game and Fish employees, Kirk Inberg and Kevin Roy, who with their pilot Ray Austin crashed in a storm while trying to locate a wounded grizzly bear. It would be hard to find a more beautiful area to pay tribute to these gentlemen.

Grand cottonwood stands and riparian shrubs border much of the Wiggins Fork River which runs through the area to the south. Rough, broken country lies above the river to the east, where sagebrush grasslands, mountain shrubs and conifers cover the hills and benches.

The area protects critical winter range for the Wiggins Fork elk herd and many other species of wildlife, and offers good fishing and other recreation, as well as archaeological sites. According to the Game and Fish access guide, "Relatively mild winters and historic abundance of big game made this area a favorite wintering site for various Indian tribes — the Sheepeater Clan of the Shoshone Tribe was the most common." A bighorn sheep trap used by the Sheepeaters is located on adjacent U.S. Forest Service lands. Remember that a permit is required for any collection of fossils or artifacts. Help preserve and protect these treasures for future generations.

There are three designated camps: two along Bear Creek and one along the Wiggins Fork River. These camps are in shady stands of trees with stone fire rings and each of the Bear Creek camps has a vault toilet and corrals for public use. While there is no potable water supply in any of these camps there is a hydrant for potable water on the side of the road in front of one of the buildings at the elk winter headquarters. The Wiggins Fork camp is in an impressive stand of Engelmann spruce near the river and in the shadow of Black Mountain. Stay limited to 14 days.

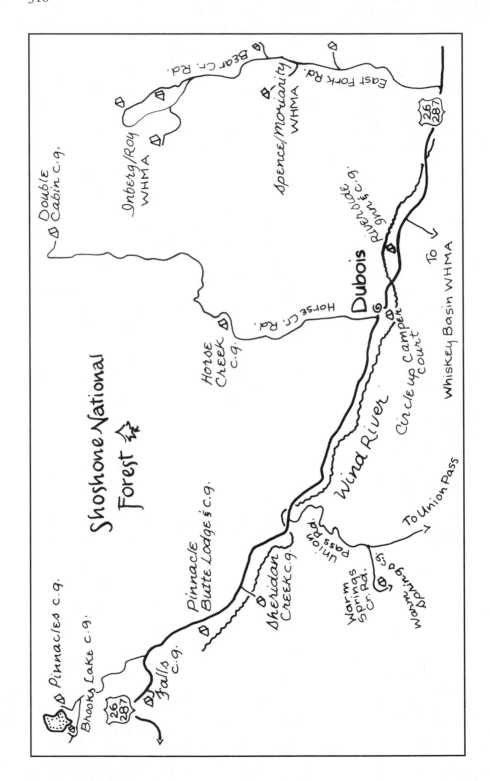

Rates – Free

Getting there – From the junction at the corner on the east end of Dubois, go southeast 10.6 miles on US 26/287 to the East Fork Road; then left 9.8 on the East Fork Road to the fork of Bear Creek Road; then left on Bear Creek Road 3.5 miles to a very hard right-hand turn; then right .4 miles to the first Bear Creek camp on the left; *[or]* continue a total of 4.2 miles on Bear Creek Road to a two-track going up hill to the left; then left 2 miles to the Wiggins Fork camp; *[or]* continue a total of 6.2 miles on the Bear Creek Road to the second Bear Creek Camp near the elk winter headquarters. *See map facing page.*

—North of Dubois—

Horse Creek Campground

(Shoshone National Forest, Open June 1 to Oct. 30)

About the camp – This camp is about ten miles north of Dubois in open and light forest along Horse Creek. The camp has a vault toilet, potable water and 9 roomy sites with tables, fire rings with grates and tent pads. Stay limited to 14 days.

Rates – Campsite per night: $6. Rates half with Golden Age or Access Passport.

Getting there – From the corner junction in Dubois, go .1 miles west to Horse Creek Road; then north 10.7 miles to the camp on the left (*the road is paved for the first 3.8 miles and good gravel thereafter*). *See map facing page.*

Double Cabin Campground

(Shoshone National Forest, Open June 1 to Sept. 30)

About the camp – This camp is about 25 miles north of Dubois above Frontier Creek in a mature forest setting on a hillside that faces a basin ringed by peaks of the Absaroka Range. The camp has vault toilets, potable water and 15 roomy sites with tables and fire rings. Four sites are pull-thrus. About .2 miles east of the camp entrance are several undeveloped overflow sites with stone fire rings and the Wiggins Fork Community Corral for public use. Trailheads here include: Wiggins Fork, Indian Point, Cougar Pass and Frontier Creek. Bear rules apply. Stay limited to 14 days.

Rates – Campsite per night: $6. Rates half with Golden Age or Access Passport.

Getting there — From the corner junction in Dubois, go .1 miles west to Horse Creek Road; then right 25.2 miles to the camp on the right (*the road is paved for the first 3.8 miles and good gravel thereafter*). *See map facing page.*

Warm Springs Campground (Undeveloped)

(Shoshone National Forest, Open June 1 to Sept. 30)

About the camp – This camp is in aspen and Engelmann spruce along Warm Springs Creek about 12 miles west of Dubois. The camp has stone fire rings which show a lot of use, and a fairly new vault toilet. Bear rules apply. Stay limited to 16 days.

Rates – Free.

Getting there – From the corner junction in Dubois, go 9.7 miles west on US 26/287 to Union Pass Road on the left; then left 5.5 miles to Warm Springs Creek Road: then right 1.6 miles to the camp on the left (*just before the bridge over Warm Springs Creek*). *See map page 318.*

Sheridan Creek Campground (Undeveloped)

(Shoshone National Forest, Open June 1 to Sept. 30)

About the camp – This primitive camp on grass in light forest is just a short distance off the highway about 18 miles west of Dubois. The camp has stone fire rings and a vault toilet, but no potable water. Bear rules apply. Stay limited to 16 days.

Rates – Free

Getting there – From the corner junction in Dubois go 18 miles west on US 26/287 to the Warm Springs Creek Road turnoff; *[or]* to the Tie Hack Memorial parking area; then south off the highway; *[or]* out of the east end of the Tie Hack parking lot, where you will see a pit toilet and a bridge spanning the Wind River; then cross the river and go .2 miles to the camp on the right. *See map page 318.*

Pinnacle Butte Lodge and Campground

(Private, Open all year)
3577 West US Hwy 26, Dubois, WY 82513 Ph: (307) 455-2506 or (800) 934-3569 Fax: (307) 455-3874

About the camp – This camp is open and level, located behind and below the lodge, overlooking a portion of the Wind River. The camp offers 15 RV sites: 1 pull-thru (12x50) and 14 back-ins (up to 20x37). 7 sites are full hookups (20/30/50amp); 4 have water and electric only and 3 electric only. Sites have gravel parking areas with native grass 'yards' and some tables and grills. Grass tent sites with some tables and grills are available. The lodge also offers 3 full-service cabins — two with kitchenettes — and motel units.

Amenities – Rest rooms and showers ($) (showers only: meter only); heated pool (June, July and August); snacks, ice, cafe, gifts, Native American jewelry, unique sweat shirts and T-shirts, and pay phone.

Rates – Full hookups per site: $19. Water and electric only or electric only per site: $15. Tents: $10. V MC D Reservations: phone or mail.

Getting there – From the junction at the corner on the east end of Dubois, go 20 miles west on US 26/287 to the camp on the left. *See map page 318.*

Pinnacles Campground
(Shoshone National Forest, Open June 20 to Sept. 3)

About the camp – This camp on a forested hillside overlooking Brooks Lake has 21 sites. The camp has vault toilets and potable water. Three sites are pull-thrus; sites 3,4,6 and 8 are the best lakeside options, and site 9 is a short walk-in. Sites have tables and fire rings with grates. Bear rules apply. Stay limited to 14 days.

Rates – Campsite per night: $9. Rates half with Golden Age or Access Passport.

Getting there – From the junction at the corner on the east end of Dubois, go 22.8 miles west on US 26/287 to Brooks Lake Road; then right 4.4 miles to the Pinnacles Campground turnoff; then right .1 miles to the fee board. *See map page 318.*

Worth mentioning – Brooks Lake Road is worth the ride for the view it provides: From this forested road there are several striking peeks of the lake, Brooks Mountain, and the sheer rock faces of the Pinnacle Buttes formations which tower over roadway and evergreens.

Brooks Lake Campground
(Shoshone National Forest, Open June 20 to Sept. 30)

About the camp – This camp has 13 sites on a rise a short distance from the shore of the Brooks Lake. Sites 1 and 2 are slightly isolated at the end of a short road with a small turn around, but farther from the lake. Similarly, sites 5-7 are located off a small cul de sac and farther from the lake. Sites 11-13, on a slight rise near the shore, offer the most picturesque views of the Pinnacle Buttes and the lake. The camp has vault toilets, potable water, a boat ramp and a picnic area. Sites have tables and fire rings with grates. Bear rules apply. Stay limited to 14 days.

Rates – Campsite per night: $9. Rates half with Golden Age or Access Passport

Getting there – From the junction at the corner on the east end of Dubois, go 22.8 miles west on US 26/287 to Brooks Lake Road; then right 5 miles to a hard right-hand turn near the gate to Brooks Lake Lodge; then right .2 miles to the fee board. *See map page 318.*

Falls Campground

(Shoshone National Forest, Open June 1 to Oct. 30)

About the camp – This camp has 45 sites, offers a good view of some of the area's formations, and is near the short trail to view Brooks Lake Creek Falls. The camp has vault toilets and potable water. Sites have tables and fire rings with grates, and 10 sites are pull-thrus. Bear rules apply. Stay limited to 14 days.

Rates – Campsite per night: $9. Rates half with Golden Age or Access Passport

Getting there – From the junction at the corner on the east end of Dubois, go 23.2 miles west on US 26/287 to the camp turnoff on the left. *See map page 318.*

Hoback Junction

Hoback Junction is a three-forks community near the confluence of the Snake and Hoback Rivers. Hoback Canyon is along US 191 to the south and east and Snake River Canyon, a mecca for whitewater devotees, is south and west along US 89. Jackson is 13 miles to the north. There are three privately-owned camps in the area and Forest Service camps along both roads going south. Businesses at the junction offer basic groceries, fuel, ice and snacks.

Lazy J Corral

(Private, Open May 1 to Nov. 1)
10755 S. Hwy 89, Jackson, WY 83001 Ph: (307) 733-1554

About the camp – This level, grassy 3-acre camp is along the highway and just north of Hoback Junction. The camp has 25 full hookup (20/30/50 amp) RV sites: 5 pull-thrus and 20 back-ins (all 25x40). All sites are gravel and native grass. No tents.

Amenities – Rest rooms and showers, laundry, and gifts.

Rates – Full hookups per site: $20. MC V Personal checks okay. Reservations: phone or mail.

Getting there – From the junction of US 26/89 and 189/191 at Hoback Junction, go north .1 miles to the camp on the left. *See map page 326.*

Snake River Park KOA

(Private, Open April 1 to Oct. 11)
9705 S. Hwy 89, Jackson, WY 83001 Ph: (307) 733-7078 or (800) KOA-1878

About the camp – This 7-acre camp is on a level grassy area just above the Snake River about 12 miles south of downtown Jackson. The camp has 50 RV sites: all back-ins (17x40), with 32 full hookups (20/30/50 amp) and 18 water and electric only. All sites are gravel and have grass 'yards' with tables and grills. There are 30 grass tent sites with tables and grills, 3 teepees and 11 Kamper Kabins.

Amenities – Rest rooms and showers, laundry; whitewater rafting headquarters, game room and playground; limited groceries and RV parts, firewood, gifts, dump station, and pay phone.

Rates – Full hookups for 2 persons: $35.95. Water and electric only for 2 persons: $32.95. No hookups for 2 persons: $28.95. Tent sites for 2 persons: $26.95. Teepees for 2 persons: $31.50. Kamper kabins for 2 persons: $44.95-54.95. Additional persons: $5. MC V D Reservations: phone or mail.

Getting there – From Hoback Junction (*US 189/191 and US 26/89 about 13 miles south of Jackson*), go north 1.3 miles on US 191 to the camp on the left. *See map page 326.*

—Southeast of Hoback Junction—

Lone Eagle Resort

(Private, Open May 15 to Sept. 30)
13055 South US Hwy 191 Star Route 45c, Jackson, WY 83001 Ph: (307) 733-1090 or (800) 321-3800 Fax: (307) 733-5042

About the camp – This 20-acre camp on two level grassy tiers next to and above the Hoback River is bordered on the rear by national forest lands. The camp has 55 full hookup (30 amp) RV sites: all pull-thrus (30x50). All sites are gravel with grass 'yards,' tables, fire rings and grills. There are grass tent sites along the river with tables, fire rings and grills. This camp also offers 15 camping cabins, 5 tent cabins (wooden floor and walls with canvas roof) and 7 deluxe guest houses (fully furnished park model RV's with slide outs).

Amenities – 2 rest rooms and showers (one handicapped-accessible), laundry; outdoor heated pool with spa, game room, playground, white water raft trips, horseshoes, archery, volleyball, basketball, trail rides, kayak rentals, mountain bike rentals, guided fishing trips and guided canoe trips (6 or more only); food court (breakfast, lunch and dinner), sandwich and soda shop, firewood, gift shop and pay phone.

Rates – Full hookups for 2 persons: $39.22. Additional persons over age 6: $4. Tent sites: $10.60 per person. Tent Cabins: $28.62. Camping Cabins: $66.78. Deluxe Guest Houses: $127.20. All rates: incl. tax. All major credit cards. Personal checks okay. Reservations: phone only.

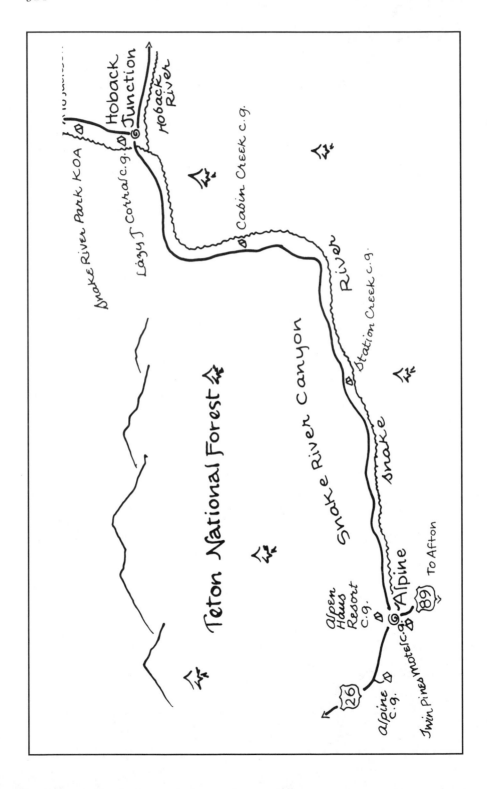

Getting there – From Hoback Junction (*US 26/89 and 189/191 about 13 miles south of Jackson*), go south 4 miles on US 189/191 to the camp entrance on the right. *See map facing page.*

Hoback Campground
(Bridger-Teton National Forest, Open June 5 to Sept. 8)

About the camp – This camp is convenient to the highway, along the banks of the Hoback River about 21 miles south of Jackson. There are 14 sites, all with tables, fire rings with grates and grills. The camp has vault toilets and potable water. Stay limited to 10 days.

Rates – Campsite per night: $12. Rates half with Golden Age or Access Passport.

Getting there – From Hoback Junction (*US 189/191 and US 26/89 about 13 miles south of Jackson*), go south 8.1 miles on US 189/191 to the camp on the right. *See map facing page.*

Granite Creek Campground
(Bridger-Teton National Forest, Open June 5 to Sept. 8)

About the camp – This camp is located on Granite Creek a short distance below the falls and Granite Creek Hot Springs, in the shadow of an interesting formation known as 'The Open Door.' There are 53 sites on three loop roads in a mixed conifer forest. The camp has vault toilets and potable water. Campsites have tables and fire rings with grates. Stay limited to 10 days.

Rates – Campsite per night: $12. Rates half with Golden Age or Access Passport. (Reservations are possible at this campground up to 240 days in advance and 10 days prior to arrival. Service fee per reservation: $8.65. Ph: (877) 444-6777 toll free.)

Getting there – From Hoback Junction (*US 189/191 and US 26/89 about 13 miles south of Jackson*), go south 11.6 miles on US 189/191 to a turn off to the left; then left about 8 miles to the camp on the right. *See map facing page.*

Kozy Campground
(Bridger-Teton National Forest, Open June 5 to Sept. 8)

About the camp – This camp is convenient to the highway, along the banks of the Hoback River about 25 miles south of Jackson. There are 8 sites with tables, fire rings with grates and grills. The camp has vault toilets and potable water. Stay limited to 10 days.

Rates – Campsite per night: $10. Rates half with Golden Age or Access Passport.

Getting there – From Hoback Junction (*US 189/191 and US 26/89 about 13 miles south of Jackson*), go south 12.9 miles on US 189/191 to the camp on the left. *See map facing page.*

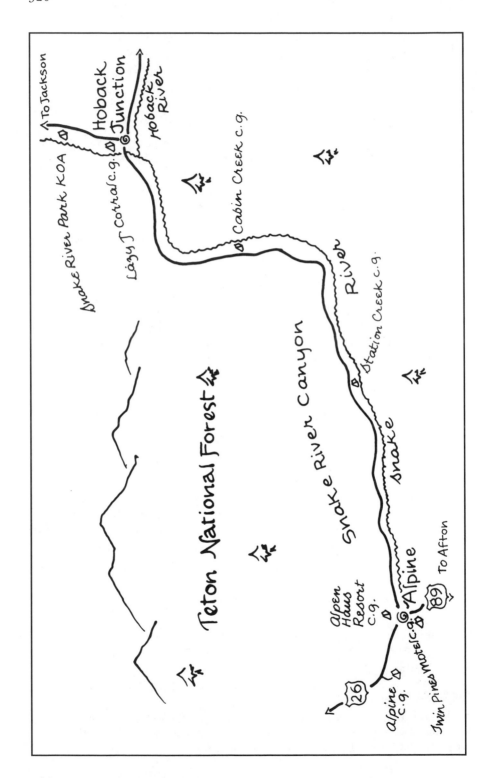

Cabin Creek Campground

(Bridger-Teton National Forest, Open May 25 to Sept. 8)

About the camp – Here there are 10 sites: all roomy with good tenting options and all on the river side of the camp road. 4 sites are pull-thrus. The camp has a vault toilet, but no potable water. Sites have tables, fire rings with grates and grills. Stay limited to 16 days

Rates – Campsite per night: $10. Rates half with Golden Age or Access Passport.

Getting there – From Hoback Junction (*US 26/89 and 189/191 about 13 miles south of Jackson*), go south 7.4 miles on US 26/89 to the camp on the left. *See map facing page.*

Station Creek Campground

(Bridger-Teton National Forest, Open June 10 to Sept. 8)

About the camp – This camp has 15 sites. Sites are roomy with good tenting options and have tables, fire rings with grates and grills. Stay limited to 16 days.

Rates – Campsite per night: $10. Rates half with Golden Age or Access Passport.

Getting there – From Hoback Junction (*US 26/89 and 189/191 about 13 miles south of Jackson*), go south 12.8 miles on US 26/89 to the camp on the left. *See map facing page.*

Jackson

Jackson is Wyoming's world-famous year-round recreation area, a hub from which to enjoy the **Snake River, Snow King Mountain, Teton Village** and both **Grand Teton and Yellowstone National Parks**. In Jackson you find boardwalks and an intimate town square with elk-antler arches on the four corners. The western flavor does little to hide a vigorous commercial community providing for every need from groceries and sporting goods to RV sales and service.

The **Jackson Hole Museum**, at 105 N. Glenwood, Ph: (307) 733-2414, is open summers M-Sat., 9-6 and Sun. 10-4 ($) and the **National Museum of Wildlife Art** just north of town, at 2820 Rungius Road, Ph: (307) 733-5771, is open daily 9-5 ($). The USFS has an office here for information, but maps are sold by the Grand Teton Natural History Association at the visitors centers in Jackson and at Moose.

Memorial Day weekend is busy with **Old West Days** in Jackson and a **Mountain Man Rendezvous** at Teton Village. For eight weeks from the end of June to the middle of August the **Grand Teton Music Festival** performs 42 concerts from their traditional and classical repertoire. From Memorial Day to Labor Day the **Jackson Hole Rodeo** shakes out the dust on broncs and bulls at 8 p.m. every Wed. and Sat. And, Jackson has a nightly (except Sunday) stage coach heist and damsel in distress shoot-out melodrama at 6:30 p.m. on the southeast corner of the square.

There are two privately-owned camps in town and another near Teton Village, as well as three Forest Service camps in the Gros Ventre area, one other high above the National Elk Refuge overlooking the valley floor, and three more over Teton Pass and near the Idaho State Line.

Even if camping here is not on your agenda, the Gros Ventre Road northeast of Jackson offers a remarkable scenic drive. In addition to the slide itself, you pass amidst mature stands of aspen, steep green valleys, hillsides fully carpeted with evergreens and rolling green and red hills sprinkled with pockets of evergreen and aspen stands. Rounding out the view are greener-than-green hay meadows marking two prosperous ranches spread across the valleys (see *'getting there'* under Red Hills Campground on page 331).

Elk Country Inn RV Park

(Private, Open all year)
(PO Box 1255) 480 W. Pearl St., Jackson, WY 83001 Ph: (307) 733-2364 or (800) 4 TETONS
Fax: (307) 733-4465 E-mail: townsquareinns@wyoming.com

About the camp – If you try to find this camp by looking for other RV's, it won't work. You can't see the camp from the street, though it's only about 4 blocks from the square in the center of downtown Jackson: It's behind the inn on an open and level gravel area fronted by a large grass park with picnic tables and grills. The camp has 12 back-in (14x45), full hookup RV sites (30 amp on city water). No tents. *Horses free: at nearby barn with own feed, small charge for boarding.*

Amenities – Rest rooms and showers, laundry; cable included, spa, rec area; snacks and ice, free hot beverages and free newspapers in office, and pay phone.

Rates – Full hookups per site: $30. All major cards. Reservations: phone, E-mail, fax or mail.

Getting there – From the junction of US 26/89/189/191 and Hwy 22, go 1 mile east on Broadway St.; then angle right onto Pearl St. for .1 miles to the Elk Country Inn on the right.

From Broadway St. at the square, go one block south on Cache St. to Pearl St.; then right about 4 blocks to the inn on the left. *See map page 330.*

Virginian RV Campground

(Private, Open May 1 to Oct. 15)
(PO Box 1052) 750 W. Broadway, Jackson, WY 83001 Ph: (307) 733-7189 or (800) 321-6982

About the camp – This camp is on the west end of Jackson, 1 mile from the heart of downtown. The open and level camp offers 103 full hookup RV sites (20/30/50 amp on city water): 64 pull-thrus (up to 25x65) and 35 back-ins (up to 25x35). All sites are gravel with grass 'yards' and tables and grills. No tents.

Amenities – Rest rooms and showers, laundry; cable included, use of pool and spa at motel; vending machines and pay phone.

Rates – Full hookups per site: $34-42. All major cards. Reservations: phone or mail.

Getting there – From the square in the center of downtown Jackson take Broadway St. west .9 miles to Virginian Way; then left one-quarter mile to the camp on the left.

From the junction of US 26/89/189/191 and Hwy 22 go .5 miles east on Broadway to Virginian Way; then right one-quarter mile to the camp on the left. *See map page 330.*

Wagon Wheel RV Campground

(Private, Open May to Oct.)
PO Box 1463 (505 N. Cache), Jackson, WY 83001 Ph: (307) 733-5488

About the camp – This camp, only five blocks north of the square in downtown Jackson, is open and level, with Flat Creek running along two edges of the camp. The camp has 33 full hookup RV sites (30 amp on city water): 1 pull-thru (20x45) and 32 back-ins (up to 20x35). All sites are gravel with some tables and grills. There are 11 grass tent sites, all along Flat Creek, with tables and grills. *Horses boarded, with camp rental, during hunting season only: $5.*

Amenities – Rest rooms and showers, laundromat nearby; cable included; pay phone on street just in front of camp.

Rates – Full hookups per site: $32. Tent sites: $15. V MC Reservations: phone or mail.

Getting there – This camp is on the west side of N. Cache St. (*US 26/89/191*) 5.5 blocks north of the square in downtown Jackson. *See map page 330.*

Teton Village KOA

(Private, Open May 1 to Oct. 15)
(PO Box 38) 2780 N. Moose-Wilson Road, Teton Village, WY 83025 Ph: (307) 733-5254 or (800) KOA-9043 Fax: (307) 739-1298

About the camp – This camp is on 15 acres of green grass with hawthorns, willows, aspens and cottonwoods providing shade for many sites. The camp has 80 RV sites: 60 pull-thrus (up to 30x80); 20 back-ins (up to 24x34), and 60 full hookups (20/30/50 amp). All sites have gravel spurs and grass 'yards' with tables and fire rings. There are 70 grass tent sites with tables, fire rings and grills. 6 kamper kabins are available.

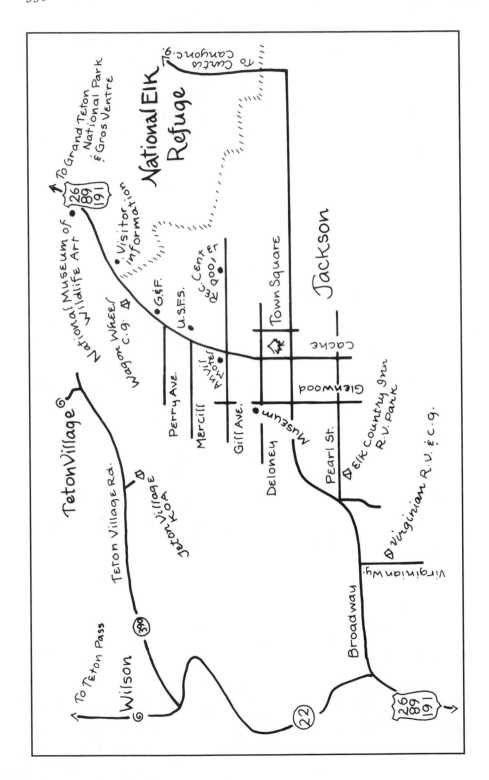

Amenities – Rest rooms and showers, laundry; cable included with full hookups, game room and playground; limited groceries and RV parts, firewood, gifts, dump station, propane and pay phone.

Rates – Full hookups for 2 persons: $34. Water and electric only for 2 persons: $30. Tent sites for 2 persons: $26. Additional persons: $5 each. Most major cards. Reservations: phone, fax or mail.

Getting there – From the junction of US 26/89/189/191 and Hwy 22, take Hwy 22; then go 4.1 miles to the Teton Village/Wilson fork; then right 1.5 miles to the camp on the right. *See map facing page.*

—Northeast of Jackson—

Atherton Creek Campground

(Bridger-Teton National Forest, Open June 5 to Sept. 8)

About the camp – This campground on Lower Slide Lake is only 21 miles, on paved roadways, from the square in Jackson. The camp has a boat ramp, vault toilets, potable water and 14 sites with tables, grills and fire rings with grates. Stay limited to 16 days.

Rates – Campsite per night: $10. Rates half with Golden Age or Access Passport.

Getting there – From the square in Jackson, go north 7 miles on US 26/89 to Gros Ventre Junction; then right 8.3 miles through the town of Kelly to Gros Ventre Road; then right 6.1 miles on Gros Ventre Road to the camp entrance on the right. *See map page 332.*

Red Hills Campground

(Bridger-Teton National Forest, Open June 5 to Sept. 8)

About the camp – This campground is on the Gros Ventre River with sites in light forest. The camp has a vault toilet, potable water and 5 sites on a short road with no turnaround. Sites have tables and fire rings and are fairly roomy with good tenting options. Stay limited to 16 days.

Rates – Campsite per night: $10. Rates half with Golden Age or Access Passport.

Getting there – From the square in Jackson, go north 7 miles on US 26/89 to Gros Ventre Junction; then right 8.3 miles through the town of Kelly to Gros Ventre Road; then right 11.7 miles on Gros Ventre Road (*the first 6.1 miles is paved*) to the camp entrance on the left. *See map page 332.*

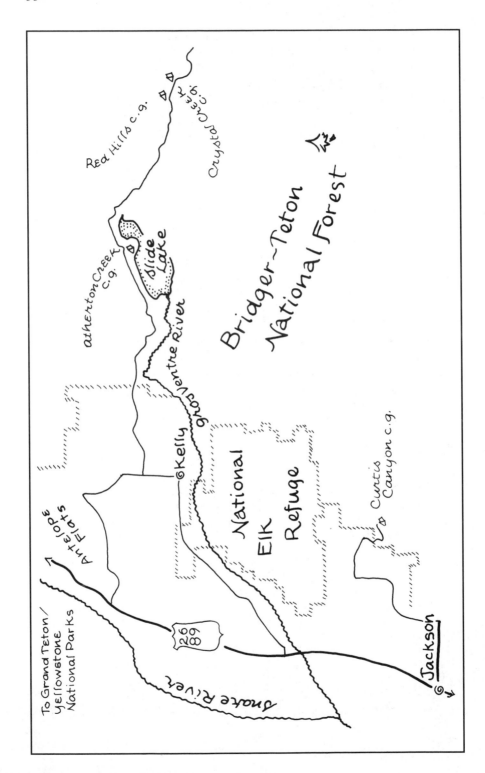

Crystal Creek Campground
(Bridger-Teton National Forest, Open June 5 to Sept. 8)

About the camp – This campground is on the Gros Ventre River with open sites in light forest. The camp has a vault toilet, potable water and 6 sites on a short loop road. Sites have tables and fire rings and are roomy with good tenting options. Stay limited to 16 days.

Rates – Campsite per night: $10. Rates half with Golden Age or Access Passport.

Getting there – From the square in Jackson, go north 7 miles on US 26/ 89 to Gros Ventre Junction; then right 8.3 miles through the town of Kelly to Gros Ventre Road; then right 12 miles on Gros Ventre Road to the camp entrance on the left. *See map facing page.*

Curtis Canyon Campground
(Bridger-Teton National Forest, Open June 5 to Sept. 8)

About the camp – This location is directly across the road from a popular but little known overlook of the Tetons and the Jackson Hole country. The camp, in a shady forest with a smattering of mature douglas firs, has 12 sites with tables, fire rings and grills along a short road with an end-of-the-road loop turnaround. The sites are roomy and offer good tenting options. Sites 2, 5 and 7 are small pull-thrus. There is a vault toilet, but no potable water. Stay limited to 16 days.

Rates – Campsite per night: $10. Rates half with Golden Age or Access Passport.

Getting there – From the square in the center of downtown Jackson, go east 1 mile on Broadway St. to the back of the National Elk Refuge; then left 4.7 miles along the back of the refuge to a turnoff to the right; then right to the base of the hill and up a switchback to the camp at the top on the right (*the overlook is at the top on the left*). *See map facing page.*

—North of Jackson over Teton Pass—

Trail Creek Campground
(Targhee National Forest, Open May 15 to Sept. 15)

About the camp – This campground, in a mostly conifer forest with a few aspen, is just inside the Wyoming State Line along Hwy 22. Trail Creek flows behind most of the 11 campsites which are roomy with good tenting options. All sites have tables, fire rings with grates and grills. The camp has vault toilets and potable water. Stay limited to 14 days.

Rates – Campsite per night: $6. Rates half with Golden Age or Access Passport.

Getting there – From Jackson take Hwy 22 over Teton Pass. The camp is on the left 6.2 miles from the summit of Teton Pass and .2 miles east of the Idaho State Line. *See map facing page.*

Teton Canyon Campground
(Targhee National Forest, Open May 15 to Sept. 15)

About the camp – The last four miles of road into this camp negotiates a valley drainage with great views of the back side of the Tetons. This camp has 21 campsites in a variety of settings from heavily shaded, cool sites in mature forest to lightly forested sites overlooking an open park or open, sunny sites. Most sites are roomy with good tenting options. The camp has vault toilets, potable water and sites with tables, fire rings with grates and grills. Stay limited to 14 days.

Rates – Campsite per night: $8. Rates half with Golden Age or Access Passport.

Getting there – From Driggs go east on Little Ave. through the town of Alta for a total of 6.7 miles to a right-hand fork at FSR 009; then right 4.3 miles on FSR 009 to the camp. *See map facing page.*

Cave Falls Campground
(Targhee National Forest, Open May 15 to Sept. 1)

About the camp – This camp is just inside the Wyoming line and just outside the Yellowstone National Park boundary along the Falls River. The camp has 23 sites and most are pull-thrus. There are vault toilets and potable water. Campsites have tables, fire rings with grates and grills. Stay limited to 14 days. *Pack it in, Pack it out.*

Rates – Campsite per night: $8. Rates half with Golden Age or Access Passport.

Getting there – From the junction of Idaho Hwys 32 and 47 near Marysville, go east 5.1 miles to 1400 N. Road; then right 18.4 miles to the camp on the right (*the pavement ends after 5.8 miles at the forest boundary and you cross the state line into Wyoming at 16.6 miles*). *See map facing page.*

Worth mentioning – Due to the proximity to Yellowstone National Park and Idaho, and less than clear boundary markers on the river be sure you're fishing with the right license or licenses.

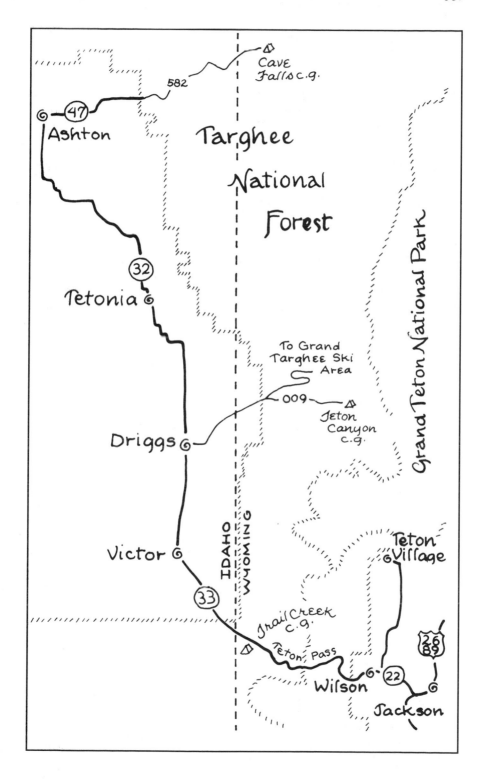

Meeteetse

Meeteetse from the Shoshone language means, 'meeting place,' or as some reports claim, it comes from the Crow words for 'meeting place of the chiefs.' In any case, prehistoric Native American presence is certain at **Legend Rock State Petroglyph Site** south of town (the gate to this site is locked, but keys with SASE and directions are available in Meeteetse at the Bank Museum). A 58-foot-long arrow of placed stones on a ridge northwest of town points to the Medicine Wheel National Historic Landmark in the Big Horn Mountains, a remarkable feat of orientation for these ancient people (as the arrow is on private property, inquire regarding permission and directions at the Bank Museum). The known history of the area centers on cattle, with several large ranches located west of town along the Wood and Greybull Rivers. Most notable is the Pitchfork Ranch, founded in 1878. Hwy 290 southwest out of town is the access to the Shoshone National Forest and the Washakie Wilderness.

In town are two free museums: the **Meeteetse Hall Museum**, at 942 Mondell St. and the **Meeteetse Bank Museum**, at 1033 Park Ave., Ph: (307) 868-2423. Though hours may vary slightly, both museums are open daily from May 15 to Sept. 30. The town kicks up its heels for three days during the **Labor Day Celebration** with rodeo, street dance, parade, barbecue and more. In late August, local historians host the **Kirwin Excursion** with four-wheel-drive explorations of this abandoned mining town.

Even if you're just passing through enjoy outstanding panoramas of the local mountain country as you navigate the agricultural land of prosperous-looking ranches in the fertile valleys along the Wood and Greybull Rivers on Hwy 290 and Wood River Road, which forks off of Hwy 290 at 6.7 miles from town. (*Hwy 290 is paved for its entire 11.4 miles and Wood River Road is paved for the first 5.3 miles.*)

There are 3 free Forest Service camps and one free Game and Fish camping areas located off of Hwy 290, as well as two privately-owned camps in town. An old fashioned soda fountain highlights the decor in the 1899 Meeteetse Mercantile where you find groceries, a small deli, meat counter and produce section, plus limited hardware and sporting goods. The school in Meeteeste has a pool at 2107 Idaho St., open to the public for rec swims in the summer. ($1)

Oasis Motel and Campground

(Private, Open all year)
PO Box 86, Meeteetse, WY 82433 Ph: (307) 868-2551 or 1-888-868-5270 Fax: (307) 868-2687

> About the camp – This camp is on 3 acres, with lots of cottonwood trees, just north of downtown Meeteetse. The camp has 11 full hookup sites (30/50 amp): 4 pull-thrus (15x35) and 7 back-ins (15x30). Sites have gravel spurs and grass 'yards' with some tables and grills. Tent sites are available. *Horses okay : $2.*

Amenities – Rest rooms and showers (showers only: $3), laundry; cable TV included in full hookups; a small but nice antique display area in office, dump station and pay phone. Full-service motel units are also available.

Rates – Any RV hookup for one person: $12. Additional persons: $2. Tent sites: $5, plus $3 per person. Motel units $26-51.

Getting there – From the junction of Hwy 290 and 120 in downtown Meeteetse, go north .1 miles (*just across the bridge*) to the camp on the right. *See map page 338.*

Vision Quest Motel and RV Campground

(Private, Open all year)
(PO Box 4) 2207 State St., Meeteetse, WY 82433 Ph: (307) 868-2512

About the camp – This camp has 8 sites: all pull-thrus (15x50) and all full hookups (30 amp on city water). No Tents. *Horses okay.*

Amenities – Cable TV available: $2.

Rates – Full hookups per site: $12.50. Electric only per site: $10.

Getting there – This camp is at Highland Ave. and State St., two blocks south of the intersection of Hwys 120 and 290 in downtown Meeteetse. *See map page 338.*

Wood River Campground

(Shoshone National Forest, Open May 31 to Nov. 15)

About the camp – This nicely forested camp sits on the banks of the Wood River. The camp has 5 sites with tables, fire rings with grates and a vault toilet, but no potable water. The camp road has a cattle guard and the area is fenced, presumably due to grazing leases in the area. Stay limited to 14 days.

Rates – No fees, but donations for upkeep and maintenance are appreciated.

Getting there – From the junction of Hwys 120 and 290 in downtown Meeteetse, go west 6.7 miles on Hwy 290 to Wood River Road (*CR 4DT*); then left 16.6 miles to the camp on the left. *See map page 338.*

Brown Mountain Campground

(Shoshone National Forest, Open May 31 to Nov. 15)

About the camp – This camp is on the banks of Wood River with steep foothills rising above the river on one side and the road on the other. The camp has 7 sites with tables, fire rings with grates and a vault toilet, but no potable water. From this area you are within sight of Mount Crosby (12,449'), Chief Mt. (12,003'), Brown Mt. (12,161'), Franc's Peak (13,158') and Jojo Mt. (12,561'). A sign near this camp indicates the road continues on for 4-wheel-drive vehicles with the Kirwin Trailhead 9 miles ahead. The camp road has a cattle guard and

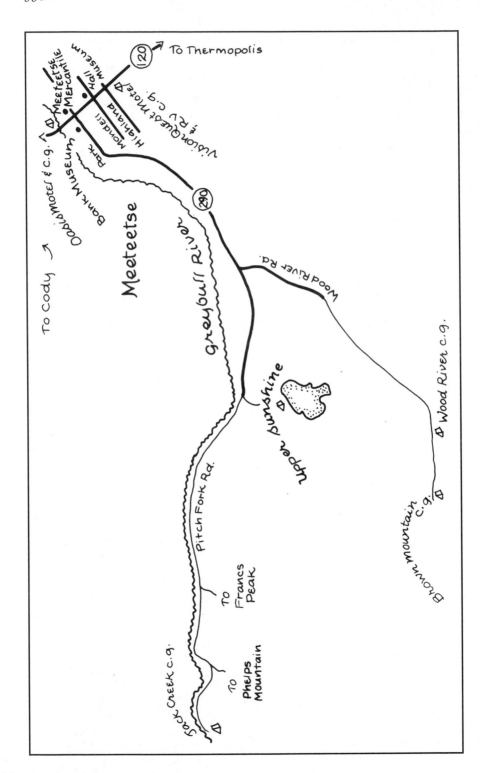

To Thermopolis

120

Meeteetse Museum
Hall
Meeteetse Mercantile
Highland Motel
Vision Quest Motel & R.V. c.g.

Mondell

To Cody

Oasis Motel & c.g.
Bank Museum
Park

Meeteetse

290

Greybull River

Wood River Rd.

upper sunshine

Wood River c.g.

Pitch Fork Rd.

Brown mountain c.g.

To Francs Peak

Jack Creek c.g.

To Phelps Mountain

the area is fenced, presumably due to grazing leases in the area. Stay limited to 14 days.

Rates – No fees, but donations for upkeep and maintenance are appreciated.

Getting there – From the junction of Hwys 120 and 290 in downtown Meeteetse, go west 6.7 miles on Hwy 290 to Wood River Road (*CR 4DT*); then left 19.1 miles to the camp on the left. *See map facing page.*

Worth mentioning – The Wood River Road is paved for the first 5.3 miles and navigates agricultural land in a fertile valley with good panoramas of the mountain country ahead.

Upper Sunshine Reservoir
(Wyoming Game and Fish and GVID, Inc., Open all year)

About the camp – These camping options are primitive with only stone fire rings: no tables, potable water or vault toilets. At this site, however, there is a network of two-tracks that lead to different settings on the water's edge. Visibility is superb, with nary a tree blocking your view of the shore or the superb panorama of this mountain country. The unprotected nature of the reservoir could be a factor making these waters ideal for the needs of wind surfers. Stay limited to 14 days.

Rates – Free

Getting there – From the junction of Hwys 120 and 290 in downtown Meeteetse, go west 11.4 miles to the fork of CR 5XS and 41X; then left 2.7 miles on CR 5XS to the reservoir; then work your way to the right to the camping option of your choice. *See map facing page.*

Worth mentioning – Hwy 290 is paved 11.4 miles to the junction and offers a nice scenic drive with magnificent mountain panoramas and prosperous-looking ranches in the fertile bottom land.

Jack Creek Campground

(Shoshone National Forest, Open weather permitting)

About the camp – This small out-of-the-way camp, about 30 miles west of Meeteese, is located in a spectacular area with substantial rewards for those willing to make the trip. The camp sits in a small basin near the confluence of Jack Creek and the Greybull River, which flows through the fertile valley below the camp on the way to Meeteetse and beyond. Several trailheads near the camp lead into the surrounding high country. The camp has a vault toilet, but no potable water. There are five tables and fire rings at parking spurs, and two spurs without tables. The camp looked under utilized, but continuing through the buck and pole fence that surrounds the camp there was another area with indications of more use, a vault toilet, corrals and plenty of parking for horse packers accessing the trailheads. Stay limited to 14 days.

Rates – No fees, but donations for upkeep and maintenance are appreciated.

Getting there – From the junction of Hwys 120 and 290 in downtown Meeteetse, go west 11.4 paved miles to the Sunshine-Pitchfork Ranch junction; then right 3.9 miles on the Pitchfork Ranch Road to a fork; then right 1.8 miles to another fork; then left across a cattle guard 1.5 miles to another fork; then right 2.4 miles to another fork; then left 8.3 miles — staying right through an oil well area — to the camp. *See map page 338.*

Moran Junction

Moran Junction, at the entrance to Grand Teton National Park isn't much more than the park's fee booth. If you're planning to camp in the area, coolers should be stocked and supplies acquired along the way in Dubois or Jackson, depending on your route. If you need additional supplies while in the area, there is **Dornan's**, a market at Moose with basic groceries and a surprising selection of coffee, cheese and wine.

One favorite wildlife viewing and photographic opportunity about three miles into the park is 'The Oxbow,' a luxurious meander of the Snake River where moose and many species of waterfowl are often nearby. With Mt. Moran (12,605') sometimes reflected in the river's still waters, it is a striking scene, especially for the few days of fall when the aspen are aflame with turning leaves.

Grand Teton Park RV Resort

(Private, Open all year)
PO Box 92, Moran, WY 83013 Ph: (307) 733-1980 or (800) 563-6469
Fax: (307) 543-0927 Web site: www.yellowstonerv.com

About the camp – This camp is just 6 miles from Moran Junction and the entrance to the Grand Teton and Yellowstone National Parks. The camp is open, level, practically surrounded by the Willow Wildlife Habitat Area, and offers a splendid view of the Tetons from most sites. The camp has 193 RV sites: 53-70 pull-thrus (up to 25x45). 65 sites are full hookups (30/50amp). Sites are gravel and grass with tables and grills. 65 grass tent sites with tables are available. *Horses okay.*

Amenities – Four rest room and three shower locations (showers only: $4.50), three laundries; spa, game room, rec room with pool table and playground; limited groceries and RV parts, firewood, fishing licences and tackle, gifts, ice, gifts, gas/diesel, two dump stations, propane and pay phones.

Rates – Full hookups for 2 persons: $29. Water and electric for 2 persons: $26. Tent sites for 2 persons: $20. Teepees for two persons: $30-44. Camping cabins for two persons: $38-44. Additional persons age 4-17: $3.50, over age 17: $4.50. MC V Reservations: phone, fax or mail.

Getting there – From Moran Junction, go east 6 miles on US 287/26 to the camp on the right. *See map page 342.*

Hatchet Campground

(Bridger-Teton National Forest, Open June 1 to Sept. 8)

About the camp – This camp is just off the highway 8.7 miles east of Moran Junction and the south entrance to Grand Teton and Yellowstone National Parks and .1 mile west of the Black Rock Ranger Station. The camp has a vault toilet, potable water and 8 sites with tables and fire rings with grates. Sites 6 and 12 are pull-thrus. Stay limited to 16 days.

Rates – Campsite per night: $10. Rates half with Golden Age or Access Passport.

Getting there – From Moran Junction, go east 8.7 miles on US 287/26 to the camp on the right. *See map page 342.*

Box Creek Campground (Undeveloped)

(Bridger-Teton National Forest, Open June 1 to Sept. 30)

About the camp – This is a primitive camp in light forest next to the paved Buffalo Valley Road and along Box Creek. The camp has stone fire rings, but no vault toilet or potable water. Bear rules apply. Stay limited to 16 days.

Rates – Free

Getting there – From Moran Junction, go east 3.5 miles on US 26/287 to Buffalo Valley Road; then left 9.3 miles to the camp on the left. *See map page 342.*

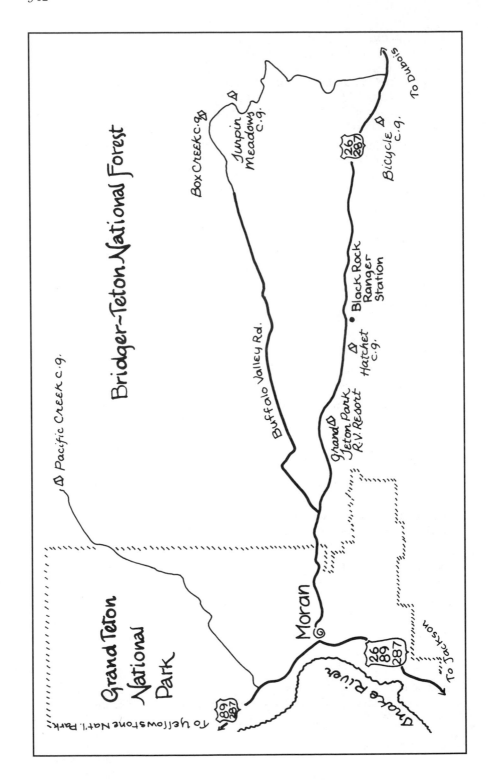

Turpin Meadows Campground

(Bridger-Teton National Forest, Open June 1 to Sept. 8)

About the camp – This camp is in light forest on a grassy park near the Buffalo Fork River. The camp has vault toilets, potable water and 18 sites with tables and fire rings with grates. Sites 6 and 12 are pull-thrus. Bear rules apply. Stay limited to 16 days.

Rates – Campsite per night: $10. Rates half with Golden Age or Access Passport.

Getting there – From Moran Junction go east 3.5 miles on US 287/26 to Buffalo Valley Road; then left 10 miles on the pavement to the turnoff to the left; then left .3 miles to the camp.

Westbound on US 287/26 go to Turpin Meadows Road (*directly across the highway from 4 Mile Meadow Picnic Area and about 13.5 miles east of Moran Junction*); then right 4.4 miles to the camp turnoff on the right (*just across the bridge over the Buffalo Fork River*); then right .3 miles to the camp. *See map facing page.*

Bicycle Campground

(Bridger-Teton National Forest, Open June 1 to Sept. 8)

About the camp – This camp is in light forest on a grassy park overlooking the valley of Blackrock Creek. The camp has a vault toilet, 4 sites with tables, fire rings with grates and a bear box (see page 8), but no potable water. These sites are all walk-in for bicyclists only. Bear rules apply. Stay limited to 16 days.

Rates – Free

Getting there – From Moran Junction take US 287/26 east 12.7 miles to the camp on the right.

Westbound on US 287/26 this camp is on the left .8 miles west of Turpin Meadows Road, which is directly across the highway from the 4 Mile Meadow Picnic Area. *See map facing page.*

Pacific Creek Campground

(Bridger-Teton National Forest, Open June 1 to Sept. 8)

About the camp – This camp is in light forest at the Pacific Creek Trailhead into the Teton Wilderness, and is an extremely popular staging area for hunters in the fall of the year. You must enter Grand Teton National Park and pay park fees to access this camp. The camp has a vault toilet, potable water, game hanging racks and horse-handling facilities. The 7 sites in this camp have tables and fire rings with grates. If the camp is full, there are several dispersed camping options along the 2 miles of road, from the forest boundary to the camp. Bear rules apply. Stay limited to 16 days.

Rates – Free. *Pack it in, pack it out.*

Getting there – From the park entrance booth at Moran Junction go into the park 1 mile to the turnoff to the right; then right 2.2 miles to a left fork; then left 6.1 miles to the forest boundary and another 2.1 miles to the camp at the end of the road. *See map page 342.*

Sheffield Campground
(Bridger-Teton National Forest, Open June 1 to Sept. 8)

About the camp – This is a trailhead camp and you might want a 4-wheel-drive. There is a rough ford and that is likely not suitable for any vehicular crossings until later in July or August when snow melt has tapered off. However, if usable it would be a great spot for an early start into Yellowstone National Park. Stay limited to 16 days.

Rates – Free. *Pack it in, pack it out.*

Getting there – From the park entrance booth at Moran Junction go about 24 miles (*about a mile south of the bridge over the Snake River*) to the camp on the right. *See map page 342.*

Flagg Ranch Campground
(Private, Open May 15 to Sept. 20)
South Entrance of Yellowstone National Park

About the camp – This camp is in the trees 2 miles from the South Entrance to Yellowstone National Park. The camp offers 93 full hookup (20 amp) pull-thru (up to 30x60) sites and 74 tent or no hookup sites. Sites are on gravel and native grass with tables, fire pads and grates.

Amenities – Rest rooms and showers (showers only: $3.25 incl. tax), laundry; limited groceries, snacks, ice, firewood and pay phone. Float trips and trail rides are available.

Rates – Full hookups per site: $19. Tent sites: $9. Yellowstone Park entrance fees must be paid to access this campground.

Getting there – From the park entrance booth at Moran Junction go 26.5 miles to the Flagg Ranch Resort turnoff on the left (*about 2 miles south of the entrance to Yellowstone National Park*); then left about .2 miles to the camp entrance on the left; then left to the camp office. *See map page 347.*

Powell

Powell was named for early western explorer, John Wesley Powell when founded in 1909 on the Shoshone Reclamation Project, the second ever irrigation project authorized by Congressional Act. It is a fair-sized commercial center serving a large farming community where sugar beets and beans are the primary crops. It also caters to the shopping needs of students at **Northwest Community College**. The history of the area is preserved in the free **Homesteader Museum**, located just one block off of US 14A at the corners of First and Clark Sts., Ph: (307) 754-9481, open May 1 to Sept. 30, Tues.-F 1-5 p.m. The Powell High School swimming pool, at 226 N. Evarts St., is open to the public at various times for lap, open and family swimming ($1.25), Ph: (307) 754-5711. The **Park County Fair** is here late July to early August and classic cars and airplanes fill the bill in mid-August during the **Wings 'N Wheels** celebration.

Hookups are available at the Park County Fairgrounds, with free overnight camping available at Homesteader Park just east of town. Groceries, sporting goods and hardware are available.

Homesteader Park

(City owned, Open all year)
On US 14A east of Powell, WY

About the camp – This camp is east of downtown Powell, located in a nice park adjacent to a rest area. The interior roads are paved with parking areas for RVs and a designated grass area for tenting with no nighttime watering. Stay limited to 3 days.

Amenities – Rest rooms at the rest area; playground and wading pool; potable water and dump station.

Rates – Free

Getting there – This camp is on the north side of US 14A just east of Powell.

Park County Fairgrounds

(County owned, Open all year - water seasonal)
PO 702, Powell, WY 82435 Ph: (307) 754-5421

About the camp – This camp is on the fairgrounds and is open to the public all but the last two weeks in July during Park County Fair activities. There are 106 total sites: 8 pull-thrus and 90 back-ins (all up to 20x40) on gravel and all full hookups (30/50 amp). 8 pull-thru sites (up to 20x40) are on grass with electric only (30/50 amp). Tent sites are available. *Horses okay: $5 in stalls. Please call ahead.*

Amenities – Rest rooms and showers.

Rates – Full hookups per site: $12. Electric only per site: $10. Tent site per vehicle: $6. Reservations: Phone or mail.

Getting there – From US 14A and Ferris St., go north 4 blocks to the fairgrounds.

Grand Teton National Park

Grand Teton National Park has five NPS campgrounds offering a total of 865 sites, with four of the campgrounds offering sites for recreational vehicles as well as tents. There are no hookups at campsites and reservations are not accepted. However, you can phone (307) 739-3603 for recorded information on site availability. Group camps can be reserved, between Jan. 1 and May 15 for 10 to 75 persons at a cost of $2 per person (write to Chief Ranger's Office, GTNP, PO Box 170, Moose, WY 83012). Backcountry camping is also allowed with a permit. For recorded information on camping in the backcountry call (307) 739-3602. The campgrounds include:

Colter Bay with 310 sites, flush toilets, showers, a laundry, dump station and propane available. There is marina on Jackson Lake and 10 group sites. This camp is open mid-May to late September and usually fills by noon.

Gros Ventre with 360 sites, flush toilets, dump station and five group sites. This camp is open early May to early October and is usually the last campground to fill.

Jenny Lake with 49 sites for tents only, and modern rest rooms. This camp is open mid-May to late September and usually fills early in the morning.

Lizard Creek with 60 sites, modern rest rooms and a dump station. This camp is open May to mid-October and usually fills by early afternoon.

Signal Mountain with 86 sites, and modern rest rooms. This camp is open mid-May to late September and usually fills by mid-morning.

Your stay at Jenny lake is limited to 7 days with a maximum stay of 14 days at the other campgrounds. A campsite per night is $12 and rates half with Golden Age or Access Passports. Maps are provided with your entrance fees, but the map on page 347 will help you decide in advance where you might prefer to camp in this park.

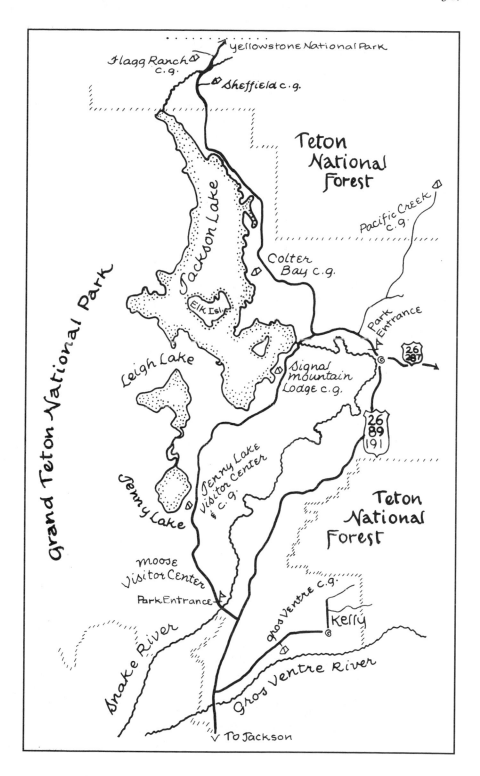

Yellowstone National Park

Flagg Ranch
c. g.

Sheffield c. g.

Teton
National
Forest

Pacific Creek
c. g.

Jackson Lake

Colter
Bay c. g.

Elk Isl.

Park
Entrance

26
287

Signal
mountain
Lodge c. g.

Leigh Lake

Grand Teton National Park

26
89
191

Jenny Lake
Visitor Center
& c. g.

Jenny Lake

Teton
National
Forest

moose
Visitor Center

Park Entrance

Gros Ventre c. g.

Kelly

Snake River

gros Ventre c. g.

Gros Ventre River

To Jackson

Yellowstone National Park

Yellowstone National Park has 1863 campsites at 11 campgrounds with 7 on a first come, first served basis, and four, with 1400 sites, where reservations are available. In addition, Fishing Bridge RV Park has 341 sites for RV only. The RV park does not have tables or fire grates. Sites in all other campgrounds have tables and fire grates and firewood is sold at the larger camps. The campgrounds include:

Bridge Bay with 429 sites and reservations available. The camp has flush toilets, pay showers, firewood sales, a dump station and boat access. Campsite per night: $15;

Canyon Village with 271 sites and reservations available. The camp has flush toilets, pay showers, firewood sales and a dump station. Campsite per night: $15;

Fishing Bridge RV Park with 341 sites and reservations available. The camp has flush toilets, pay showers and a dump station. RV site per night: $26;

Grant Village with 425 sites and reservations available. The camp has flush toilets, pay showers, firewood sales, a dump station and boat access. Campsite per night: $15;

Indian Creek with 75 sites and firewood sales. Campsite per night: $10.

Lewis Lake with 85 sites and boat access. Campsite per night: $10.

Madison Junction with 280 sites and reservations available. The camp has flush toilets, firewood sales and a dump station. Campsite per night: $15;

Mammoth with 85 sites, flush toilets and firewood sales. Campsite per night: $12;

Norris with 116 sites, flush toilets and firewood sales. Campsite per night: $12;

Grant Village with 425 sites and reservations available. The camp has flush toilets, pay showers, firewood sales, a dump station and boat access. Campsite per night: $15;

Pebble Creek with 36 sites. Campsite per night: $10;

Slough Creek with 29 sites. Campsite per night: $10, and

Tower Fall with 32 sites. Campsite per night: $10.

Your stay limited to 14 days. Backcountry camping permits are free and available from visitor centers or ranger stations. Advance reservations for backcountry camping are available at a cost of $15. For reservation services in this park call (307) 344-7311.

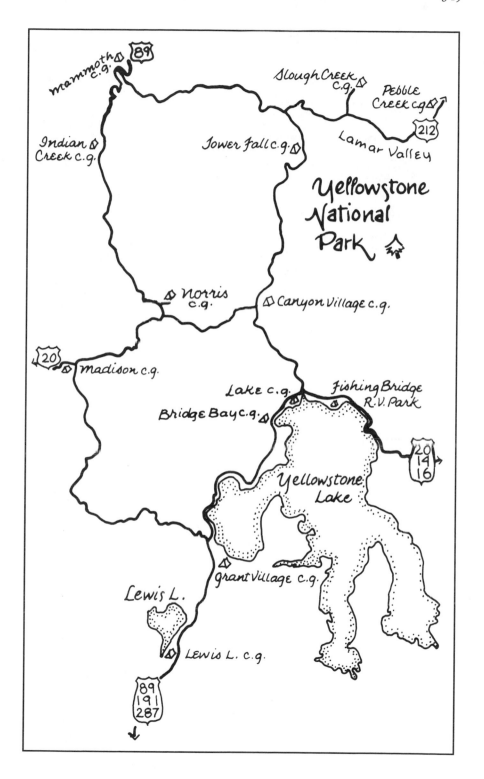

US Forest Service Offices

Big Horn Nat'l Forest
1969 S. Sheridan Ave.
Sheridan, WY 82801
(307) 672-0751

Big Horn Nat'l Forest
604 E. Main
(PO Box 367)
Lovell, WY 82431
(307) 548-6541

Big Horn Nat'l Forest
1425 Fort Street
Buffalo, WY 82834
(307) 684-1100

Black Hills Nat'l Forest
Hwy 14 East
(PO Box 680)
Sundance, WY 82729
(307) 283-1361

Bridger-Teton NF
Kemmerer Ranger Dist.
Hwy 189 (PO Box 31)
Kemmerer, WY 83101
(307) 877-4515

Bridger-Teton NF
Big Piney Ranger Dist.
Hwy 189 (PO Box 218)
Big Piney, WY 83113
(307) 276-3375

Bridger-Teton NF
Greys River Ranger Dist.
145 Washington
(PO Box 338)
Afton, WY 83110
(307) 886-3166

Bridger-Teton NF
Jackson Ranger District
340 N. Cache
(PO Box 1888)
Jackson, WY 83001
(307) 739-5570

Bridger-Teton NF
Pinedale Ranger District
210 W. Pine St.
(PO Box 220)
Pinedale, WY 82941
(307) 367-4326

Medicine Bow NF
2468 Jackson Street
Laramie, WY 82070
(307) 745-2300

Medicine Bow NF
S. Hwy 130
(PO Box 249)
Saratoga, WY 82331
(307) 326-5258

Thunder Basin National
Grassland
(Med. Bow Nat'l Forest)
2250 E. Richards
Douglas, WY 82633
(307) 358-4690

Shoshone Nat'l Forest
808 Meadow Lane
Cody, WY 82414
(307) 527-6241

Shoshone Nat'l Forest
Wapiti Ranger District
203 A Yellowstone Ave.
(PO Box 1840)
Cody, WY 82414
(307) 527-6921

Shoshone Nat'l Forest
Wind River District
1403 W. Ramshorn
(PO Box 186)
Dubois, WY 82513
(307) 455-2466

Shoshone Nat'l Forest
Greybull Ranger District
2044 State St.
Greybull, WY 82433
(307) 868-2379

Shoshone Nat'l Forest
Washakie District
333 East Main St.
Lander, WY 82520
(307) 332-5460

Chambers of Commerce for Wyoming

Basin
PO Box 599
Basin, WY 82410
(307) 568-3331

Big Piney
PO Box 70
Big Piney, WY 83113
(307) 276-3554

Bridger Valley
PO Box 1506
Lyman, WY 82937
(307)

Buffalo
55 N. Main
Buffalo, WY 82834
(307) 684-5544

Casper CVB
500 N. Center
(PO Box 399)
Casper, WY 82601
(307) 234-5311

Cheyenne CVB
309 W. Lincolnway
Cheyenne, WY 82003
(307) 778-3133

Cody
836 Sheridan Ave.
Cody, WY 82414
(307) 587-2777

Cokeville
PO Box 358
Cokeville, WY 83114
(307) 279-3200

Devils Tower
PO Box 3
Devils Tower, WY 82714
(307) 467-5395

Douglas
121 Brownfield Road
Douglas, WY 82633
(307) 358-2950

Dubois
PO Box 632
Dubois, WY 82513
(307) 455 2556

Elk Mountain
PO Box 121
Elk Mountain, WY 82324
(307) 348-7387

Evanston
36 10th St.
(PO Box 365)
Evanston, WY 82931
(307) 783-0370

Gillette
314 S. Gillette
Gillette, WY 82716
(307) 682-3673

Gillette CVB
1810-A S. Douglas Hwy
Gillette, WY 82718
(307) 686-0040
(800) 544-6136

Glenrock
217 W Birch
(PO Box 411)
Glenrock, WY 82637
(307) 436-5652

Green River
1450 Uinta
Green River, WY 82935
(307) 875-5711

Greybull
333 Greybull Avenue
Greybull, WY 82426
(307) 765-2100

Hulett
PO Box 421
Hulett, WY 82720
(307) 467-5430

Jackson
PO Box E
Jackson, WY 83001
(307) 733-3316

Kaycee
P.O. Box 147
Kaycee, WY 82639
(307) 738-2444

Kemmerer
800 Pine Avenue
Kemmerer, WY 83101
(307) 877-9761

LaBarge
PO Box 331
LaBarge, WY 83123
(307) 386-2504

Lander
160 N. 1st Street
Lander, WY 82520
(307) 332-3892

Laramie
800 S. Third St.
Laramie, WY 82070
(307) 745-7339

Lovell
336 Nevada
(PO Box 295)
Lovell, WY 82431
(307) 548-7552

Lusk
PO Box 457
Lusk, WY 82225
(307) 334-2950

Lyman
PO Box 1506
Lyman, WY 82937
(307) 787-6738

Marbleton
PO Box 4160
Marbleton, WY 83113
(307) 276-3815

Medicine Bow
PO Box 470
Medicine Bow, WY 82329

Moorcroft
PO Box 441
Moorcroft, WY 82721
(307) 756-3386

Newcastle
PO Box 68
Newcastle, WY 82701
(307) 746-2739

Niobrara-Lusk
PO Box 457
Lusk, WY 82225
(307) 334-2950

Pine Bluffs
206 Main St.
(PO Box 486)
Pine Bluffs, WY 82082
(307) 245-3645

Pinedale
PO Box 176
Pinedale, WY 82941
(307) 367-2242

Pine Haven
197 Pine Haven Road
Pine Haven, WY 82721
(307) 756-9757

Platte County
PO Box 427
Wheatland, WY 82201
(307) 322-2322

Powell
111 S. Day St.
(PO Box 814)
Powell, WY 82435
(307) 754-3494

Rawlins-Carbon County
519 W. Cedar St.
(PO Box 1331)
Rawlins, WY 82301
rcccoc@trib.com
(307) 324-4111
(800) 228-3547

Riverton
1st and Main
Riverton, WY 82501
(307) 856-4801

Rock Springs
1897 Dewar Drive
(PO Box 398)
Rock Springs, WY 82902
(307) 362-3771

Saratoga
PO Box 1095
Saratoga, WY 82331
(307) 326-8855

Sheridan CVB
5th & I-90
(PO Box 7155)
Sheridan, WY 82801
(307) 672-2485

Shoshoni
PO Box 324
Shoshoni, WY 82649
(307) 876-2389

Star Valley
P.O. Box 1097
Afton, WY 83110
(307) 886-3196

Sundance
PO Box 1004
Sundance, WY 82729
(307) 283-1000

Thermopolis
220 Park St.
(PO Box 768)
Thermopolis, WY 82443
(307) 864-3192

Torrington
350 West 21st Ave.
Torrington, WY 82240
(307) 532-3879

Upton
PO Box 756
Upton, WY 82730
(307) 468-2441

Wheatland
PO Box 427
Wheatland, WY 82201
(307) 322-2322

Wind River CVB
PO Box 1449
Riverton, WY 82501
(307) 856-7566

Worland
120 N. 10th St.
Worland, WY 82401
(307) 347-3226

Wright
PO Box 430
Wright, WY 82732
(307) 464-1312

State of Wyoming Offices

Wyoming Division of Tourism
I-25 at College Drive
Cheyenne, Wyoming 82002
(307) 777-7777
(800) 225-5996
www.wyomingtourism.org

Wyoming Game and Fish Department
5400 Bishop Blvd.
Cheyenne, Wyoming 82002
(307) 777-4600

State Parks and Historic Sites
Herschler Building — 1st Floor — NE
122 West 25th Street
Cheyenne, Wyoming 82002
(307) 777-6323

BLM Offices in Wyoming

Wyoming State Office
5353 Yellowstone Road
(PO Box 1828)
Cheyenne, Wyoming 82009-4137
(307) 775-6256 fax: (307) 775-6129
Office hours: M-F   7:45 - 4:30
Public room hours: 9:00 - 4:00

Big Horn Basin Resource Area
101 South 23rd (PO Box 119)
Worland, Wyoming 82401-0119
(307) 347-5100 fax: (307) 347-6195

Buffalo Field Office
1425 Fort Street
Buffalo, Wyoming 82834-2436
(307) 684-1100 fax: (307) 684-1122

Casper Field Office
2987 Prospector Drive
Casper, WY 82604
(307) 261-7600 fax: (307) 234-1525

Cody Field Office
1002 Blackburn (PO Box 518)
Cody, WY 82414-0518
(307) 587-2216 Fax: (307) 527-7116

Kemmerer Field Office
312 Highway 189 N.
Kemmerer, WY 83101-9710
(307) 828-4500 Fax: (307) 828-4539

Lander Field Office
1335 Main St. (PO Box 589)
Lander, WY 82520-0589
(307) 332-8400 Fax: (307) 332-8447

Newcastle Field Office
1101 Washington Blvd.
Newcastle, WY 82701-4453
(307) 746-4453 Fax: (307) 746-4840

Pinedale Field Office
432 E. Mill St. (PO Box 768)
Pinedale, WY 82941-0768
(307) 367-5300 Fax: (307) 367-5329

Rawlins Field Office
1300 N. Third St. (PO Box 2407)
Rawlins, WY 82301-2407
(307) 328-4200 fax: (307) 328-4224

Rock Springs Field Office
280 Highway 191 North
Rock Springs, WY 82901-0256
(307) 352-0256 Fax: (307) 352-0329

Worland Field Office
101 South 23rd Street (PO Box 119)
Worland, WY 82401-0119
(307) 347-5100 Fax: (307) 347-6195

Website Addresses of Interest

Big Horn National Forest: http://www.fs.fed.us/r2/bighorn/

Black Hills National Forest: http://www.fs.fed.us/r2/blackhills/

BLM in Wyoming: http://www.wy.blm.gov/

BLM maps: http://www.wy.blm.gov/Information/fai/wynf.0014(98).pdf

BLM Rec. for Wyo.: http://www.wy.blm.gov/Recreation/recreation.html

Bridger Teton National Forest: http://www.fs.fed.us/btnf/

Devils Tower: http://www.nps.gov/deto/

Grand Teton National Park: http://www.nps.gov/grte/

Grand Teton Natural History Association: www.grandteton.com/gtnha

Medicine Bow National Forest: http://www.fs.fed.us/r2/mbr/

National Recreation Reservation Services: http://www.ReserveUSA.com

Shoshone National Forest:http://www.fs.fed.us/r2/shoshone/tvisitor1.htm

Thunder Basin Grassland: http://www.fs.fed.us/mrnf/thunder.htm

Wyoming Maps: http://www.lib.utexas.edu/Libs/PCL/Map_collection/wyoming.html

Wyoming Scenic Drives: http://www.gorp.com/gorp/activity/byway/wy.htm

Wyoming State Parks: http://www.commerce.state.wy.us/sphs/index1.htm

Wyoming Wilderness: http://www.nwrain.net/~outdoor/WYOMING/WYOMING.HTML

Wyoming Write Ups: http://www.gorp.com/gorp/location/wy/wyfeats.htm

Yellowstone Backcountry:http://www.jacksonwy.com/stories/bakcntry.htm

Yellowstone NationalPark: http://www.nps.gov/yell/

NOTES

NOTES

<u>NOTES</u>

Index

<u>NOTES</u>

<u>NOTES</u>

NOTES

<u>NOTES</u>

<u>NOTES</u>

<u>NOTES</u>

<u>NOTES</u>

NOTES